A Revolutionary Year

A REVOLUTIONARY YEAR

The Middle East in 1958

Edited by
Wm. Roger Louis
and
Roger Owen

I.B. Tauris *Publishers*
LONDON • NEW YORK

Woodrow Wilson Center Press
Washington, D.C.

Published in 2002 by I.B. Tauris & Co. Ltd. in association with
Woodrow Wilson Center Press

I.B. Tauris & Co. Ltd.
6 Salem Road, London W2 4BU
175 Fifth Avenue, New York, NY 10010
www.ibtauris.com

In the United States of America and in Canada distributed by
St. Martin's Press, 175 Fifth Avenue, New York, NY 10010

EDITORIAL OFFICES

Woodrow Wilson Center Press
Woodrow Wilson International Center for Scholars
One Woodrow Wilson Plaza
1300 Pennsylvania Avenue, N.W.
Washington, D.C. 20004
Telephone (202) 691-4029
www. www.wilsoncenter.org

ISBN 1 86064 402 3
2 4 6 8 9 7 5 3 1

A full CIP record of this book is available from the British Library.

Library of Congress Cataloging-in-Publication Data

A revolutionary year : the Middle East in 1958 / edited by Wm. Roger Louis and Roger Owen.
p. cm.
Includes bibliographical references and index.
ISBN 1-86064-402-3
1. Middle East—Foreign relations—United States. 2. United States—Foreign relations—Middle East. 3. Middle East—Foreign relations—Great Britain. 4. Great Britain-Foreign relations—Middle East. 5. United States—Foreign relations—1953-1961. 6. Great Britain—Foreign relations—1945-1964. 7. Arab nationalism—Middle East. I. Title: Middle East in 1958. II. Louis, William Roger, 1936-
III. Owen, Roger, 1935-
DS63.2.U5 Y43 2002
956.04—dc21

2002000023

Contents

Contributors

Howard J. Dooley (Ph.D., Notre Dame) is Executive Director of International Affairs and Professor of History at Western Michigan University. He is the co-author of *Hesburgh's Notre Dame*. His articles and reviews have appeared in *The Middle East Journal* and *The Review of Politics*. He has recently written a chapter on the Suez crisis in Antonio Donno, ed., *Ombre guerra fredda, gli Stati Uniti nel Medio Oriente durante gli anni di Eisenhower, 1953–1961*.

Michael Graham Fry (Ph.D., London) is Professor Emeritus of International Relations at the University of Southern California. His books include *Illusions of Security: North Atlantic Diplomacy, 1918–22*; *Lloyd George and Foreign Policy, 1890–1916*; *Despatches from Damascus: Gilbert MacKereth and British Policy in the Levant, 1933–1939*; and *The North Pacific Triangle: The United States, Japan, and Canada at Century's End*.

Irene L. Gendzier (Ph.D., Columbia) is Professor of Political Science at Boston University. She works in the areas of US foreign policy in the Middle East and problems of globalization and maldevelopment. She is the author of *Frantz Fanon: A Critical Study*; *Development Against Democracy*; and most recently, *Notes from the Minefield: United States Intervention in Lebanon and the Middle East, 1945–1958*.

Rashid Khalidi (D.Phil., Oxford) is Professor of Middle East History and Director of the Center for International Studies at the University of Chicago. His books include *Palestinian Identity: The Construction of Modern National Consciousness*, which won the Middle East Studies Association's Albert Hourani Prize; *British Policy towards Syria and Palestine, 1906–1914*; and *Under Siege: PLO Decision-making during the 1982 War*.

Diane B. Kunz (Ph.D., Yale) is Adjunct Professor of International Affairs at Columbia University. She was a corporate lawyer, 1976–83. She is the author of *The Economic Diplomacy of the Suez Crisis* and *The Diplomacy of the Crucial Decade: American Foreign Relations during the 1960s*. Her most recent book is *Butter and Guns: America's Cold War Economic Diplomacy*.

Wm. Roger Louis (D.Litt., Oxford) is Kerr Professor of English History and Culture and Distinguished Teaching Professor at the University of Texas, Austin, and Honorary Fellow of St. Antony's College, Oxford. He was the Editor-in-Chief of the *Oxford History of the British Empire*. His books include *Imperialism at Bay* and *The British Empire in the Middle East*. He is a former President of the American Historical Association.

Roger Owen (D.Phil., Oxford) is a former Director of the Center for Middle Eastern Studies and the A. J. Meyer Professor of Middle East History, Harvard University. His books include *Cotton and the Egyptian Economy*; *The Middle East in the World Economy, 1800–1914*; and *State, Power, and Politics in the Making of the Modern Middle East*. He is also the co-author (with Sevket Pamuk) of *A History of the Middle East Economies in the Twentieth Century*.

Ilan Pappé (D.Phil., Oxford) is Lecturer in Political Science at the University of Haifa. He is the author of *Britain and the Arab-Israeli Conflict, 1948–1951*; *Jordan in the Middle East: The Making of a Pivotal State, 1948–1988*; *Jewish-Arab Relations in Mandatory Palestine*; and *Middle Eastern Politics and Ideas: A History from Within*. His most recent book is *The Israel-Palestine Question*.

Carol R. Saivetz (Ph.D., Columbia) is Research Associate at the Davis Center for Russian Studies and a Lecturer in the Department of Government, Harvard University. She is also the Executive Director of the American Association for the Advancement of Slavic Studies. She has written widely on Soviet and now Russian policy in the Middle East. Her books include *Soviet-Third World Relations, The Soviet Union and the Gulf in the 1980s,* and *The Soviet Union in the Third World.* Her most recent work deals with the politics of Caspian oil pipelines.

Peter Sluglett (D.Phil., Oxford) is Professor of Middle Eastern History at the University of Utah. His books include *Britain in Iraq 1914–1932; Iraq since 1958: From Revolution to Dictatorship* (with Marion Farouk-Sluglett); a translation of Bassam Tibi's *Arab Nationalism: A Critical Enquiry*; and *The Times Guide to the Middle East: The Arab World and Its Neighbours.*

Preface

The year 1958 marked the high tide of Arab nationalism. After the creation of the United Arab Republic in January, when Egypt and Syria merged into a single state under the leadership of Gamal Abdel Nasser, it seemed as though all of the Arab world might be swept into revolutionary turmoil. In May a crisis occurred in Lebanon and in July the Iraqi monarchy fell.

This book inquires into the possible links between those two events and the forces of Arab nationalism—"Nasserism" in the phrase of the time. It deals with the response to the crises in Lebanon and Iraq by the Western powers, the Soviet Union, and the United Nations, and it examines the reasons for the failure of the movement for Arab unity. In wider compass the book discusses the problem of Western access to Middle Eastern oil and the ways in which the tensions of the Cold War helped to shape the destiny of the region.

For making conferences and discussions possible over a number of years, we thank the Center for Middle Eastern Studies at the University of Texas, the Middle East Centre and Lebanese Studies Centre of St. Antony's College, Oxford, and the Division of International Studies of the Woodrow Wilson International Center for Scholars in Washington, D.C. We especially thank Jennifer O'Conner, Monica Belmonte, Renée Goings, and Stefanie Ellis for their assistance in the preparation of the manuscript.

Wm. Roger Louis
Roger Owen

Chronology

HOWARD J. DOOLEY

1952–1956

23	July 1952	Egyptian monarchy overthrown by Free Officers' coup led by Colonel Gamal Abdel Nasser.
17	April 1954	Nasser becomes Premier of Egypt.
19	October 1954	Britain signs Suez Base Evacuation Agreement with Egypt.
24	February 1955	Iraq and Turkey sign Baghdad Pact.
28	February 1955	Israeli Raid on Gaza.
5	April 1955	Britain joins Baghdad Pact.
27	September 1955	Nasser announces Czech Arms Deal.
26	July 1956	Egypt nationalizes Suez Canal Company.
29	October–7 November 1956	Israel, Britain, and France attack Egypt in Suez War.

1957

5	January 1957	Eisenhower Doctrine presented to US Congress.
9	January 1957	Harold Macmillan replaces Anthony Eden as British Prime Minister.
7	March 1957	Israel withdraws last forces from Egypt's Sinai Peninsula.
13	March 1957	Jordan terminates 1948 Treaty of Alliance with Britain.
8	April 1957	Suez Canal reopens.
13	April 1957	Jordan's King Hussein faces down a military conspiracy at Zerqa; wins backing of Bedouin troops.

24	April 1957	King Hussein appeals for US assistance. President Dwight Eisenhower and Secretary of State John Foster Dulles declare preserving Jordan "vital."
29	April 1957	US concludes aid agreement with Jordan.
	June 1957	Rigged Lebanese parliamentary elections produce victory for supporters of President Camille Chamoun.
6	August 1957	Syria concludes economic assistance agreement with Soviet Union.
12	August 1957	Damascus announces discovery of "American plot" to overthrow the Syrian government.
4	October 1957	Sputnik I launched by Soviet Union.
13	October 1957	Egyptian forces land at Latakia to buttress Syria against Turkish threats.

1958

12	January 1958	Delegation of Syrian Baathist officers fly to Cairo to plead for Egypt-Syria union.
31	January 1958	US launches its first satellite, Explorer I, four months after Sputnik.
1	February 1958	Egypt and Syria proclaim merger to form the United Arab Republic.
14	February 1958	Iraq and Jordan proclaim an Arab Union joining the two monarchies.
21	February 1958	Plebiscites in Egypt and Syria approve merger and make Nasser President of the UAR.
5	March 1958	Nasser alleges conspiracy to assassinate him organized by King Saud.
6	March 1958	Nasser appoints UAR Cabinet; Egyptians named to ministries of war and foreign affairs.
8	March 1958	Crown Prince Mohamed al-Badr of Yemen signs pact in Damascus with Nasser linking Yemen to a federation called the United Arab States.

24	March 1958	King Saud of Saudi Arabia grants Crown Prince Faisal power over foreign, internal, and financial affairs.
27	March 1958	Manifesto by Lebanese leaders warns Chamoun against seeking re-election as President.
7	May 1958	Chamoun informs US ambassador that he plans to run again for President of Lebanon.
8	May 1958	Assassination of Lebanese opposition journalist triggers riots and strikes.
12	May 1958	Anti-government forces barricade Beirut streets.
13	May 1958	Lebanese Foreign Minister Charles Malik accuses UAR of instigating rebellion. Insurrection by French Army and settlers in Algeria. US Vice-President Nixon attacked by anti-American demonstrators in Venezuela.
14	May 1958	US airlifts police equipment to help Lebanon restore order and maintain a pro-Western government.
15	May 1958	Soviet Premier Nikita Khrushchev promises Nasser that Moscow will provide all necessary help in uniting the Arab peoples as the best guarantee of keeping "colonizers" out of the Middle East.
20	May 1958	Dulles says Eisenhower Doctrine is applicable to Lebanon.
22	May 1958	Beirut charges UAR with provoking riots in Lebanon, asks urgent meeting of UN Security Council. Contingency plans discussed by US-British military teams in Cyprus.
1	June 1958	French National Assembly votes General Charles de Gaulle's return to power.
6	June 1958	Malik asks UN for help in combating the UAR's alleged effort to "overthrow the present regime in Lebanon and replace it with one more subservient to the United Arab

		Republic." UN Security Council begins debate on Lebanon.
10	June 1958	Dulles says there is "irrefutable evidence" of UAR interference in Lebanon.
11	June 1958	UN Security Council votes to form a United Nations Observer Group in Lebanon (UNOGIL) to investigate charges of external interference.
14–15	June 1958	Heavy fighting in Beirut.
19–25	June 1958	UN Secretary General Dag Hammarskjöld visits Middle East.
26–27	June 1958	Heavy fighting in Tripoli.
3	July 1958	US Sixth Fleet moves closer to coast of Lebanon. UNOGIL reports no evidence of UAR intervention.
13	July 1958	Egypt and Suez Canal Company reach compensation agreement.
14	July 1958	Iraqi monarchy overthrown by military coup; King Faisal II and Crown Prince Abdel Ilah killed. Republic proclaimed with Brigadier Abdel Karim Qasim as Premier, and Colonel Abdel Salam Aref as Deputy Premier.
15	July 1958	US Marine battalion lands over Beirut beaches. UN Security Council meets. Iraqi Premier Nuri Said killed trying to escape coup.
16	July 1958	King Hussein requests Western military assistance.
17	July 1958	British paratroops fly over Israel to land at Amman airport. Khrushchev orders Soviet military maneuvers on Turkish border.
18	July 1958	Qasim announces Iraqi oil production will continue as normal.
19	July 1958	Khrushchev proposes summit meeting to deal with Middle East crisis.
20	July 1958	US airlifts petroleum products to Jordan.

31	July 1958	General Fouad Chehab elected President by Lebanese Parliament.
	July–December 1958	Yasser Arafat lays foundations for the Fatah movement in Kuwait.
1	August 1958	Britain officially recognizes new Iraqi government. Soviet Union protests to Israel about US and British flights over Israeli territory.
2	August 1958	US officially recognizes new Iraqi government. Israeli Premier David Ben-Gurion asks US and British overflights stop.
3	August 1958	UAR (Syria) closes border with Jordan, leaving Aqaba as only access to outside world. Britain lands more paratroops in Amman, and supplies internal security equipment to Jordanian police. US forces in Lebanon reach peak of 13,300.
4	August 1958	Israel announces that it has withdrawn permission for British and US overflights to Jordan.
5	August 1958	Israel denies that Soviet note of 1 August caused withdrawal of permission for overflights.
6	August 1958	Airlift to Jordan resumes after Israel retracts ban on flights over its territory.
13	August 1958	US Marines begin departure from Beirut. UN General Assembly convenes to discuss Middle East situation.
21	August 1958	UN General Assembly adopts an Arab Resolution calling for early withdrawal of US and British forces from Lebanon and Jordan.
23	August 1958	China begins bombardment of Quemoy.
26	August–12 September 1958	Hammarskjöld visits Middle East to implement Arab Resolution.
28	August 1958	Ben-Gurion begins secret visit to Turkey to conclude cooperation agreement.

29	August 1958	Qasim announces that any Iraqi union with the UAR would be slow.
6	September 1958	Malik elected president of the UN General Assembly at the opening of the 1958 session.
12	September 1958	Qasim ousts Aref from post of Deputy Premier.
23	September 1958	Chehab takes office as President of Lebanon.
28	September 1958	Constitution of Fifth French Republic accepted by referendum.
20	October 1958	British troops begin withdrawal from Jordan.
25	October 1958	US forces complete withdrawal from Lebanon.
2	November 1958	British forces complete withdrawal from Jordan.
10	November 1958	Khrushchev announces Soviet Union wishes to terminate Four Power Agreement on status of Berlin.
11	November 1958	Plane carrying King Hussein to Switzerland intercepted by Syrian jets that attempt to force it down. Hussein returns to Amman.
16	November 1958	Lebanon asks UN Security Council to delete its complaint against UAR.
19	November 1958	Hammarskjöld announces that UNOGIL will be abolished since Lebanon has withdrawn charges against the UAR.
29	November 1958	Martial law lifted in Jordan.
21	December 1958	de Gaulle elected President of France.
23	December 1958	Nasser launches anti-Communist campaign in the UAR.
27	December 1958	Egypt and Russia sign aid agreement to build Aswan High Dam.

1959

1	January 1959	Fidel Castro leads Cuban rebel forces into Havana as President Batista flees.

8	January 1959	de Gaulle proclaimed President of the Fifth French Republic.
24	January 1959	Baghdad announces that Aref has been found guilty of treason in a secret trial.
19	February 1959	Cyprus Agreement opens way for independence from Britain.
6	March 1959	Revolt in Mosul against Qasim regime by Arab nationalist officers.
11	March 1959	Nasser attacks Qasim as the "Divider of Iraq." ("Divider" is a pun on the name al-Qasim, one of the ninety-nine names of God [ordainer, maker of order], which also has the connotation of dividing.)
17	March 1959	Nasser denounces Khrushchev for supporting Communism in the Middle East.
24	March 1959	Iraq withdraws from the Baghdad Pact.
7	October 1959	Qasim escapes assassination attempt by Iraqi Baathists led by Saddam Hussein.
22	October 1959	Egypt's Field Marshal Abdel Hakim Amer appointed Nasser's proconsul in Syria.

1960–1962

9	January 1960	Construction of Aswan High Dam begins.
28	September 1961	Syrian Army coup ends union with Egypt and dissolves the United Arab Republic.
1	July 1962	Algeria votes for independence; French occupation officially ends.

Introduction

WM. ROGER LOUIS

The year 1958 was a time of crisis in Lebanon and revolution in Iraq. The purpose of this book is to establish the relationship between those two significant events and to explore the contradictory interpretations, both at the time and in retrospect. Above all the chapters inquire into an issue that was controversial among contemporary observers and has remained so ever since: to what extent were the troubles in Lebanon and the coup d'état in Iraq—the prelude to the revolution—externally inspired? With that question in mind, the book deals more generally with Arab nationalism and the Western response. In establishing the significance of the year 1958 as a dramatic turning point in the history of the region, the authors deal in one way or another with the consequences of the Suez crisis of 1956. The chronological scope of the book in a broad sense is thus 1956–1958.

Western observers believed that Egyptian President Gamal Abdel Nasser had encouraged and led a pan-Arab movement to undermine Western influence in the region and, some suspected, to bring the countries of the Middle East into alignment with the Soviet Union. Nasser had played an important part in the Egyptian revolution of 1952. After he later emerged as the undisputed leader of the revolutionary regime, he alienated all Western countries, not least the United States, by accepting arms from the Soviet Union in 1955. In the next year he defied Britain and France by nationalizing the Suez Canal Company. In 1958 he headed a new union of Egypt and Syria known as the United Arab Republic (UAR). What was the significance of the UAR or, for that matter, Nasser's ambitions as an Arab nationalist? Was he making a bid for mastery of the Middle East? Had Egypt fallen, to some degree, under the control of the Soviet Union? From the vantage point of Britain and the United States, Nasser was not merely exploiting the tensions of the Cold War but had become dangerously anti-Western. It was commonly believed that he had stirred up the unrest in Lebanon and, perhaps, had helped to plan the Iraqi revolution. For the Arabs, however, Nasser was the hero of the day. In spite of all odds he had emerged triumphant from the invasion of Egypt by British, French, and Israeli forces during the Suez crisis of 1956. Against Western imperialism he stood as a champion whose personality and powers of rhetoric made him a charismatic leader.

How have those interpretations stood the test of time? How do archival and other historical sources help to explain the motives of Western governments in 1958 and the course of Arab nationalism? What can we now conclude about the decline of British—and French—influence and the emergence of the United States as a regional power in the Middle East? What were the aims of the Soviet Union? How did the Cold War help to shape the destiny of the region?

The chapters focus mainly on the year 1958 and the theme of the book itself is reflected in the title: the year of revolution. The phrase might well have a question mark after it. The events of 1958 were characterized by the high tide or high hopes of Arab unity, though in contradictory ways. The merger of Egypt and Syria in early February was followed two weeks later by the union of Iraq and Jordan. Dependent on the West, Jordan was an artificial state with few natural boundaries and only scarce resources. Iraq, rich in oil, was regarded in much of the Middle East as a British satellite. The union of Jordan and Iraq made sense as a counterweight to the UAR and as a consolidation of the two branches of the Hashemite dynasty. But the Iraq-Jordan marriage was foredoomed because of the revolution in Iraq in July. Would the revolution engulf Jordan and perhaps other parts of the region? The crisis in Jordan now appeared more dangerous than the one in Lebanon.

As events transpired, American troops landed in Lebanon to stabilize the Lebanese government and British forces intervened in Jordan to support the regime of King Hussein. To the British and Americans, the crisis of 1958 resolved itself in a manner more or less satisfactory. The Lebanese and Jordan governments remained, in the phrase of the day, within the Western orbit, and the Iraqi revolution did not expand into other countries. Above all, the Western petroleum companies retained control over the oil in the Persian Gulf. The leader of the military coup in Iraq, Brigadier Abdel Karim Qasim, saw that it was critical for him, at least temporarily, to remain on good terms with the Iraq Petroleum Company (a

British, Anglo-Dutch, American, and French consortium) for the survival of his own regime as well as for economic development. Was the revolutionary year turning out to be not so revolutionary after all?

The question can be answered in different ways. Between the Arabs and the peoples in the West there existed a chasm of incomprehension and suspicion. From the Western vantage point it seemed clear that Nasser had precipitated the crisis of 1958. Arab nationalism was on the march and the Western presence in the region seemed to be in jeopardy. Emotions ran high. When the civil strife in Lebanon became engulfed in the larger issue of revolution in Iraq, and when the revolution itself threatened to spill over into Jordan and other parts of the region, the Western powers perceived a plot coordinated and masterminded by Nasser. In fact, the Iraqi revolution proved to be an internal revolution, and its impact was mainly restricted to Iraq. To Nasser himself, the situation in Iraq presented dilemmas of how to respond to the revolutionary regime as well as how to deal with what he erroneously believed to be the British attempt to roll back the revolution. There was greater confusion and hesitancy in Nasser's reaction than was commonly recognized in Western countries. Nevertheless the question remains open as to what Nasser actually thought, and whether or not his leadership was a form of Egyptian imperialism. In any event, these problems can be interpreted from various points of view. This book aims at an overarching unity by examining the crises of 1958 from different perspectives, Israeli as well as Arab, and from that of certain individuals such as Dag Hammarskjöld, Secretary-General of the United Nations.

The chapters are not designed to cover all aspects of the subject, though each author attempts to define the nature of the crisis in 1958. One result is that the clash between the Western powers and those in the Middle East is sharply drawn in virtually all cases; but the atmosphere of crisis pervades the Western side more than it does the Arab, with the notable exception of Iraq after 14 July 1958. Iraq is not dealt with here except in relation to other themes. This is because the Iraqi revolution is the subject of another book in which four of the present authors are represented (Khalidi, Louis, Owen, and Sluglett).[1] Readers should turn to that work, among others, for an understanding of the revolution as a landmark in the history of the Middle East, but Albert Hourani's words in the foreword bear repeating

[1] Robert A. Fernea and Wm. Roger Louis, eds., *The Iraqi Revolution of 1958: The Old Social Classes Revisited* (London, 1991).

here because they identify the turning point in the pan-Arab movement of the 1950s:

> Those who observed the revolution of 1958 at close quarters have borne witness to the explosion of new ideas and the social forces they represented. The sense, so common at moments of great upheaval, was that everything was now possible. This proved to be a false dawn. The Communists, after a short period when they were in the ascendant, saw their power destroyed. The vision of pan-Arabism was dissolved in the struggle for influence between Gamal Abdel Nasser, who embodied it, and Abdel Karim Qasim, who had come to power in Iraq partly on a wave of enthusiasm for it.

In the present work, the chapter by Peter Sluglett deals with the Iraqi revolution in relation to the region generally and with a view to the problem of Communism, as does Carol Saivetz's chapter from a Russian perspective.

Although many of the chapters focus mainly on the year 1958, some, especially the one by Diane Kunz, trace the origins of the crisis to the confrontation at Suez in 1956. Therefore, another way of regarding the intellectual thrust is as an inquiry into the consequences of Suez. Again, however, there is a limitation because the Suez crisis is the subject of a book in its own right in which six of the present authors are represented (Dooley, Fry, Khalidi, Kunz, Louis, and Owen).[2] It is important to bear in mind that the present work is a companion volume to *Suez* as well as *The Iraqi Revolution,* and that *The Year of Revolution* carries the subject forward on the basis of fresh archival research and interpretation. The book thus represents a collaborative effort of over a decade to understand the interaction between the West and the Middle East in the 1950s.

The chapter by Wm. Roger Louis provides some of the essential background to the 1958 crisis in a British context. Here, as throughout the book, the question is asked: was the conflict in Lebanon stirred by external forces or was it more in the nature of a civil war? The answer at the time depended in part on the assessment of Nasser and the nature of Arab nationalism. These matters were controversial and hotly debated, but the consensus among British officials held that Nasser was first and foremost an anti-British Arab nationalist, as well as an Egyptian patriot who

---

[2] Wm. Roger Louis and Roger Owen, eds., *Suez 1956: The Crisis and Its Consequences* (Oxford, 1989).

regarded Egypt as the natural leader of the pan-Arab movement. He was all the more dangerous because he believed he could use the Soviet Union to achieve his own goals. When the crisis deepened in Lebanon in the spring of 1958, the British asked themselves whether the line could be held against Egyptian subversion there and elsewhere. After the beginning of the Iraqi revolution in mid-July, the Prime Minister, Harold Macmillan, himself took the matter in hand. With wild swings of mood and a penchant for historical analogy, he quickly concluded that the Iraqi revolution could not be reversed, and that the British and the Americans would have to coordinate plans for saving Lebanon and Jordan and safeguarding access to oil in the Gulf. The British could not have succeeded in the 1958 operations without American assistance. With the loss of Iraq, the British position in the Middle East further declined, but British forces had achieved a significant goal: with American help, they had managed to stabilize the situation in Jordan. The chapter demonstrates that the British believed that they had salvaged at least part of the wreckage from their position at the time of Suez, and that, in the phrase of a secret document, "Anglo-American cooperation in the Arab world is possible." By reviving the American alliance, and by treating Arab leaders "with tact and discretion," Britain could still remain a world power, though a diminished one, in an arc extending from the Middle East to South-East Asia.

Diane Kunz explicitly provides the connection between the Suez crisis and the dilemmas facing the US government in the subsequent two years. As a result of the confrontation in 1956, and against the background of overwhelming American economic and military strength, the United States emerged as the predominant Western power in the Middle East. But this would not have happened, at least at this time, had not Britain and France decided on a course of action in 1956 that placed them in collision with anti-Western nationalism throughout the Middle East and Asia. Contrary to British and French speculation, there is no evidence that the Americans deliberately aimed at hegemony in the Middle East. Their aims differed from those of their allies, or at least they had a different set of priorities. First and always in the minds of President Dwight D. Eisenhower and Secretary of State John Foster Dulles was the danger of the Arab states becoming Soviet satellites (a danger that the British and French believed to be exaggerated). This helps to explain the motive in early 1957 behind Dulles's statement, known as the Eisenhower Doctrine, which became the rationale for the American presence in the Middle East. The Eisenhower Doctrine promised the willingness of the United States to provide assistance to Middle Eastern states "against armed aggression from any country controlled by international communism." What were the origins of this momentous proclamation? To what extent was Dulles himself responsible for the wording and the underlying logic? Did it mean to imply that Nasser was a Communist? Or that he was under the control of international Communism? Did Eisenhower and Dulles take into account that Nasser might feel "encircled" by the countries who took advantage of American assistance—eventually, Lebanon, Jordan, Saudi Arabia, and Iraq? How is one to assess the consequences of the doctrine? Should it be regarded, on the whole, as contributing to the polarization of the region's politics, and thus to the origins of the Iraqi revolution, or should it be seen as achieving in some degree its principal purpose of stabilizing pro-Western Middle Eastern countries? For example, Lebanon?

In an interpretation based on an extensive review of archival and other historical sources, Irene Gendzier argues that the events of 1958 must be seen in the context of nationalist challenges to Western control of oil not only in the Middle East, but throughout the world. Such was the complexity of the oil problem that US officials in the spring of 1958 had to consider how events in Indonesia, for example, might influence those in Saudi Arabia and Lebanon, where a strategic pipeline carried Saudi oil to its terminus on the eastern Mediterranean. In answering the question of whether the origins of American intervention in July are to be found in internal Lebanese developments or more immediately in the outbreak of the Iraqi revolution, it is useful to keep in mind the fundamental aim of guarding American-owned oil installations. John Foster Dulles cloaked US policy in rhetoric of Wilsonian morality, but this lofty language concealed a concerted effort on the part of the Americans to provide a justification for intervention rather than an explanation of the actual motive "to protect their oil interests in Saudi Arabia, Kuwait, and the Gulf." The underlying economic rationale helps to explain why the United States intervened to support the Lebanese President, Camille Chamoun, who had virtually no popular following but who had aligned himself on the side of the Western powers in the Cold War. With similar logic, Dulles was hostile toward Nasser despite evidence from the CIA that he actually wanted to help resolve the conflict in Lebanon.

Believing that the anti-British sentiment in the Middle East could be a liability in the struggle against the Soviet Union, Dulles ruthlessly assessed his allies in the same way. He was not especially optimistic about the possibility that the British might intervene effectively in Jordan to buoy up the regime of King Hussein. Such was the mounting anxiety that the Middle East might spin out of control in the summer of 1958 that US nuclear weapons were kept offshore from Lebanon. The threat to the West represented by Arab nationalism seemed to diminish when it became clear that the Iraqi revolution would not be exported to other parts of the Middle East. Some American intelligence estimates even argued that Nasser and Arab nationalism were not necessarily incompatible with American aims. But this chapter reflects a sober judgment on the nature of American statecraft in 1958 and its bias in supporting conservative and reactionary regimes: "US policy-makers proved capable of exploiting divisions between radical regimes, consolidating gains secured from covert arrangements with Lebanon, enhancing collaboration with Israel, and expanding cooperation with other conservative and dependent allies from Turkey to Iran." The historical record of Lebanon as a microcosm in the Cold War thus reveals the underlying economic and political structure of postwar American imperialism.

The chapter by Michael Fry establishes the central importance of the United Nations in the crisis. One of the remarkable aspects of Dag Hammarskjöld, the Secretary-General, was his understanding of the leaders of the Middle Eastern countries as well as his mastery of the politics of the Cold War. Hammarskjöld had a difficult personality—he was secretive and measured others by his own high standards—but he bridged the Arab and European worlds. He believed that Nasser had legitimate grievances and aspirations, and that the United Nations could help to secure a stable and neutral Middle East. Hammarskjöld's sympathy for the radical Arab countries and his attempt to be even-handed put him at odds with Eisenhower and Dulles as well as Prime Minister Macmillan and Selwyn Lloyd (the Foreign Secretary), all of whom regarded him in various degrees as naive and dangerous—in the extreme judgment, a dupe of Nasser and a tool of the Kremlin. In Lebanon, for example, Hammarskjöld worked to create a neutral, independent, and peaceful country. But it would be a Lebanon as free from Western influence and control as it would be free from Egyptian interference. Hammarskjöld consequently aroused suspicion in American and British circles that the United Nations Observation Group in Lebanon (UNOGIL) might, perhaps unwittingly, have a pro-Egyptian bias that would affect intelligence estimates and thus the military outcome of the civil war.

From Hammarskjöld's own perspective, Nasser had no grand design on Lebanon or on Jordan. Nasser seemed to be as flummoxed and frustrated by the revolution in Iraq as were the British. This was an entirely different perception of Nasser from the one that prevailed in the West in 1958. That it has historically proved to be more accurate than the stereotype did not help Hammarskjöld at the time. In spite of Western suspicion and obstruction, he nevertheless managed to create a special relationship between the United Nations and the Middle East and helped to resolve the crisis of 1958 as an intermediary of extraordinary ability. By the end of the year he had individually met with more Middle Eastern leaders than any other Western statesman. "On most counts, in diagnosis and treatment, Hammarskjöld had outshone both Eisenhower and Macmillan...." This chapter provides crucial evidence of the way in which Hammarskjöld guided the United Nations and how the United Nations of that era must be regarded as a creative force in its own right.

Most Western observers of the Middle East, statesmen and journalists alike, had distorted views, which, especially on the American side, were filtered through the prism of the Cold War. The theme of Rashid Khalidi's chapter is Middle Eastern as well as Western misunderstanding, which often approached caricature. On the Arab side the stereotyped concepts of imperialism and Zionism paralleled those in the West of Communism and Nasserism. Perhaps it was the sheer complexity of Arab politics that prevented the development of any lasting movement for unity in 1958 and that also gave rise, in the West, to "far-fetched depictions of Nasserism and Communism working hand-in-glove, and Egypt and the Soviet Union collaborating in subversion." In the Middle East itself, Arab newspapers were as balanced and nuanced—or as unbalanced but just as nuanced—as their Western counterparts. In view of the lack of access to archives in the Arab states, the historian must turn to journalism for the details of the period as well as for the changing climate of opinion, which the newspapers irrepressibly portrayed. Newspapers of course are not a substitute for original documentation, but they are rich and rewarding. A study of these sources restores to the Arabs their own independent thought and fierce self-respect.

The Western archival material, especially that of the British, reveals an overbearing, paternalistic, and arrogant view of the Arabs' incapacity to manage their own affairs. Thus there was the need to help the Arabs to help themselves, if necessary by covert means, to protect them against Communism and the danger of falling under Egyptian or Soviet sway. It is one of the ironies of the revealed archival secrets in Britain and the United States that we know more of the details of Saudi, Syrian, and

Egyptian bribery and subversion in Lebanon than we do of the American or the British, or for that matter the French. But it is clear that Western sources of corruption were just as vicious as their Arab counterparts, and that covert activity on the part of the US government surpassed all others at this time. By 1957 Jordan was well on its way to becoming a client state of the CIA. One wonders how the political history of Jordan might have evolved had it not been for British intervention and the long-term American subsidizing of the Jordan government. From the vantage point of radical Arab nationalism, the aggressive Western reaction to the events of 1958 turned the tide against the surge of revolution and contributed to the failure of the movement for Arab unity.

The shattered vision of a pan-Arab state is one of the themes of Peter Sluglett's chapter, which also deals with the Iraqi revolution in relation to Nasser and the Soviet Union. There were many reasons for the failure of the movement for Arab unity, not merely those of Western dominance and intervention. This is a complex argument, but it clearly establishes that the causes of the Iraqi revolution were internal and included, above all, the deep-seated discontent at the land ownership and wealth of the country concentrated in the hands of a few. Both the British presence in Iraq and the ruling elite were generally resented, but these were Iraqi and not regional issues. The vision of a pan-Arab state had little appeal, either before or after the revolution. Over half the population were Shia Arabs, and about one-fifth Sunni Kurds, but Iraq was ruled in effect by a Sunni Arab minority. The Shia Arabs and the Kurds would be further swamped in a larger Arab state that would have an even greater "Sunni Arab dominance and discrimination." Nevertheless, in Iraq as elsewhere, Nasser had an irresistible appeal. The Egyptian revolution was the model for the army officers led by Abdel Karim Qasim. But Nasser himself had little influence on the course of events, or on Qasim. Nor was Qasim at this stage under any obligation to the Soviet Union, though he regarded the Soviets as natural allies.

The Soviet Union, like revolutionary Egypt, was admired in Iraq as it was in many other parts of the Middle East. For those who came of age in the Middle East in the 1940s and the 1950s, the Soviet Union symbolized economic and social advancement and held out hope for a better life. Both the Soviet Union and Egypt represented social justice, as well as anti-colonialism and independence. There existed, however, an irresolvable tension between nationalists and local Communists. There was no love lost between Nasser and the Communist parties in Egypt or in Syria, and no prospect of Egypt becoming a satellite along the lines of the other eastern European states. Egypt, and later Syria and Iraq, accepted Soviet arms and became dependent on the Soviet Union; but the Russians could not dictate policy in any of the Middle Eastern states. This was a wary relationship in both directions, though it was mainly Nasser who defined it and benefited from it. He knew from the experience of Suez that the Soviet Union in a major crisis with the West could offer little more than moral and psychological support. American naval and military power dominated the eastern Mediterranean. Nasser later made disastrous miscalculations about the Yemen and about Israel, but in 1958 he demonstrated a fairly shrewd knowledge of how far he could go. He was cautious about territorial annexations in the cause of the pan-Arab movement.

Though written on the basis of different sources, the conclusions reached in Carol Saivetz's chapter run parallel to those of Peter Sluglett's. The theme is the origin of the crisis from the time of the Suez confrontation. The focus is on Nikita Khrushchev, who consistently demonstrated an awareness of the limits of Soviet power, yet attempted persistently but sometimes erratically to increase Soviet influence in the Middle East. On the basis of Soviet sources—including archival material that has become available to historians after the collapse of the Soviet Union—this chapter relates in detail how events in Egypt influenced Soviet decisions during the Hungarian uprising, which coincided with the Suez crisis. In late October 1956 Khrushchev and his colleagues had decided to attempt a peaceful resolution of the Hungarian insurgency, but the invasion of Egypt by the British, French, and Israelis changed their minds. "If we leave Hungary," Khrushchev stated, "that would encourage the American, British, and French imperialists. They would understand this as our weakness and would be on the offensive." Khrushchev therefore reversed the decision to arrive at a peaceful solution to the Hungarian emergency and deployed Soviet tanks in Budapest. Otherwise the Soviets would have faced, they believed, a dual defeat.

There was never any intention on the part of the Soviet Union, either in 1956 or in 1958, to intervene militarily in the eastern Mediterranean or the Middle East. Khrushchev wanted to avoid nuclear confrontation, though he successfully exploited the Suez crisis by threatening nuclear warfare. Curiously enough, he was not beyond playing on his own reputation as an unstable, irrational, and volatile personality in such a manner that caused his threats to be taken seriously in the West. In 1958 Khrushchev held the same attitude toward intervention as in 1956, but the stakes were now higher. The Soviet Union had championed Nasser and within the two years had substantially increased economic assistance. But the political or military commitment, as previously, would not go beyond moral encouragement and proclamations of friendship with the Arab world. "We are not ready for World War III," Khrushchev said during the July crisis. His clients in the Middle East understood his priorities, but there were other reasons for tense relations. Khrushchev was exceedingly frustrated in his dealings with Nasser, and later with Qasim, because of the persecution of Communists. Khrushchev commented on the Egyptian and Iraqi revolutionary regimes: "Do you think Nasser is a Communist? Communism is outlawed in Egypt.... Take Iraq, there the leaders are not Communists. In fact they are anti-Communists. The revolt was against a feudal system." True enough, but Khrushchev assumed that Nasser had sponsored the Iraqi revolution and that the Egyptians had close links with Qasim. Misperceptions about the Middle East were not restricted to those held by the West.

What was Israel's role in the events of 1958? Ilan Pappé begins by examining the evolution of the idea of a "Greater Israel" up to the time of the crisis. He challenges the portrayal of Israel by most Israeli historians as a passive and defensive nation surrounded by hostile Arab states. He argues that, far from being merely reactive, some influential Israelis within the government believed that a "forward policy" would be necessary to secure in 1958 what they believed should have been taken in 1948. There were three goals. The first was "Greater Israel," including, specifically, the part of Palestine ruled by Jordan known as the West Bank. Another aim was to create an alliance with the West, again more specifically, with the United States. The last was to demonstrate that the Israel Defence Force (IDF) was the most efficient and powerful army in the region. The events of 1958 had a bearing on all three aims, for it was, to the Israelis, above all a crisis concerning Jordan. Long before 1958 the Israeli government held as a premise that Jordan was a potential flash point. "The moment a pro-Nasserite regime toppled Hussein, the IDF would enter the West Bank." In early 1958 the union of Egypt and Syria was far less important to the Israelis than the merger of Jordan and Iraq. It became a matter of intense concern in July whether or not the Iraqi revolution would encompass Jordan.

The Israeli Prime Minister, and Defense Minister, in 1958 was David Ben-Gurion. He sympathized with the ideas associated with a "Greater Israel," though he distinguished between the visionary and the possible and was principally concerned with Israel's day-to-day defense. Ben-Gurion was an exceedingly complex personality. He was sensitive to the issue of Arab irredentism and well aware of the danger, demographic as well as political, of territorial expansion. Yet his fertile and inventive mind turned in all directions to increase Israel's power and influence. By 1958 he had become convinced that Israel needed a series of defensive alliances that would include Turkey, Iran, and Ethiopia. Yet he also yearned for a commitment on the part of the West. "The most popular people in Israel are now the French," he had said in 1957. "But this is not good enough. We need the Americans." A security alliance with the United States was Ben-Gurion's ultimate aim. He hoped to use the crisis of 1958 to secure it. This, however, was the reverse of what Eisenhower and Foster Dulles had in mind. Their aim was to keep Israel quiet and to stabilize Jordan before the crisis precipitated a takeover of the West Bank by Israel. These frustrating circumstances perhaps help to explain Ben-Gurion's contradictory and eccentric behavior during the crisis itself. When tensions mounted in mid-July, it became obvious that the only way British paratroops could reach Jordan would be for British aircraft to fly over Israel. Thinking that they had an assurance, the British were astonished to learn that Ben-Gurion furiously protested—and demanded that Israel in return be made a member of the British Commonwealth! As a result of American pressure, Ben-Gurion acquiesced and British forces stabilized Jordan. Israel in fact played only a small part in the crisis and achieved none of the three principal aims: no "Greater Israel," no demonstration that the IDF was the most powerful army in the region, and no security alliance with the United States. All those things lay in the future, but one can understand the eventual "basis for the American commitment to Israel" as a result of the 1958 crisis.

The chapter on oil by Roger Owen analyzes the crisis by comparing it to the one of 1956 and by examining the debate on how the change of political regimes in the Middle East might or might not have disrupted the flow of oil to the West. What were the lessons drawn from the Suez crisis, when the Canal had been closed and a section of the Iraqi-Syrian pipeline had been blown up? The American and British governments had pondered measures that might have reduced Western dependence on Middle Eastern oil, but nothing had been done by the time the new crisis broke out two years later. In May 1958 the disturbances in Lebanon caused an interruption in the pipeline of the Iraq Petroleum Company at its terminal on the eastern Mediterranean. Western anxiety about oil supplies mounted at the time of the Iraqi revolution in July. What would be the oil policy of the revolutionary government in Iraq? Would the United Arab Republic under Nasser's leadership, perhaps with Soviet backing, attempt to cut off the West from Middle Eastern oil? There did occur serious shortages in Jordan, but Iraq depended on oil revenues for economic stability and development, and Nasser calculated that it would not be in Egypt's self-interest to interfere with the oil companies. Oil flowed as usual through the Suez Canal and across the trans-desert pipelines, though emergency measures to protect Western oil supplies continued to be debated in Washington and London. No consensus emerged on how best to deal with the disruption of oil supplies during a time of crisis, though Eisenhower perhaps more than anyone else helped to curb alarmist attitudes by putting forward realistic and balanced views.

The conclusion brings together the main themes of the book. It places the events of the year in wide Middle Eastern and international context by contemplating some of the consequences as well as the origins of the crisis. The wider perspective helps us to understand some of the basic issues, not merely those of anxiety in the West about access to petroleum reserves, but also of the tendency to see conspiracies where none existed. The destabilizing force of Nasserism seemed to link the three major events of the creation of the United Arab Republic, the crisis in Lebanon, and the revolution in Iraq. In fact it was the uncertainty about the fast-breaking events that itself contributed to an atmosphere of revolution. One theme of the chapter is the significance of the crisis appearing quite differently to historians than it did to contemporary observers. It was one of those rare times when it became apparent to the world at large that fundamental forces for change—above all those of Arab nationalism—clashed dramatically with British and American efforts to preserve their own influence and to hold the line against both Nasserism and the Soviet Union. The year 1958 marked an important step in the final liquidation of the British presence in the region, but it also saw the beginnings of a shift in power between the United States, Egypt, and Israel that became apparent in the next great crisis in 1967.

The book ends with a comprehensive bibliographical survey. We are greatly indebted to Howard Dooley not only for the bibliography, but also for the chronology.

1

Britain and the Crisis of 1958

WM. ROGER LOUIS

"Gamal Abdel Nasser remains the hero of the Arab world," observed the British Ambassador in Lebanon, Sir George Middleton, at the beginning of the Middle East crisis of 1958.[1] He wrote this in February just a few days before the world's attention was galvanized by the joining of Egypt and Syria into the new state of the United Arab Republic. The significance of the merger, Middleton noted later, could be made clear by a glance at the map because it "has brought Abdel-Nasser to within some fifty kilometres of Beirut."[2] Neither Middleton nor virtually anyone else in British

---

[1] Middleton to Lloyd, Confidential, 23 January 1958, Foreign Office document (hereafter cited as FO) 371/134116, Public Record Office, London. For Nasser and the crisis of 1958, one of the most useful works remains Malcolm H. Kerr, *The Arab Cold War* (London, 1971 edn.). Another work that has stood the test of time is Patrick Seale, *The Struggle for Syria: A Study of Post-War Arab Politics* (Oxford, 1965). For recent scholarship see especially Irene L. Gendzier, *Notes from the Minefield: United States Intervention in Lebanon and the Middle East, 1945–1958* (New York, 1997); Ulrich H. Brunnhuber, *Die Libanonkrise 1958: U.S. Intervention im Zeichen der Eisenhower Doktrin?* (Hamburg, 1997); Ritchie Ovendale, "Great Britain and the Anglo-American Invasion of Jordan and Lebanon in 1958," *International History Review* 16 (1994); Lawrence Tal, "Britain and the Jordan Crisis of 1958," *Middle Eastern Studies* 31 (January 1995); and Fawaz A. Gerges, *The Superpowers and the Middle East: Regional and International Politics, 1955–1967* (Boulder, CO, 1994). See also especially J. C. Hurewitz, *Middle East Politics: The Military Dimension* (New York, 1969). For historiographical interpretation see Douglas Little, "Gideon's Band," *Diplomatic History* 18, 4 (Fall 1994), pp. 513–40. I have benefited from Carolyn Attié's University of Texas Ph.D. dissertation: "Lebanon in the 1950s: President Chamoun and Western Policy in Lebanon" (April 1996).

[2] Middleton to Lloyd, Confidential, 13 March 1958, FO 371/134116.

circles questioned the assumption that Nasser himself directed, indeed motivated, an expansionist pan-Arab movement or, later in the year, that he might be the hidden hand in the Iraqi revolution of 14 July.[3] For the British, the events in the spring and summer of 1958 posed dilemmas almost as severe as those during the Suez crisis, which Nasser had precipitated—two years previously to the month—by the nationalization of the Suez Canal Company in July 1956. He now appeared to be making a territorial bid for all the Middle East, not least the Persian Gulf. According to a Cabinet discussion in May 1958, "If Lebanon was compelled to accede to the United Arab Republic, Iraq and Jordan might not be able to retain their independence."[4] As the crisis reached its peak in July, the prospects seemed even more alarming: "If we allowed the legitimate Government of the Lebanon to be overthrown and acquiesced in the armed insurrection in Iraq, disorder would rapidly develop in Jordan; Israel, Turkey and the Persian Gulf States would be isolated."[5] The question was whether Nasser could be stopped by force or whether intervention would merely repeat the disastrous Suez invasion of 1956, which stood in memory as an ignominious as well as frustrating defeat because of American insistence on the withdrawal of British and allied troops. Suez cast a shadow over all British thought and action.

In reflecting on the link between the events of 1956 and 1958, Middleton pondered the irony of the rise and decline of great powers, the winning of the Second World War, and the waning of British power. He was a man of incisive intellect and wide experience, which included tours of duty in Iran and India. His ideas represented a main current of thought. He believed that Western influence in the Middle East had gradually but ineluctably eroded. The power of the elites who had benefited from the British and French presence had diminished, thus leaving the British with only a remnant of their former power. "The Suez intervention of 1956," he wrote, "was the latest of the crises in this process of decline."[6] He urged a realistic acknowledgment of Britain's limited capacity to influence the politics of the region. Sir Gladwyn Jebb, the Ambassador in Paris, agreed with him and held that "the tough Suez type action" to prop up such states

---

[3] For recent historical accounts see Robert A. Fernea and W. R. Louis, *The Iraqi Revolution of 1958* (London, 1991).

[4] Cabinet Conclusions (58) 43, 15 May 1958, CAB 128/32 Part 1.

[5] Ibid., (58) 55, 14 July 1958, CAB 128/32 Part 2.

[6] Middleton to Lloyd, Confidential, 11 June 1958, FO 371/134122.

as Lebanon and Jordan simply would not work.[7] Those who had opposed Suez now questioned not merely the effectiveness of another intervention, but were uneasily aware of certain ethical issues. The lessons of Suez, for officials and ministers no less than for the public, were moral as well as political, at least in a minimal sense: everyone wished to avoid the "moral obloquy" of Suez, in the phrase of Harold Macmillan, the Prime Minister.[8]

On the other hand, Sir William Hayter and others who shaped day-by-day as well as long-range Middle Eastern policy at the Foreign Office refused to accept "defeatist assumptions." Hayter was the Deputy Undersecretary. "We may flop...," he wrote, "but I hope we can avoid it, particularly as we now have the Americans on our side."[9] This distinction between Suez in 1956 and the impending crisis of 1958 was vital. Had the Americans been on the side of the British in 1956, the outcome obviously would have been entirely different. In 1958 the situation reversed itself. The Americans would now take the lead. Not without an element of sardonic humor mixed with anxiety, Macmillan noted that the Americans faced a crisis comparable to Britain's own encounter with Nasser. "You are doing a Suez on me," Macmillan remarked to Eisenhower in July 1958.[10]

After the British and French collapse in the region in 1956, the United States emerged as the dominant Western power in the Middle East. As in London, officials in Washington recalled historical analogies of the 1930s and tended to see the Middle East through the prism of the Cold War. Arab politics however had a dynamic of its own, especially in relation to the Baghdad Pact of 1954 and the Eisenhower Doctrine of 1957. From Western perspectives, the Baghdad Pact would protect the Middle East against possible expansion of the Soviet Union as well as the danger of

---

7 See Jebb to Hayter, Secret, 4 July 1958, FO 371/134130.

8 Macmillan's comment in the Cabinet meeting of 16 July 1958, CC (58) 59, CAB 128/32 Part 2, Public Record Office.

9 Hayter to Jebb, Secret, 8 July 1958, FO 371/134130. Wm. Roger Louis, "Harold Macmillan and the Middle East Crisis of 1958," *Proceedings of the British Academy: 1996 Lectures and Memoirs*, 94 (London, 1996), pp. 207–28. This lecture incorporated passages from the draft of the present chapter.

10 According to Macmillan, Eisenhower laughed. (Macmillan's diary, 14 July 1958). But see Richard Lamb, *The Macmillan Years 1957–1963* (London, 1995), p. 35; and Alistair Horne, *Macmillan 1957–1986* (London, 1989), p. 93. I am grateful to Alistair Horne for allowing me to read typescript copies of the Macmillan Diaries, which have now been desposited in the Bodleian Library, Oxford. For recent assessments of Macmillan and issues of the Middle East, see Richard Aldous and Sabine Lee, *Harold Macmillan and Britain's World Role* (London, 1996); and Nigel John Ashton, *Eisenhower, Macmillan and the Problem of Nasser* (London, 1997).

internal Communist takeovers. The Pact included Iraq, Turkey, Iran, Pakistan, and Britain. The United States had acted as one of the sponsors but did not formally join the organization. John Foster Dulles, the Secretary of State, saw belatedly that Cold War alliances would divide rather than unite the Arab world and that the Baghdad Pact would have repercussions beyond the Middle East. Pakistan's adherence antagonized India and Afghanistan. Nasser regarded Iraq as a satellite of Britain. The Pact intensified Egypt's hostility to the West. In December 1955 Jordan had refused to join, thus dividing the two Hashemite monarchies of Iraq and Jordan. Saudi Arabia allowed the United States access to an air base at Dhahran but opposed the Baghdad Pact, in part out of historic antagonism towards Iraq. After the events of Suez in late 1956, those rivalries took a different turn when Saudi Arabia shifted into the anti-Nasser camp. A loose royalist alliance of Iraq, Jordan, and Saudi Arabia now confronted the revolutionary force of Nasser's populist pan-Arab nationalism. Sir Charles Johnston, the Ambassador in Jordan, described the anti-Nasser coalition as a curious "new 'Arab caravan'" with which the British now traveled.[11] The metaphor of the caravan expressed a certain reality about Middle Eastern alliances, which shifted in and around the Baghdad Pact.

The survival of British influence as well as the very existence of some of the ruling elites in the Arab monarchies in the post-1956 period now depended on American support provided by the Eisenhower Doctrine. A makeshift proclamation in the wake of Suez in January 1957, it was originally a spontaneous utterance by Dulles, who had not conferred with regional experts at the State Department, the CIA, or the Pentagon. At one stroke he rekindled Arab suspicion of American motives and diminished the goodwill that the United States had built up by opposing the British, French, and Israelis during the Suez crisis.[12] The announcement of what became known as a "Doctrine" progressed from a formal presidential address to a joint resolution by Congress. The resolution authorized the President to provide economic and military assistance to Middle Eastern countries that requested "assistance against armed aggression from

---

[11] Quoted in Elie Podeh, "The Struggle over Arab Hegemony after the Suez Crisis," *Middle Eastern Studies* 29, 1 (January 1993), pp. 91–110.

[12] In 1958 Middleton wrote that the Suez crisis remained "a vivid memory" but that "despite Lebanese adherence to the 'Eisenhower Doctrine' and some increase in American aid to Lebanon, the United States signally failed to retain the popularity achieved at the time of the Suez crisis." Middleton to Lloyd, Confidential, 3 March 1958, FO 371/134114.

any country controlled by international communism." The difficulty, which the British fully perceived, was that Nasser was not a Communist, nor could it be proved that the Soviet Union "controlled" Egypt. When Lebanon, Jordan, Saudi Arabia, and Iraq became open allies of the United States by adhering to the Eisenhower Doctrine, and thus qualifying for military and economic assistance, Nasser believed that a pro-Western alliance had encircled him. The polarization provided the regional background to the insurrection in Lebanon in May 1958 and to the military coup that liquidated the Iraqi monarchy in July.

From the British perspective there were three parts to the crisis of 1958. The first embraced the aftermath of the proclamation in Cairo on 1 February merging Egypt and Syria into the United Arab Republic. Two weeks later on 14 February an Arab Federation between Iraq and Jordan was proclaimed in Amman, Jordan. Less electrifying than the news of the Egyptian-Syrian merger, the Iraq-Jordan federation seemed to be a reflex reaction. The British doubted its effectiveness against Nasser. The second phase of the crisis began in the week of 8 May with street riots in Lebanon protesting against the pro-Western policy of President Camille Chamoun and threatening civil war. The American and British governments made contingency plans; the Security Council of the United Nations on 11 June voted to send UN observers to Lebanon to guard against illegal movement of troops or arms. The third phase of the crisis began on 14 July with the outbreak of the Iraqi revolution. Lebanon and Jordan now appeared to be on the verge of dissolution because of pro-Nasser sentiment within the two countries and because of the revolutionary atmosphere spreading from Iraq. American Marines from the Sixth Fleet landed near Beirut on 15 July and British paratroops were dropped at the capital of Jordan, Amman, two days later. This last phase encompassed the return to stability in Lebanon signified by the assumption of office by General Fouad Chehab as President on 23 September, and the withdrawal of American and British troops by the end of October.

The underlying assumption common to both British and American officials held that Nasser, like Hitler, aimed at expansion and that he had to be confronted and made to desist, by force if necessary. Sir Harold Caccia, the Ambassador in Washington, reported that Dulles believed that "Nasser was following in Hitler's footsteps" and used similar methods to pursue a policy of expansion. Nasser "could not afford to stop to consolidate the Syrian-Egyptian Union because he was bound to encounter grave practical difficulties, and his only hope of maintaining his position and popularity was to gain external successes by further coups in the Middle East."[13] The British generally agreed with that assessment. With various shades of sophistication, most British officials and statesmen, from lowly levels in Whitehall to the Prime Minister, shared the idea of Nasser as a latter-day dictator of 1930s vintage. Macmillan himself believed that Nasser was to some extent mentally unbalanced and thus, like Hitler, prone to unpredictable, irrational behavior. Macmillan wrote in his diary in May 1958:

> A great crisis is blowing up in Lebanon. Nasser is organising an internal campaign there against President Chamoun and his regime. This is partly Communist and partly Arab Nationalist.
>
> Russian arms are being introduced from Syria and the object is to force Lebanon to join the Egyptian-Syrian combination. In other words, after Austria—the Sudeten Germans. Poland (in this case Iraq) will be the next to go.[14]

The Prime Minister added, "Fortunately the Americans have learned a lot since Suez...."

Another tenet in British thought, slightly at variance with the first, held that Nasser did not fully control his own destiny because he had sold his political fortune if not his Arab soul to the Soviet Union. Though not a predominant interpretation, it vied for ascendancy. Its high priest was Sir William Hayter, who had been Ambassador in Moscow 1953–57. Hayter believed Nasser to be a dangerous dictator in his own right who had, by accepting Russian economic assistance and military advisers, forfeited some degree of political freedom and in any event had welcomed the Soviets into the Middle East as a means of undermining Britain and France. In early 1958 Hayter visited the Middle East and made a shrewd assessment of the interplay between Nasser and the Russians. In his reckoning the Soviet Union figured as the enigma within the enigma of the Arab world. He reported from Baghdad a week after the merger between Egypt and Syria that opinion throughout the region believed that neither Nasser nor the Russians had promoted the union and indeed did not want it to occur when it did. Nasser's hand had been forced by radical nationalists and military officers of the Arab Social Renaissance Party in Syria, the Baathists, who precipitated the merger. They argued that only Egypt and the pan-Arab movement could save Syria from anarchy and from the

---

13 As recounted in Caccia to Lloyd, Secret, 20 March 1958, FO 371/133789.

14 Macmillan diary, 13 May 1958.

danger of a Communist takeover. Hayter himself disparaged the idea that Nasser had merely responded to the crisis in Syria:

> My own opinion is that this is a superficial view; whether Nasser wanted it [union with Syria] or not, he is certainly now exploiting it to the full, while the Russians, through their control over Nasser, will no doubt be able to make much more of it than we ever could.
>
> Certainly the general view here [in Baghdad] is that it [the Egyptian-Syrian merger] represents a serious menace to our position in the Middle East and a still more immediate menace to the régimes in the Arab States favourable to the West.[15]

In this view Nasser may have been reckless, and perhaps even irrational, but any assessment of him had to take into account a certain amount of Russian control over his actions even though he had suppressed Communism in Egypt and banned the Communist Party.

The last strain in British thought, exemplified perhaps by Harold Beeley, held that Nasser was not a Hitler or a stooge of the Russians but first and foremost an Arab nationalist who used the Soviet Union to achieve his own goals. Beeley later became Ambassador in Cairo. Throughout his career he was an astute observer of Nasser and the historical course of the Egyptian revolution. In the first part of 1958 he was Assistant Undersecretary and, from June, Deputy Representative at the United Nations, where he exerted a moderating influence in the interpretation of Nasser and Egyptian aims. In Beeley's view Nasser was essentially opportunistic and by no means in control of Arab nationalism even though in the eyes of his followers he symbolized it. Beeley's Nasser was no demon, but neither was he benevolently disposed towards Britain. He had an inveterate suspicion of British motives and a remarkable capacity to read British conspiracies in each turn of events. He was inimical to British interests, especially those in oil. Nevertheless the British thought it might be possible to avoid confrontation.

The three interpretations were not necessarily contradictory, but it is useful to bear in mind that Beeley's was closest to the historical reality. The formative stage of Nasser's career had been before and during the Second World War, when he had graduated from the Egyptian Military Academy and had witnessed the humiliation of the Egyptians when the British forced them to create a pro-Allied government in 1942. Another motivat-

[15] Hayter to Frederick Hoyer-Millar, Secret, 10 February 1958, FO 371/133806.

ing force was the lesson he learned during the 1948 war against Israel and Egypt's humiliating defeat, which he attributed to the corruption of the old regime and specifically King Farouk. As one of the free officers in the revolution of 1952, Nasser had perfected the art of conspiracy. Those who met him were often struck by his transparent sincerity, but candor formed only one side of a complex personality. He was rational but also calculating and suspicious, especially of the British. His early experience as an anti-British nationalist continued to influence his judgement. He had great stamina, he worked long hours, and he was close to his family. Above all he restored Egyptian pride and sense of dignity after decades of subjugation to the British. Contrary to many critics, then and forever after, he was not a megalomaniac, though he concentrated all power in his own hands. His ministers were often no more than glorified civil servants. He committed himself first and foremost to the social and economic development of Egypt, but even by 1958 the Egyptian debt had outstripped the capacity of the economy to service it. In foreign affairs he upheld the principle of non-alignment, but after 1955 he had become dependent on the Soviet Union for supplies for his armed forces and, later, for the construction of the high dam at Aswan. He aspired to be the leader of the Arab world. "What he wants outside Egypt," Harold Beeley reflected some years later, "is not provinces but Satellites."[16] This may have pitched it a little high but the interpretation was understandable enough. Nasser was a charismatic orator whose rhetoric on Arab unity inspired his followers and caused Western observers to draw conclusions about his ambitions. His aims were not modest; neither were they especially coherent. As later reports were to make clear, he was as baffled and frustrated by the course of events in 1958 as were the British and Americans.

The United Arab Republic and the Creation of the Arab Union of Iraq and Jordan

In a comment that perhaps reflected a consensus in British thought, Sir Michael Wright described what he believed to be Egyptian motives in cre-

---

[16] Beeley to Butler, Confidential, 19 August 1964, FO 371/178580. In a forecast in the 1958 crisis Sir George Middleton in Beirut wrote in similar vein that the Lebanese Muslim leaders aimed at "the 'satellization' or 'Nasserization' of Lebanon." Middleton to Lloyd, Confidential, 11 June 1958, FO 371/134122.

ating the United Arab Republic (the British generally underestimated the Syrian initiative). It was a bid for regional economic hegemony: "one of Colonel Nasser's objectives was probably the control of the oil resources of the Mesopotamian plain and the Persian Gulf." Wright was the Ambassador in Baghdad. He held views heavily influenced by Nuri Pasha al-Said, the long-standing British ally, veteran premier of Iraq, and champion of plans for Arab unity in harmony with British interests. In British eyes, Nuri represented the counterweight to Nasser. Wright and his colleagues took a critical view of Nuri's weaknesses and limitations. Obsessed with political control, and perpetually on guard against conspiracies, Nuri paid only lip service to long-range social and economic development. He represented an older generation that at any time might have to yield to younger, anti-British nationalists. Yet Wright and others recognized in him the attributes of political leadership that could not be found elsewhere in the Middle East except in his rival, Gamal Abdel Nasser. Nuri was not a puppet. He often created dilemmas for the British. In the estimate of the British Embassy in Baghdad, King Hussein of Jordan had taken the initiative in the creation of the Arab Union, but Nuri had become the driving force. If the new union were to collapse, "the situation for Britain and America in the Middle East would be worse in the short term than it would have been if Iraq and Jordan had not come together."[17] On the other hand there were grounds for optimism. The new union might succeed. General Sir Gerald Templer, the Chief of the Imperial General Staff, viewed the initiative as a stroke of luck that might help to sustain British power: "the Arab Union presented us with our very last chance to retain our position in the Middle East and to safeguard our oil."[18]

From the Iraqi vantage point, the union of Egypt and Syria marked an historic event. Wright placed the significance in the perspective of the evolution of power politics in the Middle East:

> In Iraqi eyes a new pattern has been taking shape since the beginning of the year and the map of the Middle East is being redrawn. Frontiers and groupings of population... decided by the West without full freedom of choice for those involved are now being called into question, and what may have been more or less sacrosanct since 1913, 1919 or the end of the second world war is no longer necessarily so. The map will be redrawn to their own

[17] Wright to Lloyd, Confidential, 25 February 1958, FO 371/134025.

[18] Chiefs of Staff Meeting, Confidential Annex, 7 May 1958, DEFE 4/107.

> liking by Nasser or the Communists or both, if they are not resisted jointly by those who wish to maintain their freedom.[19]

Nuri believed that the key to the struggle lay in the oil resources of Kuwait. Only by Kuwait's accession would the Iraq-Jordan combination be economically viable. Otherwise Jordan would be a financial incubus to Iraq. At the idea of Kuwait joining the union, "Iraqi eyes tend to light up."[20] Unfortunately for Nuri and his colleagues, the Ruler of Kuwait, Sheikh Sir Abdullah as-Salim as-Sabah, regarded himself as a broker between Nasser and the West and seemed blind to the regional danger of the new Egyptian-Syrian merger. By contrast, Nuri and Hussein saw themselves as upholding principles of Arab unity that ultimately offered the only alternative to Nasser. In this vision of the Middle East, Iraq and Jordan formed a shield of resistance against Egyptian encroachments in Yemen, in Lebanon, and possibly in Kuwait. According to Wright:

> In this situation the Iraqi and the Jordanian Governments and régimes are fighting, not only for their own survival within the new Union based on friendly partnership, but also for the principles both of Arab unity on a basis of this kind and of the maintenance of active friendship with the West.
>
> If they fail, not only they themselves but Lebanon and Kuwait are likely to go the way of Syria or at least of Yemen. Already Lebanon is in critical danger and Kuwait might be so at any moment. If they succeed, Lebanon and Kuwait may be saved and Syria may be retrieved.[21]

The fate of the Middle East thus hung in the balance.

Shortly after the Iraq-Jordan union in mid-February 1958, Nuri had been in London. Macmillan wrote in his diary:

> Nuri Pasha came to see me.... He is full of plans—some of them rather dangerously vague—for detaching Syria from Egypt. He wants us to get the Ruler of Kuwait to join, in some form, the Irak-Jordan union.
>
> The problem we have is to head Nuri off impossible or dangerous schemes, which are bound to fail, without losing his confidence or injuring his will to resist Egypt and Russia.[22]

---

[19] Wright to Foreign Office, Secret, 8 June 1958, FO 371/132776.

[20] Sam Falle to R.M. Hadow, Confidential, 4 February 1958, FO 371/134387. On Kuwait and the crisis see Mustafa M. Alani, *Operation Vantage: British Military Intervention in Kuwait 1961* (The Gresham Press, Old Woking, Surrey, 1990), chapter 2.

[21] Wright to Foreign Office, Secret, 8 June 1958, FO 371/132776.

[22] Macmillan diary, 17 February 1958.

Nuri's plans bordered on the visionary. He hoped that the Iraq-Jordan union might lead to the incorporation not merely of Kuwait but also Saudi Arabia. The Arab Union eventually might succeed in wooing Syria away from Egypt. Nuri expected and demanded British support. But the British knew that to assist Nuri in furthering his extreme aims might lead to Soviet intervention on behalf of the Egyptian-Syrian union. According to Sir William Hayter: "This would create a Spanish civil war situation, with dangerous consequences...for general peace in the Middle East."[23]

One further comment on the Kuwaiti dimension of the regional problem helps to establish the atmosphere of intellectual effervescence and commercial prosperity that characterized parts of the Middle East in the 1950s. The Ruler of Kuwait believed that "the destiny of Kuwait is to become something like another Beirut." Beirut was much more than a thriving center of trade and commerce: intellectual debate and freedom of the press seemed to contribute to the ability of a small nation to prosper despite great power rivalry and regional tension. The Ruler of Kuwait cared little for freedom of the press and still less for intellectuals, but the mystique of Lebanon exerted considerable influence on him. According to Bernard Burrows, the Resident at Bahrain who was on close terms with the Ruler of Kuwait, the Kuwaitis recognized "that they cannot hope to rival the Lebanese climate but they think of Kuwait as a centre of communications and as a free market for finance and trade, which with its much greater natural resources might fulfill some of the functions of Beirut in these matters."[24] The idea of Kuwait as another Lebanon lasted at least until the troubles began in the spring of 1958. After the Iraqi revolution in July, the Ruler faced the prospect, which seemed real and by no means imaginary, that "Kuwait might find itself entirely surrounded by a Nasser-controlled Iraq and a Nasser-controlled Saudi Arabia."[25] Sir

[23] Minute by Hayter, 29 May 1958, FO 371/134119.

[24] Burrows to Riches, Secret, 1 April 1958, FO 371/132775.

[25] Memorandum by Hayter, 14 March 1958, FO 371/132774. The assessment on Saudi Arabia pursued similar themes: "If a pro-Egyptian Government" were installed in Saudi Arabia, it would probably join the United Arab Republic, "and this would have the following effect:

(i) The Hashemite Union would be outflanked, not to say more or less surrounded;

(ii) the previous benevolent attitude of the Saudi Government towards the three shaikhdoms of Kuwait, Bahrain and Qatar would be replaced by pressure to join the United Arab Republic.... The Ruling Families in Kuwait and Qatar would be ill-placed to resist such pressures given the state of public feeling. Bahrain would be a somewhat better case.

William Hayter had expressed that alarming thought as a worst-case scenario in May 1958. His words revealed the uncertainty of mood and the possibility of ominous events.

The British were willing to consider membership of Kuwait in the Iraq-Jordan union, but, the more they pondered the possible consequences, the less they were inclined to support Nuri's demands to exert pressure on the Ruler. Kuwait supplied the major part of Britain's oil, more than that of Iraq and Iran combined.[26] Nevertheless there were certain things to be said in favor of Kuwait's merger with Iraq and Jordan. It might not alter the oil relationship with Britain, and it might help the most impoverished of the three states, Jordan, by a sharing of the oil revenues. Kuwaiti accession, Hayter wrote, might give the Iraq-Jordan union more "sex appeal" by helping to correct the public impression that the merger had been brought about by the British in an attempt to preserve influence rather than by Iraq and Jordan in a genuine manifestation of Arab nationalism. According to Hayter, still on a positive note:

> The Iraqis, of course, see it [Kuwaiti accession] largely as a way of dealing with Jordan's chronic financial difficulties. For the Kuwaitis it would have at any rate the advantage that it might no doubt be possible as part of the bargain to extract from Iraq recognition of Kuwaiti sovereignty and frontiers.[27]

On the other hand, any assessment had to take into account the personality of the Ruler and the general anti-Iraq sentiment in Kuwait. The Ruler, in Hayter's view, held Nasser in esteem as a fellow Arab nationalist. "He does not fear Nasser nor does he accept the thesis that his own fate is bound up with that of Iraq and the Union."[28] On the contrary, the Ruler looked to Nasser for protection against the expansionist aims of Iraq:

> The Ruler does not see the need to stand with his fellow rulers of monarchical states in a common front against the threat of the United Arab

---

(iii) The American tenure of Dhahran would become at the best insecure." Minute by D. M. H. Riches, 18 March 1958, FO 371/133154.

[26] The relative production of crude oil by the three states in 1957 in metric tons: Kuwait 57 million, Iran 35 million, and Iraq 20 million. Value of total exports to Britain in 1957 including cotton, fruit, and grain as well as oil: Iran £35 million, Iraq £12 million, Kuwait £134 million.

[27] Hayter to Hoyer-Millar, Secret, 10 February 1958, FO 371/133806.

[28] Minute by Hayter, 14 March 1958, FO 371/132774.

> Republic. He is suspicious of Iraqi policy in view of past history and sees no advantage in association with the Iraq-Jordan Union either politically or economically—rather the reverse.
>
> Popular feeling in Kuwait is strongly in favour of the [United Arab] Republic and indifferent or hostile to the Hashemite Union.[29]

Any British effort to persuade the Ruler to join Iraq and Jordan would jeopardize good relations between Britain and Kuwait. Better to have oil in hand than to risk the consequences of pushing Kuwait into an unpopular union. Ultimately the calculation on oil determined the attitude. As will be seen, the British could even reconcile themselves to the loss of Iraqi oil if the oil of Kuwait remained secure.

It helps to see the Jordanian view of the possible membership of Kuwait in the Union, just as it is useful to focus briefly on Britain's specific relationship to Jordan as distinct from Iraq.[30] Jordan had become an independent kingdom in 1946 and had expanded its frontiers into former British Palestine by absorbing the West Bank during the war of 1948. Jordan then consisted of some 40,000 square miles with two million inhabitants, one-third of whom were refugees, in a country in which only one tenth of the land was arable. The Palestinian issue dominated Jordanian politics. The radical pro-Nasser and anti-British atmosphere helps to explain the mood in 1951 at the time of the assassination of King Abdullah, the ruling Hashemite monarch since the creation of the state after the First World War. The element of radical nationalism weighed heavily in the calculations of his eventual successor, Abdullah's grandson, King Hussein, age eighteen at the time of his accession in 1953. In March 1956 Hussein dismissed General Sir John Glubb, the commander of Jordan's army, the Arab Legion, thereby sending a shock tremor throughout the Middle East. A Hashemite King had defied the British and disarmed critics who had denounced Jordan as a client state. In April 1957 Hussein ended the Anglo-Jordan treaty of 1946 and in the following month successfully suppressed a plot to depose him led by the pro-Nasser nationalist Suleiman al-Nabulsi. Hussein thus proved himself to be a dexterous, effective, and ruthless force in Jordan's internal politics.

---

[29] Foreign Office memorandum, 3 March 1958, FO 371/132774.

[30] In general see Uriel Dann, *King Hussein and the Challenge of Arab Radicalism: Jordan, 1955–1967* (New York, 1989); and more specifically Tal, "Britain and the Jordan Crisis of 1958."

When Egypt and Syria merged into the United Arab Republic in January 1958, the external threat heightened. Damascus was little over an hour's drive from Amman. Hussein took the original initiative in the Arab Union as a means of countering Nasser. He appears not to have placed as much hope as Nuri in the prospect of Kuwait joining the Iraq-Jordan merger. As the ruler of one of the poorest states in the Middle East, he continued to look to the West for economic and military support. British influence, despite the ending of the formal treaty relationship a year earlier, remained significant, though Jordan relied increasingly on US economic assistance. According to the British Ambassador, Sir Charles Johnston in 1957, Hussein "seems to have perceived that his country could not survive economically on the basis of Arab aid only, and he therefore made no secret of his view that Jordan should at least consider the Eisenhower doctrine very carefully."[31]

When Johnston commented on American assistance, he did not refer to a coherent policy of economic and military aid to pro-Western governments of the Middle East but rather a confused program that nevertheless produced critical economic support. By the phrase "Eisenhower Doctrine," he and others understood that the United States would come to the assistance of Middle Eastern states threatened by "international communism," a phrase commonly assumed to have more meaning in American domestic politics than in the geopolitics of the Middle East. Nevertheless the economic aid was vital. Looking back in December 1958, Johnston wrote: "Jordan could never have survived without the financial and economic support of the United States."[32]

Sir Charles Johnston himself is of interest because he consistently presented a closely-reasoned case that the British must cooperate with the United States if Britain herself were to remain a regional power in the Middle East. The corollary was that Arab nationalism, especially in the case of Jordan, was not necessarily anti-Western or anti-British. Johnston perhaps more than any of his contemporaries saw that Hussein had to present himself as a full-blooded Arab nationalist, and to some extent as an anti-British nationalist. But Johnston knew also that Hussein's own inclinations were moderate, that he was essentially conciliatory towards Israel as well as Britain, and that he still looked to the British for guid-

[31] Johnston to Lloyd, Confidential, 8 May 1957, FO 371/127880.

[32] Johnston to Lloyd, Secret, 4 December 1958, FO 371/134011.

ance and assistance even though he might depend on the United States for economic aid. In this view Jordan remained part of Britain's informal empire in the Middle East. The British had managed to free themselves from costly subsidies and military commitments, now assumed increasingly by the Americans. The significance of the crisis of 1958 for Jordan lies in part in the clear formation of alignments of power in the Middle East in relation to Britain, the United States, and Israel. From the time of the Suez crisis through the period of the termination of the Anglo-Jordan treaty in April 1957, according to Johnston, "we were neither liked here nor respected." By the end of 1958, however, "We were once more Jordan's greatest outside friend."[33] Yet the British had always to bear in mind that "the Jordanian Nasserites are more extreme than Nasser himself."[34]

The issue of Palestine fueled extremist sentiment in Jordan and elsewhere. In Jerusalem the British Consul, Charles Stewart, observed that the Arab inhabitants of the city displayed virtually no enthusiasm for the creation of the union of Jordan and Iraq. "The Arabs are an emotional people who love celebration, yet the establishment of the Arab Federation aroused less spontaneous rejoicing than is normal during any of the Muslim holidays." Stewart went on to explain that in time Jordan might benefit economically from the union, and thus might be in a stronger position against Israel. Palestinians generally would welcome the presence of Iraqi troops on Israel's borders. Yet there were underlying reasons why the Palestinians had reacted apathetically to the merger of the two Hashemite countries and why they continued to sympathize with Nasser:

> In the first place [Jordan's] union with the United Arab Republic would have been more logical from the point of view of geography (at least in so far as Syria is concerned).
>
> Secondly, the Palestinians have a greater cultural and racial affinity with the Syrians than with the Iraqis.
>
> Thirdly, Egypt is regarded as the leader of Arab nationalism and the leading exponent of neutralism, both real forces here [in Jerusalem].

---

[33] Johnston to Lloyd, Secret, 4 December 1958, FO 371/134011.

[34] Johnston to Lloyd, Secret, 18 August 1858, PREM 11/2381. "Whatever Nasser's own private attitude may be, there is no doubt about the violent anti-Israeli fanaticism of his Jordanian supporters." Johnston to Lloyd, Confidential and Guard, 22 January 1959, FO 371/142100.

> Fourthly, an united Arab Republic composed of Egypt, Jordan and Syria would encircle Israel, thus making more effective her containment and bringing nearer the day when the Arabs would be able to force the Jews to make the concessions or "be swept into the sea."[35]

Not all Arabs by any means held such extreme views on the destruction of Israel, but, if given the option, Palestinian Arabs would choose the United Arab Republic over the Arab Union.

For all its intensity, the Palestine issue became relatively muted in the early months of the year 1958. "The decision of Egypt and Syria to form a United Arab Republic," wrote Sir Michael Wright in words that summed up everyone's preoccupation, "changed the whole atmosphere."[36] As the crisis deepened in Lebanon, the British asked not merely whether Jordan and Iraq could hold the line against Egyptian expansion but whether the United States would recognize the gravity of the issues at stake. Sir William Hayter believed that behind Nasser lay the hand of the Soviet Union and that one could detect a historical pattern that could be traced to the interwar years. In a sense the Egyptian revolution could be seen as an extension of the Russian revolution, which as an ongoing world revolution continued to have an anti-British thrust to it. Hayter exaggerated the extent of Soviet control over Nasser but his comment reveals a major element in British thought:

> [A]ny extension of Nasser's influence means really an extension of Soviet influence. However much he and the Russians may distrust and dislike each other they seem bound to work together.
>
> The Russians are using him as Stalin used Chiang Kai-shek in the twenties, as a Nationalist leader who can be relied upon to get rid of "Western Imperialism influence" in what the Russians would regard as a semi-colonial area. They do not much mind if in so doing he is pretty rough with the local Communists too. But Nasser is much less capable than Chiang then was of turning against the Russians and standing on his own.[37]

In view of such danger, why did the Americans, in Hayter's words, regard the situation with such "torpor" and "lethargy"? Did the Americans not sense the danger of revolution, held precariously at bay by Iraq and

---

35 A. C. Stewart to E. M. Rose, Confidential, 19 February 1958, FO 371/134025.

36 Wright to Lloyd, Confidential, 25 February 1958, FO 371/134025.

37 Hayter to Sir Harold Caccia, Secret and Personal, 28 March 1958, FO 371/133799.

Jordan?[38] As the British approached the abyss in the spring of 1958, they regarded Jordan as more vulnerable than Iraq, certainly an ironic view in light of the revolution in July. One of the most remarkable comments on Britain's relationship with Jordan was made by David Ben-Gurion, the Prime Minister of Israel, a few days after the outbreak of the revolution: "The Lebanon was basically a democracy and would survive as such; Jordan was only the King and one bullet would finish him"—and the Jordan state.[39]

Background to the Crisis in Lebanon

Lebanon was not merely a democracy but also, at least to the public at large in Britain and America in the 1950s, a sort of Christian Israel.[40] This was a misleading idea. But it formed part of the general view of Lebanon as a small but vital bulwark against Communism in the Middle East. Here British and American views differed. Despite Sir William Hayter, whose ideas about the Middle East had crystallized during his time as Ambassador in Moscow, the British did not generally take the line that the Soviet Union used Nasser as a pawn. During the crisis in the spring and the summer of 1958 there developed, in the words of a Foreign Office assessment, "a basic but hitherto submerged difference between ourselves and the Americans." It came into sharp focus during and after the Iraqi revolution but had been implicit throughout:

> They [the Americans] have regarded Nasser as bad primarily because he seemed to be a tool of the Russians. We have regarded him as basically inim-

---

[38] In fact the State Department at this time had concluded a balanced assessment of Middle Eastern dilemmas concluding, among other things that "The Arab Union has, undoubtedly, been handicapped by the bellicose and unrealistic policy which Nuri has pursued toward the United Arab Republic" but nevertheless that "The present regimes of Iraq and Jordan, while not popular, have created stability and appear to be the best able to bring about an alternative union to the United Arab Republic." Memorandum drafted by David Newsom, 26 March 1958, *Foreign Relations of the United States Series* (hereafter *FRUS*), 1958–1960, XI, pp. 282–86.

[39] As related in Sir Francis Rundall to Foreign Office, 19 July 1958, FO 371/134284.

[40] For a useful essay that establishes the complexity of the situation in Lebanon in the present context, see Malcolm Kerr, "The Lebanese Civil War," in Evan Luard, *The International Regulation of Civil Wars* (London, 1972). See also especially J. C. Hurewitz, "Lebanese Democracy in its International Setting," *Middle East Journal*, 17, 5 (Autumn 1963), pp. 487–506, for an acute analysis of the confessional politics and system of government.

> ical to Western strategic, economic and political interests in the Middle East...particularly in the short run and especially in regard to oil.[41]

Though the crisis in Lebanon had many dimensions, oil was one of them. Tripoli was the terminal of the Iraq Petroleum Company's pipeline bringing crude oil from Iraq. Saida was the terminal of the Trans-Arabian Pipeline for oil from Saudi Arabia.

Despite the oil terminals, the British generally regarded Lebanon as a country not worth the bother that it caused in international affairs. Lebanon (3,400 square miles) was half the size of Israel (7,993 square miles) and by the same measure less than half the size of Wales. The country had a population of only 1.4 million divided between Christians and Muslims, though these communities were by no means monolithic. The Lebanese exported citrus fruits, apples, olives, and tobacco, but the imports to Britain in 1957 amounted only to £2 million versus £11 million from Israel. The British Overseas Airways Corporation was Beirut's largest single customer. Nevertheless even the most jaded British observer had to admit that Lebanon possessed an astonishing intellectual vitality as well as the commercial hustle and bustle of Beirut, which was already a principal financial center of the Middle East. There were 34 daily newspapers with a circulation of 100,000. Beirut was a thriving commercial port, the principal point of entry into Syria. As a strategically situated country that faced both sides in the Cold War, and as a Mediterranean as well as a Middle Eastern country, Lebanon attracted intelligence operatives. Beirut was thus a center of the Arab cold war as well as the larger Cold War between West and East.

Summing up Lebanon's years of independence since 1943, Sir George Middleton in 1958 observed that the country had "achieved a quite remarkable level of material prosperity." But affluence was a mixed blessing, the Christian half of the population benefiting more than the Muslim half. The economic disparity reflected and to some extent caused a basic tension: "The Moslem element...resents the Western patronage and protection under which their Christian fellow-Lebanese have grown fat and seeks to redress the balance through a patron of its own (nowadays Nasser)."[42] Middleton's comment went to the heart of the matter. The 1950s were a period of economic growth and prosperity, but there never-

[41] Minute by R. M. Hadow, 18 December 1958, FO 371/133958.

[42] Middleton to Lloyd, Confidential, 11 June 1958, FO 371/134122.

theless existed a grievance on the part of the less privileged who now looked to Nasser. According to a later British comment: "This Christian-dominated Lebanon rested on the assumption of Western support, the efficiency of which was generally taken for granted until the emergence in Egypt of Gamel Abdel Nasser."[43]

In the stereotype common in Western countries, Lebanon represented an embattled Christian fortress in an Arab mass. But the Muslim population ranked substantially close numerically, and both Christians and Muslims regarded themselves as Arab. The official language of the country was Arabic. There were 792,000 Christians, 424,000 of whom were Maronites, the remainder Greek Orthodox, Armenians, and others forming altogether some ten Christian communities. The Christians were indigenous since the earliest time of Christianity. The Muslims numbered 536,000 of whom 286,000 were Sunnis and 250,000 Shias. The other principal community was that of the Druze of some 90,000. The country was divided along communal lines weighted since independence in 1943 in favor of the Christians. By rigid convention the President was always a Maronite Christian while the Prime Minister was always a Sunni Muslim. The Speaker of the Chamber of Deputies was always a Shia Muslim. In what Middleton described as a delicately-balanced religious and political mosaic, "the rise of Arab nationalism with its pan-Islamic overtones" now instilled fear in the Christian community.[44] But it was a basic mistake to regard Lebanese Christians as anything other than Arab. In slightly paternalistic tone he commented on the better part of the population:

> The intelligent Christians do not want protection by the West from their Moslem Arab neighbours; they too are Arabs, resent colonialism (from which they have only recently emerged) and, for all their fears of Egypt, are mostly anti-Zionist and deeply shocked by attacks on other Arab peoples.
>
> The best elements in Lebanon are in sympathy with Western culture and philosophy, but Western policy sometimes appears to them as merely selfish and opportunistic and leading to the ruin of their small country as well as setting back the progress of the Arab world.[45]

The country's political system received a major shock after the merger of Egypt and Syria in early 1958, when Middleton reckoned that eighty-

[43] P. M. Crostwaite (Middleton's successor) to Lloyd, Confidential, 24 April 1959, FO 371/142208.

[44] Middleton to Lloyd, Confidential, 11 June 1958, FO 371/134122.

[45] Middleton to Lloyd, Confidential, 7 February 1957, FO 371/127996.

five percent of the Lebanese Muslims "must be counted as ardent supporters of the United Arab Republic."[46]

The key to Lebanon's intricate political system was the "National Pact" of 1943, which essentially represented a compromise between the Maronite and Sunni communities on the issues of Lebanese independence.[47] It reflected the common denominator within the context of internal Lebanese political rivalries and regional Arab politics. The National Pact eventually symbolized peaceful, democratic, religious co-existence as well as a reconciliation of the two faces of Lebanon, one side looking to the West, the other side to other Arab countries. In the first decade of independence the National Pact held, though precariously, in part because of the system of checks and balances, established in the constitution, with a classic separation of powers between a President, a single Chamber of Deputies, and an independent judiciary. On the surface the system worked well but it ossified the sectarian solution of 1943. Thereafter the general Christian interpretation of the Pact remained unchanged while regional developments greatly affected the Muslim view of it. Middleton made a perceptive comment in 1958 when he observed that the Lebanese political system probably needed to be basically revised: "the Pact of 1943, which seemed the logical solution of sectarian differences when it was written, has with the passage of time had the unfortunate effect of freezing those divergencies and perpetuating the political fragmentation of Lebanon rather than resolving it."[48] On another occasion he summed up what he believed to be the essence of the problem by stating that "effective power remains in the hands of the Christians."[49]

In 1952 the Chamber of Deputies elected Camille Chamoun for a six-year term. Chamoun regarded himself as a friend of Britain and the United States but above all he viewed himself as an Arab nationalist and Lebanese patriot. As the British saw it, his style of Arab nationalism, at its best, was a throwback to an earlier, more moderate type compatible with British interests and thus out of harmony with the radical nationalism of Nasser. Chamoun too had a problem of scarcely concealed ambition and an

---

[46] Middleton to Lloyd, Confidential, 13 March 1958, FO 371/134116.

[47] See Farid el-Khazen, "The Communal Pact of National Identities: The Making and Politics of the 1943 National Pact" (Centre for Lebanese Studies, Oxford, Papers on Lebanon 12, 1991); see also Albert Hourani, "Lebanon: Development of a Political Society," in Albert Hourani, *The Emergence of the Modern Middle East* (Berkeley, CA, 1981).

[48] Middleton to Lloyd, Confidential, 11 June 1958, FO 371/134122.

[49] Middleton to Lloyd, Confidential, 7 February 1957, FO 371/127996.

instinct for what the British described as Levantine intrigue. In the 1956–58 period he stood uncompromisingly for a pro-Western alignment, thus becoming the main target for those who sympathized with closer Arab unity. He was also, according to Middleton, "a man of stubborn, sometimes obstinate, courage." Unless he could find a successor who could be counted upon to follow his line of policy, he would succeed himself.[50] In the last phase of his career, Chamoun, in the British view, was almost in a class by himself in political ability and leadership. But by choosing to violate the conventional six-year term, he brought together Christians as well as Muslims who increasingly held that "whatever else may happen, the present President should not be re-elected."[51] The resolution of this issue by Chamoun's eventual though hesitant withdrawal from politics, and the restoration of the ever-more fragile balance of the 1943 pact, helps to explain the success of the American intervention in the summer of 1958.

Until the time of Suez, the British had thought Chamoun to be a weak and indecisive personality. According to the collective wisdom of the confidential "Personalities" report prepared each year by the Embassy in Beirut, "he proved for a long time either too weak or too idle to pursue a persistent policy on the domestic front, and was a disappointment to the Opposition and the despair of the old political bosses whom he refused to consult, relying largely on his personal popularity and his talent for intrigue."[52] Chamoun in some circles had the reputation of being a British tool. He disliked the French, having been arrested by them during the war. He had served as Minister in London 1944–47, a critical period in the shaping of his general political outlook. But from the British point of view he was "basically Lebanese and pro-Arab." That was an essentially accurate judgement, though it hardly inspired confidence in the British who, at least in the period up to 1956, underestimated his strength. Chamoun's dominant sympathy, to the British, seemed to lie with Arab nationalism.[53] Perhaps because he was "arabisant," the phrase of Middleton's predecessor,

---

50 As Middleton reflected on one of the reasons for the May crisis in a despatch of 11 June 1958, FO 371/134122.

51 Middleton to Lloyd, Confidential, 3 March 1958, FO 371/134114.

52 The "Leading Personalities" reports are usually subjected to a fifty rather than a thirty year period of access, but one that eluded the censor's net is dated 18 July 1959 in FO 371/142209.

53 See Chamoun's memoir, *Crise au Moyen-Orient* (Paris, 1963), in which pro-Arab sympathies are a prominent theme.

the British tended to underestimate the strength of his commitment to the Western powers. Middleton assessed Chamoun's strengths and weaknesses during the Suez crisis in August 1956, a little over two months before the invasion of Egypt:

> President Chamoun has done his best to exercise a moderating influence but he is basically a weak man and given to compromise and so far his voice has not been particularly effective. Indeed, if it should come to a show down in Egypt and we have to intervene with armed force, I am by no means sure that Chamoun will be strong enough to stand up to the outcry which is bound to follow and I should not be altogether surprised if he were to resign in such circumstances.[54]

Chamoun's resolute pro-British stand in November 1956 thus came as a welcome surprise. "At this juncture," Middleton wrote, "President Chamoun moved with gratifying courage and decision." Despite earlier phases of indecision, he had proved himself a man of character and had transcended the limitations of what Middleton and others referred to as the Levantine personality: "The President, frequently accused of weakness, vacillation and other Levantine failings, has shown himself able to take strong action when such action was needed."[55]

It was the Suez crisis that gave Lebanese politics an international significance and shaped the background for the events of 1958. During the crisis itself the development of conspicuous importance was, to British eyes, the sudden and ominous growth of the influence of Nasser. Middleton reported in August 1956:

> There is no doubt in my mind about the tremendous impetus which the Nasser bandwagon has now gained. All the latent anti-Western resentments, Arab xenophobia and "anti-imperialist" hysteria is being given free rein.... The Christian element especially feels that the very existence of πLebanon as an independent State is in danger....
>
> Portraits of the Egyptian dictator are beginning to appear in all the shops and I should think that nearly half the taxis in Beirut also have his portrait displayed on the rear window.[56]

---

[54] Middleton to Ross, Secret, 20 August 1956, FO 371/121607.

[55] Middleton to Lloyd, Confidential, 7 February 1957, FO 371/127996.

[56] Middleton to Ross, Secret, 20 August 1956, FO 371/121607.

In November, after the British and French invasion of Egypt in concert with Israeli forces, the Lebanese Cabinet divided on the issue of whether or not to support Nasser. As President, Chamoun championed the Western powers but the Prime Minister, Abdallah Yafi, and the Minister of the Interior, Saeb Salam, vehemently favored Egypt. Chamoun rejected their recommendation to break relations with Britain and France, at which point they tendered their resignations. Middleton described this crucial development:

> Yafi and his more powerful and sinister henchman, Saeb Salam, were strongly inclined towards a pro-Egyptian, pan-Arab and pan-Islamic policy. In Lebanon where communal affairs are so delicately balanced, whose trade and prosperity depend upon free communications with the West and whose cultural and educational ties are largely European, this policy threatened to split the country into opposing camps....
>
> At this juncture President Chamoun moved with gratifying courage and decision....The significance of the fall of the Yafi Cabinet lies in the fact that success for the pro-Egyptian section of the Moslem Arabs of Lebanon would have inevitably called into question the continuance of the Convention of 1943 under which effective power remains in the hands of the Christians. Once that position had been turned, it could probably never have been recovered.[57]

The Suez crisis thus touched the heart of Lebanese domestic politics while injecting a volatile element that would remain internationally significant.

There were two main aspects of Lebanese domestic politics, in Middleton's judgment, that had to be analyzed against the changing international background. Chamoun had emerged from the Suez crisis as one of the few champions of the British in the Middle East. How did he stand in consequence in Lebanon itself? In answering that question Middleton detected what he described as "the underlying contradiction of the Lebanese political system."[58] Chamoun's opponents had to be studied in this context. The second question was: how might the army respond in a prolonged crisis? Here the answer turned on the Commander-in-Chief of the Armed Forces, General Fouad Chehab.

---

[57] Middleton to Lloyd, Confidential, 7 February 1957, FO 371/127996. F. B. Richards, First Secretary in Bahrain but temporarily in the Foreign Office, commented: "That our relations with Lebanon should now be as sound as they were a year ago is largely due to the efforts of President Chamoun." Minute by Richards, 14 February 1957, FO 371/127996.

[58] Middleton to Lloyd, Confidential, 5 June 1957, FO 371/127999.

Chamoun's position as President had to be understood in terms of the Lebanese constitution of 1926. Modeled after the French constitution, it provided for a President and a Council of Ministers responsible to a Chamber of Deputies, but the President had inherited the executive authority of the High Commissioner in the mandate period and was thus a more powerful figure than his French counterpart in the Third Republic. Though the system worked in favor of the Christians, they faced, in Middleton's slightly odd comment, a "frustrating restriction" because they could never hope to have a Christian Prime Minister. From anyone's point of view, however, Chamoun was an active and aggressive President and his rivals accused him of being "un-neutral." His opponents denounced him for violating the consensus of the National Pact, which rested on the assumption that a Muslim Prime Minister would be able to represent the Sunni Muslims in the face of the extensive authority vested in a Christian President. Middleton dismissed the accusations against Chamoun as "specious" because, in the Lebanese political system, "no President...can fail to play an active part in internal politics." The question was whether or not Chamoun would overstep his authority to the point of destroying the consensus of the 1943 Pact. Middleton warned that there was serious "confusion" between "the chief executive and the chief legislative powers" and that this confusion of authority would be "a source of weakness as regards future stability."[59]

General Chehab had been brought into the government as Minister of Defense after the fall of the Yafi government in November 1956. According to Middleton, "He commands respect among all communities, less because of his personal abilities than for his honesty and lack of ambition." In 1952 Chehab had refused to allow the armed forces to become involved in politics, but by doing so had contributed to the collapse of the government. He had then served temporarily as Prime Minister. "At that time," Middleton wrote, "he loyally kept the ring and made no attempt to seize personal power or advantage."[60] In general, Middleton made measured assessments. Most of his colleagues in the Foreign Office would have agreed with him in 1956:

> The commonest estimate of General Chehab is that he is weak. He is certainly more given to reflection than to action but he has a strong streak of obstinacy and a well-known reluctance to commit himself hastily....

---

[59] Middleton to Lloyd, Confidential, 5 June 1957, FO 371/127999.

[60] Middleton to Lloyd, Confidential, 29 November 1956, FO 371/121607.

> In private conversation General Chehab is discursive, philosophic and, risking a pun, given to broad generalities. In all that does not immediately concern the Army he is by inclination cynical. But even as a military leader whose first concern is to maintain his beloved Army intact he allows himself no illusions and I was surprised when, at our first meeting...[in 1956] he quite cheerfully suggested that the Lebanese Army was capable, as a military force, of resisting the Syrians for one day and the Israelis for one hour....
>
> To sum up his character, General Chehab is too aristocratic to be ambitious, too lazy to descend to the common arena, too comfortable to seek martyrdom and too average to arouse jealousy.[61]

Chehab held as an axiom that any political intervention by the army would cause its disintegration into Christian and Muslim factions and might thereby destroy the Lebanese state itself. He resisted Chamoun's political overtures and indeed, according to Middleton, held Chamoun in contempt as a politician who put ambition before country. Middleton's judgment may have been generally too negative on Chehab himself, but on one point, at least, it was certainly accurate: "The General is a good Maronite Christian but I think he is also very conscious of his Arab heritage and of the need for Lebanon to be on good terms with its neighbours."[62]

Middleton respected Chehab as "a sincere patriot," but he knew that the mutual distrust of Chehab and Chamoun would lead to uneasy relations and perhaps trouble. What part might the army play in time of political turmoil? The British Chiefs of Staff held the Lebanese armed forces in low esteem.[63] The army had a strength of only about six thousand officers and men and seemed to resemble a gendarmerie more than an effective military force. The Army would, however, determine the balance in any civil disturbance. Some months after Chehab had left the government in January 1957 and continued his duties as Commander-in-Chief, Middleton commented on his leadership in relation to the lessons to be drawn elsewhere in the Middle East:

> General Chehab has been much praised publicly as the impartial guarantor of political freedom but the fact is that the Lebanese Army is a largely

[61] Middleton to Lloyd, Confidential, 27 August 1956, FO 371/134133.

[62] Ibid.

[63] For the "low opinion of the value of Lebanese forces held by the Chiefs of Staff," see Chiefs of Staff minutes and estimates in FO 371/110969.

> static body which can never expect to have a properly military function and whose duties are largely confined to the maintenance of internal order, in which promotion is almost non-existent and where dissatisfaction among the younger officers must exist.
>
> There have been the examples in neighbouring countries of the preponderant part which the Army has been able to assume during time of political evolution, if not revolution. Hitherto the Lebanese army has fortunately remained largely divorced from day-to-day politics. But I seriously doubt whether this will remain the case in future and there is the real danger that...military cliques may be tempted to take over where politicians have failed.[64]

With the benefit of hindsight, it is clear that Middleton underestimated Chehab's political skill as well as his determination not to allow the army to become a political instrument. Middleton's judgment, however, was representative. There was a general tendency among the British to underrate Chehab.[65]

To understand the crisis of 1958 it is necessary to study briefly the nature of post-Suez Lebanese politics. The prominent members of the November 1956 government, apart from Chamoun and Chehab, included Sami Solh (a Sunni Muslim) as Prime Minister, and Megid Arslan, one of the leaders of the Druzes who had previously been Minister of Defense but was now relegated to a minor post. Sami Solh had served before as Prime Minister, the first time as early as 1942. The son of an Ottoman official, he had been educated in Istanbul. The British regarded him as an aged and increasingly ineffectual politician with limited intellectual horizons. His loyalty to Chamoun made him vulnerable in his own Sunni-Muslim community. He carried the portfolios of Interior, Justice, Information, and, after Chehab left the Cabinet in early 1957, Defense. To the British, Sami Solh appeared to be out of his depth, as did Megid Arslan, whom Middleton described as an affable nonentity. Arslan had been anti-German during the war and had resisted the Vichy régime. He had repeatedly represented the Druzes since 1943. According to the Personalities report, he

---

64 Middleton to Lloyd, Confidential, 5 June 1957, FO 371/127999.

65 A notable exception was Lord Mountbatten, from 1956 Admiral of the Fleet and from 1959 Chief of the Defence Staff. He stated to the Chiefs of Staff Committee in May 1958: "General Chehab...in his view...was the only leader in the Lebanon whose patriotism and moral principles could be relied on. His army would be fully capable of maintaining internal security if the General wanted to do so." Chiefs of Staff Committee, Confidential Annex, 13 May 1958, DEFE 4/107.

was "A cheerful, uneducated and highly venal feudal chieftain with a boyish passion for dressing-up and firearms."[66] In the British view, both Solh and Arslan were being used by Chamoun.

Part of the further political significance of Sami Solh and Megid Arslan lay in the way they had antagonized fellow politicians. By forcing the resignation of Abdallah Yafi and Saeb Salam, Chamoun had embittered two of the most prominent Muslim leaders, who now took an increasingly acerbic line towards both the British and himself. Yafi drifted more and more into the pro-Nasser camp. Saeb Salam, who was the far abler of the two, became one of stalwarts of the Muslim Opposition in 1958 and commanded the Basta quarter of Beirut, the central, Moslem district in the heart of the city. By including Megid Arslan in the Cabinet, Chamoun alienated Kemal Jumblatt, the highly intelligent and active Druze leader who stood in opposition to the Arslan clan. Jumblatt was the leader of the Socialist and Progressive Party and the foremost exponent of socialism in Lebanon. He urged radical reform of what he viewed as a corrupt political system. It was difficult for the British to ascertain whether his influence derived more from his ideological views or from his position as a Druze chieftain, but in any event he was a dangerous opponent to Chamoun.

A special word needs to be said from the British perspective about Charles Malik, who became Foreign Minister in November 1956. He had been educated at the American University of Beirut and at Harvard University. A man of outstanding ability, Malik had returned from America to become Professor of Philosophy and Science at American University in Beirut. From 1945 to 1955 he had served as Ambassador in Washington and as Permanent Representative at the United Nations. He seemed, to the British at least, to fit awkwardly in the rough and tumble of Lebanese domestic politics. He had an unswerving commitment to what he called the values of Western society and more particularly those of the United States, which Middleton once described as "the mecca of so many Lebanese."[67] In a sense Malik shared the same passion for America as many of his countrymen, but he was in a class by himself. He had intellectual range and humane vision. Unfortunately, for the British, he seemed temperamentally akin to the Americans and intellectually he shared an outlook similar to that of John Foster Dulles. Middleton did not find him an easy colleague. Malik himself was politically vulnerable because of his long

[66] FO 371/142209.

[67] Middleton to Lloyd, Confidential, 7 February 1957, FO 371/127996.

period as Ambassador in Washington. He had no substantial political base in Lebanon. Nor was his identification with the Americans a political asset despite the number of Lebanese who had emigrated to the United States. In the aftermath of Suez, Anglo-Lebanese relations revived much more quickly than most contemporary observers would have believed possible. "The United States," according to Middleton, "signally failed to retain the popularity achieved at the time of the Suez crisis."[68] Malik nevertheless supported wholeheartedly the Eisenhower Doctrine and the opportunity to associate Lebanon with the United States.

The post-Suez Lebanese political alignments seemed ominous because of the Lebanese elections to be held in June 1957. In view of the changed circumstances, the elections were bound to have international as well as local significance. At the external level, the conflict reflected Chamoun's support of a pro-Western policy against the wishes of his opponents who wanted to bring Lebanon into the orbit of Egypt and Syria. At the internal level, much revolved around Chamoun himself. His term of office was due to expire in October 1958 but Chamoun's predecessor, Béchara el-Khoury, had set a precedent for re-election. Chamoun was anxious to consolidate support in the new Chamber of Deputies. Therein, in Middleton's view, lay one of the dangers. Chamoun had already acquired a reputation for manipulating people and rigging elections. He had a Byzantine instinct for intrigue and a consuming suspicion of others—above all of General Chehab. Though Chamoun was a man of great charm, he also had a capacity that was astonishing, to Middleton at least, for earning political enemies in all communities. One was Hamid Frangié, a Maronite who had several times served as Minister for Foreign Affairs and who dissented from the pro-Western stance of the government. Another was the Maronite Patriarch, His Beatitude Boulos Meouschi, who was a relative of Béchara el-Khoury and who came in increasing conflict with Chamoun. If Chamoun too blatantly rigged the elections, Middleton commented, "the Patriarch may feel impelled to side more and more openly with the political opponents of the President."[69] Frangié and the Patriarch represented different strains of Lebanese political thought. But they held in common that Chamoun and Malik had tilted too far towards the West.

Middleton believed that the British should support Chamoun to the hilt: "we must bring our weight to bear in support of the President and

[68] Middleton to Lloyd, Confidential, 3 March 1958, FO 371/134144.

[69] Middleton to Lloyd, Confidential, 27 February 1957, FO 371/127999.

his followers and do what we can to frustrate the activities and influence of his opponents." Opposition would not be confined to Lebanese factions: "The Russians, the Egyptians and the Syrians are all making their preparations."[70] Middleton attempted to rally the Americans to the cause. In May 1957 he reported that the American Ambassador now believed that "full support" must be given to Chamoun. "This is satisfactory," Middleton commented, "as [the] American attitude towards the President has tended at times to be equivocal." Middleton became increasingly alarmed at the extent of "Egyptian, Syrian and possibly Russian interference, including bribery and distribution of arms."[71] What kind of assistance did the British lend Chamoun? These matters are usually difficult to prove, and one of the ironies is that the British archives hold more evidence about the arrival of a consignment of arms at the Egyptian Embassy and the half a million Syrian pounds distributed by the Egyptians than about the support by the British themselves.[72] British assistance, however, must have been substantial. Sir William Hayter noted afterwards: "We were quite active in the recent elections."[73]

The elections of June 1957 resulted in an overwhelming victory for Chamoun's supporters. The number of seats in the Chamber had been increased from 44 to 66. Fifty-three of them went to government sponsored candidates. Among those returned were the Prime Minister, Sami Solh, and the Foreign Minister, Charles Malik, the latter despite his lack of domestic political experience or popular following. Yafi, Salam, Frangié, and Jumblatt were defeated. Chamoun's foremost political rivals had been driven into the political wilderness. They had not gone without protest. The elections had been marred by violence leading to thirty-one deaths. Middleton in fact described the violence as an attempted coup d'état because some of the leaders of the "Opposition" including, he believed, Yafi and Salam, had brought in bands of supporters from southern Lebanon for demonstrations and had recruited Palestinian refugees to throw up barricades in the Muslim parts of Beirut. General Chehab had managed to restore order. The phrase "Opposition" is significant. It included Muslims who refused to reconcile themselves to the events of

---

70 Middleton to Lloyd, Confidential, 27 February 1957, FO 371/127999.

71 Middleton to Lloyd, Confidential, 31 May 1957, FO 371/127999.

72 For Middleton's discussion of the evidence of Egyptian bribery and consignment of arms, see Middleton to Lloyd, Confidential, 5 June 1957, FO 371/127999.

73 Minute by Hayter, 20 December 1957, FO 371/128000.

Suez but allied to Christians who wished to bring about a change of régime in Lebanon and to ensure that Chamoun would not be re-elected.

Middleton was dismayed by the results of the elections. He acknowledged that one of the problems in Lebanon was "the subversive activities of outside Powers."[74] But the real problem he believed to be internal. Chamoun had rigged the elections to an extent that had done irreparable damage to his own cause. His most vigorous opponents—including Yafi, Salam, Frangié, and Jumblatt—had been excluded from the Chamber of Deputies. "I am afraid," Middleton wrote with considerable understatement about the charges against Chamoun of fraud and corruption, "that I have some doubt in my own mind as to whether some of these allegations may not have a basis of truth."[75] Middleton was not naive. By Foreign Office standards the Lebanese election had, on the whole, produced the desired results. What caused Middleton concern was the failure of Chamoun to see the wider issues at stake. Despite his electoral success, Chamoun faced more determined opposition than previously. Political figures from all sects, Christian as well as Muslim, now gathered in loose alliance against Chamoun personally. Some, but not all, protested against the pro-Western orientation that he and Charles Malik represented. Others bore personal as well as electioneering resentments. In retrospect, Middleton viewed the elections of 1957 as the beginning of the troubles of 1958.

"The future looks black," Middleton reported in January 1958. A wave of terrorism, which had begun in the previous December, continued unabated with time bombs, dynamite detonations, and random murders. In themselves these incidents hardly constituted matters of international significance; but he believed them to be instigated by Syrian, Egyptian, and Russian agents who aimed "to increase the public feeling of insecurity, disaffection and lack of confidence in the Chamoun régime."[76] After the explosive news of the Egyptian-Syrian union in February, the public mood swung from jittery uncertainty to excitement.

> [T]here is no doubt that the announcement of this Union does much to satisfy a deeply-felt longing in the hearts of all Moslem Arabs. All Lebanese

[74] Middleton to Lloyd, Confidential, 31 May 1957, FO 371/127999.

[75] Middleton to Lloyd, Confidential, 12 June 1957, FO 371/127999. See the chapter by Rashid Khalidi.

[76] Middleton to Lloyd, Confidential, 23 January and 13 March 1958, FO 371/134116.

> Moslems support it; and many of the Lebanese Christians who are dissatisfied, for a variety of reasons, with the way things are going in Lebanon or with President Chamoun personally are also prepared to support it.[77]

With the enemy within the gate, and with emotions now at high pitch, how would Chamoun respond?

> [I]f Chamoun is goaded too far he will become more, rather than less, determined to stand for re-election. He has in his political make-up a courageous, almost reckless, streak and a readiness to take risk which is rare in his compatriots; and he is quite capable of allowing his irritation and amour-propre to affect his political judgement, and thus of overestimating his power to control "the street."[78]

The test came on 8 May with the assassination of an anti-government, left-wing newspaper editor.

The Lebanese Troubles of May 1958

Strikes and violence immediately broke out in the cities of Sidon and Tripoli. The riots then spread to Beirut and other parts of Lebanon. Saboteurs cut the Iraq Petroleum Company's pipeline at Tripoli. The frontier with Syria closed. Opposition leaders demanded the resignation of Chamoun. From the British perspective the source of the agitation was obvious. According to a Foreign Office estimate:

> There is no doubt that these disorders are being fermented and supported from the United Arab Republic. Arms have been smuggled in large quantities into the Lebanon, an Egyptian boat from Gaza has been caught landing arms and 500 armed men from Syria have attacked a Lebanese frontier post.[79]

Much of the situation now hinged on the President and on the Commander of the Armed Forces. Chamoun and Chehab not merely distrusted each other but were on exceedingly bad terms. Unless the British,

---

[77] Middleton to Lloyd, Confidential, 6 February 1958, FO 371/134387.

[78] Middleton to Lloyd, Confidential, 13 March 1958, FO 371/134116.

[79] Memorandum by the Levant Department, 13 May 1958, FO 371/134117.

Americans, and perhaps the French took immediate action, according to Sir William Hayter, Chamoun would lose power. "Chehab might then hold the ring for a little but there will be a slide towards Nasser." The key would be with the Americans. "American forces...will have to bear the burden." In the wake of Suez the British could lend support but could not take the initiative. Hayter, who continued to supervise Middle Eastern affairs, believed that the Americans should be urged to take action. "Otherwise the Lebanon will drift into Nasser's camp and his forward march will become unstoppable."[80]

On the day of the riots, Chamoun informed Middleton that he would seek re-election. The two issues of impending civil war and Chamoun's ambition were thus joined. Both the British and the American governments had been acutely aware of the buildup to the crisis. "Mr. [John Foster] Dulles is worried about the situation in the Lebanon, which he thinks is critical," the Foreign Office recorded in early May.[81] Though the two governments had previously resisted Chamoun's demands for military assistance, they now prepared urgently to deliver six fighter aircraft and eighteen tanks. Even before the outbreak of the crisis on 8 May, the affairs of the Lebanon had acquired great significance. "Chamoun has come to symbolize...the forces of resistance to Nasser," Middleton reported.[82] In ringing words the Secretary of State himself, Selwyn Lloyd, had written earlier in the year that "the continued independence of Lebanon is a pillar of British foreign policy."[83]

The Cabinet gave urgent attention to the Lebanese crisis on 13 May 1958. Macmillan's view coincided with Lloyd's. The Foreign Secretary took the lead in the discussion. The Commonwealth Secretary, Lord Home, and the Defence Minister, Duncan Sandys, contributed respectively to the wider discussion on international affairs and the mobilization of military forces. As during the Suez crisis, R. A. Butler, the Home Secretary, remained mostly passive but tacitly supported Macmillan and Lloyd. The latter stated that the situation continued to deteriorate. Syria and Egypt had "deliberately fomented" strikes and disorders. Speaking to his brief, Lloyd described the political impasse created by Chamoun's insistence on seeking re-election and by Chehab's refusal to lend him polit-

80 Minute by Hayter, 13 May 1958, FO 371/134116.

81 Memorandum by the Levant Department, 1 May 1958, FO 371/134116.

82 Middleton to Foreign Office, Secret, 5 May 1958, PREM 11/2386.

83 Lloyd to Middleton, Secret, 8 February 1958, PREM/11/2386.

ical support. The Lebanese army still controlled the situation, but unless the British, American, and French governments responded to Chamoun's request for military assistance to preserve Lebanese independence, "President Chamoun would probably be overthrown and the Lebanon would be compelled to accede to the United Arab Republic."[84]

In the ensuing discussion, the lesson of Suez prevailed. Britain would act only in concert with the United States. Despite emphatic agreement on Nasser's responsibility for the crisis, and despite the premise of a free Lebanon as a "pillar" of British foreign policy, the Cabinet would not intervene unilaterally. After the failure of the Suez expedition, Britain could no longer take the lead in major military operations in the Middle East. If the Americans were prepared to intervene, the British would offer their co-operation. This offer however contained a qualification. Western intervention would have to be acceptable to Britain's principal client, Nuri. The Cabinet warily cast an eye also towards the United Nations. It might be advisable for Chamoun to bring a case against Syrian aggression before the Security Council. But the British did not intend to get involved in "procedural discussions" that would delay effective action. Nor were they convinced that France should be invited, as Chamoun suggested, to act along with the United States and Britain. The members of the Cabinet eventually concluded that the French should be dissuaded from taking part "since their participation would be liable to prejudice the attitude of the Arab States to the Western intervention."[85]

Macmillan skillfully handled this phase of the crisis, but Lebanon by no means monopolized his attention. In mid-May 1958 an impending railway strike engaged much of his activity and he nervously watched also the rise in the cost of potatoes and tomatoes as an index to politically unacceptable inflation. In Algeria the French Army had revolted against the Algerian policy of President Charles de Gaulle. In colonial affairs Macmillan faced the problems of both Cyprus and Malta. Placing Lebanon in the context of his other overseas preoccupations, he wrote in his diary on 16 May:

> Lebanon still holds. Our forces are in readiness, in case the request for help comes. Malta is quieter—for the moment. Cyprus may boil over again at any moment. There have already been one or two murders. France is in a

[84] Cabinet Conclusions (58) 42, 13 May 1958, CAB 128/32 Part 1.
[85] Ibid.

turmoil—no one knows whether it will lead to the collapse or the revival of the 4th Republic. The only solid thing we have to rely on is the Anglo-American co-operation, which is closer and more complete than ever before.[86]

It is a measure of Macmillan's success in restoring goodwill and trust between the British and American governments in the period after Suez, and an equal measure of Eisenhower's need for British collaboration, that the military experts almost immediately began planning joint operations. They anticipated having to deal with some 6,000 to 9,000 insurgents and some 1,000 armed "volunteers" infiltrating from Syria. Estimates would vary, but the "rebels" held one half the country and all of the Basta quarter of Beirut. The US Sixth Fleet was in the Mediterranean. The British forces included an aircraft carrier and infantry as well as other troops in Cyprus.[87] There would be an American Commander-in-Chief, Admiral James L. Holloway. Some 2,000 British forces and 3,000 American troops would be deployed.[88]

The creation of an operational force, still in place at the time of the Iraqi revolution in July 1958, shaped perhaps more than anything else the outcome of events. Selwyn Lloyd remarked at one stage that the British during the Suez crisis would have done better to have responded immediately rather than to endure the buildup both of domestic and international protest. Failing to act immediately against Nasser, the British never again found the right moment to intervene. The pattern now seemed to be repeating itself. "It is not clear that even our NATO allies would support us," Lloyd commented in June 1958. Yet if the crisis were resolved to Egypt's advantage then the consequences would be as damaging as at the

---

[86] Macmillan diary, 16 May 1958.

[87] The Defence Minister, Duncan Sandys, had sent the following message to the Prime Minister on 13 May 1958 (PREM 11/2386):

Prime Minister

1. You asked to be informed what forces could be sent rapidly to the Lebanon to support an American intervention....
   (a) Within 24 hours. 1 Marine Commando (600 men) and 2 Infantry battalions from Cyprus.
   (b) Within 2 days. 1 Parachute Brigade (3 battalions) from the United Kingdom.
   (c) Within 3 days. A small naval force including 1 aircraft carrier.
2. We are standing ready to alert these forces.... D.S.

At the height of the interventions in July the troop levels were 15,000 Americans in Lebanon and 3,000 British in Jordan.

[88] See *FRUS*, 1958–1960, XI, p. 138 note 3.

time of Suez. "If Nasser picks up the Lebanon like a ripe plum in three or four months' time, he will have won an even bigger victory than our evacuation from Port Said."[89] British assumptions still rested on the premise that Nasser planned to annex Lebanon come what may, despite conflicting reports on his aims. The British assumed also that the experience at Suez offered enduring lessons. To the world at large a genuine effort had to be made to present any intervention, in Middleton's words, as an action "through the United Nations with Anglo-United States forces in the van."[90] Only by keeping in step with the United Nations could the British hold together the Commonwealth and such "difficult" members as Canada. "We cannot be sure of Canadian support," the Commonwealth Secretary, Lord Home, wrote in June. He described the Canadians as "obsessed" with the United Nations.[91] Beyond the Commonwealth lay the even greater problem of Britain's allies. Any action with the French, not to mention the Israelis, would cause the Arab countries to rally to Nasser. In the context of the Middle East, France was now an unwelcome ally because of Arab protest against French colonial rule in Algeria and elsewhere. According to Selwyn Lloyd, French participation would be "disastrous" since "it would alienate all friendly Arabs."[92]

The French knew of course about the concentration of military forces in the eastern Mediterranean. How could the British keep on good terms with President de Gaulle while discouraging any thought of the French joining in the intervention? Iraq played an important part in the equation. Sir Michael Wright reported from Baghdad that "Nuri was staggered by the idea that Chamoun might invite or accept French participation" and Nuri left no doubt "that French participation would be ruinous."[93] Chamoun in turn contributed to the complexity of the problem because he dealt with the French Ambassador in Lebanon on equal terms as the British and American ambassadors. There was a certain logic in Chamoun's attitude because the Tripartite Declaration of 1950 by Britain, the United States, and France, served to guarantee, at least in theory, the peace of the region. The French had every right to be consulted. Sir Gladwyn Jebb in Paris warned that if the "Anglo-Saxon" powers landed

[89] Lloyd to Caccia, Secret, 23 June 1958, PREM 11/2387.
[90] Middleton to Lloyd, Top Secret, 29 May 1958, PREM 11/2386.
[91] Memorandum by Home, 26 June 1958, PREM 11/2387.
[92] Lloyd to Jebb, Top Secret, 24 June 1958, PREM 11/2387.
[93] Wright to Lloyd, Top Secret, 16 May 1958, PREM 11/2386.

troops in Lebanon, the French independently would send an expeditionary force. Jebb remarked that de Gaulle had a long memory. He recollected how the British had helped to evict France from the Levant during the Second World War. "Syria is still written on his heart." There was only one way, according to Jebb, to prevent de Gaulle from intervening: "by threats or bribes, or both."[94]

The Foreign Office ingeniously proposed to treat intervention as merely a hypothetical issue but in the meantime to discuss fully with the French all issues concerning the local situation in Lebanon and political strategy at the United Nations. If it came to a showdown, then the British and Americans, presumably the latter more than the former, "might frighten the French off."[95] Macmillan and Lloyd in fact used the tactic of the "hypothetical" in a conversation with de Gaulle in late June 1958. De Gaulle as usual confronted the issue directly. What did the British propose to do in "the Orient"? "Did we intend to intervene?" With considerable under-statement Macmillan answered that the situation had become "difficult.... At present our only possibility was to support any United Nations action." Lloyd's response indicated how the ghost of Suez continued to find a presence at virtually all important discussions. He elaborated on the problem of changing mood and the importance of finding the right moment to intervene:

> The Secretary of State said that operations of this kind were always easier if they were done at an early stage. If the Suez intervention had been carried out at the end of July, 1956, it would have been accepted by world opinion.
>
> But now the moment has passed in the Lebanon. The present Lebanese Government had shown themselves ineffective, Arab opinion had turned against us, and if we went in now we should find it very difficult to get out.[96]

In the timing of the intervention, the British in a sense were saved by the Iraqi revolution and by being able to act immediately. In the meantime de Gaulle's views coincided with those of the British, at least on the future of Lebanon. "Lebanon must not be allowed to disappear." Macmillan agreed, adding that "what must be avoided was control of the Lebanon by Nasser."

---

[94] Jebb to Lloyd, Top Secret, 17 June 1958, PREM 11/2386.
[95] Lloyd to Jebb, Top Secret, 24 June 1958, PREM 11/2387.
[96] Record of conversation, 29 June 1958, PREM 11/2387.

In early June 1958 Nasser himself offered his services as peacemaker. He told the American Ambassador in Cairo, Raymond Hare, that Egypt had not stirred up the trouble in Lebanon, but that he would help to end it. Chamoun would finish his term of office, Chehab would succeed him, and amnesty would be granted to the rebels.[97] These were reasonable terms. The British and Americans, however, greeted them with extreme suspicion. Macmillan happened to be in Washington on 11 June when Dulles broke the news. What were Nasser's motives? If Nasser succeeded in bringing peace, Dulles asked, would it not bring him further prestige and discourage Western allies such as Nuri? Macmillan suggested that the Russians might have told Nasser to call off the adventure lest it escalate into world war. Macmillan himself, always fond of historical analogy and always taking a hard line, at least tentatively, believed that American counsels divided between those who saw the need to stand up to the Egyptian dictator and those who wanted to appease him, such as William M. Rountree, the Assistant Secretary of State. Not only the ghost of Suez but the specter of Munich appeared as Macmillan, Dulles, and Eisenhower debated Nasser's intent. Suspicion prevailed. The United States and Britain would not stand by while the United Arab Republic took over Lebanon as Germany had dismembered Czechoslovakia.

A more sophisticated minority view also existed. Nasser's solution of Chehab replacing Chamoun represented the best solution that the Western powers could hope for. The problem of internal subversion would always be present, but failure to offer amnesty would further envenom Lebanese politics. Beyond the domestic Lebanese part of the problem, the British knew from various sources, including those at the United Nations, that Nasser might genuinely fear Anglo-American intervention. At Suez the British and Americans had been divided. The year 1956 had been Nasser's year for a miracle. In the year 1958 the combination of external forces did not augur a favorable outcome, nor could Nasser be certain that the Syrian initiative in Lebanon would work to his advantage. Selwyn Lloyd gained this perspective from Dag Hammarskjöld, the Secretary-General of the United Nations.

> [T]he Lebanese were geniuses at compromise and would find some way out which did not involve them in joining the United Arab Republic. In fact

[97] See Macmillan to Lloyd, Top Secret and Guard ["Guard" means "not for American eyes"], 11 June 1958, PREM 11/2386; Hare to Dulles, 7 June 1958, *FRUS*, 1958–1960, XI, pp. 101–103.

> he [Hammarskjöld] thought the Syrians were much more in control of the operation than the Egyptians and might quite possibly even have the idea at the back of their minds of making things more difficult for Egypt.
>
> Nasser was not happy about the situation....[98]

Despite this subtle, persuasive, and essentially accurate interpretation, the prevailing view simplified Nasser as a villain. Sir Harold Caccia, the Ambassador in Washington, summed up the dominant Western interpretation: the confrontation "had become a personal contest between Chamoun, backed by the West, and Nasser by the Communists."[99]

In the drama of forces of darkness and light, Charles Malik played an important part. As Minister of Foreign Affairs, he projected into the international dimension of the struggle a vision as stark as that of John Foster Dulles. On 11 June the United Nations adopted a resolution calling for an observer team to be despatched to Lebanon. By late that month it consisted of ninety-four military officers from eleven nations. Lebanon thus became, in Macmillan's phrase, a "test case" for the United Nations. Malik however believed that the Secretary-General sympathized with Nasser, that the UN force represented subversion, and that "a Munich was being prepared for his country." He suspected Hammarskjöld of undermining Lebanon's alignment with the Western democracies:

> Hammarskjoeld evidently had exalted ideas about his role as a Scandinavian peace-maker in the Middle East, and Dr. Malik was sure he had been in continuous contact with Cairo. He feared that Hammarskjoeld might return from Beirut and Cairo with a scheme for a political settlement involving large concessions to Nasser....
>
> Chamoun, like Benes in [Czechoslovakia] would have to submit, and Nasser would have scored another victory which would have serious consequences for the West and all its friends.[100]

In late June 1958 Malik visited Washington where he met with Dulles. The two men were intellectually matched and both had an interest in historical analogies, which ranged from Manchuria and Abyssinia to Munich and, more immediately, Beirut. Malik ably championed Chamoun's posi-

---

[98] As related in Lloyd to Caccia, Top Secret, 19 June 1958, PREM 11/2387.

[99] Caccia to Lloyd, Top Secret, 19 June 1958, PREM 11/2387.

[100] As recounted in Sir Pierson Dixon (United Nations), Top Secret, 19 June 1958, PREM 11/2387.

tion. But he went too far even for Dulles in attacking the United Nations. "The activities of the UN and Hammarskjold," Dulles stated, "have brought about a large cessation of infiltration."[101] Nor did Malik carry conviction with either the Americans or the British when he spoke of "something rotten in the Kingdom of Denmark," by which he meant the state of Lebanon and the hesitant part played by Lebanon's Hamlet, General Chehab.

By late June 1958 Chehab appeared to be the only person who could hold the delicate balance in Lebanese politics, though the "Chehab solution" had evolved gradually since the time of the outbreak of the insurrection in May. Against this background of a deteriorating political situation, Chamoun had only with extreme reluctance accepted that he could not stand for re-election. Chehab was the only figure in Lebanese public life who commanded unanimous respect. Middleton and others regarded him as the only possible candidate. Chamoun's impending withdrawal from politics and the election date of 24 July 1958 prepared the way towards a national reconciliation, in Middleton's phrase, of "all but the extremists." Yet Chehab took no steps to consolidate his position or, in Western eyes, to exercise sufficient control over the armed forces. Middleton reported that the army as well as the Chamoun government was "impotent." Chamoun repeatedly contemplated sacking Chehab. Nevertheless the only person who continued to command confidence was Chehab. But he appeared to suffer from several fatal defects. He was indecisive. He vacillated. He failed to come to grips with the situation. Furthermore his political ascendancy would mean a shift in the international alignment of Lebanon from a pro-Western state to one genuinely neutral with a government composed of "Lebanese of all colours and tendencies."[102] Chehab, in other words, seemed to possess deficiencies of character that made the British and Americans themselves hesitant. But these were precisely the characteristics of moderation, caution, and fair-mindedness that made him the savior of his nation. He believed that Lebanon should be genuinely neutral. Chehab's presence represented a return to the 1943 spirit of compromise. The British and Americans only slowly recognized his virtues.

---

[101] Memorandum of conversation, 30 June 1958, *FRUS*, 1958–1960, XI, p, 187.

[102] Middleton to Lloyd, Top Secret, 30 May 1958, PREM 11/2386.

The British and the United Nations

If the British got it wrong about Chehab, they got it even more disastrously wrong about Hammarskjöld. Little more than a decade old in 1958, the United Nations commanded respect in part because of the prestige of the Secretary-General, who in one sense took a minimalist attitude towards UN functions. If the United Nations were to survive, it had constantly to be on guard against taking on more than it could manage. Hammarskjöld strenuously resisted plans for converting the United Nations into a world police force or for adopting countries as permanent wards. In another sense, Hammarskjöld saw the potential of the United Nations as an independent institution that might achieve peaceful solutions to international problems in a way that would complement or surpass the efforts of individual states, large or small, which were each locked in narrow visions of self-interest.[103] Hammarskjöld worked relentlessly towards UN goals with creativity and resourcefulness. By careful calculation, the United Nations might play a critical part in solving not merely the problem of Lebanon, but even the more intractable problems of the Middle East. In Lebanon the United Nations might establish a permanent observation team.

In all his affairs, Hammarskjöld held that absolute impartiality was essential. He embodied that attribute. But he combined with it a suspicious frame of mind and a certain intellectual and ethical condescension that won him enemies, especially among those with equally strong personalities. Sir Pierson Dixon, the British Ambassador at the United Nations, was only one of several to collide with him. In his attempt to remain unbiased towards all parties, Hammarskjöld acquired among British officials a reputation for having a "notorious penchant for the Egyptians."[104] In mid-June 1958 on his way to the Middle East he paid a visit to Selwyn Lloyd. Both men had experienced the Suez crisis, the one as Secretary-General upholding the ideals of the United Nations, the other as Foreign Secretary of one of the countries that had flouted them. Hammarskjöld and Lloyd regarded each other warily, but they seemed to see eye-to-eye on Lebanon. Hammarskjöld explained to Lloyd that the "effective" members of the observation team would be from Europe and

[103] See the chapter by Michael Fry.

[104] Dixon to Lloyd, Top Secret, 19 June 1958, PREM 11/2387.

Canada and that "in view of Suez" he would not ask Australia and New Zealand to participate. Lloyd wrote afterwards:

> I wanted to assure him [Hammarskjöld] that there was no truth in any ideas current in some American quarters that we were longing to go into the Lebanon with the United States to prove how right we had been over Suez and how wrong the United States.[105]

Hammarskjöld then mentioned that he believed there would be revolutions in Iraq and Jordan. Lloyd disagreed, and the conversation moved on to the prospect of intervention in Lebanon. He attempted to make clear that intervention would be the last resort. "Mr. Hammarskjoeld repeatedly said that everything I had said to him convinced him the more of the importance of making a success of the present United Nations operation. He saw our dilemma...."

If Hammarskjöld seemed to Lloyd to be favorably disposed towards the British predicament, evidence to the contrary soon reached the Foreign Office. From London Hammarskjöld went on to the Middle East, where he stopped in Amman and visited the Jordanian Foreign Minister, Samir Rifai. In a report that the British acquired second-hand from the American Ambassador in Jordan, Hammarskjöld reportedly said "that he was unalterably opposed to foreign intervention in Lebanon," and that he would attempt to persuade Nasser "to take the heat off." If Nasser refused, Hammarskjöld would consider economic sanctions by the United Nations.[106] He had thus contradicted the impression of sympathy for the British dilemma and seemed to imply that the British would force the Americans to act. Hammarskjöld had, Lloyd wrote, "rather a devious mind."[107] Lloyd wrote him the following letter:

> I have been told that you have said, after your arrival in the Middle East, that you were very depressed as a result of your conversation with me in London.... I am told that you said you believed I was eager to involve America in an adventure in the Middle East to prove that I had been right about Suez and the United States wrong.[108]

---

[105] Lloyd to Dixon, Top Secret, 19 June 1958, PREM 11/2387.
[106] Mason to Lloyd, Top Secret, 23 June 1958, PREM 11/2387.
[107] Lloyd to Middleton, Secret, 24 June 1958, PREM 11/2387.
[108] Lloyd to Hammarskjöld, Secret, 24 June 1958, PREM 11/2387.

Hammarskjöld took the letter as an insult. Responding with a spirited defence of the UN observation team, he commented that during the Suez crisis he had been accused of being "fooled by, if not the stooge of, Nasser." Hammarskjöld believed that the record clearly spoke for itself. He concluded with a stinging rebuke to Lloyd: "The straight line often looks crooked to those who have departed from it."[109] On the eve of the Iraqi revolution, Britain's relations with the United Nations, or at least with Hammarskjöld, were tense.

The same theme of ethics during the Suez crisis had clouded Lloyd's dealings with Foster Dulles, who emerges with increased historical stature as one reads the records of the 1958 intervention. During the Suez crisis, Dulles had often contradicted himself and had certainly misled the British about his true intention of negotiating a solution with Nasser rather than forcing him, in Dulles's inimitable phrase, to disgorge. In any event Dulles warned the British Ambassador at an early stage in the 1958 crisis that the public at large suspected the British of pushing the United States into intervention in revenge for Suez. Caccia responded indignantly but the air was cleared.[110] There evolved a harmony of British and American aims. They would work together to sustain a Lebanon friendly to the West if possible, or failing that, a neutral Lebanon, but in any event a Lebanon free from domination by the United Arab Republic. The ultimate step of military action would be taken only if all else failed. Foster Dulles consistently followed that line, as if setting a precedent for defending all small nations against insurrection caused by foreign powers, and as if bearing in mind at all times the historical precedents of Manchuria, Abyssinia, and Czechoslovakia. He weighed all sides of each issue, he moved ponderously, as was his nature, but he moved decisively. On the whole his relations with the British in early July 1956 were satisfactory. Britain and the United States were prepared to intervene, if necessary, with a massive force that had been on standby for about two months. In Dulles's mind one thing was clear above all else. The British would have regarded it as ironic. If troops went in, "it was important to avoid getting bogged down as the British had in Suez."[111]

---

[109] Hammarskjöld to Lloyd, Secret, 10 July 1958, PREM 11/2387.
[110] See Caccia to Lloyd, Top Secret, 23 May 1958, FO 371/134119.
[111] *FRUS,* 1958–1960, XI, p. 252 note.

The British Response to the Iraqi Revolution

There is nothing like a revolution to concentrate the mind. After two months of deliberating, the British and American governments now acted immediately in response to the news on 14 July 1958 that about five o'clock that morning a group of young army officers in Baghdad led by Brigadier Abdel Karim Qasim had overthrown the monarchy and the government of Nuri Pasha. Though at first the situation was obscure, it soon became clear that the members of the royal family had been executed and Nuri killed while attempting to escape. The British Embassy was set ablaze. The Royal Air Force tenuously held the base at Habbaniya, and King Hussein in Amman spoke brave words to encourage Iraqi royalist forces, but the idea of a counter-revolutionary force received only fleeting attention. What the British at first called an "insurrection" became at once a thoroughgoing social and political revolution that overturned the old order and broke the British connection of four decades. British policy now lay in ruins. The revolution threw the situation in Lebanon into entirely new relief. Chamoun had immediately requested the landing of troops. But according to the Cabinet, the problem was now regional rather than restricted to Lebanon: "A temporary Anglo-American intervention confined to the Lebanon alone would be to our disadvantage rather than to our benefit."[112] The British urgently needed to defend their remaining clients in the Middle East, especially Jordan and above all Kuwait.

In Washington the reaction was the same as in London: if the Western powers failed to act, "Nasser would take over the whole area."[113] Foster Dulles prepared for the worst. He had always believed, he remarked to Eisenhower, that the Arab world might be lost, but the United States had to consider the consequences for Turkey, Iran, and Pakistan.[114] "Our failure to respond would destroy the confidence in us of all the countries on the Soviet periphery throughout the Middle and Far East."[115] The strategic aspect was also supremely important. The United States now held the edge militarily. As Dulles later explained in perhaps his clearest formulation of the problem, the Soviets "had gambled on not developing many long-range bombers and had not yet adequate missiles in operation. We

[112] Cabinet Conclusions (58) 55, 14 July 1958, CAB 128/32 Part 2.

[113] Record of meeting of Dulles and others, 14 July 1956, *FRUS*, 1958–1960, XI, p. 210.

[114] Dulles and Eisenhower telephone conversation, 14 July 1958, ibid., p. 209.

[115] Memorandum of conversation, 22 June 1958, ibid., p. 167.

would probably not have another such chance."[116] The balance might never again be so favorable. "If we do not respond to the call from Chamoun," Dulles said on the critical day of 14 July, "we will suffer the decline and indeed the elimination of our influence—from Indonesia to Morocco." Eisenhower shared those cataclysmic thoughts: "we must act, or get out of the Middle East entirely." Vice President Richard Nixon warned of the danger of the United States now acquiring a "Suez" reputation and urged that the President and Secretary of State meet with congressional leaders. Dulles agreed, commenting that "many will say we are simply doing what we stopped the British and the French from doing at the time of the Suez crisis."[117] At the congressional meeting, only Senator William J. Fulbright expressed scepticism about the extent of external aggression. Fulbright was a conspicuous exception. In Washington as in London virtually everyone assumed, in the words of the British Cabinet discussion, "that Lebanon was not primarily a civil war, but was a form of covert aggression promoted by the United Arab Republic."[118]

Macmillan aimed to persuade Eisenhower that the Lebanon operation must now be expanded to include, if necessary, all of the Middle East. The showdown had come. In a telephone conversation with the President, Macmillan said: "If this thing is done, which I think is very noble, dear friend, it will set off a lot of things throughout the whole area. I'm all for that as long as we regard it as an operation that has got to be carried through." They would be driven into a much larger operation. Eisenhower would have none of that:

> Now, just a minute, so that there is no misunderstanding. Are you of the belief that unless we have made up our minds in advance to carry this thing on through to the Persian Gulf, that we had better not go in the first place...?
>
> If we are now planning the initiation of a big operation that could run all the way through Syria and Iraq, we are far beyond anything I have [the] power to do constitutionally.[119]

Macmillan reminded Eisenhower that crises could have unpredictable outcomes. "I have seen these things go wrong," Macmillan said. "I feel

[116] Ibid., p. 356, note 5.

[117] White House conference, 14 July 1958, ibid., pp. 211–15.

[118] Cabinet Conclusions (58) 59, 14 July 1958, CAB 128/32 Part 2.

[119] Telephone conversation between Eisenhower and Macmillan, 14 July 1958, ibid., pp. 231–34.

only this, my dear friend..., it is likely that the trouble will destroy the oil fields and the pipelines and all the rest of it, and will blaze right through.... [W]e are in it together."[120] Eisenhower held firm. He could not commit the United States to more than the operation in Lebanon. But privately he told Dulles he agreed with Macmillan that the crisis was a showdown between the West and Nasser. Though Eisenhower steeled himself to keep the conflict localized, he had to face the prospect of a widening conflict and possible engagement, at least indirectly, with the Soviet Union.

Macmillan now knew that Eisenhower would attempt to limit the crisis to Lebanon, that he would proceed step by step in consultation with Congress and, so far as possible, move forward in concert with the United Nations. Macmillan himself, as if consciously attempting to avoid Eden's mistakes during the Suez crisis, had kept all members of the Cabinet as fully informed as possible and had tried to move not merely in concert with the United States but the United Nations, where British motives were generally suspect. But it was more than mere skullduggery in the General Assembly. Macmillan and Hammarskjöld operated on different assumptions. Contrary to the predominant view held in British and American circles that Egypt or the United Arab Republic had inspired the insurrection in Lebanon, Hammarskjöld reckoned that Nasser had been wary of Lebanese politicians using him to their own advantage, that he had been drawn in reluctantly, that he feared great power involvement, and that he questioned whether the Syrian initiative would serve Egyptian purposes. Perhaps Hammarskjöld manipulated the intelligence reports, but the UN observation team found scant evidence of Syrian staff officers leading rebel troops armed with mortars and bazookas. On the other hand the meager reports perhaps only reflected the limited team the UN could field along the Syrian-Lebanese border. In any event UN sources reported rival factions and fabricated estimates. Much of the trouble could be traced to the politicians ousted by Chamoun and to Chamoun himself, who exaggerated the strength of the opposition in order to secure external assistance. Hammarskjöld believed that if foreign influences were curtailed, and if the Lebanese were left more or less alone in their own goldfish bowl, they would devise their own solution.[121] On the exotic Lebanese

[120] Record of conversation, Top Secret, 14 July 1958, PREM 11/2387.

[121] Many of these aspects of Hammarskjöld's thoughts are related in a conversation with Cabot Lodge, 26 June 1958, *FRUS,* 1958–1960, XI, pp. 175–80.

goldfish bowl stirred by foreign hands, Hammarskjöld and Macmillan could both agree.[122]

Where they disagreed, with Eisenhower concurring with Macmillan and vice versa, was on the extent of external intervention. Even between Macmillan and Eisenhower there were differences, the latter regarding Nasser as a tool of the Soviets.[123] Macmillan acknowledged a degree of Soviet influence over Nasser, but, like the Foreign Office, regarded Arab nationalism as the principal problem. As if all of this were not complicated enough—with Macmillan, Hammarskjöld and others acting on different assumptions—there must be added the view that Chehab himself was a far more subtle person than commonly supposed, and that his motivations were to hold together the Lebanese army and beyond that the Lebanese nation. Towards that end he withheld intelligence reports from the United Nations. According to the American Deputy Undersecretary of State, Robert Murphy, who was sent to Lebanon at the height of the crisis, Chehab had telephone intercepts "showing that Damascus is giving direct orders" to the rebel leaders in the Basta district of Beirut.[124]

Those conflicting interpretations were put to the test on 15 July 1958, when two battalions of US Marines landed on the beaches of Beirut to the ringing of Christian church bells. Hammarskjöld had a certain point when he commented on the extent to which the Lebanese problem above all else reflected domestic tensions. He believed that Lebanese of all political colors deliberately overestimated Nasser's influence. Middleton summed up Hammarskjöld's impression: "the Lebanese were exaggerating the importance of the alleged infiltration from across the Syrian border in order to conceal their internal political disintegration."[125]

The story of the landing of the US Marines has been told many times from the American vantage point, but it gains fresh irony when related by Sir George Middleton. Middleton later recounted how "the first wave of the American force, amounting to some 2,000 assault troops of the United States Marine Corps, land on Khaldé beach at about 2.30 P.M. on the 15th of July." He went on:

> The ensuing scene which, but for the inherent gravity of the situation, must have come perilously near the ridiculous, was somehow symbolic of

---

[122] See the chapter by Michael Fry.

[123] Eisenhower stated on 15 July that Nasser "is so small a figure, and of so little power, that he is a puppet, even though he probably doesn't think so." Ibid., p. 245.

[124] Murphy to Dulles, 18 July 1958, ibid., p. 327.

[125] Middleton to Lloyd, Confidential and Guard, 30 July 1958, FO 371/134132.

> the whole crisis. The marines had been trained to land on enemy beaches in the face of stiff opposition; even those who had received some briefing expected to find some signs of civil war.
>
> They were totally unprepared for having to pick their way over recumbent sunbathers in their "bikinis" or for grinning youths trying to help them drag their jeeps ashore. Still less were they prepared for the second shock wave of regiments of small boys jostling round to sell them chewing-gum while their older brothers followed with Coca-Cola.[126]

The American troops made their first contact with the Lebanese army at the airport, where Chehab negotiated a tense withdrawal of his forces. Middleton confirmed that Chamoun had not informed his Commander-in-Chief of the impending American invasion. Chehab had learned of the landing of troops from the American Ambassador, Robert L. McClintock, only two hours before. These were momentous transactions in Lebanese politics beyond Western comprehension. No less serious, McClintock had to intervene also with Chehab to prevent an army takeover against Chamoun. Middleton and the British generally had regarded McClintock as an impulsive though eloquent American Ambassador, but on this occasion they had nothing but praise for the way in which he responded to the crisis. For the disciplined comportment of the American troops, Middleton wrote retrospectively in mild astonishment:

> In spite of their numbers I have nothing but praise for the Americans' behaviour. On the 9th of August they were given leave passes into the town, and for the first time in many months the enormous American taxis of Beirut came into their own with full cargoes of marines and sailors. Bars overflowed with white and grey-green uniforms, and everywhere one looked some grey-haired Turkish-trousered shoe-shine "boy" was putting a final gloss on a pair of trans-Atlantic shoes.[127]

When British paratroopers were dropped in Amman on 17 June 1958, they faced difficulties of a different sort. In Macmillan's words, British forces had "no port, no heavy arms, and no real mobility."[128]

The same problem of validity of intelligence sources arose in Jordan as it had in Lebanon. After a flicker of hope that all might not be lost in Iraq, British attention concentrated on Jordan and the Gulf. The British

---

126 Ibid.

127 Middleton to Lloyd, Confidential, 26 August 1958, FO 371/134133.

128 Macmillan to Eisenhower, 18 July 1958, *FRUS*, 1958–1960, XI, p. 329.

assumed, like the Americans, that "the revolution in Iraq is clearly fostered and supported from Cairo."[129] In contrast with Lebanon, Nasser had good reason to throw his support behind those plotting to overthrow Hussein. The point of ambiguity, as Hammarskjöld had pointed out, was the extent of Nasser's involvement. Nasser himself was a conspirator as well as an opportunist and he also calculated his self-interest against a possible British reoccupation of Jordan, as did Hussein. Nasser did greatly increase his propaganda attacks against Jordan after the outbreak of the Iraqi revolution. For Jordan the proof of the danger, though not of its ultimate source, lay in Hussein's reckoning that he must obtain foreign assistance. But Hussein wanted American as well as British troops to guarantee a limited British presence. Dulles and Eisenhower were unwilling to expand the operation and thought that British intervention might have the opposite of the intended effect. The King might be overthrown rather than saved. The American Embassy in Amman had warned of a "tidal wave" of Arab nationalism engulfing Jordan.[130] After the outbreak of the revolution in Baghdad, Hussein had sent word requesting British and American military support if necessary. The next day, 15 July, British and American intelligence services learned "that Nasser had instructed his agents in Jordan to assassinate Hussein and overthrow the Jordanian Government on July 16 or 17."[131] Did these intercepts reflect Nasser's orders or did they reveal the ambitions of anti-Hussein officers in the Jordan army? In any event, the British Cabinet decided, after prolonged and agonized deliberations of over three hours, to send in troops.

The British force in Amman consisted of two battalions of paratroopers at the strength of twenty-two hundred men with the support of a Guards Brigade, thus giving the total potential of four thousand troops.[132] The object was to secure the airfield, the strategic bridgehead for all operations. Without the airfield, according to the British Cabinet minutes of 16 July, the British could not protect either the King or the government and "the opportunity for effective intervention would be lost." Without intervention, "Jordan would pass under the influence of the United Arab Republic." Without Jordan, "our position in the Gulf would at once be in jeopardy." It was imperative to act immediately. "Even a day's delay might

---

[129] According to Macmillan in a message to Eisenhower, 14 July 1958, ibid., p. 301.

[130] Embassy in Jordan to Department of State, 16 July 1958, ibid., p. 314.

[131] Ibid., p. 309 note 2.

[132] US forces assisted the British by airlifting oil and in other logistical support.

rob us of the opportunity of seizing the airfield at Amman and establishing a bridgehead in Jordan." But it was, in the Prime Minister's phrase, "a difficult and dangerous operation." If the Jordan Army attacked British troops, the only opportunity to counter-attack would be by aircraft based on Cyprus.[133] Macmillan interrupted the Cabinet meeting to try to persuade the Americans to commit troops or at least airplanes to strengthen the tactical position at Amman and lend strategic support in the Eastern Mediterranean. Dulles agreed only to "moral support" and "if needed, logistic support."[134] At least the British were moving forward with American approval, but Macmillan nervously referred to it as "a quixotic undertaking." It was quixotic in the sense that British motives might be misunderstood in the House of Commons, in the United Nations, and in America. It would be erroneously assumed that the British wished to reoccupy Jordan and launch a counter-revolutionary attack against Iraq. Macmillan was correct in assuming that these aims would be attributed to the British government.

As it later transpired, Macmillan and Dulles had entirely different conceptions about the purpose of intervention both in Lebanon and in Jordan. What would be the conditions of American and British withdrawal? Macmillan held that "real United Nations safeguards" for both Lebanon and Jordan would have to be secured. Otherwise "if as soon as we withdrew, those countries fell into Nasser's lap our whole operation would have been a failure." Dulles disagreed in a statement that lucidly established the differences between British and American views on intervention:

> Nothing could cancel out the fact that we had achieved our main objectives which were, not so much to preserve Jordan and the Lebanon, as to show that our friends did not call on us for help in vain, to demonstrate to the Soviets that we could move quickly if we so wished and to show Nasser that he would not always assume that his plots could succeed without a reaction by us.[135]

Macmillan believed that the purpose of intervention went beyond the demands of the Cold War. The purpose was to save the two countries, especially Jordan, from Nasser. Dulles by contrast expressed ambivalence

---

133 Cabinet Conclusions (58) 59, 16 July 1958, CAB 128/32 Part 2.

134 *FRUS*, 1958–1960, XI, p. 316.

135 Record of a meeting between Macmillan, Dulles, and others, 27 July 1958, PREM 11/2388.

towards intervention, often recalling in 1958 the reasons he had opposed the British and French in 1956. Getting in was always easier than getting out, he said, and the presence of American troops in the Middle East would create "strong anti-Western feeling and anti-Americanism." No stable government there or elsewhere could last long if it were merely held in place by American or British bayonets. Dulles thus had two sharp reactions to a complex situation. The one pulled him in the direction of the British as part of a response to the Cold War, the other tugged him towards the position held by Henry Cabot Lodge, the US Ambassador at the United Nations, who believed as a matter of principle that intervention was fatal and that the United States should not be tainted by association with such powers as Britain and France. All in all, the British had good reason to be satisfied with the manifestation of what Selwyn Lloyd called the "robust and realistic" side of Dulles's personality.[136]

In part to keep memories of Suez subdued, Britain now attempted to keep a distance from the two allies in 1956, France and Israel, even though the latter was directly concerned with the fate of Jordan. Dealing with the French had proved to be easier than originally imagined because of the American insistence that the interventions in Lebanon and Jordan be kept separate. Sir Gladwyn Jebb had anticipated either failure of the operation, if the French participated, or "a blood row with de Gaulle," if they did not.[137] After the American invasion of Lebanon, Jebb could say that the British would not participate but would reserve forces for action elsewhere—in other words, Jordan. Events then moved so fast that the British could but brace themselves against French protests against less than full consultation before the paratroop drop. "It is impossible not to offend the French," Jebb wrote on 18 July. Nevertheless the separation of the two ventures helped considerably in arguing that it was not an allied operation under the terms of the Tripartite Declaration of 1950 but distinct maneuvers. "Given the General's determination to achieve tripartite consultation," Jebb reported, "we must try to meet him somehow, or face the risk of his reverting to his 1940 methods."[138] The answer was to involve the French as fully as possible in plans for the future of the Middle East. The British eventually took the same line with the Israelis, though with considerably more difficulty.

In the meeting on 16 July that decided in favor of the Jordan intervention, "The Cabinet were informed that there was good reasons to believe

---

[136] Lloyd to Macmillan, Top Secret, 19 July 1958, PREM 11/2388.
[137] Jebb to Hoyer Millar, Top Secret, 19 June 1958, FO 371/134125.
[138] Jebb to Foreign Office, Secret, 18 June 1958, PREM 11/2388.

that in all the circumstances the Israel Government would find no difficulty in acquiescing in our over-flying their territory...."[139] The assumption proved too optimistic.[140] Most of the British force arrived at Amman airport at noon, 17 July, but Israeli fighters fired on the last of the transports and forced them back to Cyprus. The permission to fly over Israeli airspace still stood pending in Tel Aviv. The remainder of the brigade waited five hours in Cyprus until the United States government, responding to urgent British requests, secured permission from the Israelis for the over-flight into Jordan. The British quickly discovered that the problem went directly to the Prime Minister, David Ben-Gurion, who found it "humiliating" that "we should ask to over-fly Israel at short notice." Ben-Gurion believed that the British reaped the advantage of an alliance without having concluded one. As during the Suez crisis, he placed great emphasis on being the "moral equal" of Britain. He wanted a "close working partnership" along the lines of the one between Israel and France.[141]

By acquiescing in the British overflight, the Israelis had exposed themselves more than ever. They were aligned with the Western powers and increasingly opposed Egypt and the Soviet Union. As Macmillan and Dulles both acknowledged, Ben-Gurion's "tacit agreement to the airlift was building up a backlog of Russian and Arab resentment.... [W]hen American and British forces withdrew he would be left with no hard Western guarantee of Israel's position."[142] Were Jordan to collapse, Israel would be sucked into the vortex of great power confrontation. What did the British propose to do about it? Selwyn Lloyd attempted to answer that question in a surprisingly candid discussion with the Israeli Ambassador in London. Britain would consult closely with Israel on the question of the future of Jordan.[143] As to the "partnership," the proposal produced some remarkable minutes in the Foreign Office. Sir Evelyn Shuckburgh, one of the key figures in British Middle Eastern policy in the earlier part of the decade, opposed closer association with Israel:

> [I]f we actually went on to create some sort of partnership on the lines proposed by the Israelis, it seems to me that we should simply be adding another heavy link to the chain hanging round our neck which started with the Balfour Declaration and has been steadily drowning us ever since.

139 Cabinet Conclusions (58) 59, 16 July 1958, CAB 128/32 Part 2.

140 See the chapter by Ilan Pappé.

141 Sir Francis Rundall (Tel Aviv) to Foreign Office, Top Secret, 19 July 1958, FO 371/134284.

142 Record of a meeting between Macmillan, Dulles, and others, 27 July 1958, FO 371/133823.

143 Lloyd to Rundall, Secret, 23 July 1958, FO 371/134284.

> Whichever policy we adopt in the Middle East—whether to build up Iraq as a counter-weight to Egypt or to seek a *modus vivendi* with a more united Arab world under Egyptian leadership, association with Israel will be a fatal obstacle to its success....[144]

On the other hand Sir William Hayter took a high moral line that coincided with British *realpolitik*:

> I confess I do not much like the idea of sucking up to the Israelis now when we need them and dropping them as soon as this need is over. It seems to me highly dishonest, and also liable to destroy any lingering trace of respect or confidence in us that the Israelis may retain....
>
> Our future relations with the Arabs will, or in my opinion at any rate should, be on the basis of hard-headed cooperation founded on mutual interests. They will need us, by which I mean the Americans and ourselves, as a counterpoise to Russian influence and as a market for their oil, and we shall need to buy their oil. We shall neither be able, nor be obliged to prop up unpopular regimes and to try to make them as little unpopular as possible by anti-Israeli gestures. It therefore seems to be clear that we can even in the long term afford to be much less standoffish with the Israelis than we have been in the past.[145]

Britain emerged from the crisis of 1958 with a slightly more pro-Israeli, or, more accurately perhaps, a slightly less anti-Israeli policy than previously, in part for reasons concerning the Soviet Union.

Five days after the outbreak of the revolution in Iraq, Nikita Khrushchev wrote to Eisenhower protesting the "armed intervention" by the United States in Lebanon and by Britain in Jordan. To prevent a conflagration in the Middle East, he proposed a conference to resolve the Middle East crisis to be attended by the heads of government of the Soviet Union, the United States, Britain, France, and India. Khrushchev suggested that Hammarskjöld participate. Sir William Hayter was extremely active in Washington and New York as well as London in devising a reasoned course of action in response to what he believed to be Khrushchev's purpose. Assuming that Khrushchev would act rationally—as always, as with Nasser, a large assumption in the British view—the British did not think that the Soviet Union intended to go to war

[144] Minute by Shuckburgh, 28 July 1958, FO 371/134285. John Foster Dulles also described Israel as "this millstone round our necks." As reported in Hood to Hayter, Top Secret, 9 September 1958, FO 371/134279.

[145] Minute by Hayter, 29 July 1958, FO 371/134285.

over Lebanon or Jordan, but that Khrushchev intended to make it clear that the Western powers must not embark on a counter-revolutionary invasion of Iraq. Hayter believed that there should be a United Nations solution.[146] This was the governing idea. He saw eye-to-eye with Hammarskjöld that Jordan, not Lebanon, was the heart of the problem. According to a record of a meeting between Hayter and other British officials with Hammarskjöld in New York, the Secretary-General "viewed our presence in Jordan in a quite different light from the American presence in Lebanon." The situation in Jordan was incomparably more serious.

> [Hammarskjöld]...sees that a collapse in Jordan, bringing it within Nasser's sphere of influence would at once create an acute problem for the Israeli Government and would probably lead them to occupy the West Bank, with incalculable consequences for the peace of the area.[147]

The British discussed among themselves and with others various solutions, including Nasser's proposal for the division of Lebanon along the lines of Vietnam or Korea and for the division of Jordan with the absorption of the Palestinian part in the United Arab Republic and with the pre-1948 state of Transjordan remaining independent. The Levant Department of the Foreign Office, agreeing with Hammarskjöld, commented on the Jordan part of the proposal:

> Transjordan would be politically more viable, and economically no more unviable, than the present Jordan—and cheaper to maintain. But what on earth would the West Bank do—except fall into Israeli hands?[148]

The British discussed various other proposals in the wake of the Soviet demand for a conference. A neutralized Lebanon might become a ward of

---

146 See e.g. memorandum of conversation at British Embassy, 19 July 1958, *FRUS*, 1958–1960, XI, pp. 340–43.

147 Dixon to Foreign Office, Secret, 21 July 1958, PREM 11/2388. In a conversation between Macmillan, Dulles, and others, Dulles commented:

> The disintegration of Jordan would lead probably to the Israelis seizing the West Bank and this in turn would mean an Arab/Israel war with a very dangerous chain reaction in the international field. It was possible that Khrushchev could be made aware of the dangers of such an upheaval and might agree to co-operate to prevent it. This, of course, was presupposing that Khrushchev was motivated by reason. But there were grave dangers that both Khrushchev and Nasser were inclined to act spontaneously without any rational approach.

Record of meeting, 27 July 1958, PREM 11/2388.

148 Minute by Robert Tesh (Levant Department), 7 August 1958, FO 371/133826.

the United Nations, Jordan might be neutralized along the lines of Austria, and Kuwait might be guaranteed independence as a Switzerland in the Middle East. Whatever the solutions, they would be found through the United Nations. Thereby the British would have the support or at least the acquiescence of the international community that they had so sorely lacked during the Suez crisis. As Macmillan described the plan to Dulles, the grand strategy bore a striking resemblance to Dulles's own maneuvers in 1956 when he had attempted to let the crisis peter out through protracted negotiations. Macmillan wrote:

> If...the Russians accept a meeting of the Security Council, then I think it unlikely that desperate action will be taken by Nasser or the new Iraq Government to precipitate a crisis in the Middle East. We might look for a few weeks' pause before any further serious trouble develops—such as a coup in Jordan or a move against the Western interests in the Gulf.[149]

The immediate problem, however, was to be sure that Khrushchev did not misunderstand the intent of Britain and the United States. They would not intervene in Iraq. But they would defend at virtually any cost their access to the oil in the Gulf.

From beginning to end, the British aimed above all to preserve their position in the Gulf. They found to their great relief that the Americans agreed that this point had transcendent priority. After the outbreak of the revolution in Iraq, Selwyn Lloyd had flown to Washington. He reported jubilantly to Macmillan:

> One of the most reassuring features of my talks here has been the complete United States solidarity with us over the Gulf. They are assuming that we will take firm action to maintain our position in Kuwait. They themselves are disposed to act with similar resolution in relation to the Aramco oilfields in the area of Dhahran.... They assume that we will also hold Bahrain and Qatar, come what may. They agree that at all costs these oilfields must be kept in Western hands.[150]

Eisenhower himself wrote to Macmillan that, beyond Lebanon and Jordan, "we must also, and this seems to me even more important, see that the Persian Gulf area stays within the Western orbit. The Kuwait-

[149] Macmillan to Dulles 27 July 1958, *FRUS*, 1958–1960, XI, p. 405.
[150] Lloyd to Macmillan, Secret, 20 July 1958, FO 371/132776.

Dhahran-Abadan areas become extremely important...."[151] Dulles entirely agreed: "The thing we want to preserve is that Persian Gulf position...."[152] With the oil of the Gulf remaining in Western hands, the loss of Iraq could be taken more philosophically. Lloyd stated the problem at its most basic when he wrote of the agreement between him and Dulles: "he was quite definite that the Gulf was the essential area, and that so long as we could hold it and its oil resources, the loss of Iraq was not intolerable."[153]

In both Kuwait and Jordan the British had to face the prospect that the rulers might be swept away by waves of pro-Nasser Arab nationalism. "If a coup could be carried out in Baghdad, as it had been," Lloyd remarked to Dulles, "there was an equal danger of one in Kuwait."[154] In that event US Marines based on Okinawa would secure Kuwait and, if the revolution reached Saudi Arabia, the oil installations at Dhahran. What would then happen? One course might be to rule Kuwait directly as a Crown Colony, though Lloyd pointed out the difficulties of occupying the country against the wishes of the ruling family:

> The labour force working in the oil area may strike. To produce tolerable conditions for a long-term operation, we should have to take control of the whole of Kuwait and run it as a Crown Colony. For a short-term operation we could hold the oil area alone, but that would no doubt mean a Nasserite régime in the rest of Kuwait with the inconveniences and pressures that happened when we held the Suez base but not the rest of Egypt.[155]

Prudence prevailed.[156] British contingency planning proceeded on the basis that Kuwait would become a sort of Switzerland. But the mere mention of the phrase "Crown Colony" caused tremors in Washington, especially among those who viewed the new Anglo-American combination with distaste. The British were aware of a strong element of dissent from the general line expressed by Foster Dulles. It extended all the way from

---

151 Eisenhower to Macmillan, 18 July 1958, *FRUS*, 1958–1960, XI, p. 330.

152 Record of telephone conversation between Dulles and Eisenhower, 19 July 1958, ibid., p. 332.

153 Lloyd to Foreign Office, Secret, 20 July 1958, PREM, 11/2388.

154 Lloyd to Foreign Office, Top Secret, 18 July 1958, FO 371/133823.

155 Lloyd to Macmillan, Secret, 20 July 1958, FO 371/132776.

156 The head of the Eastern Department, D. M. H. Riches, minuted: "The political effects of running Kuwait as a colony are I think understated. I think that unless we can secure some kind of request for going into Kuwait we shall be in queer street not only with the Arab but also with the rest of the world." 22 July 1958, FO 371/133808.

upper echelons to low levels in the State Department, where one Edwin M. Kretzmann caused the British anguish. Kretzmann held strong opinions, especially about the Middle East. Recent commitments to the British, he said, by no means meant that the United States would maintain "British political and military positions" in the Gulf.[157] What galled the British was not the existence of such views but that they were so blatantly and publicly expressed. "I find this disturbing evidence of the lack of discipline amongst State Department officials in dealing with policy issues on an off-the-record basis," wrote P. H. G. Wright in the Foreign Office. "There is nothing that we can do to alter what is in fact a fundamental American trait." Suez as usual was part of the explanation for such robust views. Kretzmann merely vented openly what many other American officials expressed privately. To the British, the return to the subject of Suez was extremely unfortunate because it undermined the British position not merely in the Gulf but throughout the Middle East:

> One of the strongest propaganda cards which we can play at the present time in the Middle East is the fact that there is a joint Anglo-American policy, and that the Anglo-American difficulties of the Suez era are a thing of the past. But of course the value of this card is greatly weakened if the American part of this position is going to be undermined by an impression that the Americans themselves are not wholeheartedly behind their own policy.[158]

If Kuwait were to become the Switzerland of the Middle East, it would require strong backing of both the American and British governments. The trends in American policy by no means reassured the British.

The principal exponent of an alternative to Dulles's policy appeared to be William M. Rountree, the Assistant Secretary for Near Eastern and South Asian Affairs. Dulles himself liked and encouraged controversy. It provoked him to further thought and in any event his own will always prevailed. But it disturbed the British to hear such a highly placed and influential adviser voice opinions at variance with Dulles's. Similar dissent was a vital part of the British tradition as well, but once policy had been decided, ministers and civil servants upheld it or resigned. To the British, Rountree represented an acute danger because he seemed to want to

---

[157] As quoted in Willie Morris to Riches, Secret and Guard, 6 August 1958, FO 371/132770.

[158] Minute by P. H. G. Wright, 12 September 1958, FO 371/132770.

appease Nasser. In reality Rountree's views were not far removed from Dulles's, but he did distrust the British and he did believe that eventually there had to be a reconciliation with Egypt. What drew British wrath on Jordan was Rountree's proposal that a referendum be held to determine the country's future. The British Ambassador in Amman, Sir Charles Johnston, wrote with scarcely veiled contempt that Rountree knew nothing of the country or its traditions:

> Mr. Rountree perhaps imagines that the alternative to King Hussein could be a nice cosy pro-American and anti-British republic. If he does, he could not be more mistaken.... If King Hussein went now there would be no halting the slide towards extremism.... The result would be not only that Jordan would promptly join the UAR, but that its accession would give the whole UAR a sharp twist to the left and indeed might replace Cairo's influence by Moscow's throughout Greater Syria. Mr. Rountree's advice would, in my view, lead straight to the establishment of Communist control over the Levant.[159]

The problem for the British in this case was one of mistaken identity. It was not merely Rountree but Dulles himself who wanted to examine the possibility of a referendum on Jordan. Dulles had become increasingly alarmed at the British position in Jordan. He now took the view that he had opposed the British intervention from the outset.[160] This was an exaggeration. He had been skeptical, and his skepticism had grown. He did not believe the British could now extricate themselves without pulling down the King and in consequence bringing about a Nasserite takeover. Dulles's doubts were fed by Macmillan and Lloyd, who also were extremely uneasy at the precarious British position in Jordan. Only Sir Charles Johnston took the vigorous stand that Hussein, and the British, could weather the storm.

Macmillan once said, agreeing with Foster Dulles, that "it is not really Jordan but Iraq which is the real problem."[161] By the end of the year it was still not clear whether the revolutionary regime in Iraq would emerge as pro-Nasser or pro-Soviet. But there appeared to be the possibility, at least to the British, that Abdel Karim Qasim might be first and foremost an

[159] Johnston to Foreign Office, Secret, 18 August 1958, PREM 11/2381.

[160] Dulles stated on 23 July 1958 at a meeting with Eisenhower and others that "we had not wanted the British to go in." *FRUS*, 1958–1960, XI, p. 377.

[161] Macmillan to Eisenhower, 18 July 1958, ibid., p. 329.

Iraqi patriot and thus an Arab nationalist with whom they could do business.[162] As it eventually transpired, they found him to be an erratic and oppressive tyrant, but certainly not the tool of either the Egyptians or the Soviets. Qasim apparently puzzled Nasser as well. As the British and Americans learned more of Nasser's reactions to the general crisis, the more they began to suspect that he had not been, after all, the mastermind behind the Iraqi revolution, or even in control of the anti-Hussein movement in Jordan, and still less directly involved in Lebanon. In a remarkable interview with Robert Murphy in August 1958, Nasser stated that "frankly, as a military man, he just could not believe it earlier but was quite willing now to be convinced that US military intervention [was] limited to Lebanon." He believed the Americans and certainly the British "intended to attack Iraq." Obviously, misperceptions were not limited to the West. On Jordan, Nasser stated that he simply did not know how to solve the problem, but that he failed to see how King Hussein could survive with ninety percent of the population opposed to him. Nasser undoubtedly exaggerated the size of the opposition, but when he began talking about his own part in the plot against King Farouk in 1952, his words rang true. Nasser said that the overthrow of Farouk was in itself the best example of how wrong Hussein might be in his confidence in the fidelity of the Jordanian army.[163] Sir Charles Johnston would have disagreed. He believed not only that British intervention had strengthened Hussein's position but had also consolidated the loyalty of the army.

The American and British interventions came to an end with the withdrawal of the last troops in late October, early November 1958. General Chehab's election as President on 31 July had begun a new era in Lebanese national history. In Jordan, King Hussein's regime did not collapse, contrary to fears in London and Washington. A United Nations "presence" helped to stabilize Jordan's relations with the neighboring Arab states and the United States agreed to economic assistance, thus providing the basis for Jordan's survival.

It is appropriate to end with the reflections by the two British officials most closely concerned with Lebanon and Jordan, Sir George Middleton

---

[162] Macmillan remarked that "Iraq was a country of diverse elements, some of whom might be possible Kerenskys. We should not appear to drive them out, but rather see whether we could not gradually wean them away from Nasser." Record of a meeting between Macmillan, Dulles, and others, 27 July 1958, PREM 11/2400.

[163] Murphy's report of his interview, 8 August 1958, *FRUS*, 1958–1960, XI, pp. 439–43.

and Sir Charles Johnston. Both were extraordinarily able men and their thoughts help to provide perspective on the general crisis of 1958. Middleton was essentially a humane sceptic, both about Lebanon and about Britain's future in the Middle East. Johnston was robustly optimistic about Jordan. He was one of the last of a long line of British Proconsuls who believed that Britain's presence in the region could be compatible with Arab nationalism.

The end of the crisis coincided with the end of Middleton's tenure. In his valedictory despatch he wrote of Lebanon with warm memories: "It is impossible not to enjoy the splendid and dramatic scenery, the sparkling climate, the quick wit and innate courtesy of the country folk, the urbanity of the French-speaking upper class." Nevertheless he wrote in despair. He believed that the national ordeal since May had been "a moral crisis which had its origins in the independence of the Lebanon." The internal crisis was basically a confessional issue. "Christian and Moslem live in uneasy concord only so long as there is no obvious advantage to either side in seeking to change the balance or so long as one side has the clear mastery. So long as Islam and the West are not in conflict in the wider sphere of world politics, Lebanon manages to live quietly at home."[164] He had written earlier of how the less privileged Shia had built up a standing grievance against the more affluent parts of the population, how the Suez crisis had injected an explosive element in Lebanese politics with many Muslims turning to Nasser as the leader of the Arab world, and how Chamoun had tilted the country too far to the West while driving his political opponents into armed opposition. Throughout the crisis, Middleton remained essentially favorably disposed to Chamoun and ambivalent if not hostile to Chehab. He recognized in Chamoun, for all his faults, a patriot who had his country's interests at heart. He saw in Chehab a cynic who, though also a sincere patriot, could or would not rise to the occasion. This was a basic misjudgment. In fairness it must be said that Middleton acknowledged Chehab's potential greatness:

> General Chehab is descended from the emirs who once ruled much of south-central Lebanon and I think he is conscious of his inherited part in the history of this country. To his aristocracy of birth has been added the habit of command deriving from some twelve years as the senior officer in the Lebanese Army. Moreover he is conscious that by his aloofness from day-by-

[164] Middleton to Lloyd, No. 129 Confidential, 27 August 1958, FO 371/134133.

> day affairs he has become something of a figurehead in Lebanese national life and widely regarded as a symbol of all that is most worthy in the Lebanese character....
>
> History is his chosen reading and his family name is woven into the history of Lebanon in the same way as the name of Cecil is woven into that of England.[165]

With guarded words Middleton summed up by stating that Chehab "is by no means the ideal President but he is probably the best we can hope for in the circumstances." This was a low assessment, for in Middleton's own words Chehab more than anyone else had worked "to restore the national unity which had brought independence to the Lebanon in 1943, and which had inspired the National Pact."[166] In their own way, the Lebanese had again achieved a precarious balance of national unity with Chehab as their leader.

Though Middleton acknowledged the skill and the discipline of the American intervention, he believed it had only momentarily stabilized Lebanese politics and that the country might yet drift into Nasser's orbit. In their haste to patch together an accord, to outpace even the Lebanese in pursuit of a compromise that would allow for the withdrawal of the troops, the Americans underestimated the tenacity of the pro-Nasser Muslims. Middleton remained pessimistic:

> I do not see Lebanon settling down easily or quickly. I suspect that under American pressure the General [Chehab] may seek a drastic and pro-rebel solution to the present crisis rather than one of compromise which would be more natural to him. If he does, he may find himself faced with a new rebellious element on his hands and the temptation will then be to throw in his hand in disgust.
>
> This will be exactly what the present Opposition have always wanted; first to get rid of Chamoun and then the General, so that the field is left open to the Moslem pro-Nasser nationalists.[167]

This again was too low an estimate of Chehab, but Middleton's comments revealed the suspicion prevalent in British circles that the Americans would eventually want to appease Nasser in order better to carry on the

---

[165] Middleton to Lloyd, No. 128 Confidential, 27 August 1958, FO 371/134133

[166] Middleton to Lloyd, Confidential, 26 August 1958, FO 371/134133.

[167] Middleton to Hayter, Confidential, 13 August 1958, FO 371/134133.

Cold War against the Soviet Union. The submerged differences between the British and the Americans in assessing Nasser in relation to the Soviet Union had now come to the surface.

Those differences emerged sharply in the case of Jordan. In Jordan British priorities ranked much higher than in Lebanon, which Middleton referred to as a "not very valuable" country.[168] Jordan lay in the strategic arc that had extended through Iraq to Kuwait. After the revolution in Iraq, Sir Charles Johnston gave two reasons why Jordan continued to be important: "if we did not hold on, first this whole area would go Nasserite, and secondly the remaining friends of Britain and America in the Arab World would regard us as useless and effete."[169] Johnston believed that the Americans throughout the crisis had been defeatist. He complained especially about the US Chargé d'Affaires in Amman, Thomas K. Wright, whom Johnston regarded as "the voice of doom." Wright held that neither the United States nor the United Nations could continue to underwrite a deficit regime propped up by Bedouin bayonets. Wright happened to share that view with the Secretary of State himself. Dulles became increasingly nervous about the British position in Jordan. "The British are getting into a dangerous situation in Jordan," he commented a few days after the arrival of the British forces in Amman. "They cannot leave without the situation collapsing...."[170] In London Macmillan was jittery and Lloyd was pessimistic.[171] Despite those doubts and differences, the British and American combination held. Johnston drew a far-reaching conclusion: the intervention "proved that Anglo-American cooperation in the Arab world is possible."

Without the intervention, according to Johnston, "Jordan would now be either Nasserite or Qassimite or a bit of both." Again the conclusion was far-reaching:

> As it is, we have succeeded in preserving in the Arab world a régime which is both outspokenly pro-Western and at the same time acceptable in

---

[168] Middleton to Lloyd, No. 129 Confidential, 27 August 1958, FO 371/134133.

[169] Johnston to Foreign Office, Secret, 12 August 1958, FO 371/134009.

[170] Record of a meeting at the White House, 20 July 1958, *FRUS*, 1958–1960, XI, p. 348. Dulles said on another occasion to Eisenhower that "We are hooked for 30–40 million a year to pay the budget deficit of Jordan" and that he would "rather Nasser or the Soviets do that." Ibid., p. 332.

[171] On 23 July Eisenhower remarked that Macmillan seemed to have "lost his nerve"; and Lloyd at the end of September expressed the fear that "Jordan would collapse shortly after the British withdrawal." Ibid., p. 377 and p. 580.

> its country; at least it maintains normal stability by civilian methods and without the support of martial law, which is more than can be said for most other Middle East régimes. We have showed both types of Arab extremists [Nasserites and Qassimites] that we (the West in general and the British in particular) are people to be reckoned with.[172]

Too much should not be made of Johnston's description of Jordan as a liberal regime or for that matter of Jordan's independence. He recognized that Hussein presided over a police state and that, "to put it crudely, the Hashemite Kingdom is still a horse in the Western stable."[173] Nevertheless the instincts of King Hussein quite apart from Western influence were conciliatory, as if, Johnston wrote, he had inherited the realistic attitudes of his grandfather, King Abdullah, especially regarding Israel.

> If King Hussein's régime collapsed, the Israelis would feel strongly tempted to seize some at least of the Jordanian territory on the West Bank, thereby at once transforming a Middle East dispute into a world crisis....
>
> To allow an Arab Government with such views [as Hussein's]...to be ousted by a gang of chauvinistic, irredentist demagogues like the Jordanian Nasserites...would be about the worst mistake that the West could commit.[174]

Johnston attributed the success in sustaining Hussein through the crisis in large part to Hussein himself, who possessed "a certain doggedness which is rarely found in the Arab character." Hussein, in Johnston's judgment, "has now emerged as a leader of undoubted quality." Such leaders might be rare in the Arab world, but they could be found. Johnston had written on numerous earlier occasions that it was defeatist to believe it impossible for Britain and the United States to reach an understanding with Arab nationalist leaders. "The Arabs have more sense than their behaviour sometimes suggests. If properly handled by us, treated as equals, and helped where possible, but with tact and discretion, there is no reason why they should gravitate to eastward."[175] Those ideas led to Johnston's ultimate conclusion, which helps to explain the British view on the significance of the 1958 intervention. Arab nationalism was not necessarily anti-Western. With the help of the United States, Britain could remain a great power in the Middle East.

---

[172] Johnston to Lloyd, Confidential and Guard, 22 January 1959, FO 371/142100.

[173] Ibid.

[174] Johnston to Lloyd, Secret and Guard, 4 December 1958, FO 371/134011.

[175] Ibid.

2

The Emergence of the United States as a Middle Eastern Power, 1956–1958

DIANE B. KUNZ

The year 1958 was a pivotal one for American policy toward the Middle East. Two years earlier, the Suez crisis had forced Washington to attempt a larger role in a region it had long regarded as a backwater. When the administration launched the Eisenhower Doctrine early in 1957, it had hoped that a sturdy American response would stop the Nasserite surge and block further inroads by the Soviet Union. It did not turn out that way, as the events of 1958 proved. The successful Iraqi revolution in July, the threats to staunchly pro-Western rulers in Jordan and Lebanon, and the seemingly unstoppable popularity of Egyptian leader Gamal Abdel Nasser posed serious problems for US officials as they tried to achieve regional policy goals.

Coming at the height of the Cold War, the events in the Middle East were viewed in Washington through an East-West prism. President Dwight D. Eisenhower and his officials believed that the Suez crisis and its aftermath had jeopardized the economic and diplomatic well-being of America's key Western European allies. American policy, then, first and foremost would concentrate on rectifying the situation. That meant securing continued access to Middle Eastern petroleum reserves for increasingly oil-hungry Western Europe.

The Eisenhower administration, in fits and starts to be sure, developed a nuanced approach to accomplish its goals. Writing off Jordan and Iraq, it decided to concentrate its attention on the Northern Tier states. It would also attempt to work with Nasser and other newly-emergent Middle East rulers including the leaders of Iraq's bloody revolution. And Washington would try to promote regional stability by exerting its influence on Israel so that the Jewish state did not upset the status quo.

As in other areas, economic diplomacy would provide the means for US policy implementation. Money and oil lay at the heart of American concerns and proved critical to Washington's response. In that sense, the 1958 crisis provides a paradigm of American tactics in secondary regions during the Cold War and into the post-Cold War future.

From Crisis to Crisis

The Suez crisis of 1956 forever changed the Middle Eastern mosaic—both objectively and in the American decision-making mindset. The catastrophically ill-planned Anglo-French invasion of Egypt destroyed any hopes of a European colonial renaissance in the region. In 1954 the British Foreign Secretary, Anthony Eden, in an attempt to craft a "new look" imperialism, shepherded the British government towards relinquishing the mammoth Suez Canal base. A year later Eden, by then Prime Minister, utilized economic diplomacy to further improve Anglo-Egyptian relations.[1] British officials convinced their American counterparts as well as the US-dominated World Bank to offer President Nasser a financing package for the long-cherished Egyptian goal of a high dam at Aswan.

In early 1956 the kaleidoscope shifted again. Previously the Cold War had taken a back seat to other divisive issues separating the West from Arab nations in the Middle East. But when Nasser, eager to improve Egypt's chances in the anticipated next round with Israel, accepted Soviet arms, the Cold War moved to the foreground. American pique at Nasser's attempt to play both sides against each other, combined with British anger at Nasser's meddling in Jordanian politics, turned both Washington and London against the Aswan offer. On 19 July 1956, the Secretary of State, John Foster Dulles, leveled the blow—informing Egyptian Ambassador Ahmed Hussein that the United States would not fund the dam.[2]

---

1 See Diane B. Kunz, *The Economic Diplomacy of the Suez Crisis* (Chapel Hill, NC, 1991).

2 Kunz, *Economic Diplomacy*, pp. 71–72.

One week later Nasser retaliated. On 26 July he nationalized the Suez Canal Company and ordered Egyptian troops to seize the Suez Canal itself. By this coup Nasser accomplished a series of goals. Once a hated symbol of arrogant Western imperialism, the Canal now became tangible proof of Nasser's right to lead the Arab world to its treasured objective of unity. At the same time seizing control over the Canal, which carried eighty percent of Europe's oil, put an economic gun to the head of the Western Europeans. Not least, Nasser garnered for Egypt's exchequer the Suez Canal Company's hefty canal fees.

Although the Canal Company was privately run, the British government owned forty-four percent of its shares. Eden, egged on by French Premier Guy Mollet who sought to end Nasser's support for Algerian rebels, immediately urged the American government to support a military attack on the upstart Egyptian regime. But believing that this was the wrong fight in the wrong place, Dulles and Eisenhower stalled for time, agreeing only to economic sanctions against the Egyptian government and the Bank of Egypt.[3]

As months passed the British and French governments, fearing that the status quo would become permanent, took matters into their own hands. These Western European allies conspired with Israel, whose government wanted to strike at the Egyptian army before it could make good use of its new Soviet arms. The result: a hapless scheme launched on 29 October. The Israeli army did what was required of it, but British and French leaders learned to their regret that they should have heeded Dulles's advice to British Foreign Secretary Selwyn Lloyd earlier that month: "in this particular situation [the use of force]...would be a fatal mistake."[4]

Immediately upon learning of the Anglo-French-Israeli collusion, the Eisenhower administration lashed out at Britain, supposedly its closest ally. Eisenhower made it clear that "he did not see much value in an unworthy and unreliable ally and that the necessity to support them might not be as great as they believed."[5] The weapons of choice were economic. Britain, still reeling from the Second World War, had placed its economic diplomacy at the center of its foreign policy. Foolishly believing that retaining the pound as a trading and reserve currency allowed London to

---

[3] By contrast the British and French governments froze all Egyptian assets.

[4] Kunz, *Economic Diplomacy*, p. 95.

[5] Memorandum of Conversation, 30 October 1956, Dwight D. Eisenhower Library, Abilene, Kansas, Ann Whitman Files, Eisenhower Diaries.

exert an international influence unjustified by other measures of strength, the British government and Bank of England had backed the world's most-used currency with wholly inadequate dollar and gold reserves.

Any political crisis drives traders out of weaker currencies. In the era of fixed rate currencies, selling short was a no-lose proposition.[6] London had bet that Washington would back the pound with a blank check written on the US Treasury if a run on sterling occurred. To Whitehall's horror, Eisenhower and his administration, outraged at being diverted by the imperialistic Suez ploy at the same time that the Soviet Union sent tanks to crush the Hungarian uprising, stuck to its decision: no aid for the pound, no oil for Western Europe. Washington's terms were humiliating and non-negotiable. The British and French governments had to set a definite timetable for withdrawal from Egypt, whose shores they had finally reached a week after the Israelis had first launched their attack.

This economic diplomacy proved successful. The British government, dragging its French counterparts behind it, agreed to depart from Egyptian territory on 3 December. With them went any notion that either Britain or France could generate an independent policy in the region. Only then did the administration grant Britain the economic support package that it desperately needed.

The Eisenhower Doctrine

The Eisenhower administration now faced a foreign policy juncture. Heretofore Washington had been content to play a secondary role in the Middle East. Before World War II, the United States had developed meaningful relations with only one Middle Eastern nation, Saudi Arabia. The early onset of the Cold War, in full swing by 1947, kept the American focus on Europe. In June 1950, the outbreak of the Korean War, which forced American attention eastwards, provided yet another reason for Washington's reluctance to take on a major role in the Middle East.

The creation of the state of Israel in 1948 was the exception that proved the rule. The permanent members of the American bureaucracy, whether at the State Department or the new Department of Defense, as well as military leaders, had almost unanimously opposed American support for the

[6] If the target currency were devalued, traders would make a "killing." If it was not, they could buy it back at its original price.

Jewish state. As far as they were concerned, any US endorsement of Israel would needlessly alienate Middle Eastern Arabs as well as require American military assistance for hapless Jewish fighters.

The Truman administration had ignored this advice, and recognized Israel immediately after the Tel Aviv government announced its independence. Washington responded to Israel's victory in the 1948 war by joining with Britain and France in promulgating the Tripartite Declaration, an attempt to impose an arms blockade of the Middle East. It was Nasser's decision to break out of this Western *cordon sanitaire* and ask the Soviet Union for arms that triggered the Suez crisis.

With Britain, America's closest ally, taking the lead in the Middle East, the US assumed a minor role. To be sure, Washington could not totally avoid involvement in the region. But US interventions during the first term of the Eisenhower administration—notably the American part in the Iran coup of 1953, the Project Alpha peace project, and the American offer of economic assistance for the Aswan High Dam project—came in response to British prodding and were done in conjunction with the British Foreign Office. For willing as it was to take charge, Britain could no longer afford to pay for its foreign policy.

The Suez debacle convinced the Eisenhower administration that hiding behind British foreign policy maneuvers was poor policy planning. On 21 November 1956, with the Suez crisis as yet unresolved, the President convened a meeting of senior advisors to discuss future American policy in the Middle East and to coordinate US diplomatic moves with American oil and financial policy. Once again, US priorities put Europe first and foremost. If officials shined a new spotlight on the Middle East, it was not for the region itself, but because the Suez crisis posed both a direct and an indirect Cold War threat to Western Europe. The massive propaganda coup scored by Nasser against Britain and France increased the prestige of his Soviet allies. At the same time the closure of the Suez Canal and the destruction of various oil pipelines jeopardized Western Europe's oil supply. The challenge for America, as the President informed the group, was no less than to "prevent the dissolution of Western Europe." As Eisenhower put it, "We must face the question, 'What *must* we do in Europe?' and then the question, 'How do we square this with the Arabs?'"[7] Moreover, the blow to British prestige, resulting from the

[7] Memorandum of a Conference with the President, 21 November 1956, *Foreign Relations of the United States* (hereafter *FRUS*), 1955–1957, XII, pp. 340–42.

botched Suez invasion, had left an ominous vacuum. Without American action, an unfettered Nasser, backed by an emboldened Soviet Union, would triumph. Eisenhower's instinct was to build up King Saud as a counterweight to Nasser, a goal which marked American policy maneuvers for the next fourteen months.

Eisenhower had asked the State Department to prepare an outline of short-term and long-range American plans in the Middle East. His request prompted a series of planning papers that examined three main approaches for the new activist US regional policy. The first was American adhesion to the Baghdad Pact. This symbol of American "pactomania" had first taken shape as the Turco-Iraqi Pact the previous year. While Dulles had actively promoted the Pact and encouraged Britain to join with Iraq, Turkey, and Pakistan, Washington had shied away from actual membership. If Saudi Arabia and other important Middle Eastern states joined, perhaps American membership would prove the answer to the current dilemma.

This method had the virtue of simplicity. Joining an existing organization was much easier than creating something new. And Eisenhower favored the idea of America joining the Pact, as long as Saudi Arabia and Lebanon did so concurrently. But even if so large a hurdle could be overcome, the United States would have to face Israel's objection to America's allying itself with nations pledged to destroy the Jewish state. The President's solution to that problem, a bilateral security agreement with Israel, might mollify Prime Minister David Ben-Gurion and his colleagues but would not be acceptable to Arab nations.[8] Moreover, American adherence to the treaty would require Senate ratification by a two-thirds vote at a time when the Republicans did not command a majority.

Another form of engagement was needed. If the existing agreement was flawed, why not jettison the Baghdad Pact and form another regional grouping? The United States could join as a founding member and exclude both imperialist Britain and Jewish Israel. Unfortunately, as Deputy Undersecretary of State Robert Murphy pointed out, it was doubtful whether "the organization of an additional international grouping in the area will really help achieve American objectives."[9]

---

[8] Memorandum of telephone conversation between the President and the Secretary of State, 8 December 1956, *FRUS* 1955–1957, XII, pp. 395–96.

[9] Memorandum for the Undersecretary of State, 3 December 1956, *FRUS* 1955–1957, XII, p. 368.

That left option three, a more limited American approach. It would follow the line advocated by Dulles and take the form of an American pronouncement of future policy, with congressional assent and funding. This policy, while less ambitious than either an expanded Baghdad Pact or a new regional grouping, had a number of virtues to commend it. First of all, it was unilateral. American foreign policy in the Cold War came in two varieties: completely unilateral, and unilateral in the guise of multilateral. The former was always preferable. Moreover, the Truman Doctrine and Formosa Resolution provided useful precedents of ambiguous policy statements designed for the maximum flexibility and minimum duties abroad that the United States sought. US officials had supported the policy revolution embodied by the permanent entangling alliance of NATO because the Cold War demanded US protection of the frontline Western European states. But the secondary status of the Middle East warranted only a more limited commitment.

After some internal debate, the administration decided to frame a resolution solely against Communist threats, excluding intra-Arab hostilities. Murphy captured the logic of this approach when he asserted that intra-state hostilities had been and would always be endemic to the region, while Communist penetration was "the main source of difficulty at the present moment." More to the point, Murphy continued, "Communist imperialism is a clear and present danger and is so recognized by the American people and their representatives in Congress." In other words, it would be impossible to get legislative approval for an initiative aimed at Arab-Arab disputes, but beating the Communist drum would make champions of intervention, albeit reluctant ones, of the vast majority of legislators who were part of the bipartisan foreign policy consensus that reigned during the 1950s and into the late 1960s. Ten years earlier Republican Senator Arthur Vandenberg had advised President Truman to scare the hell out of the country when he made the appeal to Congress for economic assistance to Greece and Turkey known as the Truman Doctrine. Now the Eisenhower administration would take the same tack and hope that Democratic Senate Majority Leader Lyndon Johnson would be as accommodating.[10]

On 5 January the President unveiled the result of six weeks of feverish deliberations. What the administration tried to label the American

---

10 Memorandum from the Deputy Undersecretary of State for Political Affairs to the Secretary of State, 15 December 1956, *FRUS*, 1955–1957, XII, pp. 410–12.

Doctrine for the Middle East was almost immediately dubbed the Eisenhower Doctrine. It promised $200 million "to secure and protect the territorial integrity and political independence of such nations, requesting such aid, against overt armed aggression from any nation controlled by International Communism."[11] Eisenhower always remained convinced that military action should remain a last resort. He and his colleagues hoped that the hardline American response to the Anglo-French-Israeli actions, together with this well-funded new program, would woo the Arabs away from the Soviet orbit as well as lessen the appeal of Nasser's pan-Arab rhetoric.[12]

Regional Woes

The Eisenhower Doctrine received congressional assent in March. Within the year it become clear that the United States had not garnered the prestige in the Arab world that it had counted on. Instead, Nasser's fiery rhetoric was carrying the day. No matter that the Egyptian army had been trounced by Israel yet again. Nasser had stood up to the British and French, had forced them to withdraw from Egypt with their tails between their legs, and had retained possession of the Suez Canal.

The administration responded by trying to win regional favor for its own Arab leader, King Saud. As the President had explained to Dulles in late 1956, "If we can build [Saud] up as the individual to capture the imagination of the Arab World, Nasser would not last long."[13] Unfortunately the Saudi monarch possessed neither Nasser's charisma nor his popular appeal.

And yet the administration could not abandon the region. American Middle Eastern policy was embodied in National Security Council Report NSC 5801/1, approved by the President on 22 January 1958. This wide-ranging document began with an obvious declaration: "The Near East is of great strategic, political, and economic importance to the Free World." Moreover, believed administration planners, "the strategic

---

[11] Kunz, *Economic Diplomacy*, p. 160.

[12] The Eisenhower administration threatened economic sanctions against Israel if it did not withdraw from the territory it conquered from Egypt in its successful Sinai campaign.

[13] Salim Clyde Yaqub. *Containing Arab Nationalism: The United States. the Arab Middle East. and the Eisenhower Doctrine 1956–1959* (unpublished Ph.D. dissertation), p. 142.

resources are of such importance to the Free World, particularly Western Europe, that it is in the security interest of the United States to make every effort to insure that these resources will be available and will be used for strengthening the Free World." Not only did Middle Eastern oil sources supply the bulk of Western Europe's oil needs, but also "the geographical position of the Near East makes the area a stepping stone toward the strategic resources of Africa." For these reasons, "The security interests of the United States would be crucially endangered if the Near East should fall under Soviet influence or control."[14]

Throughout the tumultuous year that followed, American objectives would remain clear. Washington had to protect Western Europe's oil resources and stave off Soviet control or influence in the region."[15] Heightening the challenge for Anglo-American planners were "the recent indications that the Arabs were going to emphasize the need for keeping the transit as well as the production of Arab oil in Arab hands."[16] But while all eyes remained on the prize, what changed over the months was the means US officials used to achieve their aims. The traumatic Middle Eastern events of 1958 engendered in official US circles a far more nuanced understanding of the region's politics. NSC 5801/1 is a tough Cold War document, replete with anti-Communist rhetoric. The American goal is to "Provide Free World leadership and assume, on behalf of the Free World, the major responsibility toward the area." The enumerated objectives all feature a Manichean comparison between Western light and the dark dangers posed by the Communist threat.

But by November US officials had significantly altered their stance. The introduction to the policy guidance in the revised administration blueprint set the United States on a course to

> Endeavor to reestablish an effective working relationship with Arab nationalism while at the same time seeking constructively to influence and stabilize the movement and to contain its outward thrust, and recognizing

---

[14] National Security Council 5801/1, 24 January 1958, *FRUS,* 1958–1960, XII, pp. 17–32.

[15] That these two factors were always central to American policy is demonstrated by a spate of documents. See, e.g., NSC Planning Board paper, "Factors Affecting U.S. Policy Toward the Near East," 19 August 1958, *FRUS,* 1958–1960, XII, pp. 182–86, and NSC 5820/1, which constituted a revised version of NSC 5801/1, approved by the President on 4 November 1958, *FRUS,* XII, pp. 187–199.

[16] Memorandum of Conversation between Evan Wilson and Adam Watson, 28 July 1957, National Archives (hereafter "NA"), Washington, DC, 780.00/6-2857.

that a policy of U.S. accommodation to radical pan Arab nationalism as symbolized by Nasser would include many elements contrary to U.S. interests.

The administration resigned itself to dealing with Nasser because, in the President's words, "we have not yet seen an avenue out of our over-all problem in the Middle East in light of the Arab sympathies toward Nasser."[17]

These Little Local Difficulties

The events that shifted American policy had begun early in the year 1958. While the Middle East by no means headed the administration's priority list, Nasser presented Western leaders with a startling demarche which raised the alarm in Washington as well as in London. He announced a union of Egypt and Syria under Egyptian control, to be known as the United Arab Republic (UAR). Launched officially on 1 February, this combination had the potential to transform the political and economic topography of the region.

For decades pan-Arabism had been an empty rallying cry in the region. Now Nasser had taken the first tangible step. At the same time, the creation of the UAR meant that one leader would control both the Suez Canal, soon to reopen under undisputed Egyptian sovereignty, and the oil pipelines of the Iraq Petroleum Company (IPC), which ran through Syria. As a result, for the first time, Nasser was now a significant player in the most important game of all—Middle East petroleum politics. Whether or not Nasser could parlay his new advantage into a credible weapon against Western Europe, for his own purposes or for those of the Soviet Union, remained to be seen.[18]

Not only had Nasser expanded his base, but in the process, he had knocked King Saud, the putative Western white knight, from the board.

---

[17] Memorandum of Conference with President Eisenhower, 20 July 1958, *FRUS*, 1958–1960, XII, p. 82.

[18] See in this regard an intelligence report made for ARAMCO by Colonel William A. Eddy, and given to Ralph Lewis, American Counsel in Dhahran, "The most revealing of all reports which I secured on this trip are those which concern Russia's plan to use Egypt primarily to control and to exercise a veto on shipment of Middle East oil to Europe. If Egypt can be used successfully for this purpose, that may be all that Russia expects her to accomplish." Lewis to SD, 17 April 1957, NA, 780.00/4-1757.

In March, the Saudi King relinquished his powers to his brother Feisal after the Syrians exposed a Saudi plot to assassinate Nasser.[19]

The Nasserite expansion to francophone Syria, among other things, threatened Lebanon. Formerly part of Syria, this Christian-dominated redoubt presented Nasser and his allies with a tempting target. Lebanon, headed by staunchly pro-Western President Camille Chamoun, had embraced the Eisenhower Doctrine. For that reason the Lebanese leader and his allies grew fearful of the threat next door. At the same time Chamoun's political machinations exacerbated the crisis atmosphere that soon surrounded discussions in Beirut. Split between the Muslim and Christian communities, Lebanon was governed by an unwritten National Pact promulgated in 1943 that mandated confessional power-sharing. Now Chamoun sought to undermine the Constitution, which embodied this fragile compromise. Even more alarmingly, Chamoun and Foreign Minister Charles Malik, described by US Deputy Chief of Mission Randolph Higgs as "Pirandello characters...in search of a policy," attempted to lure the Eisenhower administration to come to their aid by cloaking their intrigues in a guise of anti-Communism.[20] But the United States remained wary of commitment; as US Ambassador Robert McClintock put it:

> A Lebanon which did not take into full account [the] need for cooperation with [the] Moslem population would become, so far as [the] Arab world was concerned, a sort of Christian Israel beleaguered by its neighbors and incapable of sustaining itself except under guns of foreign warships.[21]

Eager as ever to avoid military involvement, Eisenhower still believed that "it was much cheaper to try to hold the situation than to try to retrieve it." Grant aid or PL-480-Title-2 aid (surplus commodities distribution) seemed the best solution.[22]

According to the CIA chief, Allen Dulles, the Lebanese government welcomed the idea of economic assistance all too enthusiastically. On 8 May he informed the National Security Council that the amount of aid

19 Peter Mansfield, *A History of the Middle East* (London, 1991), p. 262.

20 US Embassy, Lebanon (USEL) to the Department of State (SD), 9 January 1958, *FRUS*, 1958–1960, XI, pp. 1–3.

21 USEL to SD, March 20, 1958, *FRUS*, 1958–1960, XI, pp. 18–19.

22 Memorandum of Conversation between the President and the Secretary of State, 2 May 1958, *FRUS*. 1958–1960, XI, pp. 27–28.

requested by the Lebanese government "was very far beyond the needs of Lebanon, and really constituted a kind of economic blackmail." McClintock believed that Chamoun would immediately appeal for the US Marines if forces from Syria, be they army regulars or guerrillas, landed on Lebanese territory.[23]

When Chamoun made it clear that his formal request for troops from the United States as well as Britain and France was only a matter of time, Eisenhower sat down with the Dulles brothers and Generals Nathan Twining and Alfred Gruenther on 13 May to discuss the American response. The points laid down in this meeting remained central to American policy thereafter.

No one present wanted to intervene in Lebanon but the consensus was that the United States might have no alternative. For, as Eisenhower commented, "we also had to take into account the apparently much larger problems which would arise if the Lebanese needed our intervention and we did not respond." On the other hand, as Foster Dulles observed, "once our forces were in it would not be easy to establish a basis upon which they could retire and leave behind an acceptable situation."

Finding a satisfactory legal basis for sending American troops would not be easy, either. Dulles observed to his colleagues on 22 June that "[t]he question of our possible intervention posed a difficult problem from a juridical standpoint."[24] As American diplomat George Kennan has observed, American foreign policy is uniquely concerned with legal questions. This is not surprising because lawyers are often appointed Secretary of State—Henry Stimson, John Foster Dulles, and William Rogers are only a few examples. Equally relevant, the United States can rarely rely on self-defense as a justification for its foreign policy. But attempting to create a legal basis for foreign policy actions is a tricky business. Furthermore, drafting legislation that will explicitly fit the needs of the next crisis rather than the ones just past has proven a difficult task.[25] The language of the Eisenhower Doctrine appeared unsuited to the 1958 crisis because the administration could show neither that the UAR had fallen under the control of international communism nor that it had invaded Lebanon. When

23 Editorial Note, *FRUS*. 1958–1960, XI, p.35; McClintock to SD, May 12, 1958, *FRUS* 1958–1960, XI, pp. 41–43.

24 Memorandum, 22 June 1958; NA, 783a.00/6-2258.

25 During the 1930s, the most significant attempt to keep the United States out of European conflicts, the 1935 Neutrality Act, was inapplicable to the brutal conflict that developed the year after its passage, the Spanish Civil War.

Eisenhower inquired as to the basis for "our former so-called 'gun-boat' policy," the Secretary of State stated the obvious: "this policy in the world today no longer represented an acceptable practice...."[26]

While the administration had every intention of excluding the French from any intervention in Lebanon, Washington officials accepted the fact that the British had a part to play. Anglo-American relations had recovered rapidly from the nadir of December 1956. In large measure the change resulted from Eden's exit and his replacement as Prime Minister by Harold Macmillan. Not only was Macmillan able to draw upon his wartime relationship with Eisenhower, but the wily half-American Prime Minister understood that Britain needed always to demonstrate its subservience, even if feigned, to Uncle Sam.

Joint planning for an Anglo-American military mission to Lebanon had begun in May, yet another demonstration of the tangible fruits of the relationship between Macmillan and Eisenhower. For his part Macmillan believed that Nasser "is organizing an internal campaign there against President Chamoun and his regime. This is partly Communist and partly Arab Nationalist."[27] Still the eagerness with which British officials jumped upon the possibility of a Lebanese mission led Dulles to warn British Ambassador to Washington Sir Harold Caccia that "some of our people, not just in Washington, but elsewhere, had the impression that we were being crowded by our British colleagues into intervention in Lebanon."[28]

One of the hallmarks of the Eisenhower administration's Middle Eastern policy was the tendency to stall in the hope that any crisis would resolve itself without the need for American intervention. Though they ultimately failed, Eisenhower and Dulles had come up with various strategies during the Suez crisis to fend off Anglo-French military planning. Now they played for time again.

Against this backdrop the sense of crisis spread to Jordan and Iraq. By mid-June, the Secretary of State had already written off both countries—

---

26 Memorandum of a Conversation, White House, 13 May 1958, *FRUS*, 1958–1960, XI, pp. 45–48.

27 Alistair Horne, *Macmillan 1957–1986*, vol. 2 of the official biography (London, 1989), p. 92.

28 Memorandum of a Conversation Between Dulles and Caccia, 21 May 1958, *FRUS*, 1958–1960, XI, p. 70. See also, Memorandum of a Meeting in the State Department, 19 May 1958, *FRUS*, 1958–1960, XI, pp. 63–66. For his part Caccia believed that "Foster [Dulles] and others here are going through a bout of that chronic American phobia: the fear of being seen alone with the British. They badly want an assignation and a secret liaison. But they are scared stiff that we are going to ask for marriage bells." Horne, *Macmillan*. p. 94.

telling his colleagues that whether or not the United States intervened in the Lebanese crisis, the current regimes in Baghdad and Amman were doomed.[29]

British leaders found it harder to be so cavalier. These countries had long provided a pivotal base for British interests in the region. Hashemite kings—descendants of Abdullah ibn Hussein and Faisal ibn Hussein al-Hashim, who had led the Arab revolt with Lawrence of Arabia—headed these nations. Since 1955 the young King Hussein had ruled in Jordan. His youth and inexperience as well as the disruptive presence in the kingdom of hundreds of thousands of unhappy Palestinians left Western leaders dubious about his long-term prospects.

By contrast the real power in Iraq was Nuri Pasha al-Said. This increasingly out-of-touch Prime Minister had first taken office in the 1930s.[30] In 1955, with the ardent support of the British and the initial enthusiasm, soon waning, of the Eisenhower administration, Nuri had joined Turkey in the Baghdad Pact. This elderly statesman had remained in the British orbit even as he tried to work with the new radical forces winning adherents in the region. In fact, Nuri and King Faisal were being entertained by Prime Minister Anthony Eden on 26 July 1956 when they jointly learned of Nasser's seizure of the Suez Canal. Nuri did not dissent from Eden's strong reaction. But the failed British attempt to remove Nasser weakened Nuri and Faisal even as it strengthened the Egyptian leader. As Allen Dulles informed his CIA colleagues on 21 November 1956, "the situation is worsening very seriously in Iraq, and Nuri may not be able to survive very long."[31]

But Iraq, closely aligned with the West, occupied a crucial place in Britain's Middle Eastern policy and was important to the United States as well. The formation in early 1958 of a formal Iraq-Jordan alliance, the "Arab Union," created a possible counterweight to Nasser's UAR. In the best-case scenario, its existence would co-opt pan-Arabism for the West. Unfortunately the CIA's prognosis was bleak. Analysts believed that the union would fail economically because the Jordanian economy was "not

---

29 Memorandum, 22 June 1958, NA, 783a.00/6-2258.

30 Right after the coup US officials reflected that "It was generally known for some years that the regime had little popular base." But as they also pointed out, "this is, however, characteristic of Arab governments." Memorandum, 16 July 1958, NA, 787.00/7-1658.

31 Memorandum of a Conference with the President, 21 November 1956, *FRUS*, 1955–1957, XII, p. 341.

viable," and politically due to the destabilizing influence of Palestinian radicalism.[32]

Doubts there may have been, but former ties and future hopes mandated US support for the Arab Union. For that reason Assistant Secretary of State for Near Eastern Affairs William Rountree recommended to Foster Dulles that the United States greet the formal announcement of the Union, scheduled for May, with a grant of $10 million in American economic assistance.[33] Nuri wanted more, seeking double the promised American financial support to Jordan.[34] This request was to be one of the Iraqi Prime Minister's last to Washington.

A New Kind of Revolution

In March 1958 the British Foreign Secretary, Selwyn Lloyd, told Foster Dulles that Iraqi leaders were in a "very jittery state and [were] acting as though they expected to be gone in six months."[35] Their premonitions were well-founded. On 14 July a group of military officers led by General Abdel Karim Qasim overthrew the regime. Unlike the Egyptian military coup of six years earlier, the officers' clique did not permit the former leaders to retire peaceably to the French Riviera. Instead, in a move that terrified regional leaders, they failed to protect King Faisal and Nuri Pasha as well as other members of the Iraqi royal family from gruesome deaths at the hands of the Baghdad mob. One day after the Iraqi coup, the Eisenhower administration sent thirty-five hundred troops to Lebanon.[36]

Over the next few days, official Washington debated how to deal with this serious challenge both to regional stability and to Western oil supplies. It was one thing to send the Marines, but as Foster Dulles told Vice President Richard M. Nixon, "we don't want to get bogged down like the Br[itish] in Suez and have to pull out."[37]

---

32 According the administration the Jordanian economy was "not viable." See SNIE, 30–58, "Prospects and Consequences of Arab Unity Moves," 20 February 1958, *FRUS*, 1958–1960, XII p. 41; Assistant Secretary of State William Rountree to Dulles, 16 April 1958, *FRUS*, 1958–1960, XII, p. 58.

33 Rountree to Dulles, 16 April 1958, *FRUS*, 1958–1960, XII p. 59.

34 Memorandum of Conversation, 9 June 1958, *FRUS*, 1958–1960, XII, p. 301.

35 Dulles to SD, 11 March 1958, *FRUS*, 1958–1960, XII, p. 294.

36 Editorial Note, *FRUS*, 1958–1960, XII, p. 71.

37 Telephone Conversation between Dulles and Nixon, 15 July 1958, *FRUS*, 1958–1960, XII, p. 321.

Foster Dulles, throughout these meetings, tended towards belligerence, advocating the use of force to preserve access to petroleum. Eisenhower generally inclined toward what in an earlier age would have been labeled a policy of appeasement: "it was clear that we must win [the new Arab groups] to us, or adjust to them." For that reason the President believed that the best bet might be to make a deal with Iraq and Kuwait, repository of much of Britain's oil.

With the Iraqi monarchy overthrown, both the royal families of Jordan and Saudi Arabia seemed endangered. In Eisenhower's words, "If our policy is solely to maintain the Kings of Jordan and Saudi Arabia in their position, the prospect is hopeless, even in the short term." So where did America's true interests lie? On the one hand the administration had no doubt that it must do everything possible to shore up its most reliable regional allies, Turkey and Iran. To this end, the administration opened up its purse and liberally spread its economic and military assistance. The normally parsimonious President believed that "they should have all the assistance they can absorb."[38]

At the same time, American officials considered how to help protect the British regional military presence as well as the vital oil leases. Macmillan, on 14 July, had made it clear that he desired a combined operation in the manner of the landings he and Eisenhower had launched in the Second World War. But the President resisted the British pressure as well as Dulles' intermittent hawkish instincts. It was crucial, said Eisenhower, "to get indigenous people as well as governments on our side if possible. Otherwise our policies would stand on a foundation of sand, and the arms and economic assistance we sent to these governments will eventually be used against us."

On 16 July Macmillan called Dulles and asked if the British should send troops to Jordan. In London King Hussein's regime could not be easily dismissed. Having placed his grandfather on the throne of that nation, unilaterally carved from the Palestine mandate in 1922, Britain was bound to Jordan both for reasons of state and sentiment. When the Secretary of

[38] Footnote relating telephone conversation between Eisenhower and Dulles, 16 July 1958, *FRUS*, 1958–1960, XII, p. 579. Also see Memorandum of Conversation with President Eisenhower, 23 July 1958, No. 30, pp. 98–100, Memorandum of Discussion at the 373rd Meeting of the National Security Council, 24 July 1958, pp. 100–109, and NIE 30–59, August 25, 1959, pp. 230–32.

State told him that the administration could not take any military action because it had promised Congress not to act without consultation, Macmillan said he was "unhappy doing it alone tonight—we may get separated when we are beautifully together." But despite the Prime Minister's lack of enthusiasm for going it alone, he acceded to Hussein's wishes and authorized an airlift of two battalions of British troops to protect Amman, King Hussein, and "Western interests in Jordan."[39]

The United States quickly endorsed the British action but London, with the strong backing of King Hussein, pressed on for "a truly joint operation." This Washington was reluctant to approve because of continuing doubts about the durability of both Hussein's government and the state of Jordan itself. The American Chargé d'Affaires in Amman, Thomas Wright, believed that "every argument advanced by Hussein and British for United States troops is [a] good reason we should stay out."[40] For his part, Eisenhower believed that "For the West to save Jordan may be largely a 'beau geste.'"[41]

During the week that followed, Dulles grew increasingly pessimistic about the chances of Hussein's survival. On 23 July he told the President that he had never supported the dispatch of British troops—which would have come as quite a surprise to Macmillan—but feared the potential results of Jordan's disintegration, namely that Israel would invade Jordanian territory and take over the West Bank for itself.[42]

Once again, the administration played for time. In response to King Hussein's urgent request for the United States to subsidize two additional brigades, Undersecretary of State Christian Herter made it clear that the United States would neither abandon Jordan nor enthusiastically support the regime "until we can see more clearly how [the] situation in the Middle East is going to develop...."[43]

On 6 August Herter briefed Murphy, serving as Special American Envoy to Egypt, and told him to explain to Nasser that despite Hussein's

---

[39] Memorandum of Telephone Conversation, 16 July 1958, *FRUS*, 1958–1960, XI, p. 314; Editorial Note, p. 316.

[40] Amman to SD, 22 July 1958, *FRUS*, 1958–1960, XI, p. 364.

[41] Memorandum of Conference with the President, 20 July 1958. *FRUS*, 1958–1960, XI, p. 348.

[42] Memorandum of a Conference with the President, 23 July 1958, *FRUS*, 1958–1960, XI, p. 377.

[43] SD to Delegation at the Baghdad Pact Council Meetings, 26 July 1958, *FRUS*, 1958-1960, XI, p. 404.

hostility to the Egyptian leader and his decision to sever diplomatic relations between Jordan and Egypt, Nasser should understand that any violence directed toward Hussein's kingdom "could not be confined to Jordan itself.... [I]t is in [the] interests of everybody concerned that necessary steps be taken to prevent creation of a situation which might result in such hostilities."[44]

Dulles, for his part, made no effort to hide his feelings regarding Jordan's prospects. He told Soviet Foreign Minister Andrei Gromyko that "Jordan was not a viable country. The only reason for assuring its existence was that if it disappeared suddenly, there might be serious effects that could have other consequences."[45]

King Hussein, understanding the American position, played the Russian card for all it was worth, telling Wright that he was "convinced that Nasser was Russia's 'handmaiden.'" But Dulles remained unpersuaded, advising Herter on 23 August that "he did not see how we could keep the show going. To maintain this citadel is not profitable and the Sec. said he did not think we could succeed even if we spent all this money.... [W]e must concentrate on the peripheral areas—Lebanon, Tunisia, Libya, Sudan (if willing to stand up) and Ethiopia."[46]

The ongoing problem of Israel also loomed. The Eisenhower administration looked upon the Jewish state not as a strategic ally but as the proverbial millstone dragging down American policy.[47] Eisenhower had reflected that had it been up to him, the United States might not have recognized Israel in 1948 and lamented that "except for Israel we could form a viable policy in the area."[48] As the National Security Council analysts, expanding on the President's sentiments, put it: "The U.S. role in the United Nations and elsewhere and the circumstances surrounding the emergence of the State of Israel, subsequent U.S. official and private eco-

---

[44] SD to Cairo, 6 August 1958, *FRUS*, 1958–1960, XI, p. 435.

[45] Memorandum of a Conversation, 12 August 1958, *FRUS*, 1958–1960, p. 462.

[46] Amman to SD, 23 August 1958, *FRUS*, 1958–1960, XI, p. 516; Memorandum of Telephone Conversation, 23 August 1958, *FRUS*, 1958–1960, XI, p. 519.

[47] Although Eisenhower observed at a White House conference on 16 July that "the strategic action in the circumstances would be to turn Israel loose on Egypt, thus going for the head of the snake. This did not seem possible, however." Memorandum of Conference, 16 July 1958, *FRUS*, 1958–1960, XI, p. 310.

[48] Steven L. Spiegel, *The Other Arab-Israeli Crisis: Making America's Middle East Policy from Truman to Reagan* (Chicago, University of Chicago Press, 1985), p. 92.

nomic assistance to Israel and U.S. political support of Israel, are the primary bases for criticism of the United States in the Arab world."[49]

True, the harsh line taken by the United States in the immediate aftermath of the Suez crisis had temporarily ameliorated this problem. And the United States was the primary provider of financial aid to Palestinian refugees. But unless the United States abandoned the Jewish state, Washington's policy would never satisfy the vast majority of Arabs who found implacable opposition to the existence of Israel indispensable during this period of domestic and regional upheaval. Neither would it do much for relations with the Arab leaders who exploited this sentiment.

The Iraqi revolution had ominous implications for Israel. If the new regime should federate with the UAR, the combined states would pose a serious military threat. The danger to Jordanian stability was equally alarming to Israeli officials. King Hussein's state included the holiest sites of Judaism and his regime was the most moderate in the region. Should it fall, the strategic temptation for Israel to seize the West Bank would be virtually irresistible.

Washington, during the 1958 crisis, faced the same imperatives it would deal with during the Persian Gulf War of 1990–1991. The administration needed to strike a balance between supporting Israel (albeit more tepidly under Eisenhower than three decades later) and keeping sufficient distance from the Jewish state to avoid further tainting America's mission in the eyes of the Arab world. And it had to prevent the Israeli government from taking advantage of the regional crisis to fulfill military aims of its own.

Intervention with No Nasty Aftertaste

During an Anglo-American summit at Camp David held on 22 March 1959, Macmillan observed that "Lebanon and Jordan had been a risky performance and that we had been lucky to get out as well as we did, but that it had stabilized the area somewhat." The President replied that "it had been the kind of intervention which had not left a nasty aftertaste."[50] The decisions made by the Eisenhower administration during the second half of 1958 illustrated how cautious policies, combined with fortuitous

[49] NSC 5801/1, 24 January 1958, *FRUS*, 1958–1960, XII, p. 19.
[50] Memorandum of Conversation, *FRUS*, 1958–1960, XII, pp. 217–18.

external events, can propel what seems like a hopeless mission to a safe harbor. Notwithstanding American rhetoric, Eisenhower and his officials understood that the Middle East was on the periphery of the Cold War. As the President told former Treasury Secretary George Humphrey, "The basic reason for our Mid-East troubles is Nasser's capture of Arab loyalty and enthusiasm throughout the region."[51] Understanding that the outcome of the Cold War was not directly at stake allowed the administration the freedom to use modest means to obtain the limited results it sought.

The immediate American objective remained a quick withdrawal from Lebanon. Eisenhower directed his officials to continue to work on a compromise solution to the Lebanese political crisis. The installation of Muslim General Fouad Chehab as President allowed all American troops to leave Lebanon at the end of October without ever having to fire a shot. More broadly, the administration continued its policy of constructive engagement with the new brand of nationalist Arab ruler in order to stabilize the region and maintain an unimpeded flow of Middle East oil.

At the same time the Iraqi regime, after the first blood bath, proved less threatening than Western leaders had feared. For one thing, after three months in power, "no government in [the] Western conception of that term exist[ed]."[52] While Qasim was preoccupied with maintaining his insecure hold on power, the new Baghdad regime had little time to incite trouble amongst its neighbors.

The Qasim regime relieved Western minds with other glad tidings. The Iraqi Foreign Minister assured Rountree in October that while his nation desired close relations with the UAR, it would not join Nasser's union.[53] Of equal importance, the revolutionary government also promised that it would honor all contracts, including the IPC agreements.[54] The explanation behind this decision was primarily economic, for the chief characteristic of the petroleum environment during this period was that it continued to be a buyer's market. Developing nations, eager to enlarge their oil revenues, put more and more oil fields on stream and pressured the oil companies that ran the concessions to pump ever-greater amounts of oil. The resulting glut drove prices down. In the short run, then, the Iraqi

---

[51] Eisenhower to Humphrey, 22 July 1958, *FRUS*, 1958–1960, XI, p. 365.

[52] Waldemar Gallman to SD, 14 October 1958, *FRUS*, 1958–1960, XII, p. 344.

[53] Memorandum of Conversation, 11 October 1958, *FRUS*, 1958–1960, XII, pp. 342–43.

[54] See, e.g., W. J. Handley Memorandum, 19 July 1958, NA, 783.00/71958.

government had little leverage, a fact which greatly pleased the British government, as well as American officials who knew that Washington would have to make up any deficit in Western European oil supplies.[55] For their part, oil company executives followed the approach advocated by George Allen, Director of the US Information Agency: "The oil companies should be able to roll with the punches and will in fact be on a firmer foundation in Iraq than under the old regime."[56]

This was not quite the case. The long run effects of the Iraqi revolution were less positive for the West. The poor economic outlook for producer nations, in combination with resentment at their helplessness in the face of multinational oil companies, spawned the creation of the Organization of Petroleum Exporting Nations (OPEC), a development that would damage both the British and American economies some fifteen years later. While the oil shortage of the early seventies was the most important factor in the success of the 1973 Arab oil boycott, the humiliation suffered by oil-producing states at the hands of Western companies and governments alike for the preceding fifty years also contributed to the oil shocks of the 1970s and early 1980s.

The Eisenhower administration could also take comfort in the fact that neither the government of Turkey nor the Shah's regime in Iran appeared imperiled by the events of 1958. The Northern Tier retained pride of place in American planning. As the fears generated by the events of July receded, the administration recognized a fact that would remain true for decades to come: that the most pressing threat to the Shah's regime lay in "the widespread dissatisfaction of many Iranians with domestic conditions."[57] For too long, American officials would remain confident that they could persuade the Shah to remedy these difficulties. For its part, Turkey, a NATO member under a Western-looking government, showed little signs of Nasserite infection.

The British venture in Jordan ended happily as well. Despite Dulles's doubts, King Hussein refused to follow the Secretary of State's script and continued to cling to power, even after the withdrawal of all British troops. This time the administration's habit of stalling had benefited the

---

[55] As Dulles had pointed out to the Cabinet on 18 July, "there would be no problem so long as alternative resources are held in Iran, Kuwait and Saudi Arabia." Minutes of a Cabinet Meeting, *FRUS*, 1958–1960, XII, p.80.

[56] Memorandum of Discussion, 24 July 1958, *FRUS*, 1958–1960, XI, p.384.

[57] NSC 5821/1, 15 November 1958, *FRUS*, 1958–1960, XII, p. 605.

indigenous ruler as well as long-term American policy. By allowing inertia to direct American policy toward Jordan, the administration enabled King Hussein to survive. Not even his obsequious line toward Saddam Hussein during the Gulf War could completely sever the plucky little King's connection with the West and by the time of this death in 1999, King Hussein had become the West's favorite Arab leader.

The British battalions left Jordan as the Americans departed Lebanon. This British throwback to gunboat diplomacy again demonstrated the erosion of Britain's power. Not only did the United States need to provide the economic ballast to Jordan that Britain could not afford to give one of its few remaining client states, but the small British airlift only occurred with American military assistance. Gromyko had remarked to Dulles that "the British seemed to want to continue sitting on a war horse, but all that they had was a dead horse." Under the circumstances, this unkind observation was not far from the truth.[58]

Yet this second revelation in two years of the paucity of British power served in the short run to buttress American power. No administration need fear another Suez. The British would advise, they might even pontificate or patronize, but they would never limit US freedom of action in the region. It was only at the end of the next decade, when the Vietnam War exhausted the American public's tolerance for international involvement and when the British government decided to withdraw completely from East of Suez, that Washington regretted this evolution.

Once again a Middle Eastern crisis had drawn the United States closer to Israel. In the wake of the Suez crisis, as part of the price for Israeli withdrawal from the Sharm el-Sheik region, the United States had given to Israel an aide-memoire guaranteeing Israeli right of passage through the strategic waterway. This written commitment, however reluctant and restricted, was the most significant step that the Eisenhower administration had yet proffered to the Jewish State. The Israeli government had only allowed British over-flights of its territory after much American persuasion and with great reluctance. In exchange, Prime Minister Ben-Gurion, nervous about the Soviet as well as Arab reaction, had wanted "assurances that, if Israel got into difficulties like Lebanon's, we [the United States] would give them help." While the Eisenhower administration steered clear of a specific guarantee, Eisenhower and Dulles now

[58] Memorandum of Conversation, 12 August 1958, *FRUS*, 1958–1960, XI, p.466.

affirmed that the Eisenhower Doctrine covered Israel. Prior to this point, they had avoided this clarification. America had taken another small step in the direction of the special relationship that the United States and Israel would have after the Six-Day War.[59]

Ironically, the Anglo-American military intervention contributed to the growing détente between the Eisenhower administration and Nasserism. If the show of American force alarmed the Egyptian leader, the quick US withdrawal eased his obsessive fears for his own security. As Nasser told Special American Envoy Robert Murphy, "as a military man he just could not believe it earlier but was quite willing now to be convinced that [the] US military intervention [was] limited to Lebanon." Murphy concluded quite rightly that "effective US military intervention may exercise [an] excellent effect on Nasser's outlook and attitude."[60] For by sending troops on a limited mission, the administration proved that it had the capability and the will to intervene in the Middle East but no desire to dethrone Nasser.

The general drift in the Eisenhower administration in favor of expanding American economic assistance to developing nations had repercussions in the Middle East as well.[61] Addressing a special General Assembly session devoted to the Middle East on 13 August, Eisenhower proposed a new Arab development bank under Arab control.[62] While the plan came to nothing, it represented another American olive branch directed toward Egypt.

The Egyptian leader's imperial overstretch also contributed to the mellowing of tensions. Syrian economic problems proved a drag on the union while the much-vaunted Communist assistance to the UAR came with increasingly onerous strings. In December 1958 the United States resumed sales of PL 480 wheat to the UAR while Nasser began arresting suspected Communists, denouncing them as betrayers of the Arab cause.[63] American economic diplomacy, in evidence throughout the crisis, now resumed its earlier form. Eisenhower and Dulles turned once more to the carrot-and-stick approach to containing Nasserism, which had failed so

59 Memorandum of a Conference with the President, 25 July 1958, *FRUS*, 1958–1960, XIII, p. 73.

60 Murphy to State Department, 8 August 1958, *FRUS*, 1958–1960, XI, p. 442.

61 It was at this time that the Eisenhower administration began considering a serious economic aid program to Latin America.

62 Yaqub, *Containing Arab Nationalism*, pp. 382–87.

63 Ibid. p. 398.

markedly prior to Suez. Whether it would now be more effective remained a perennial question for future American administrations.

And what of the Eisenhower Doctrine? The Suez debacle had forced the administration to improvise a new approach to a region officials believed was now "in play," so to speak. But the American view of the Soviet role in the Middle East grew increasingly nuanced after the promulgation of the Eisenhower Doctrine. That is to say, although Dulles and Eisenhower had no doubt that the Soviet Union would take advantage of any loosening of the Western hold on the Middle East, neither of them saw the Soviets behind every regional setback, despite the Eisenhower Doctrine which cited "International Communism" as the only threat.

For one thing Dulles thought that "it was not possible to maintain a country in the status of a Soviet satellite when it was not geographically connected with the USSR and could be threatened or occupied by adjacent states."[64] And the President, for his part, repeatedly remarked that the problem for the United States was that Nasser was genuinely popular in the region while the conservative, pro-American regimes were not.

The transcripts of discussions between Dulles and his Soviet counterpart, Andrei Gromyko, reveal the words not of bitter rivals but of two lawyers trying to negotiate their differences over a business transaction.[65] Perhaps this development was the most important legacy of the 1958 crisis. The events of that year made it clear to American officials that the spread of "International Communism" was hardly the most serious problem in the Middle East. This realization made it possible for both Washington and Moscow to step back from the brink when their various client states lured them into trouble. As a result none of the later Middle Eastern conflicts led to the wider conflagration that was always the nightmare hovering over Cold War–era diplomacy.

64 Memorandum of Conversation, 8 October 1957, NA, 780.00/10-857.

65 See, e.g., Memorandum of Conversation, 12 August 1958, *FRUS*, 1958–1960, XI, pp. 461–67.

3

Oil, Politics, and US Intervention

IRENE L. GENDZIER

In a work published in 1971, historian Arno Mayer described the controversy over war aims during World War I in terms of the tension between "parties of order" as opposed to "parties of movement."[1] The former were generally on the Right, whereas the latter were more often on the Left. In the context of World War I, Mayer viewed President Woodrow Wilson as leading the forces of movement that favored the "New Diplomacy," which in Wilson's terms included support for ideas such as self-determination and a popular-based foreign policy. Despite clear contradictions between the practices of the "revered apostle of self-determination" and his claims,[2] the rhetorical promise of a democratic foreign policy and support for self-determination remained "necessary illusions" in the public language of post-World War II US foreign policy.[3] Their systematic violation led to deceptions justified as necessary in the cover-up of US policies that have included covert action, intervention, and counterinsurgency.

The double tensions between the forces of order and movement, and the "necessary illusions" as well as the justifications of their violations, resonate in the conduct of US foreign policy in the Middle East in the 1950s. These tensions are exemplified in US policy in Lebanon in 1958, when the

1 Arno J. Mayer, *Political Origins of the New Diplomacy, 1917–1918* (New York, 1959), p. 371.

2 See Noam Chomsky, *Turning the Tide: US Intervention in Central America and the Struggle for Peace* (Boston, 1985), p. 86 for references to Wilson's policies.

3 The title is taken from Noam Chomsky's book, *Necessary Illusions: Thought Control in Democratic Societies* (Boston, 1989).

United States intervened in the midst of Lebanon's first civil war on behalf of a President with virtually no popular support, and in favor of a regime committed to maintaining the access to power of the privileged at the expense of the mass of the population. That policy, undertaken on the basis of calculations that conformed with the prerequisites of US interests, was long justified as a response to the Baghdad coup that opened the way to revolution in Iraq in 1958. In practice, such justification has served to perpetuate the illusion of a disinterested US policy in Beirut, as well as to mask the covert policies jointly undertaken by Britain and the US to assure their oil interests in Saudi Arabia and Kuwait.

What does the evidence suggest as to why the United States intervened in Beirut in July 1958? Was this a result of the Iraqi revolution or a response to internal Lebanese developments? What indeed was the relationship between the developments in Iraq and Lebanon? And how was US intervention in Lebanon justified?

This chapter argues that American intervention in Beirut was a function of US interests in Lebanon and more generally in the Middle East.[4] Oil and its transport system were paramount. The need to maintain a compatible political and economic environment in the region to protect these and other related interests explains the interventionist character of US diplomacy. It is in this context that the American courtship of Lebanon's pro-Western political and economic elite must be situated. The policy was not unique to Lebanon. Reproduced across the region, this courtship promoted the existence of an informal structure of allies who, in exchange for protecting American investments and other assets, were the beneficiaries of US support. Any threats, internal or external, to the stability of such regimes were viewed with suspicion by American as well as British officials. The emergence of nationalist movements throughout the decade of the 1950s was alarming to Western policy-makers precisely because they threatened to alter the uneven relationships of power and profit with multinationals and their government protectors.

This concern for oil is critical to the Western response to Middle East developments. But the international oil economy transcended regional

[4] With the addition of new evidence, this chapter develops the argument elaborated at greater length in *Notes from the Minefield: United States Intervention in Lebanon and the Middle East, 1945–1958* (New York, 1998, and paperback edition, Boulder, CO, 1999). I am grateful for the cooperation of the publishers in permitting me to cite passages from this work. All citations are from the paperback edition. I wish to thank Michael L. Schur, Boston University Computing Consultant, for his technical assistance.

boundaries. Anglo-American oil policy planners devoted considerable attention to this problem in the mid-1950s. Indeed, the successive crises of the decade—including those involving nationalizations of oil and international oil companies in Iran and Egypt, respectively—validated the importance of thinking globally while acting locally where oil was concerned. More specifically, these and other related crises underscored the urgency of planning for alternative sources of oil and transport. Developments in the spring of 1958 reinforced the significance of these regional and international coordinates of US policy.

At first glance, the dual crisis involving the United States, Saudi Arabia, and Indonesia might appear remote from Lebanese politics or US policy in Beirut. Yet upon closer examination it becomes clear that the overlapping crises involving oil and US policy across the globe had a direct effect on Middle East politics, prompting US action on behalf of its regional allies, including Lebanon. Months before the outbreak of the civil war in Lebanon or the revolution in Baghdad, a local scandal exposed Saudi intrigue in Syria, which alarmed US officials lest it inspire retaliation against American oil interests. That scandal, however, coincided with a more protracted conflict involving US efforts to undermine the Sukarno regime in Indonesia. It was in that context that fears for the safety of US oil installations arose. The coincidence of the two crises confronted US officials deliberating on the Middle East situation with what they regarded as an unacceptable predicament in which the security of their oil interests appeared to be at stake. Whether or not this was so, the conviction that such a danger existed influenced US policy.

In reconsidering the nature of US intervention in Lebanon, then, the first step is to identify relevant aspects of Middle East developments through the 1950s that shaped the reaction of Western powers. It is against the background of nationalist challenges to Western control of oil that US officials viewed the emergence of the United Arab Republic (UAR) in the winter of 1958 with increasing disquiet. The Saudi attempt to subvert the Syrian regime, which was part of the UAR, can be viewed in this light. The attempt failed but in the process it aroused opposition to the United States and its allies in the region, while in Washington it inspired fears of possible retaliation against American oil interests. At this point, news of the ongoing crisis in Indonesia, where the United States was deeply involved as well, exacerbated the situation from the perspective of officials in the National Security Council. Two months later, civil war broke out in Beirut and Washington wasted no time in providing assistance to the regime of Lebanese President Camille Chamoun. American intervention in favor of maintaining the status quo in Beirut took place long before the Iraqi revolution. That historic turning point, however, triggered a full-scale military intervention. Operation Bluebat, as it was known, was above all a calculated response to domestic conditions in Beirut, which were assessed in reference to developments that heightened Lebanon's political and economic value as an ally. Thus the attempt to reduce US intervention in Beirut to a response to the Iraqi revolution is inadequate. There is a sharp difference between the justification of policy before the US public—a matter of great concern to US policy-makers—as opposed to its internal explanation. It was the perceived nationalist threat to Western oil interests that was central to US policy calculations.

Consider the following sequence of events. In 1951 Iran's Prime Minister nationalized the Anglo-Iranian Oil Company (AIOC). In 1956 Egypt's President nationalized the Suez Canal Company. In the spring of 1958 civil war broke out in Beirut, followed several months later by revolution in Baghdad. The West responded by mobilizing its allies, promoting pacts, issuing doctrinal pronouncements, and intervening. In retaliation for Iran's nationalization of the AIOC, US and British intelligence in 1953 carried out the covert coup known to American officials by the acronym AJAX and in British parlance as Project Boot. In Egypt the nationalization of 1956 was followed by the tripartite invasion of Egypt by Britain, France, and Israel. These were not the only Western interventions on record, as the examples of US machinations in Syria in 1949 and later in the 1950s indicate. Indeed, the Syrian coup of 1949 was, according to some analysts, carried out in order to assure Syrian approval of the negotiations for the US-owned Trans-Arabian Pipeline Company, TAPLINE.[5] And it was the future of TAPLINE, among other considerations, that concerned US policy-makers as they provided military assistance to Chamoun in the days following the outbreak of civil war in Beirut. Neither the Americans nor the British launched a military intervention directly in Iraq in July 1958, although they did intervene separately in Jordan and Lebanon, and they made covert plans for intervention in the oil-rich zones of Saudi Arabia and Kuwait. The events of the 1950s,

---

[5] See Gendzier, *Notes from the Minefield*, pp. 97–98. See also "Personalities in the Public Eye," from *The Illustrated London News*, 9 April 1949. I am grateful to Borre Ludvigsen for bringing this to my attention.

then, contributed to Western fears that nationalist regimes were increasingly willing to contest their control of critical resources, and the multiple crises of 1958 greatly contributed to Western anxieties.

The dual crises involving Saudi Arabia and Indonesia in March 1958 affected US deliberations on the Middle East because of the impact on Lebanon, a staunch American ally and indispensable actor in the regional oil economy. The Saudi crisis contributed to Lebanon's domestic tensions which led to the outbreak of civil war in May. And that event, as American sources so clearly demonstrate, was to be a continuing source of concern to US policy-makers. Would the future Lebanese regime be as compliant with US policies? And if not, what would be the consequences? Such questions explain the circumstances that led Secretary of State John Foster Dulles to provide Chamoun with the necessary military assistance to remain in power. Such assistance was earmarked for the Lebanese gendarmerie only as opposed to the Lebanese military; thus, it was reserved for purposes of internal security. Still, US aid could not contain the overwhelming opposition to the regime that even officials in Washington recognized. These were the conditions which gave rise to considerations of intervention months before the Iraqi revolution. The effect of the Iraqi revolution on Eisenhower and his advisors was to determine the timing for the implementation of such preexisting contingency plans. But as American and British records indicate, that was only one part of a more comprehensive response to Iraqi developments.

The Iraqi revolution of 14 July, clearly the defining event of the period, profoundly altered the political contours of the region.[6] The critical question on the minds of Western policy-makers in Washington and London was whether the revolution would spread. Would those presumed to be at the source of Iraqi developments, such as Gamal Abdel Nasser and his Soviet supporters, pursue their victory in the rest of the Middle East? As Western leaders came to realize, the Iraqi revolution was not the result of external manipulation. And while the UAR's impact on the region was unmistakable, the leader of the UAR was not committed to the revolutionary transformation of Egypt, nor were his Syrian colleagues so inclined in Damascus.

Yet the evidence of the undeniable solidarity—albeit temporary—of revolutionary Iraq and the UAR reinforced the impression of a new Middle

[6] See also the chapter by Peter Sluglett.

East, one in which Western power had been dealt a fatal blow. That impression continued to influence those in the region who remained deeply apprehensive about the impact of these developments on the existing social and political order. And it obviously continued to haunt Western policy-makers who assessed their losses in the Middle East. These were not evenly distributed. The predicament of British power in the region, after Iran, Suez, and Baghdad, was acute. There was little consolation for London in the realization that Washington benefited from these crises, enhancing its own influence so that by the end of 1958 it was the undisputed Western power in the Middle East. US multinationals, for example, had profited from their place in the consortium arrangements in Iran. They had gained also from the non-belligerent status of the United States in the Suez-Sinai crises, as did Washington itself. Moreover, while comparisons of the Anglo-American relationship in 1956 and 1958 invariably underline the collaboration of the two in 1958, as opposed to 1956, this is a partial view. In 1958, British Prime Minister Harold Macmillan proposed a rollback policy in the Middle East. It was not feasible without US support, but that support was not proffered. For Eisenhower, the objectives of US policy were attainable with less risk.

Resisting counterrevolution in Iraq, Eisenhower was prepared to countenance US military intervention in Lebanon. Yet US policy-makers carefully maintained the distinction between its justification and its explanation. They sought to preserve the "necessary illusion" of a US foreign policy respectful of self-determination by the "necessary deception" of presenting US policy as devoid of self-interest. When political leaders speculated about what was to be done in the Middle East as a result of 14 July, Eisenhower, Dulles, and Vice President Richard M. Nixon, among others, focused on how intervention was to be justified as anti-intervention. The answer was the formula of intervention by invitation.

When Dulles became Secretary of State, he observed in obeisance to Wilsonian ideals that the days of the "Old Diplomacy" were gone and that it was no longer possible to act in the colonial manner. In 1958 when deliberating with the President on the Lebanese crisis, he made note of the allergic reaction that Latin American leaders had to talk of intervening, doubtless the result of their experience at US hands. Dulles advocated caution on public discussion of US intervention in other countries. He was sensitive to the risks of the US being labeled as an imperialist power as a result of its policy in Beirut, as the British, French, and Israelis had been at Suez. That analogy had been made by the Joint Chiefs of

Staff in 1957.[7] At the time, the JCS warned that the results of that invasion had been detrimental to British and French prestige and correspondingly favorable for the Soviet Union. Once the decision had been made to intervene in Lebanon, Dulles warned US diplomats against making, supporting, or condoning such an analogy.

There were other explanations to be eliminated from public debate, such as those that justified US intervention in the name of economic interests. The exchange between Eisenhower and Nixon on the subject is particularly revealing. Eisenhower was unprepared to have American policy publicly explained in terms of the protection of US economic interests. He considered the economic theme as crass, inappropriate, and morally unacceptable. Instead he wanted to offer a statement that would put US efforts in a good light, such as emphasizing that the US sought access to oil, "without hindrance on the part of anyone."[8] The troublemakers, it was to be emphasized, were Arab leaders such as Nasser. Eisenhower pursued the matter with Generals Nathan F. Twining and Andrew J. Goodpaster, insisting that it was essential to find "a moral ground on which to stand if we have to go further."[9] The point, Eisenhower explained, was that if the only explanation offered by the US was in economic terms, "this would be quite different, and quite inferior to a purpose that rests on the right to govern by consent of the governed."

This accorded with Nixon's position. The Vice President thought it important not to give the impression that "the Mid East countries are simply a pawn in the big power contest for their resources."[10] Nixon offered the following formula, well in keeping with the "necessary illusions": "Any nation ought to have the right to revolution. We recognize the right of revolution. We also say every people has the right of self-determination—that right of self-determination is one that carries with it the right not to have outside interference that stimulates it." Nixon claimed that it was necessary to explain that civil war was not really a civil war when it was the product of outside intervention. From the US and Lebanese perspectives, the UAR was responsible for Lebanon's civil war. Hence, UAR intervention justified that of the US, which was thus morally superior, according to this logic. The Lebanese regime's reliance on the alleged responsibility

[7] See Gendzier, *Notes from the Minefield*, p. 325.
[8] Ibid., p. 325.
[9] Ibid., p. 326.
[10] Ibid., p. 326.

of the UAR for Lebanese civil conflict provided the missing link, with its insistence that civil strife in Lebanon was a product of UAR intervention. The ensuing invitation by Chamoun to the United States to intervene conformed to the favored formula of intervention by invitation, which later apologists of US policy in Lebanon and elsewhere exploited.

Against this background, the United States sent the marines into Beirut. On 14 July, as he learned of developments in Iraq, Chamoun pleaded for intervention, and Macmillan agreed with Eisenhower that the altered circumstances legitimated US intervention in Lebanon.[11] By then US forces were already on their way to Beirut. In spite of Macmillan's appeal to Eisenhower, there was to be no counterrevolution in Iraq. In both capitals, however, there was speculation that the Iraqi coup was the result of Egyptian and Soviet involvement. These possibilities were discounted by US intelligence, but that in no way dampened anxieties about the impact of these developments on Western interests, concerns which continued to influence public talk on the subject. Given the overt signs of solidarity between Iraqi and UAR leaders, the internal differences between the two Arab states were not readily apparent. What appeared beyond doubt was that 14 July was the beginning of a process whose end was not yet in sight.

Four days after the Iraqi coup, Eisenhower conveyed his assessment of the situation to Macmillan:

> Whatever happens in Iraq and other parts of the area, we must, I think, not only try to bolster up both the loyalties and the military and economic strength of Lebanon and Jordan, we must also, and this seems to me even more important, see that the Persian Gulf area stays within the Western orbit. The Kuwait-Dhahran-Abadan areas become extremely important and Turkey and Iran have become more important.[12]

Eisenhower's pronouncement clarified US priorities. It distinguished between the protection of economic interests in Saudi Arabia, Kuwait, and Iran, thereby underscoring the importance of keeping the Gulf area "within the Western orbit," and the objective of protecting non-Arab allies on the periphery. This echoed Dulles's "northern tier" notion. Turkey and Iran were central to the US structure. At the core of the Arab heartland were Lebanon and Jordan, the two states singled out by the President as

---

[11] Ibid., p. 299.

[12] Ibid., p. 295.

those specifically to be protected and bolstered by US support. Unlike Jordan, Lebanon served US economic and political as well as strategic interests. The first was a function of the role of TAPLINE, which was indispensable to the transport system of the regional oil economy. The second was a product of the ideological compatibility between Lebanese political and economic elites and their US counterparts. And the third corresponded to Lebanon's role in the network of US intelligence, among the "assets" highly valued by Dulles.

The Saudi-Indonesian Crises and Their Impact on US Policy

The 14 July crisis, in sum, called for the urgent reinforcement of forces, that is, the formal and substantive increase of previously offered military assistance, critical to the protection of US interests in the Middle East. The implicit purpose of such coordination was the containment of radical forces in the region represented by Nasser and Arab nationalism. Their role in 1956 was not forgotten. Indeed, it was the fear of a repeat of Suez that was evoked in the different environment of 1958 when multiple crises of relatively minor proportions raised questions concerning the safe access and transport of Middle East oil. One crisis involved a Saudi attempt to finance the overthrow of the Syrian government. Another unnerving development for US officials was the simultaneous crisis in Sumatra, Indonesia, a major alternative source of oil outside of the Middle East.

The Saudi Affair is of particular interest, as it affected both US-UAR relations and Lebanese domestic politics. US civilian and defense officials feared a Nasserist counterattack that could jeopardize American oil interests. At the level of Lebanese politics, the crisis exacerbated opposition to the regime, while the Saudi king continued to warn Washington of Soviet-Syrian meddling in Lebanon's domestic affairs.

The Saudi crisis unfolded in early March 1958, against a background of pervasive US caution regarding the progressive expansion of Arab nationalism, notably, the union of Egypt and Syria in the UAR, in February 1958. That historic development, which did not long survive, provoked a cynical response from CIA Director Allen Dulles. He considered the UAR as potentially divisive in Arab politics, and thus, an advantage for the US. This was not the outlook of Foster Dulles or his subordinates at the State Department. William Rountree, Assistant Secretary of State for Near Eastern, South Asian and African Affairs, considered radical Arab nationalism as a force "inimical to our interests" and not susceptible to US control. Nasser's brand of Arab nationalism opened the door to "international Communism" according to Rountree, thereby jeopardizing Western access to oil. Nasser was castigated for his incendiary political language. The Egyptian leader was accused of calling for the "eventual overthrow of pro-Western Arab leaders in the area [that] can only be interpreted as an invitation for assassination and civil commotion."

On 3 March, Ambassador Donald Heath reported from Jidda that the Saudi King wanted the Secretary of State and the President to be informed of the impending "successful military revolution" in Syria.[13] Nasser publicly disclosed the details concerning Saudi efforts at subverting the regime in Damascus on 5 March in the opening remarks of a speech he gave in the Syrian capital. Further, Syrian Major Abdel Hamid Sarraj implicated the Saudi King "as the source of three checks paid to Sarraj for the purpose of overthrowing the Nasser control of Syria and establishing a new regime under Sarraj."[14] According to Sarraj's report, "he had been informed that the United States knew of the plot and had agreed to recognize the new government."

US-sponsored covert intervention in Syria had a long history, as already noted, and reached back to 1949. According to former CIA agent Miles Copeland, whose claims have been substantiated in American sources, he and another CIA officer who was Assistant Military Attaché at the US Embassy in Damascus, "engineered the March 1949 coup in which Chief of Staff Husni Zaim overthrew (President Shukri al-) Quwatli...."[15] Other sources have suggested, as noted above, that the objective of such a coup was to obtain Syrian approval of the TAPLINE contract. The *Illustrated London News* of 9 April 1949 claimed that Syrian Colonel Zaim "was the instrument of the coup financed by TAPLINE carried out by the CIA." And the same newspaper underlined the importance of TAPLINE, which it described as constituting the "the greater part" of US interests in the Middle East in the 1950s and 1960s. Wilbur C. Eveland verified such claims in 1988.[16] Writing of an earlier period, Eveland credited the CIA

---

[13] Department of State to the Embassy in Saudi Arabia, *Foreign Relations of the United States Series* (hereafter *FRUS*), 1958–1960, XII, p. 714, notes 1–3.

[14] Memorandum from the Assistant Secretary of State for Near Eastern, South Asian, and African Affairs, ibid., p. 719.

[15] Douglas Little, "Cold War and Covert Action: The United States and Syria, 1945–1958," *Middle East Journal* 44, 1 (Winter, 1990), p. 55.

[16] Interview with the author, 27 October 1988, Boston.

with "agreeing to fund King Saud's part in a new area scheme to oppose Nasser and eliminate his influence in Syria" in 1957.[17]

On the subject of covert operations, Eveland also claimed that the CIA ran "the multinational intelligence-planning group" in Beirut consisting of British, Iraqi, Jordanian, and Lebanese intelligence agents. The Lebanese regime's tolerance of this group was regarded as invaluable, and it was one that Eveland thought sufficiently important to warrant continued support for President Chamoun. One may assume that Dulles, who shared Eveland's view of Lebanese politics, was in total agreement. Indeed, Lebanon's role as host to the intelligence group may well have been among those "assets" to which Dulles regularly referred in citing the importance of Lebanon in US Middle East policy.[18]

In the wake of the 1958 Saudi crisis, the immediate response of US officials was to deny involvement. Rountree adopted such a posture, insisting that "we have denied any involvement in the plot and have protested to the United Arab Republic Government on its continuing insinuations that the United States is seeking to overthrow that government." Suffice it to note that the US Ambassador to Syria also acted along these lines. Several days later, at the National Security Council (NSC) meeting of 6 March Dulles informed the council of the "abortive plot in Syria" and the predictable reaction it inspired. "Nasser was now fully engaged in an all-out battle with the remaining pro-Western Arab leaders," according to Dulles.[19] Deletions in US sources indicate that more was afoot. What was not deleted was Dulles's concern lest the scandal adversely affect US allies and lead the USSR to seize Middle East oil. To compound the difficulties, the State Department's Undersecretary, Christian Herter, reported that the Saudi King appeared totally disconcerted by developments and uncertain as to whether to break with Nasser or, on the contrary, move closer to him. Neither option appealed to Washington.

On 13 March, the Saudi crisis was again discussed at a meeting of the National Security Council. Dulles introduced a further development in the Saudi situation by referring to the critical position the King now found him self in, "as the result of his implication in the plot to assassinate Nasser."[20]

[17] Wilbur C. Eveland, *Ropes of Sand* (New York, 1980), p. 244.

[18] Ibid., p. 245.

[19] *FRUS*, 1958–1960, XII, Editorial Note, p. 715.

[20] Memorandum of Discussion at the 358th Meeting of the National Security Council, ibid., p. 46.

Dulles proceeded to give his assessment of the regional impact of Saud's predicament, referring to the increased vulnerability of Jordan and Iraq, but concluding that the King would do well as he "was such a wily individual." The discussion then turned to how the United States could assist the King. The Eisenhower Doctrine, which provided assistance to states threatened by international Communism, was obviously inapplicable. Yet Eisenhower and the Treasury Secretary, Robert Anderson, made it clear that under existing circumstances the inapplicability of the Eisenhower Doctrine was irrelevant, as "the loss of Near Eastern oil to the West, particularly to Europe, would be catastrophic." The world should be informed, Anderson continued, that neither the United States nor NATO would tolerate such an outcome. The Secretary of Defense, Neil H. McElroy, agreed, adding: "especially in view of what we might have to face in *Sumatra* in the near future" (emphasis added). Accordingly, Eisenhower urged that the State Department explore assistance to US allies in the region, which included Iraq, Jordan, Saudi Arabia, and Lebanon.

Following the meeting, Herter, McElroy, Allen Dulles, and the Chief of Staff of the US Army, Maxwell Taylor, pursued the subject. McElroy concluded that the seriousness of the crisis warranted a shift in policy toward Nasser. "We ought to buy into Nasser, to try to recapture whatever remaining potential of good will that there was there and turn it to our own purposes. Allen agreed this should be studied at once." Rountree was asked to prepare a review of the options and "see what could be done."[21]

There was no mention of the precise connection between the Saudi and Indonesian crises on this occasion, perhaps because it was the subject of discussion at another session of the same NSC meeting. The Sumatran crisis was clearly part of a far more complex story involving the role of the mineral-rich island archipelago in US postwar policy in southeast Asia. In the context of the Middle East crisis, however, the impact of the Sumatran crisis was more limited. Its relevance was a function of Indonesia's place in Anglo-American oil planning. Indonesia was repeatedly cited in reports as one of the prime alternative sources of oil outside of the Middle East. The prospect of Indonesia being rendered inaccessible loomed before US officials. Events in Sumatra encouraged them to contemplate the merits of seeking a rapprochement towards Nasser to preclude any possible retaliatory actions on his part.

---

[21] Ibid., p. 47.

US efforts to undermine the Sukarno regime in Indonesia, which was labeled pro-Communist, by threatening retaliation for attacks on American oil installations therefore coincided with Washington's attempt to blunt the effect of Saudi subversion on the security of American oil interests in the Middle East. Such maneuvers to protect US interests encourage further analysis of the relation of oil and politics in US policy.

Securing oil and its transport was what US planners were committed to in the years prior to the twin crises of 1958. Before the Suez crisis of July 1956, a working group of representatives of the Departments of the Interior, Defense, and State, under the leadership of the Director of the Office of Oil and Gas of the Interior, Hugh A. Stewart, issued a memorandum on the "Effects on the Free World Petroleum Economy Under Certain Assumed Conditions in the Middle East Area." The reference was to conditions deemed to constitute risks to Western access and transport. Sent by the Director of the Office of International Trade and Resources to the Assistant Secretary of State for Policy Planning on 30 March 1956, the memorandum outlined the risks as consisting of either full or partial cuts in oil production or transport, or both.[22] Under such circumstances, the importance of having access to alternative sources of oil in the United States, Canada, the Caribbean, and Indonesia, was evident.[23]

Several months after the Suez crisis, Eisenhower inquired at an NSC meeting as to "whether any oil could be got from Sumatra or elsewhere in Indonesia."[24] At their meeting in Bermuda in the spring of 1957, American and British officials continued their examination of planning for access to Middle East oil. Questions of production and transport dominated such discussions, along with the options of reducing dependence on Middle East oil through alternative stockpiles and sources. In their May 1957 review of the problem, US and British officials once again identified Indonesia in their listing of alternative sites, along with Canada, Venezuela, Colombia, North Africa, and Burma.[25]

In 1957, Dillon Anderson, who was consultant to Eisenhower and the Cabinet Committee on Crude Oil Imports, reiterated some of the major concerns of oil planners. He urged that the NSC, Commerce, and Interior

[22] Foreign Aid and Economic Defense Policy *FRUS*, 1958–1960, X, p. 590.

[23] Ibid., p. 592.

[24] Memorandum of Discussion at the 303rd Meeting of the National Security Council, 8 November 1956, ibid., p. 630.

[25] "Review of Middle East Problems Bearing Upon the Supply of Oil to the Free World," 10 May 1957, 14 May 1957, ibid., pp. 682–89.

Departments reconsider US dependence on Middle East oil in the light of Soviet policy, Middle East politics, and the existence of alternative sources. The key to a successful US oil policy, according to Anderson, consisted in cultivating the dependence of Middle East producers, and keeping them "more dependent on us than we are on them...."[26] Failing this, the use of force would be justified. Anderson recommended a policy that would assure the dependence of oil producers on Western markets. This was to be achieved by manipulating tax and tariff policies, as well as keeping the refining and processing of oil—as opposed to its extraction—in consuming countries. In addition to such devices, there were other sources outside of the Middle East, such as "Sumatra (a vast lode)," in Anderson's language. The lode was the site of US oil multinationals which had branches operating in the Middle East, including Lebanon. In 1958, the "vast lode" appeared to be endangered.

Why this was the case compels a brief detour into the situation of US oil multinationals as well as US policy in Indonesia. US oil companies had been active in Indonesia since the nineteenth century. Standard Oil Company of New Jersey was one of the companies to explore the territory in this period, though it was eventually thwarted by the Dutch colonial regime as well as by the Royal Dutch Petroleum Company.[27] In 1918 Standard nonetheless discovered oil in Sumatra. Thirty years later, Indonesia's importance as a source of oil, rubber, and tin was assured. So was the cooperation of US multinationals with the State Department. In 1949, officials of the Standard Vacuum Oil Company (STANVAC) urged US officials to take a hard anti-Communist line in order to prevent Communists from playing a role in the Indonesian nationalist movement.

Throughout 1957–1958, US oil multinationals persistently complained to Washington of the regime's reluctance to approve new concessions. What their compaint failed to reveal were the political conditions under which the regime labored, namely, the covert efforts of the United States to subvert the Sukarno regime by supporting rebel forces. In the fall of 1957, the CIA transferred funds to Indonesian military officers in Sumatra and Sulawesi, two areas of rebel concentrations.[28] In its Special Report on

---

[26] Letter from the President's Consultant (Anderson) to the President, 9 August 1957, ibid., p. 737.

[27] Robert J. McMahon, *Colonialism and Cold War* (Ithaca, 1981) pp. 47–48.

[28] Audrey and George McT. Kahin, *Subversion as Foreign Policy: the Secret Eisenhower and Dulles Debacle in Indonesia* (New York, 1995). I am grateful for George McT. Kahin's generous criticisms of my discussion on Indonesia.

Indonesia, the NSC advised "all feasible covert means to strengthen the determination, will and cohesion of the anti-Communist forces in the outer islands, particularly in Sumatra and Sulawesi, in order through their strength to affect favorably the situation in Java, and to provide a rallying point if the Communists should take over Java."[29]

Several months later US forces were providing direct support to the anti-Sukarno forces and considering intervention in Sumatra. And by the winter, the Revolutionary Government of the Republic of Indonesia (PRRI) was proclaimed by the anti-Sukarno movement in Padang, Sumatra. US covert arrangements for the delivery of arms through the Philippines, Taiwan, Thailand, and Malaysia to Sumatra were implemented through this period. In late February, Foster and Allen Dulles, along with Herter and the Chief of Naval Operations, Arleigh Burke, reconsidered sending a naval force to Indonesia.[30]

By early March, the US Seventh Fleet task force was on its way to Singapore "as the Eisenhower administration was still groping for the most plausible excuse for using it on behalf of the Sumatran rebels."[31] What occurred next coincided with the exposé of the Saudi scandal in the Middle East, setting off the double alarm. As historians George and Audrey Kahin explain, "on March 4 Dulles had privately suggested to the CIA chief that a threat by Jakarta 'to bomb US property and people' might provide 'a case for usefully doing something' and asked him whether he did not think it desirable 'to send forces in to protect American lives and property.' "[32] According to US sources, Dulles "referred to the threat to bomb US property and people and said he thinks we should see if that is a case of usefully doing something or not. A [Allen Dulles] said if they try it they might get a bloody nose. The Sec said then you don't think it desirable to send forces in to protect American lives and property. A said no, he is inclined to think it good if they did it—then we have a good basis for yelling and screaming and also get a better reception."[33]

The same source reports that the Indonesian regime acted out of fear of US intervention. It requested that the oil companies—such as the California-

[29] "US Policy Toward Indonesia," Memorandum from the Special Assistant to the Joint Chiefs of Staff for National Security Council Affairs (Trievel) to the President's Special Assistant for National Security Affairs, *FRUS*, 1958–1960, XVII, p. 31.

[30] Kahin, *Subversion as Foreign Policy*, pp. 148–149.

[31] Ibid., p. 149.

[32] Ibid., p. 149.

[33] Editorial Note, *FRUS*, 1958–1960, XVII, p. 54.

Texas Oil Company (CALTEX)—remove their dependents from Pekanbaru, the main center of CALTEX operations, and it promised compensation. CALTEX, on the other hand, let the Assistant Secretary of State for Far Eastern Affairs, Walter S. Robertson, know "that both the Indonesian Government and the insurgents are very friendly to his company's representatives." Both the regime and the rebels, in short, recognized the value of oil royalties and were careful to protect the oil installations.

The critical point that emerges from the full-scale inquiry into US policy in Indonesia undertaken by the Kahins is that the Secretary of State sought a pretext for intervention. That pretext involved US oil installations, whose bombing whether by the forces of Sukarno or those of the rebels would presumably constitute a justification for intervention. According to the main representative of the rebels in Singapore in this period, "As far as those in charge of the 7th Fleet themselves were concerned, given their attitude towards Jakarta, they would say [to us] 'go ahead and blast the oil fields.' "[34]

While the SEATO Foreign Ministers' meeting was held in the Philippines on 11–12 March, the Indonesian regime conducted preemptive strikes in Sumatra. The PRRI did not retaliate by burning oil fields. The prospect of direct American intervention was thus aborted, as recognized by US naval officials at the time. The conflict in Indonesia was ongoing, however, as Allen Dulles duly reported to the NSC on the same day that US officials considered the Middle East crisis.[35] Allen Dulles's reminder that neither the Sukarno regime nor the "dissidents" were prepared to lose oil revenue does not appear to have altered this response.[36]

Oil was not in jeopardy and direct American action was aborted. But to Foster Dulles, intervention remained the objective of American policy in Indonesia, and he and Eisenhower continued to deliberate on its legality if Sukarno "seized the oil installations." In the interval, however, there was an evident disjuncture between the ideological bent of US policy and the profit-seeking politics of US multinationals. That gap did not prevent American companies from supporting US policy or American officials from extending the companies official protection. But such collaboration, which was a key element of US policy, did not preclude tactical differences

---

[34] Kahin, *Subversion as Foreign Policy*, p. 151.

[35] Editorial notes regarding the 13 March 1958 NSC meeting, *FRUS*, 1958–1960, XVII, p. 65.

[36] Ibid., p. 65.

of the kind exhibited in the Indonesian and Lebanese cases. In much the same way that CALTEX and STANVAC officials recognized that their product was invaluable to all sides of the Indonesian conflict, so in the Middle East in July 1958 TAPLINE's Executive Vice President William Chandler rejected US military protection, arguing that it was not only politically undesirable but practically unnecessary in the light of TAPLINE's relations with both the Lebanese regime and the "rebels."

There are doubtless other analogies of interest in the relations of US multinationals and the Lebanese and Indonesian regimes, on the one hand, and the US government, on the other. Suffice it to note one such situation that is particularly meaningful in terms of Lebanese domestic politics. CALTEX, which was a product of the merger of Standard Oil of California and the Texas Company, was the owner of the Mediterranean Refining Company (MEDRECO) in Lebanon. Its Sidon refinery was indispensable to Lebanon's oil transit role.[37] In 1952, CALTEX officials were among those that pressured the newly elected President Chamoun to make sure that Kemal Jumblatt, the leader of the Progressive Socialist Party, was kept out of the cabinet.[38] Derisively labeled the Mossadeq of Lebanon, Jumblatt appears to have been a marked man as far as oil company executives were concerned. With the Iranian case in mind, they clearly wanted no repetition of what had transpired in Tehran to recur in Beirut. Six years later, Jumblatt was among the Lebanese leaders of the opposition to the regime.

Dulles found it expedient to play off officials in the Middle East with those in Jakarta in the course of the following months. He must have assumed that those in one capital had little information as to what US policy was in the other. Whether or not this was an accurate assessment, it barely disguised the Secretary's self-serving claims. On 13 May, for example, Dulles warned the Indonesian regime that it ought to seriously consider the manner in which the Soviet Union exploited the independence of sovereign states. Dulles pointed to Soviet policy in eastern Europe to argue that the USSR was prepared to ignore the independence of states "if it is able, directly or indirectly, to impose its will."[39] What he failed to disclose to his Indonesian interlocutors was that at the very time he was issu-

[37] John M. Blair, *The Control of Oil* (New York, 1978), p. x.

[38] For further details, see Gendzier, *Notes from the Minefield*, chapters 5 and 8.

[39] Department of State to the Embassy in Indonesia, 13 May 1958, *FRUS*, 1958–1960, XVII, p. 165.

ing such a reminder, he was coaching the Lebanese President on how to request US military intervention, while circumventing the UN role in Lebanon and avoiding reference to the Eisenhower Doctrine.[40] Two months later, on 15 July, the very day on which US Marines landed in Beirut to support an unpopular regime, Dulles once again used the Lebanese example, this time warning Jakarta against bringing charges in the United Nations against the United States. Indonesia would find itself isolated at the United Nations, warned Dulles, since the international community was preoccupied with developments in the Middle East.[41]

US Policy in Beirut

The United States had been preoccupied with developments in Beirut in the period from March through July. The controversial question of Presidential succession in the winter of 1958, the unnerving Saudi crisis in the spring, and the consistent growth of political opposition leading to civil war, all combined to weaken the regime. This, in turn, magnified US concerns lest the regime on which it depended for support of its interests be critically undermined. US policy-makers clearly relied on President Chamoun as an unquestioned ally whose compatibility with US policy was regarded as virtually axiomatic. But US Lebanese interests predated Chamoun's political ascendancy in Beirut.

Prominent among those interests was TAPLINE, which carried ARAMCO oil to the Mediterranean and beyond. As of 1952, "through Lebanon passed 78 percent of Saudi and Iraqi crude [oil], on its way to Western Europe, and approximately 22 percent going to the United States and Canada." TAPLINE was not only an engineering feat, it "cut the cost of tanker transport by 50 to 75 percent while increasing the political rent value of its territory, along with that of the region."[42] While Lebanon, was oil-poor, then, it was nonetheless a major player through its transit role that had a ripple effect on the economy, affecting aviation, commerce, and finance, sectors that continued to thrive irrespective of political conditions within the country. The Lebanese political and economic elites that bene-

---

[40] Gendzier, *Notes from the Minefield*, pp. 245–46.

[41] Embassy in Indonesia to the Department of State, 15 July 1958, *FRUS*, 1958–1960, XVII, p. 242.

[42] Gendzier, *Notes from the Minefield*, p. 91.

fited from Lebanon's transit role and with its impact on the nation's economy were the same elites on which US policy relied. On the other hand, as a result of his domestic and regional policies, Chamoun alienated many of these prominent figures, who subsequently joined the opposition to the regime, albeit without becoming radical critics in the process.

From first to last, then, Chamoun was a reliable US ally. Some of his closest advisers, such as Lebanese Foreign Minister Charles Malik, had consistently supported a rapprochement with Washington that would have embedded Lebanon even more firmly in the American structure of Middle East politics than it was. Malik shared Dulles's view of the Cold War and of the dangers to Lebanese stability. The two were joined in their suspicion of Arab nationalism and the figure of Nasser, the *bête noir* of both the Lebanese Right and the Secretary of State. It was Malik who appeared to have a monopoly on presenting the Lebanese position in the United States, whether at the United Nations or in such influential circles as the Council on Foreign Relations. In endorsing Malik's views, Washington reinforced the Lebanese regime's resistance to political change. In spite of the barrage of warnings that Dulles aimed at Chamoun concerning the risks should the United States intervene, there was no break in US support for the Lebanese President.

With the crises of Suez and Sinai in 1956, however, Chamoun found himself increasingly in difficulty at home, as members of his political establishment mobilized against his domestic and regional policies. The mood worsened when Chamoun accepted the Eisenhower Doctrine in the beginning of 1957. His move swelled the ranks of a diversified opposition that called for the reaffirmation of the 1943 National Pact, the formal basis for national unity. The call was a statement of support for a united Lebanon free of sectarian conflicts and foreign entanglements as in the 1943 Pact, even though Lebanon's neutrality in international politics had long been violated as had the ideal of a state united despite religious and communal differences.

Without reviewing Lebanon's tangled history since 1943, suffice it to note that few US officials working in Beirut or the State Department had illusions about the nature of the Lebanese state or the system which kept it going. They understood the inherently biased character of the existing system and its favoritism towards Christian elites. They were aware of the operations of the client system, its corruption as well as its capacity to provide services neglected by the state. They knew, in sum, that Lebanon was a precarious state and a divided society, both before and after 1958. But they also knew that their support in Lebanon was based on the very elites whose power was guaranteed by the Lebanese system and its confessional arrangements. The United States supported the perpetuation of this system in the name of protecting US interests, irrespective of the social consequences for the Lebanese. As opposition to the system mounted, so did American efforts to maintain it. Hence, Washington covertly subsidized the parliamentary elections in 1957, and covertly provided military assistance to Chamoun in 1958.

From the fall of 1957, the opposition intensified its demands for reform. Although mostly conservative at the top, the opposition had a more radical mass base that was largely but not exclusively Muslim, and included Christians who were outspoken in their conviction that reform was the prerequisite for a united Lebanon. At the leadership level, the opposition was pro-American, divided on the question of Chamoun's foreign policies, supportive of a more representative political system though opposed to fundamental reform, and united in its opposition to Chamoun's succeeding himself in office. Among Chamoun's critics were business elites who believed that he was isolating Lebanon from the Arab hinterland. The Saudi scandal furthered this trend, much as it strengthened Washington's commitment to support its regional allies, including Lebanon. Nonetheless, by the spring of 1958—which was the height of the Saudi affair—the Lebanese opposition was continuing to mobilize an increasing number of political dissidents representing political and economic elites as well as the more radical partisans who were part of the heterogeneous political coalition opposing Chamoun. The opposition included the United National Front (UNF), the Third Force, and the Progressive Socialist Party. In addition, there were smaller political parties and groupings opposed to the regime, including those allied with Baathists, supporters of the Arab Nationalist Movement, and Communists. Arrayed against this broad and disunited coalition were Chamoun loyalists, members of the Phalangist Party (the Kataeb), and the Syrian Social Nationalist Party (the PPS).

To describe the opposition leadership as pro-American, as did Nasser in his talks with US officials and former CIA agents in Cairo, does not adequately convey what this elite represented in Lebanese politics. At the top of the United National Front leadership was Saeb Salam, the Sunni leader of uncontested political influence in Beirut. A highly successful entrepreneur, he was one of the founders of Middle East Airlines, the premier Lebanese airline whose operations were closely linked to the increasing oil wealth of Saudi Arabia and the Gulf states. Hussein al-Uwaini, who emerged as Foreign Minister in the first post-civil war cabinet of President Fouad Chehab, was viewed by US officials in Lebanon in the early 1950s as one of the key figures responsible for Lebanon's emergence as the center of regional finance and commercial development. He had a history of close ties to French capital, Saudi interests, and connections with TAPLINE.[43] Even Jumblatt, though much maligned in US circles, was sympathetic to the United States although not to its intervention, a position he shared with the more conservative leaders of the opposition.

In April 1958, Foreign Minister Malik requested economic assistance from Washington. The urgent message that the Lebanese Ambassador, Nadim Demechkié, conveyed to Rountree was based on "the need for the present pro-Western regime in the Lebanon to receive a further indication of US support in the form of grant aid if it is to remain in power and triumph over the efforts of disruptive pro-Nasser elements."[44] Rountree's reply was unequivocal: "We believe, on balance, that the political stakes in the Lebanon are of such importance as to warrant our making a further gesture at this time. The pro-Western elements headed by President Chamoun are under very heavy pressure and we think that we should do everything within our power to demonstrate to the Lebanese the advantages of close relations with the West."

With the outbreak of civil war on 8 May, Chamoun increased his requests for assistance and the US complied, providing incremental military to the gendarmerie which was crucial to keeping the regime in power. On 13 May, Dulles informed Chamoun as to how to request US military intervention. Further, he informed Chamoun that the United States was

> prepared upon appropriate request from President and Rpt and GOL [Government of Lebanon] to send certain combat forces to Lebanon which would have the dual mission of (a) protecting American life and property and (b) assisting the GOL in its military program for the preservation of the independence and integrity of Lebanon which is vital to the national interests of the United States and to world peace. They would of course also be authorized to act in self-defense. FYI [for your information] We believe these two courses are clearly within the President's constitutional authority without further congressional action but that the President is not authorized

43 For additional information see the discussion of "Who Rules? The Anatomy of Power and Wealth," in Gendzier, *Notes from the Minefield*, pp. 80–89.

44 Memorandum from the Assistant Secretary of State for Near Eastern, South Asian, and African Affairs, 16 April 1958, *FRUS*, 1958–1960, XII, p. 57.

> by Section 2 of the Joint Resolution to send armed forces to fight for Lebanon's independence since there has not occurred "armed aggression from any country controlled by International Communism."[45]

Months before the Iraqi Revolution, the United States prepared to intervene in Beirut in an effort to shore up the regime. "According to the U.S. Joint Chiefs of Staff, U.S. assistance materially altered the political as well as military balance of power" in Beirut.[46] Such assistance involved the provision of arms and police equipment, allowing Lebanese government forces to assert their control over much of the country. Further, as the JCS analysis of US policy in Lebanon indicated, the presence of US troops facilitated the role of the Lebanese military in defending the regime during the civil war. On 13 May, Admiral James L. Holloway Jr., who was Commander in Chief, US Specified Command, Middle East, received instructions to head towards Beirut.

Confirmation of US involvement in Lebanon's civil war came in the form of a reply to King Saud who, at the end of May, communicated an alarmist message about UAR and USSR plans to take over the region. Syria was to be its focus and Lebanon was among its targets.[47] But Dulles reassured Saud that the United States was cognizant of the risks. It was, in fact, providing support to the Lebanese regime. Thus, according to Dulles: "[The] support given [to the] established government of Lebanon to restore order, maintain Lebanese independence, and frustrate outside efforts to interfere should in itself assist in restricting advances of destructive elements in Syria. This [is] perhaps [the] most important action anyone can take at [the] present time." This judgment was shared by Lebanese loyalists, as well as by a coterie of US regional allies, which included Israel, Iran, Turkey, and Iraq, as well as select US business interests, and CIA operatives who were persuaded that Lebanon's role in US regional intelligence activity would cease with the political eclipse of Chamoun.

By late June, US officials acknowledged that Chamoun controlled less than a third of Lebanese territory. Kemal Jumblatt was leading the military forces of the opposition who were advancing on the presidential palace

---

[45] Gendzier, *Notes from the Minefield*, p. 246.

[46] Ibid., p. 247.

[47] Department of State to Embassy in Saudi Arabia, 6 June 1958, *FRUS*, 1958–1960, p. 729, ftnt.1.

and the international airport. In the two weeks prior to the coup in Iraq, the United States conducted surveys throughout the country, and Israel conducted covert naval operations in the port of Beirut. US military preparations for intervention were already underway at this stage, according to the US Task Force in Lebanon Report of 1959.[48]

Among those who had earlier sought to arrest the course of Lebanese civil strife and avert the prospect of US military intervention were a number of Lebanese political and religious figures such as Paul Meouschi, who counseled Lebanon's Christians to support political reform out of self-interest. Meouschi's views were regularly communicated to Washington and as regularly ignored, to judge by US policies. But there were others, including Lebanese entrepreneurs, who sought to engage US officials and Nasser in mediation efforts.

Nasser and the United States in Lebanon

Throughout the course of Lebanon's civil war and the American occupation that followed, Egypt and Syria were accused by the Lebanese regime and the United States with supporting the opposition through its "massive intervention." To those in London, Washington, and the Middle East who thought of Nasser as Hitler on the Nile, Lebanese accusations merely confirmed their fears. Investigations undertaken by the United Nations Observation Team in Lebanon (UNOGIL), however, failed to confirm such charges, to the chagrin of Chamoun as well as US and British officials, who recognized the UN presence as an impediment to intervention.

Nasser's efforts to engage Washington in a public mediation effort on the Lebanese crisis offers an image of the UAR leader entirely at odds with the venomous portrait of the Egyptian leader as bent on absorbing Lebanon. In practice, as US officials in Cairo, Beirut, and Washington knew, Nasser's views on the Lebanese crisis did not fundamentally contradict their own. Nonetheless, the Egyptian leader failed to persuade Washington of the advantages of openly collaborating with him, a position that would certainly have posed a challenge to the formal logic of US Middle East policy, which was rationalized in terms of anti-Nasserist, anti-Arab nationalist, and anti-neutralist pronouncements.

---

[48] See footnote 55 below.

Nasser's repeated and ultimately frustrated attempts to persuade the Secretary of State to join him in mediating the Lebanese crisis were obviously undertaken as a result of political calculations. Was this an expression of Nasser's desire to distance himself from the Soviet Union at this stage? If so, such a plan found little favor in Washington, where the risks of such collaboration evidently exceeded its advantages. Yet American officials in Cairo conceded that Nasser's positions on the crisis were not irreconcilable with those of Washington. They were incompatible, however, with those of President Chamoun, whose objections were sustained by Dulles.

Miles Copeland, the former CIA agent then resident in Cairo, emerged as a useful intermediary between the Egyptian leader, US officials, and Lebanese business figures who sought Nasser's intervention in an effort to stem civil strife. The discussions that ensued between Nasser and US officials disclosed the common ground between the two on how to resolve the Lebanese crisis, but to no avail. Dulles systematically undercut the possibilities of cooperating with Nasser in the face of Chamoun's strenuous objections. Chamoun and his supporters consistently opposed any negotiations with the opposition leadership in Beirut or with Nasser. Yet as Copeland and the US Ambassador in Egypt, Raymond Hare (who had previously served in Lebanon), reported, Nasser was not an unconditional ally of the Lebanese opposition leadership. Relations between the United National Front leadership and Nasser were problematic. Nasser preferred to deal with members of the Third Force, the most conservative of the opposition coalitions, a grouping identified primarily by its opposition to Chamoun's tampering with the constitution. The Lebanese figures who sought Nasser out in the late spring of 1958 belonged in this category. Emile Boustani and Fawzi el-Hoss, millionaire contractors bent on arresting the course of Lebanon's civil war, were not radical partisans of revolution or reform. But their purpose was thwarted by the combined resistance of the United States and Lebanon.

In May, Ambassador Hare conveyed Nasser's views on the Lebanese crisis to the State Department. Reporting on Nasser's critical appraisal of US policy in Beirut, Hare also informed Dulles that Nasser had vigorously denied intervening in Beirut, arguing that his intelligence budget was too modest for such adventures. More important, Hare reported that Nasser wanted to cooperate with the US in Lebanon. Nasser proposed the following positions:

> (1) An amnesty for opposition. This is of first importance because [the] greatest preoccupation of opposition leaders is that they will be court-

martialed and, as long as there is [the] prospect that [Chamoun] will take his revenge, they obviously will not talk of settlement.

(2) General [Fouad] Shehab [Chehab] to become Prime Minister since he is respected and enjoys confidence of both Christians and Moslems.

(3) [Chamoun] to disclaim intention to seek [to] change [the] constitution but to serve out term. Nasser said [he] understood [the] opposition insisting on his [Chamoun's] resigning now but this would obviously present complications and he saw no reason for insisting on this provided there was fully guaranteed amnesty.

(4) Possibly have new elections.[49]

The above points were among the key elements in US-UAR discussions. They served to clarify areas of agreement and discord between the two parties. On amnesty, Nasser's support for a guarantee of safety for the opposition was endorsed by the United States. On the Chehabist formula, an unorthodox recommendation that ignored the practice of naming a Sunni to the position of Prime Minister, there was accord between the two, as well. The third point was more contentious. It was rejected in Beirut by Chamoun with the backing of the US Ambassador. Robert McClintock claimed that the Lebanese President had already renounced his ambitions in favor of the Chehabist formula. Moreover, McClintock, opposed concessions to the United National Front (UNF). He feared a new election, since new deputies would most likely be in "favor of a line of strict neutrality, some of them of the "positive" variety."[50] McClintock, in short, was critical of both the UNF and Chamoun, whom the US continued to support. From Washington, Dulles instructed Hare in Cairo to persuade Nasser to convince the Lebanese opposition to drop its demands for Chamoun's resignation prior to the end of his term. Washington was pledged to "assist Lebanon to defend its integrity, and we remain determined to do so."[51]

The efforts of Copeland as well as Lebanese mediators to persuade Chamoun to meet with the opposition leadership failed. Copeland proved unable to obtain Chamoun's approval "to quote him to President Nasser as agreeing to meet with Raschid Keramé, Sabri Hamadé and Kemal Jumblatt and to make an honest effort to obtain a truce with them in

[49] Gendzier, *Notes from the Minefield*, p. 259.

[50] Beirut to London, No. 600, 24 May 1958, FO 371/134119.

[51] Herter to American Embassy in Cairo, Beirut, London, Paris, 27 May 1958, No. 14927, RG 59, Box 3750, 783A.00/5-2058.

exchange for Nasser's agreeing to discontinue support of the Beirut Four [United National Front leaders]."[52] The frustrated talks nonetheless continued. Nasser agreed to exclude the UNF leadership from any political solution while additionally denying any plans to absorb Lebanon into the UAR. Nonetheless, Dulles withdrew from the discussions, and left Nasser with the recommendation that he undertake bilateral meetings with the Lebanese President. Dulles's maneuver in effect scuttled the negotiation since he knew that Chamoun would not agree to meetings with the UAR leader or the Lebanese opposition.

From Chamoun's perspective, the end of the abortive talks removed an unwelcome predicament. Moreover, he interpreted the American position as an indication of support for the level of military intervention he repeatedly urged Washington to consider. When that intervention materialized, Chamoun succeeded in obtaining the political and military protection that he desperately needed to maintain himself in power in the short term. Where he obviously failed was in retaining sufficient US support to assure his own continuation in power over the long term. That bitter end was doubtless unexpected. But US military intervention achieved its political objectives in the civil war.

Baghdad and Beirut

By 15 July, the US Marines were in Beirut. Anglo-American deliberations immediately following news of the collapse of the Nuri Said regime at the hands of the Iraqi military that seized state power on 14 July set the stage for the timing of the dual interventions in Jordan and Lebanon. As Macmillan understood, the Iraqi revolution provided an unexpected legitimation of US intervention in Lebanon. The timing made it necessary, according to the Prime Minister. While Macmillan and Eisenhower agreed on this, they were far apart on the question of rollback in Iraq. Nonetheless, the President made it clear that the Iraqi situation was in Britain's lap, while the question of protecting Western oil interests in the eastern Arab world was a matter of joint responsibility. Intervention to that end was planned.

In the Middle East, the sequence of events led some knowledgeable leaders to conclude that US action in Lebanon was a counter-intervention,

---

[52] Miles Copeland, *The Game of Nations* (New York, 1969), p. 236.

in the words of Saudi Prince Faisal, whose rise to power in Saudi Arabia was one of the by-products of the earlier Saudi crisis.[53]

The counter-intervention that Faisal described was not directed at Iraq, however, but at the course of Lebanon's ongoing civil war. US military historians shared this view. They argued that the United States intervened in "Lebanon's internal political affairs to support a pro-Western government that was endangered by a crisis largely of its own creation."[54] Further, according to the report of "The U.S. Army Task Force in Lebanon" (1959):

> Long before the President [Eisenhower] announced the U.S. intervention, preparations had been made for such an eventuality. In addition to the preparatory steps taken by the Army, the U.S. Sixth Fleet, with embarked Marines, was getting ready for action in the Mediterranean. Thus, in the mid-afternoon of 14 July CINCNELM [Commander in Chief, U.S. Naval Forces, Eastern Atlantic and Mediterranean] directed the Sixth Fleet Task Force 61 (TF 61) to operate east of 30 degrees east longitude (roughly the position of Alexandria, Egypt, or halfway from Crete to Cyprus), with 1 amphibious squadron remaining within 12 hours' sailing time of Lebanon.[55]

Macmillan worried that such intervention was bound to set off anti-Western reactions, thus risking further political deterioration. Macmillan's view was that individual action, be it in Lebanon or Jordan, was inseparable from the situation of the Middle East as a whole. As he explained to Eisenhower, things "are all tied up together now, and if this thing is done [US intervention in Lebanon], which I think is very noble of you, in the Lebanon, —all the same it will set off a whole series of things throughout the whole area. The oil will be in jeopardy. [The] operation has got to be carried through to the end." Macmillan got even more specific. US action in Lebanon, he thought, was capable of provoking attacks on Tripoli (Lebanon) as well as pipelines in Syria. The losses to "international com-

---

[53] Embassy in Saudi Arabia to the Department of State, 25 July 1958. *FRUS*, 1958–1960, XII, p. 732.

[54] #1, V.E. 23.2.58, Lebanon, July 1958, Marine Corps Historical Center, Washington, DC.

[55] "The US Army Task Force in Lebanon, 1958 Headquarters, United States Army, Europe, G3 Division, 1959." I want to thank Sean Morris of Boston University, indefatigable researcher, for drawing my attention to this report in the online archive of the Military History Institute at Carlisle, Pennsylvania; and Dennis Vetock of the Military History Institute for his assistance in making this material accessible.

panies and particularly upon us who depend on sterling oil" would be considerable, the Prime Minister warned.[56] Macmillan indicated that he was prepared to accept such risks provided that Eisenhower agreed that "it is part of a determination between us both to face the issues and be prepared to protect Jordan with the hope of restoring the situation in Iraq."

At the same time, Macmillan conceded that "intervention in the Lebanon in response to Chamoun's request is certainly made much more necessary by what has happened in Iraq," adding that Eisenhower would doubtless justify US action in terms of the UAR. Yet he clearly considered Lebanon, where the United States and Britain had been cooperating prior to the Iraqi coup, as a secondary matter, "not very important in itself," but part of a larger project.[57]

Vice President Nixon shared Macmillan's attitude. Nixon advocated marching on Iraq and expelling those US Ambassadors—such as McClintock—who opposed US intervention.[58] In this he was countered by the Secretary of State who reminded Nixon of Suez and the flaws of British policy.

As to Lebanon, as John Foster Dulles pointed out, the United States had "assets in Lebanon we don't have in other places." Dulles supported the proposal for unilateral as opposed to joint intervention in Lebanon. He concurred that it was advisable for the British to maintain reserves "to deal with trouble elsewhere," which to the British meant Iraq and Kuwait.[59] Dulles conceded the importance of helping Britain avert future oil shortages, in the event of attacks on pipelines, for example. TAPLINE sources proved useful in this regard. But the Secretary of State was in accord with Eisenhower that full-scale intervention in the region entailed problems "that we have not even considered." When he appeared before congressional leaders in an urgent meeting on 14 July, Dulles was an unconditional advocate of intervention in Beirut. He introduced that plan, however, as a joint Anglo-American intervention, in which British forces would be reserved for a possible move on Iraq, an idea he attributed to General Twining. In so doing, Dulles shifted responsibility for the decision to go it alone in Beirut to the US military, but he remained committed to unilateral intervention in Lebanon to protect US "assets."

---

[56] FO telegraph # 44477 to Washington, 15 July 1958, FO 371/134130.

[57] For a full discussion of the British side of the question, see the chapter by Wm. Roger Louis.

[58] Nixon telephone call to Dulles, 15 July 1958, John Foster Dulles Papers, Eisenhower Library, Telephone Call Series, Box 8.

[59] 15 July 1958, *DDQC*, 7, No. 4 (October–December 1981), 627B.

But despite Dulles's testimony, Eisenhower and Dulles had no further interest in a joint policy but were planning only for a dual policy, with American and British forces operating in parallel but separate spheres in the Middle East.[60] Macmillan too was set on intervention. He left no doubt about the urgency of Britain's responding to the pleas from its royal client in Amman, one of "two little chaps" who had requested urgent help. The other was Feisal, who, the British learned, had already been killed in the coup in Baghdad.

Such considerations affected the Anglo-American response to the Iraqi coup. But there were other factors involving Western oil interests. Four days after the military seized power in Baghdad, on 18 July, the Iraqi revolutionary regime under Abdel Karim Qasim assured the West of its commitment to the continued production and flow of oil. Such welcome assurances aside, Eisenhower considered it imperative to protect Western oil and political interests in the region. To Macmillan he sent the assessment cited earlier in this chapter in which he identified US priorities. The first priority of seeing that "the Persian Gulf area stays within the Western orbit" involved the "extremely important" Kuwait-Dharan-Abadan areas. The second was protecting such reliable allies as Turkey and Iran as well as Lebanon and Jordan. For Beirut and Amman Eisenhower recommended fostering loyalties and bolstering economic as well as military strength.[61]

British sources of this period are more revealing than American ones on the subject of keeping the Gulf within the Western orbit. Not only do they provide considerable information on the thinking of British officials, they disclose the extent of US support and collaboration in this project.

The British position in Kuwait had been under discussion for some time prior to 14 July. US officials in charge of Saudi and Iraqi affairs had raised concerns similar to those of the British with regard to the need for political, social, and professional advances for the ruling classes of Kuwait. That was in late March.[62] But British discussion of increased autonomy for Kuwait, which had been on the agenda before 14 July, was subsequently dropped. Security became the uppermost issue, not modernization or

[60] Department of Defense Memorandum for the Record, 14 July 1958, *DDQC*, 12, 2, (March–April 1986), 00759; and "Joint Chiefs of Staff and National Policy, 1956–1958," chapter 8, p. 445.

[61] Eisenhower to Macmillan, signed Dulles, to American Embassy, London, 18 July 1958, *DDQC*, 12, 3, (May–June 1986), 1416.

[62] Memorandum for the Officer in Charge of Arabian Peninsula-Iraq Affairs (Newsome) to the Director of the Office of Near Eastern Affairs (Rockwell), 31 March 1958, *FRUS*, 1958–1960, XII, pp. 774–75.

development. Foreign Office records are of interest in this connection, particularly since they also disclose Dulles's views on intervention and the use of force.

On 15 July, the Foreign Office cabled the Kuwaiti Ruler with instructions "to take all necessary precautions to protect oil installations and British buildings against demonstrations and sabotage."[63] In the event that the Ruler was not up to the task, British military assistance—intervention, in short—would be necessary. In the opinion of Lord Hood in the British Embassy in Washington, intervention held out irresistible advantages since "we would get our hands firmly on the Kuwaiti oil," he explained to Macmillan on 19 July.[64] But the risks of such action were evident. It would invariably arouse resistance, which could take the form of strikes in the oil fields. That contingency might, in turn, lead to a more permanent occupation and the change in status of Kuwait to that of a Crown Colony. The alternative, according to the same source, was a "kind of Kuwaiti Switzerland," where even "mildly pro-Egyptian sentiments" would be tolerated as long as they did not lead to "an Iraqi type coup...." Hood left no doubt that such developments might entail the use of force. In that eventuality, he explained, "we must also accept the need, if things go wrong, ruthlessly to intervene, whoever it is has caused the trouble. The alternative course of immediate British occupation would bring a lot of political trouble in its wake and result in the permanent involvement of at least two brigades."[65] But as in the case of the Americans in Lebanon, British officials sought a plausible cover for intervention. The preferred form was an invitation to intervene from the Kuwaiti Ruler. Otherwise, as a British official, D. M. H. Riches, put it, "we shall be in queer street not only with the Arab but also with the rest of the world." The absence of such an invitation did not preclude intervention. As Riches explained, this was "no reason for not going into Kuwait if we have to."[66]

Dulles gave his approval. British records indicate that the Americans "are disposed to act with similar resolution in relation to the Aramco oilfields in the area of Dhahran, although the logistics are not worked out. They assume that we will also hold Bahrain and Qatar, come what may. They agreed that at all costs these oilfields must be kept in Western

[63] 15 July 1958, #427, FO 371/134158.
[64] Washington to Foreign Office, 19 July 1958, FO 371/132779.
[65] Ibid.
[66] 22 July 1958, FO 317/133808.

hands."[67] The British scenario, then, was the following. If "everything blows up at once," the British would go into Kuwait, the Americans into [the province of] Hasa, and by then, "presumably normal restraints on action from Bahrain will have to disappear."[68]

On the very same day, 23 July, Rountree sent a memorandum to Dulles in which he indicated that "we have given further consideration to the possible necessity for US-UK military intervention or other resolute steps in the Persian Gulf area."[69] Rountree indicated that the occupation of Saudi Arabia was not then being considered since there was no present threat. In the event that this changed, he recommended obtaining an invitation to intervene from the proper sources. Ever-concerned with adverse publicity, he urged utmost secrecy with respect to military movements into the Gulf and Kuwait, particularly since intervention in Lebanon was now an open matter. In Rountree's words: "one reinforced U.S. Marine battalion is now en route to the Persian Gulf and may arrive within the next two weeks" [two following lines of source text have not been declassified].[70]

Then there was the matter of protecting TAPLINE, which had undertaken a dramatic twenty-five percent expansion of its pipelines from Saudi Arabia to the Mediterranean. TAPLINE had extended its radio-controlled, unmanned pumping stations and tanker capacity, and had expanded storage tanks at Sidon, the Mediterranean port city that was the TAPLINE outlet to the sea.[71] Working through the winter and spring, TAPLINE officials anticipated completion of the project in the summer. Several days after US intervention in Beirut, Allen Dulles reminded Eisenhower that "there are three million barrels of oil stored at Sidon. The Secretary [Foster Dulles] thought perhaps we should move up to guard this oil (although this will have bad connotations). He said he had asked Murphy for his recommendation. The President recalled that Chamoun had suggested moving the Marines into additional areas."[72] There had been earlier discussion

---

[67] Lord Hood to Macmillan, 19 July 1958, FO 371/132779.

[68] D. M. H. Riches to W. Morris, 23 July 1958, FO 371/132779.

[69] Memorandum from the Assistant Secretary of State for Near Eastern, South Asian, and African Affairs (Rountree) to the Secretary of State, 23 July 1958, *FRUS*, 1958–1960, XII, p. 93.

[70] Ibid., p. 94.

[71] Communication to the author from Professor Bare Ludvigsen, 12 April 1999. Professor Ludvigsen is the author of the unique online TAPLINE history project: http://almashriq.hiof.no/borrel/

[72] Memorandum of Conference with President Eisenhower, 20 July 1958, *FRUS*, 1958–1960, XII, p. 85.

of this option, according to TAPLINE Executive Vice President William Chandler. The day after the US Marines landed, Rear Admiral Howard A. Yeager, who was in charge of US Naval Forces, proposed a further landing of US Marines in Sidon to protect the TAPLINE terminal. He was deterred from doing so by Chandler's urgent recommendation. TAPLINE had its own security arrangements. It had the protection of the Lebanese Army and, through one of its political informants, it was well-connected with General Chehab. Given Chehab's continued access to the opposition leadership, a matter of contention in Beirut and Washington, the connection was invaluable for TAPLINE. Proposals for protecting the pipeline with US Marines were subsequently abandoned.[73]

Other preparations were also underway in this period. Eisenhower ordered the redeployment of the Strategic Air Command (SAC), with a "Composite Air Strike Group," which would be redirected from Europe to Turkey, along with Marine combat missions ordered to the Gulf.[74] Nuclear weapons were considered in the eventuality of an Iraqi move into Kuwait, according to a well-informed source.[75] Nuclear weapons were similarly in reserve for Lebanon, though in deference to the anticipated political reaction they were kept offshore.

Operation Bluebat and After: Fixing the Cabinet, Organizing Troop Withdrawal, and Providing for Internal Security

The codename of US intervention in Lebanon was Operation Bluebat. Evidence of its nature and the purpose of the ensuing US occupation scarcely conforms to the media and academic image of US intervention as a benign adventure in the catalogue of postwar military successes. The record of the crises that occurred between US civilian and military officials and the Lebanese military are entirely at odds with conventional accounts. US forces achieved their political purpose, however, which was to support the regime in the course of a civil war, to contain dissident elements of the

[73] Personal communication from William R. Chandler to the author, 25 April 1997.

[74] Alan Dowty, *Middle East Crisis: U.S. Decision-Making in 1958, 1970, and 1973* (Berkeley and Los Angeles, 1984), p. 49.

[75] William Quandt, "Lebanon, 1958 and Jordan, 1970," in B. Blechman and S. D. Kaplan, eds. *Force without War: U.S. Armed Forces as a Political Instrument* (Washington, DC: Brookings Institution, 1978), p. 85.

opposition, and, in collaboration with US civilian officials in Beirut, to assure an acceptable political solution.[76]

Other aspects of the military operation in Lebanon, including the use of aerial photography over Lebanon and the region, served the interests of US military strategists. Eleven thousand air sorties were ordered over Lebanon. How can this be explained in light of the ostensibly limited purposes of US action? The historian of the Sixth Fleet in the Mediterranean explained that although "photographic coverage of key targets throughout the Middle East was available," and "target intelligence for air strikes" was satisfactory, "coverage of internal areas of Lebanon was inadequate. To overcome this deficiency, extensive photo reconnaissance operations of all of Lebanon and portions of the Syrian interior and coastal areas were undertaken."[77] The project was approved by Chamoun, it appears, reluctantly. Lebanon, in this instance, appears to have served the purposes of those in the US military bent on finding justification for the endorsement of "limited war" operations. How such reconnaissance operations fit the stated purpose of US intervention offered by Eisenhower is another matter.

The role of US troops in Lebanon, the President stated, was to "protect American lives and by their presence help sustain [the] Lebanese government in its defense of Lebanon's sovereignty and integrity. They do not go as combat forces and not in any act of war. They will be withdrawn as soon as possible."[78] The US Marine Corps Historical Center account of the Lebanon operation differed. The operation, according to this source, was a "show of force" that had "psychological overtones." These included "shows" by Air Force and Naval air units. The operation's goals were "achieved by demonstrations of combat capabilities, training assistance to the Lebanese Army, positioning of combat outposts, opposing sources of harassment, and operating numerous strong tank-infantry patrols in areas of civil disturbance."[79]

CIA Agent Eveland's account of the encounter between Chehab and Robert Murphy, the Special Envoy of the President, further illustrated Eisenhower's true intentions. Responding to Chehab, who as Commander-in-Chief of the Lebanese Army opposed US intervention,

---

[76] The discussion that follows is based on material that either appears in, or is adapted from, Chapter 14 ("By Mutual Consent: July-October 1958") of Gendzier, *Notes from the Minefield*.

[77] Ibid., p. 313.

[78] Ibid., p. 324.

[79] Ibid., p. 312.

Murphy adopted an aggressive attitude. He remarked to Chehab that it would take no more than "one of the aircraft, armed with nuclear weapons" in the *Saratoga* that sat in Beirut harbor to "obliterate Beirut and its environs from the face of the earth."[80] Yet Murphy followed the none-too-subtle threat with the observation that he had been sent to Beirut to be certain that it would be unnecessary for US troops to "fire a shot." Murphy wanted to be certain that Chehab would "ensure that there were no provocations on the Lebanese side."

The presence of US forces in Beirut, along with the vigorous action of Ambassador Robert McClintock and Robert Murphy, provided an effective "show of force," though not precisely of the type expressed in formal justifications of US intervention. Such a show nonetheless achieved its objective, which was to obtain a politically acceptable outcome to the civil war, defined in terms of American interests.[81] Due credit for this outcome must be given not only to the military officers who remained in Beirut, but to Murphy and McClintock. The Ambassador was so outspoken in his reports to the Secretary of State about his role as intermediary between the new President and opposition leaders Chamoun and Pierre Gemayel, the Phalangist Party leader, that Dulles cautioned him about the need for discretion. While Murphy appears to have played a critical role in persuading Eisenhower and Dulles of the need to marginalize Chamoun, McClintock worked to assure Chamoun's constituency of representation in the new cabinet. That task, obviously undertaken to assure US interests, proved onerous due to continuing tensions, as he reported to Washington. Further, McClintock's job as he saw it was to appease Dulles and his partial vision of Lebanon which owed much to his chief Lebanese interlocutor, Charles Malik. Dulles and Malik were both persuaded that the UN Secretary General was an avowed partisan of Nasser and not to be trusted in the Lebanese situation.

McClintock's intervention in Lebanese politics, like that of the US military, was by invitation. This time it was not Chamoun but Chehab who requested the Ambassador's assistance. No stranger to the internal conflicts of Lebanese leaders, McClintock strenuously applied his efforts in mediating among the interests of the principal wartime protagonists. His opportunistic role in supporting Gemayel's political ascendance reinforced—but did not create—the Phalangist leader's political base. Such positive reinforcement at a critical phase in Lebanon's postwar politics was clearly of inestimable value to Gemayel, Chehab, and the United States. Without

---

[80] Ibid., p. 316.

[81] For details, see ibid., chapter 14.

McClintock's interference, which is to say that of the United States, would the configuration of the new cabinet have been the same? Would there have been a resumption of civil war? McClintock had few illusions about Gemayel's contribution to Lebanese politics. He recognized the Kataeb leader's hostility to compromise which was a prerequisite to a political solution of prewar conflicts. Months earlier, the Ambassador had sent Dulles a blunt portrait of Gemayel as one who "denied [that] Christians enjoy [a] privileged position in Lebanon and rejected any settlement with respect [to] government positions, gratuities, et cetera."[82] Chehab had additional concerns, namely that the discontented political leaders would opt for military rule.[83] That prospect sealed Chamoun's fate in the eyes of US officials who rejected the invitation to military assistance.

It also appears to have affected Chehab's outlook on US troop withdrawal. The bitter struggle over withdrawal was therefore muted given the unresolved political tensions and the anticipated resumption of conflict.

Murphy and McClintock, meanwhile, turned to the opposition, meeting with those the United States had formerly classified as anti-American rebels. The resulting arrangements that were finally approved included Pierre Gemayel as Minister of Education, Health, Public Works, and Agriculture in the four-person cabinet responsible for some fifteen ministerial posts. Having consulted with the future Prime Minister Raschid Keramé, US officials were persuaded that he was no threat. Neither was Hussein al-Uwaini, the new Foreign Minister who had been among Nasser's recommended appointments in past negotiations. Raymond Eddé, Minister of the Interior, Post and Telegraph and Social Affairs, was singled out by McClintock as a friend. The new arrangements were soon to be reinforced by American funds and plans for internal security.

Before these appointments were announced, the question of troop withdrawal was addressed with Britain. The delay was a function of British and American concern with a possible Israeli movement into Jordan should King Hussein's position prove to be at risk. As Dulles explained to the UAR Foreign Minister, Mahmoud Fawzi, in the fall of 1958, Jordan was a key to stabilizing the Arab-Israeli situation:

> We were paying tribute to hold Jordan so that war would not break out. Jordan had nothing of interest to us. It was of interest to all, however, that there be no chaos in the area. We did not know Israel's purposes, but there

[82] Ibid., p. 351.
[83] Ibid., p. 345.

> was a fifty-fifty chance that if Jordan collapsed, the Israelis would occupy the West Bank. This could start a lot of other things. There was a common interest to try to preserve peace so that Jordan's future could evolve peacefully. The Secretary admitted, however, that he was at a loss to know how such a peaceful evolution might take place.[84]

In subsequent talks, Dulles shared his sense of frustration about Amman, particularly since the Chargé d'Affaires in Jordan, Thomas K. Wright, made clear that the United States needed to decide if it would support "'fortress Jordan' as a non-viable Western satellite in the heartland [of] Nasser['s] hoped-for Middle East empire with [the] clear understanding this can only be accomplished by force and against [the] will [of the] majority [of the] Jordanian people...." The other option was that the UAR be allowed to absorb Jordan, which Wright clearly thought would occur if the existing Jordanian cabinet fell.[85] US sources indicate that Fawzi suggested a revival of the Iraqi-Jordanian union, this time in the form of an Iraqi takeover of the Jordanian state. Dulles did not categorically reject the idea, provided that Jordan would not be absorbed by the UAR and that Israel did not object to the arrangements.[86] If the former contingency in fact occurred, Dulles explained, US funds for Amman would be cut, thus shifting the burden to the UAR.[87] That, in turn, as Fawzi made clear, was not in the UAR's interests. The Dulles-Fawzi meetings continued, with both men convinced of the urgency of avoiding the collapse of the Jordanian regime, which continued to be subsidized by the United States and Britain.

In mid-September the Joint Chiefs of Staff and State Department officials confirmed that US troop withdrawal from Lebanon continued to be delayed by the British position in Jordan. Stuart Rockwell of the State Department conceded that "we have made clear to the British that we will not leave their forces in Jordan alone in the Middle East. The political problem in Jordan is more difficult and withdrawal might not be possible as early as in Lebanon."[88] Withdrawal was therefore delayed until the end of October. The announcement of plans for joint withdrawal of British

---

[84] #270, *FRUS*, 1958–1960, XI, p. 471.

[85] Embassy in Amman to DOS, #281, 19 August 1958, ibid., p. 503.

[86] Ibid., #279, p. 493.

[87] Letter from Foreign Secretary Selwyn Lloyd to the Secretary of State, 25 August 1958, ibid., p. 524.

[88] Memorandum DOS-JCS, Pentagon, 12 September 1958, ibid., p. 564.

forces from Jordan on 24 October and American forces from Lebanon by 31 October signaled the final stages of Anglo-American collaboration in the Lebanon-Jordan interventions.

The withdrawal of US Air forces had begun on 29 August and by mid-September Admiral Holloway agreed to the evacuation of military equipment and accompanying service units, as a preface to the departure of combat forces. Withdrawal was expected to be completed by 10 November, although "the two U.S. Marine battalions will remain afloat in the Eastern Mediterranean."[89] Most troops were withdrawn by 23 October. Holloway had moved to his London headquarters, after which the last vestiges of US military presence were removed from Beirut. On 2 November, British forces withdrew from Jordan.

The next step was the termination of the Lebanese question in the United Nations. US Representative to the United Nations Henry Cabot Lodge, Lebanese Foreign Minister Hussein al-Uwaini, and Dag Hammarskjöld, in turn, announced the withdrawal of troops, requested the removal of the Lebanese Government's complaint against the UAR, and declared the mission of the United Nations Observation Group in Lebanon (UNOGIL) to be at an end. Thus, on 6 November, Cabot Lodge informed the Secretary General that American troops had been withdrawn from Lebanon. He was careful to emphasize that their departure was in compliance with the General Assembly Resolution of 21 August, which by its language had vindicated Lebanese claims against the UAR, claims about to be deleted from the record. The United Nations now called on member states to respect each other's sovereignty and territorial integrity.

On 16 November, Al-Uwaini officially closed the Lebanese case in his letter to the Security Council, formally requesting that the Security Council delete the Lebanese Government's complaint against the UAR, which had been submitted on 22 May.[90] This was followed by Hammarskjöld's announcement to the Security Council on 17 November that pursuant to the completion of UNOGIL's assignment in Lebanon, it was to be officially terminated. The UN phase of the Lebanese crisis was thereby ended. It had been a seven-month trial in which the United

---

[89] Staff Notes, Mem Conf. President, 15 October 1958, Box 36, Dwight D. Eisenhower Diaries, Eisenhower Library.

[90] Letter of 16 November from the Lebanese Minister of Foreign Affairs to the President of the Security Council, 25 November 1958, 840th UN SCOR.

Nations had been undermined, its reports ignored by the major powers as well as Lebanon.[91] At its peak, "UNOGIL had 591 observers, 49 posts, 12 planes and six helicopters," which it subsequently withdrew in the period between 28 November and 9 December.[92] Rajeshwar Dayal, who had been in charge of UNOGIL, went on to another debacle, this time in the Congo, where he now found himself between the United States and Belgium, and became the target of their dealings to retain control of the Congo's mineral wealth.

At about the time that the United Nations was being apprised of US and British troop withdrawal from Lebanon and Jordan, the US National Security Council addressed the Lebanese situation. The report NSC 5820/1 of 4 November 1958 is of interest because of the nature of US policy, and particularly because of the security arrangements put in place in the same period. While such arrangements assured a continuing relationship with Lebanon at the highest levels, the NSC report recommended the following:

> a. Provide Lebanon with political support and with military assistance for internal security purposes, stressing our support for the country as a whole rather than for a specific regime or faction.
> b. Reduce grant economic assistance as feasible and emphasize Lebanon's capacity to borrow from international lending institutions for purposes of economic development.
> c. Where appropriate seek to encourage the acceptance of Lebanon's unique status by its Arab neighbors, and, if desired by and acceptable to the people concerned, be prepared to subscribe to a United Nations guarantee of the continued independence and integrity of Lebanon.[93]

US policy at this juncture was based on the premise that the regime would continue to be unstable. Intelligence sources claimed that US intervention had prevented the emergence of a pro-Nasserist regime, but conceded that this did not resolve internal Lebanese problems. The future of Lebanon's President was considered uncertain, and Lebanon's Christian

---

91 For a more favorable assessment, see the chapter by Michael G. Fry.

92 Michael G. Fry, "The Uses of Intelligence: the United Nations Confronts the United States in the Lebanon Crisis, 1958," *Intelligence and National Security* 10, 1 (January 1995), p. 89, n. 36.

93 US Policy Toward the Near East, 4 November 1958, *DDQC*, 6, 4 (October–December 1980), 00386B.

population was viewed as weakened but unbowed and unprepared for political compromise.[94] As a consequence, steps were taken to ensure the new regime's security and financial stability in the first months of its existence. McClintock made arrangements for internal security in discussion with the US Army Attaché, the State Department, the Country Team, and the Office of Public Safety Program (OPS) of the International Cooperation Administration (ICA).

US officials recommended that non-American personnel be found to train the Lebanese "because of the differences in systems and public attitudes as between Lebanon and the United States in respect of police activity."[95] Further, the same source, identified only as "I [Edwin H. Arnold]" indicated that he had "dealt separately...on the possibility of providing technical advisors to the Lebanese Sûreté." The ICA was reluctant, in practice, to provide assistance to the Lebanese Gendarmerie without prior agreement "to assignment of at least one US Public Safety representative to screen civil police needs and provide technical advice and program control." The Office of Public Safety specialized in the "modernization" of police forces and in counterinsurgency training. The candidate identified for the Lebanese position, Albert E. DuBois, had experience in the civil police and military, and was at the time Chief Public Safety director in Thailand where the United States had a major OPS operation supporting the Thai military dictatorship.[96] McClintock made plans for DuBois to be on the embassy staff. The Ambassador considered such arrangements unproblematic because of the identity of the Minister of the Interior and because the Lebanese Gendarmerie was then "under the command of a thoroughly capable and honest officer, one Colonel...who has had some military training in the United States."[97] McClintock asked for "prompt word if ICA/W plans to so assign Mr. DuBois so that maximum effect from his assignment could be achieved by discreet conversation with President Chehab." The Army Attaché prepared an itemized list of equipment and the probable cost, some $925,000, which was to cover three categories of materials.

[94] SNIE 30-6-58, 28 October 1958, *FRUS*, 1958–1960, XI, p. 618.

[95] Assistance to Lebanese Gendarmerie, Status Report for November 1958, *DDQC*, 7, 2, (April–June 1981), 217B.

[96] N. Chomsky and E. S. Herman, *The Washington Connection and World Fascism*, 1:219, see pp. 218–30.

[97] Status Report for November 1958, *op. cit.*

Priority one embraces rifles, ammunition, cots, trucks, batteries, and trailers estimated to cost $350,000. Priority two embraces revolvers, bayonets, helmets, belts, blankets, Thompson sub-machine guns, jeeps, personnel carriers, and ammunition at an estimated cost of $350,000. Priority three embraces grenade launchers, hand grenades, machine guns, rifles, jeeps, trucks, ambulances, tents, and ammunition at an estimated cost of $225,000.[98]

Action on "priority three" was deferred until the Public Safety Official was securely in place. Materials that plainly constituted military assistance were to be justified in terms of the "military internal security objectives" of the gendarmerie. The US European Command Report to the President's Committee to Study the U.S. Military Assistance Program (MAP) for North Africa and the Middle East (the Draper Committee Reports of 1958–1959) confirmed such objectives as integral to US military policy in Lebanon.[99] In 1958, the US provided Lebanon with $3.6 million in military supplies, including engineering and communications supplies as well as the assistance offered in this connection by the Richards mission in pursuance of Lebanon's acceptance of the Eisenhower Doctrine. In the winter of 1958, under the MAP and International Military Education and Training Program, a modest sum of grants and credits for the purchase of US arms was offered, while military training for Lebanese students was provided, bringing the total personnel affected by such programs between 1950 and 1976 to 1,521. The number was comparable to that for Jordan and Saudi Arabia, though far below that for Iran (11,025) or Turkey (19,150).[100]

In 1954–1958 Lebanon received $7.5 million for military aid, of which only $3.4 million was delivered prior to July 1958. The figure offered for fiscal year 1959 was $500 thousand.

With the exception of the $.5 million, no U.S. military aid is now programmed for Lebanon for FY 1959 or beyond. On the assumption that a certain amount of military aid will be necessary to maintain the independ-

---

[98] Ibid.

[99] The Draper Commission Reports, 1958–1959, U.S. European command, Report to the President's Committee to Study the US M.A.P., North Africa and the Middle East, 18 December 1958. Box 18, Eisenhower Library.

[100] M. Klare and C. Arnson, *Supplying Repression* (Washington, DC: Institute for Policy Studies, 1977) p. 36, cites the US Defense Security Assistance Agency, Foreign Military Sales, and Military Assistance.

> ence of the government of Lebanon, $5.0 million a year for the period FY 1959–1961 has been projected as a probable program. The expenditures of $14.6 million for FY 1959–1961 reflect this illustrative program.[101]

In December 1958, $10 million in Development Loan Funds was also under consideration, in addition to the $2.5 million provided in September, and $5 million worth of wheat set aside for delivery to Beirut.[102] McClintock informed Chehab of these plans on December 1, 1958, indicating that such assistance was intended to guarantee that the new regime could deal with the post-civil war economic problems it faced. In the estimates of U.S. allocations through the Development Loan Fund for 1959, Lebanon's share was some $17.1 million out of a projected $114.5 million.

Conclusion

What was the US position at the end of 1958, a year of crises that culminated in the Iraqi revolution, Lebanese civil war, and the British intervention in Jordan, as well as the American invasion of Lebanon? Arab nationalism, which had been regarded as a threat to US interests, was—in late July—viewed by the Secretary of State as a flood whose course could not be altered but against which the US could "put up sand bags" in states such as Israel and Lebanon, as well as Saudi Arabia and the Gulf.[103] A Special National Intelligence Estimate (SNIE), went even further, concluding that the objectives of "radical Arab nationalism are not invariably in conflict with U.S. interests. Thus, the Arab objectives of maintaining independence and of utilizing the profits of Arab oil are compatible with two crucial US interests—denial of the area to Soviet domination and maintenance of Western access to Middle East oil."[104] And the same estimate maintained that "we do not believe that Nasser is a Communist or sympathetic to the Communist doctrine." His relationship to the Soviet Union was explained as a function of the mutual interests existing between Egypt and those of a major power.

---

[101] NSC 5820/1, Financial Annex, p. 23.

[102] McClintock to DOS, #2534, 2 December 1958, RG 319, SCSI Message File 1950s, Parts 1 and 2, Box 34, Centre for Lebanese Studies, Oxford University.

[103] Memorandum of Conference with the President, 23 July 1958, *DDQC*, 8, no. 1 (January–March 1982), 00341.

[104] Special Intelligence Estimate, 12 August 1958, ibid., p. 142.

Arab nationalism, in sum, appeared as less of a major threat by the late summer of 1958, whatever public discourse on the subject continued to be. US fears about the regionalization of the Iraqi revolution appeared diminished. At regional as well as international levels, the United States emerged in a position of enhanced power. There was no doubt of US supremacy in the Middle East in relation to Britain. US policy-makers proved capable of exploiting divisions between radical regimes, consolidating gains secured from covert arrangements with Lebanon, enhancing collaboration with Israel, and expanding cooperation with other conservative and dependent allies from Turkey to Iran.[105]

Here was the realization of Eisenhower's list of priorities in the Middle East, which he had conveyed to Macmillan on 18 July. In the broader context of US foreign policy there were other urgent issues to deal with, such as the looming crisis in Quemoy and Matsu, and the struggles over US policy in southeast Asia. Middle East oil, however, continued to constitute "the jugular of the world economy," which explained Washington's continuing commitment to maintaining the balance of regional power in favor of the forces of order. [106]

---

105 Gendzier, *Notes from the Minefield*, p. 367.

106 Franz Schurmann, *The Logic of World Power* (New York, 1974), p. 200.

4

The United Nations Confronts the United States in 1958

MICHAEL GRAHAM FRY

The Context

Two maps drawn simultaneously after 1945—one charting Cold War alliances, another identifying United Nations membership and activity—would reflect the consequences of the Second World War. The former map captures the bipolar world, the overarching USA-USSR strategic balance, while the latter conveys the process of decolonization. The Cold War was not simply the context of decolonization. Rather, each phenomenon—the Cold War and decolonization—was part of the explanation of the other, if not equally so. The intricate relationship between the Cold War and decolonization posed the fundamental predicament for US policy. Britain and France were the indispensable allies of the United States in its competition with the Soviet Union. Possession of empire seemed crucial to their post-war economic revival and their strategic reach. Yet the United States could not defy the march of history, the moral history of the twentieth century. If it endorsed the perpetuation of empire, if it opposed decolonization, the USSR and radical nationalist regimes, those beyond US experience and tolerance, would benefit. In some cases, in the face of this dilemma, the United States could stay relatively detached and avoid choice, especially if the French and not the British empire were at issue. When detachment was not possible, the United States explored the challenging middle ground where decolonization, the process of reducing the burdens of empire but preserving Anglo-French interests, would serve Western not Soviet purposes, moderate not radical nationalist preferences. That was how decolonization bred neo-empire. On one occasion, in the Suez crisis of 1956, the United States brought Britain and France, and their co-aggressor, Israel, to heel.

Little of US policy was palatable to the controversial UN Secretary General of the era, Dag Hammarskjöld. He saw, in his vision and naiveté, the prospect of a secure, moderate, stable, and independently neutral Middle East prospering under UN auspices. It would be led by Gamal Abdel Nasser and the newly-forged United Arab Republic. These preferences put Hammarskjöld at odds with the United States and Britain. His inclinations reflected his maturing view of the United Nations' role in the Middle East.

From its inception in 1945 to the Congo Crisis in 1960, the United Nations undertook five major initiatives, not all of which were strictly peacekeeping operations. Three of the five operations took place in the Middle East—United Nations Truce Supervision Operation (UNTSO), from June 1948, preventing the escalation of conflict on Israel's borders with its Arab neighbors; United Nations Emergency Force (UNEF) from November 1956, securing the cease-fire between Egypt and Israel and overseeing the withdrawal of Israeli, French, and British forces from Egypt; and United Nations Observation Group in Lebanon (UNOGIL), from June to December 1958, deterring the illegal infiltration of arms and men from Syria into Lebanon.[1] In addition, the United Nations was attending to the plight of the Palestinian refugees.

In the Suez crisis of 1956, action in the Security Council and particularly in the General Assembly, and the initiatives of Hammarskjöld, had helped to contain the crisis, drain it of potential for escalation and exploitation, and, beyond the mandate of UNEF, provide for the clearing of the Suez Canal and the creation of a regime for its operation. In 1957 the United Nations had been involved in the settlement of the future of Gaza and Sharm-el-Sheikh and the Syrian crisis. By 1958 Hammarskjöld had met with every Middle Eastern leader of consequence except the Syrians, a marked contrast with President Dwight D. Eisenhower, his Secretary of State, John Foster Dulles, Prime Minister Harold Macmillan, and his Foreign Secretary, Selwyn Lloyd. Hammarskjöld's relationship with President Nasser was particularly

[1] United Nations, *The Blue Helmets: A Review of United Nations Peacekeeping* (New York, 1990); Alan James, *Peacekeeping in International Politics* (London, 1990); and Thomas A. Weiss and Jarat Chopra, *United Nations Peacekeeping* (New York, 1992).

important. From this involvement came credibility, experience, and expertise for the institution and its Secretary General, a presence in the field by UN personnel, and a commitment from officials in New York. It all constituted a special relationship between the United Nations and the Middle East.

In a broader but no less profound sense, the United Nations had become both a mirror and a heliograph of issues and trends in the international system outside the immediate and direct agenda of the Cold War and decolonization—the claim to influence of the Afro-Asian states, itself reflected in the changing face of the British Commonwealth; the relative balance between the small, middle, and great powers; the use of force in inter-state relations; indirect aggression; and the permissibility of intervening in the internal affairs of member states. The United Nations was coming to be understood as providing a second set of norms, precedents, and rules, not a substitute for established diplomacy and statecraft, not displacing traditional foreign policy, but a complement to established rules of international conduct. In this coexistence between old and new rules there was ample room for harmony and discord, as respective boundaries were adjusted and jurisdictions were worked out. Eisenhower, for example, on rare occasions, yearned for the days when the great powers, in unison, enjoyed the freedom to manage the international system, but he accepted the fact that the world had changed after the Second World War. In the final analysis, with respect to the Middle East in 1958, he would not allow the United Nations to constrain US policy excessively. Hammarskjöld understood that to be the case and acquiesced, not out of despair but with calculation.[2]

The United Nations was, as a consequence, a source of complexity, uncertainty, and unpredictability in a way the League of Nations had rarely been. This situation of unavoidable complexity sired a series of problems. What issues could and could not appropriately be handed to the United Nations? And at what point? How could the United Nations be made centrally relevant without being overburdened and overtaxed? The United Nations could not be asked to achieve the improbable single handedly, but

[2] Dulles-Hammarskjöld telephone conversation, 14 July 1958, *Foreign Relations of the United States* (hereafter *FRUS*), 1958–1960, XI, 126, p. 217. They agreed that if the United States decided to intervene militarily, it would be wise to convene the Security Council. "The Secretary said we wanted to work under the Charter as much as we can and would not want to move without reporting it to the United Nations. Hammarskjöld said we are facing a wide revolution...that he hoped they would be kept informed and they will do what they can to keep things on the rails."

how could it be used efficaciously rather than merely being "used" by the superpowers, for example, to prosecute the Cold War? When its member states used it as they should, to what extent were they creating an actor of consequence, a source of influence and constraint on themselves? These questions applied equally to the institution and the Secretary General. It would be folly to under-utilize him, irresponsible to overburden him, and futile to expect his obsequious compliance.

There was, most assuredly, an intelligence dimension to all of this. What access did the Secretary General have to the intelligence communities of the powers in the Security Council? What personal relationships had he developed with those who headed those communities? To what extent did and should the United Nations rely on the intelligence provided by the various states? Was it not wise to develop independent sources of intelligence, and were not the observation and peacekeeping forces in some ways ideally suited for this purpose? And what would transpire when UN intelligence challenged that of the United States, for example, especially on the Middle East? After all, the United States was, among other things, the principal paymaster of peacekeeping efforts in the region.

These questions also ensured that the United Nations would be controversial, beyond serving as "an institution for the organization of collective chaos." Its critics, from their various perspectives, found much to deplore. Some despaired of that flawed instrument, the Security Council, which had become little more than a public forum to air the controversies of the Cold War, and a tool of the United States, albeit of declining relevance as it gave way to the General Assembly. Others felt irritation with a General Assembly that grew in pretentiousness as it gathered influence, became a vehicle for the decolonized world to assault the West, and thus, even despite itself, served the mischievous purposes of the Soviet Union. Suspicion of the Secretary General was marked in London, Paris, and Tel Aviv; opinions differed in Washington with Allen Dulles, Director of the CIA, one of his covert detractors.[3] And where Allen trod, Foster, on occasion, followed.

---

[3] Allen Dulles statement, National Security Council, 19 June 1958, *FRUS*, 1958–1960, XI, p. 155. Dulles, forecasting difficult days ahead, noted that "Hammarskjöld had been in touch with Nasser which could prove to be a serious matter if true." The CIA concluded later, quite unjustifiably, that Hammarskjöld had failed to implement the General Assembly Resolution of 21 August and that the effectiveness of the UN "presence" in Jordan was doubtful (National Security Council, 18 and 25 September, ibid., 323, pp. 572 and 332, pp. 579–80.

The Suez crisis, prompting the flawed but remarkable performance of the United Nations, had made Hammarskjöld as controversial as the organization. He had been judged both irresolute and decisive, devious and straight, and well on the way to becoming a stooge of Egypt. In 1957 he had participated in the resolution of the future of Gaza and Sharm-el-Sheikh and the Syrian crisis, to mixed reviews. But the General Assembly had re-elected him unanimously in September 1957, and Hammarskjöld was decidedly *persona grata* with the Security Council. Yet he could be blunt in his exchanges with, and remarkably indiscreet in his comments on, various prominent statesmen. Hammarskjöld, however, grew in stature as he gained the confidence of governments; he became more creative and accepted risks as the prestige of his office blossomed. He had a precision of mind that matched a clarity of purpose. He was deeply committed to UN processes and could see how to improve on them. He found satisfaction in demonstrating that the United Nations was working. Indeed, his immediate entourage, Ralph Bunche, Andrew Cordier, and Brian Urquhart, worried lest the "leave it to Dag" thesis circulating in the international community became an axiom. There were grounds for these concerns amidst talk, for example, of making Jordan a ward of the United Nations when it seemed to be crumbling, irreparably crumbling, in the summer of 1958. Yet Hammarskjöld's feet never left the ground. He was well aware of the United Nations' limitations. As he told Henry Cabot Lodge, the US representative at the United Nations, on the critical evening of 14 July 1958, "you and we were in a jam" and "some gifts the United Nations received were too big for the UN lap."[4]

Controversy continued to stalk Hammarskjöld as he helped to manage the Lebanese crisis in 1958. After pleading with Hammarskjöld to resolve the crisis, Camille Chamoun, Lebanon's beleaguered President, denounced the Secretary General as "the most conceited man in the world or the most deceitful."[5] Hammarskjöld, a fool to trust Nasser, had become Nasser's boy, Chamoun concluded. King Hussein of Jordan too found ample reason to trust neither the United Nations nor the Secretary General.

---

[4] Lodge to Dulles, reporting Hammarskjöld-Lodge conversation, 14 July 1958, *FRUS*, 1958–1960, XI, 133, p. 237, note 2.

[5] McClintock (Beirut) to Dulles, 28 June 1958, *FRUS*, 1958–1960, XI, 109, p. 183; and Dulles-Malik conversation, 30 June, *FRUS*, 111, p. 185–86. Early biographies of Hammarskjöld are of limited value: Joseph P. Lash, *Dag Hammarskjöld: Custodian of the Brushfire Peace* (New York, 1961); but see Israel E. Levine, *Champion of World Peace: Dag Hammarskjöld* (New York, 1962).

US policy preferences, whether applauded or deplored, were decisive in many ways in 1958. In deciding on policy, Eisenhower, like all US Presidents, was driven in part by the legitimation imperative. In other words, he had to explain and justify policy to his several constituencies. The United Nations enjoyed wide popular support in the United States in the mid- and late 1950s. Dues were paid and resources were made freely available to the organization. Congress expected the administration to take the lead in the United Nations. Eisenhower and Dulles, in their devotion to maintaining bipartisan support for foreign policy, paid considerable and sustained attention to managing Congress. They consulted congressional leaders before acting. Eisenhower knew that visible support for the United Nations was good politics.[6]

For that and other compelling reasons, the debate within the US policy community in 1958 on the Middle East crisis involved, persistently and essentially, consideration of the United Nations and its Secretary General. That is why it is helpful initially but ultimately unsound analytically to view involving the United Nations as a discrete policy option, entirely separate from other courses of action, such as mobilizing Arab or Turkish support for US policies in the Middle East. It is equally flawed to depict legitimating policy at and through the United Nations as merely wrapping US preferences in the UN flag with unrelieved cynicism when reporting, for example, the decision of 14 July 1958 to intervene militarily in Lebanon to the Security Council. To involve the United Nations, of necessity, was to invite a spectrum of repercussions, to incur both costs and benefits, not all of which were predictable but with which Eisenhower and other world leaders had to live.[7] The United Nations Observation Group in Lebanon, the decision to create it, and the results of its presence in Lebanon became an object lesson in the management of complexity.

The Decision to Create UNOGIL, 11 June 1958, and the Consequences

On 7 May Chamoun informed Robert McClintock, the US Ambassador, of his decision to run again for the presidency of Lebanon. The decision

[6] Michael Graham Fry, "Eisenhower, Dulles and the Suez Crisis of 1956," in S. Warshaw, ed., *Reexamining the Eisenhower Presidency* (Westport, CT, 1993).

[7] Accountable political leaders cannot avoid the legitimation imperative, but the place of the United Nations in the legitimation process varied widely. Macmillan used the United Nations less than Eisenhower. David Ben-Gurion, Israel's Prime Minister, reaped political benefits by flouting the United Nations.

was sufficiently provocative in the context of Lebanese politics to incite something akin to civil war. That, in turn, resurrected in critical form the issue of external intervention in Lebanon's affairs. Although "Nasser would continue his subventions to newspapers and politicians, while Syria would continue sending of clandestine arms," Chamoun agreed that "there is as yet no evidence of a concerted UAR plan or campaign against Chamoun once his decision to stand for re-election had been announced."[8] But that could change, in fact or in Chamoun's imagination. If the United Arab Republic (UAR) intervened to oust Chamoun and solve the Christian-Moslem confrontation to serve its own interests, then Chamoun would demand US countervailing support. That demand, unavoidably, would involve the United Nations in various ways, unless the Arab League crafted a solution. Lebanon, its government and armed forces led by General Fouad Chehab and not merely Chamoun, must, Eisenhower and Dulles insisted, register a complaint against the UAR with the Security Council or invoke the most applicable article of the UN Charter as the essential preface to asking for US military assistance. They very emphatically wanted Lebanon to solve its problems without US intervention. They were cool towards military involvement.

If that proved impossible to avoid, US action must bear the stamp of legality, a stamp that could be imprinted credibly only by the Security Council or the UN charter. There were compelling domestic and international reasons to act in and through the United Nations. The UN imprimatur would cement bipartisan support in Congress, but neither erase doubts about the consequences of military involvement nor eliminate fears of entrapment. It would probably earn the endorsement of Jordan, Iraq, Pakistan and Turkey, but, just as predictably, outrage the UAR and the Soviet Union. The threat of a military confrontation with the USSR, however, was throughout the crisis judged to be minimal. Votes in the United Nations were more critical to Foster Dulles than facts, but much seemed to depend on uncovering evidence that was both credible and usable about a UAR conspiracy to destroy Lebanon's independence. The case, as Lodge insisted, must be as airtight as possible.[9] US intelligence

[8] McClintock to State Department, 7 May 1958, *FRUS,* 1958–1960, XI, 20, pp. 31–33.

[9] McClintock to State Department, 13 May 1958, Dulles to McClintock, 13 May, Dulles-Caccia (British Ambassador) conversation, 18 May, Policy Community Meeting (State, CIA and Defense) and National Security Council meeting, 29 May, ibid., 27, pp. 41–43; 31, pp. 49–50; 41, p. 61–63; 42, pp. 63–66; and 53, pp. 79–80; Policy Community Meetings (Eisenhower, Dulles, Dulles), 13 and 15 May, Dwight D. Eisenhower Papers (hereafter DDE), White House Memoranda Series, Box 6, and Ann Whitman Files, Diary Series, Box 32.

must not be seen to be competing with other and perhaps more credible sources of information—the United Nations for example.

Officials in Washington, Lodge among them, harbored doubts about the wisdom of an Arab state lodging a complaint in the Security Council against another Arab state. Resolution of the Lebanese crisis through the Arab League was clearly preferable. Guided apparently more by Britain than the United States, the Chamoun government, for its own purposes, rejected immediately what the UAR did not oppose, the three-point Arab League Council resolution of 4 June. Chamoun personally may still have thought that the United States equated perpetuating his presidency with preserving Lebanon's independence and pro-Western international posture.[10] On 6 June, Charles Malik, Lebanon's Foreign Minister, a man of formidable intellect and enormous ambition, brought the issue of UAR subversion back to the Security Council.[11]

Malik's submission was eloquent if not moving, elaborate if not convincing, a veritable catalog of indirect aggression. He made three "claims" and presented six "facts." The UAR had been and was still the source of "massive, illegal and unprovoked" intervention in Lebanon. This undermining of Lebanon constituted a threat to its independence. The perpetuation of that threat put international peace and security in jeopardy. If Lebanon was not safe, no small country was safe. Malik's six "facts" were predictable—the UAR, from Syria, was supplying arms on a large scale to rebel elements in Lebanon; armed bands, Lebanese "elements" trained in subversion in the UAR, were being sent back into Lebanon from Syria to overthrow the legitimate government; and UAR civilians, in or passing through Lebanon, were active in subversive and terrorist activities. The UAR was conducting a violent and utterly unprecedented radio campaign against the Lebanese government, and attempting through strikes and demonstrations to incite the people to overthrow the Lebanese government.

The ensuing debate in the Security Council ranged the UAR and the USSR against Lebanon and its supporters, the United States, Britain, France, Iraq, and China, with Canada, Colombia, Japan, Panama, and

[10] The Lebanese government took the issue of UAR intervention to the Arab League and the Security Council on 21 and 22 May 1958 (K. Azkoul to President of the Security Council, 22 May 1958, UN, Security Council, Official Records, S/4007). On 27 May the Security Council deferred to the Arab League (UN, Security Council, Official Records, 818th meeting, 27 May).

[11] UN, Security Council, Official Records, 823rd meeting, 6 June 1958.

Sweden neutral or undecided. Gunnar Jarring's resolution of 10 June, which owed something to Hammarskjöld, proposed that a UN observation group proceed to Lebanon "so as to ensure that there is no illegal infiltration of personnel or supply of arms and materials across the Lebanese borders," and authorized Hammarskjöld "to take the necessary steps to that end." It was adopted on 11 June by a vote of ten to none, with the USSR abstaining. Arkady Sobolev, the Soviet Ambassador to the United Nations, explained that the absence of UAR objections to the Swedish resolution made a veto unnecessary.[12] The establishment of UNOGIL, a cautious but promising step, was regarded initially by all concerned as preferable either to drift or to US military intervention. It would stay in Lebanon as long as it proved useful, not requiring periodical renewals and being, therefore, self-terminating.

Chamoun was elated, very briefly, at the decision to despatch UNOGIL, and at Hammarskjöld's prompt and effective implementation of the Security Council resolution. Support for Lebanon's integrity and independence seemed to be a victory, an opportunity perhaps for him to succeed himself, and a personal triumph for Malik. The United Nations, in fact, would "save" Lebanon from the UAR. But such euphoria unavoidably faced, almost instantaneously, two realities. To accomplish what Chamoun expected of it, UNOGIL had to become what it was not, a police, peacekeeping force, controlling Lebanon's borders and intervening in the civil war in his favor. Hammarskjöld, despite pressure from Lebanon's supporters, resolutely, deftly, and successfully resisted any such expansion of UNOGIL's responsibilities. Instead, he worked with Nasser privately to end the Lebanon crisis. Yet to the extent that UNOGIL, enlarged and augmented, was effective in fulfilling its limited mission, while evading an expanded mandate, Chamoun was less likely to wring a commitment out of the United States to intervene militarily. UNOGIL's competence gave Eisenhower every reason, at home and internationally, to ward off Chamoun's requests for US military action. Thus Chamoun had a compelling and urgent motive to challenge UNOGIL's competence, question its effectiveness, and risk turning on Hammarskjöld, while

12 UN, Security Council, Official Records, 823rd, 824th, 825th meetings, 6, 10, 11 June 1958 and resolution S/4023, 11 June; Policy Community Meetings (Eisenhower, Dulles), 15 and 16 June, DDE, Ann Whitman Files, Diary Series, Box 33. See also Brian Urquhart, *Hammarskjöld* (New York, 1972), pp. 264–65.

demanding that either a UN peacekeeping or a US military force, or both, proceed to Lebanon.[13]

That situation, in turn, left the US policy community, and the British, grappling with uncertainty. Nasser had not objected to the Security Council Resolution of 11 June. Indeed, Dulles, the same day, passed on to the Chamoun government for its sole consideration a "Nasser formula," the origins of which remain obscure. It may have been presented through Hammarskjöld. In any event, Nasser was reported as being "willing to use his influence" to try to end dissidence within Lebanon provided it was understood that (a) Chamoun would finish his term, (b) Chehab was to become Prime Minister, and (c) amnesty would be offered to those in opposition, whom Nasser believed would otherwise be unwilling to come to terms. The initiative must be kept secret; Nasser must not be betrayed. If he were, Nasser would repudiate the initiative and increase his attacks on the Chamoun government. The firmness of US support for the Chamoun government would also be called into question. Nothing came of such explorations until after Hammarskjöld had returned from the Middle East in the last week of June.

By that time, the brothers Dulles were experiencing moments of acute pessimism, fed by doubts about UNOGIL, lingering distrust of Hammarskjöld, and Israel's contrived apprehensiveness. Lebanon was "slipping down the drain"; UNOGIL, acting as a mediator, would confer status on the rebels; and Hammarskjöld was "not bucking it up very much...; he is just stopping the fighting while there and he may have taken some of the morale away from our side.... They fear he is going to produce a Munich and...the fear is not without justification." If Hammarskjöld championed "the Munich proposal" and successfully prevented military intervention to assist Chamoun, then Chamoun's spirit would be broken "and we have to build it up or let the mission go."[14] If it enabled Chamoun to triumph over the rebels but not necessarily retain

---

[13] McClintock to State Department, 13, 15, 19 and 28 June 1958; *FRUS*, 1958–1960, XI, 71, pp. 113–14; 80, pp. 124–26; 96, pp. 156–58; and 109, pp. 183–84; Rountree-Malik conversation, 15 June, *FRUS*, 78, p. 122–23, and Dulles-Malik conversation, 30 June, *FRUS*, 111, p. 185–90; Hammarskjöld press conferences, 12 and 17 June 1958, Andrew Cordier and Wilder Foote, eds., *Public Papers of the Secretaries-General of the United Nations, Vol. IV, Dag Hammarskjöld, 1958–1960* (hereafter *Public Papers)* (New York, 1974), pp. 101–106 and pp. 110–116; and Hammarskjöld statement, 26 June, ibid., pp. 116–117.

[14] Dulles to McClintock and Cairo embassy, 1 June 1958, John Foster Dulles Papers, Eisenhower Library (hereafter JFD), Chronological Series, Box 16; Dulles-Caccia conversation,

office, however, UNOGIL would remove the need for US military assistance, and thus it merited support. A promising initiative, vigorously implemented, UNOGIL must be given a fair chance. The United States must do nothing to bring about UNOGIL's failure; to undermine it would be catastrophic.

On the other hand, if it could be demonstrated that the opposition to Chamoun was a threat to UNOGIL, that the situation in Lebanon was deteriorating sharply, and that UNOGIL's ineffectiveness confirmed that Lebanon required further assistance, then the United States could intervene militarily. But it was "almost a *sine qua non*" that Lebanon ask the Security Council again for assistance before the United States could act. Eisenhower did not need Hammarskjöld's personal concurrence—the Secretary General was not the Institution, but US intervention must have the moral support of the United Nations. The United States must act only within the framework of UN legality. Moreover, to ensure Arab support, UNOGIL must confirm, incontrovertibly, evidence of UAR-sponsored infiltration tantamount to UAR responsibility for the Lebanese civil war. In other words, for some US purposes, UNOGIL must be ineffective, and for others, effective.

The brothers Dulles, in their pessimism, worried lest this unavoidable procedure—Chamoun approaching the Security Council as the necessary preface to US military intervention—result in a delay which would make the request for assistance moot and a US response well-nigh pointless, as Chamoun would by that time have fallen. One way out of this dilemma, described on occasion as an ideal solution, would be for Hammarskjöld to ask the United States and other powers to supply additional forces to support UNOGIL. Such a contrivance, and variations on it, took on irresistible appeal every time it appeared unavoidable that Chamoun would ask, formally and publicly, for US military intervention, such as on 17 June. A positive response to that appeal would lay the United States open to charges of imperialist behavior, and to an assault at the United Nations from the USSR. It would probably result in a wave of anti Western demonstrations which would undermine Chamoun further and threaten

18 June, *FRUS*, 1958–1960, XI, 94, pp. 153–55; Dulles-Lodge conversation, 15 June, *FRUS*, 79, p. 124; Dulles to McClintock, 19 June *FRUS*, 97, pp. 158–66; and Foster Dulles-Allen Dulles telephone conversations, 20 June, *FRUS*, 99, p. 163–64, and 19 June, JFD, Telephone Call Series, Box 8. See also Ben-Gurion to Hammarskjöld, 30 June, Urquhart, *Hammarskjöld*, p. 273. Ben-Gurion warned of a Middle East Munich and indicted the UAR for its subversion of the Lebanon.

the governments of Iraq and Jordan. Even the Western powers would be divided over a US military response, and most UN members opposed it while UNOGIL appeared to function effectively. Lodge had warned Dulles on 15 June that US military intervention would be very badly received at the United Nations; UNOGIL must be given its opportunity. Malik must not be allowed to mislead the Secretary of State on this point. Yet a negative response to Chamoun would damage the United States" reputation in the region, and would also accelerate the fall of friendly Arab governments and hand a triumph to Nasser.

That dilemma brought Dulles and Selwyn Lloyd back to the United Nations, whatever the costs and risks. Chamoun, they hoped, would neither misinterpret the advice nor abuse the opportunity. Through Hammarskjöld, he must appeal to the Security Council. The rebels were flouting its preferences and subverting UNOGIL. The USSR would veto a Security Council resolution calling for a UN police force and would cause a brief delay. The United States, with ready plans to protect US lives and property, could then act to support the Security Council's preference and intervene so as to cooperate with UNOGIL. Or Chamoun might appeal directly to the United States, which would respond in conformity with the UN charter while denying any attempt to determine Lebanon's political future. The USA was not the USSR. Alternatively, in consultation with Iraq and Jordan, Lebanon and the United States could activate General Assembly procedures under the "Uniting for Peace" resolution. The United States could then intervene militarily, avoiding any hint of collaboration with Britain and particularly France, thereby avoiding any whiff of Suez as well. Again, the United States would act only under UN auspices, with its moral support, and in Dulles's eyes, in conformity with international law. Congress would approve. It was not at all clear, of course, either whether Chamoun would survive or Lebanon would have a neutral rather than a pro-Western government. Little wonder that Eisenhower asked, where was Lebanon's strong man? Moreover, Dulles, likening Lebanon to Manchuria in 1931 and looking for a "Korea type" action (that is, a multinational force under the United Nations, requested by Hammarskjöld), simply misunderstood Hammarskjöld's preferences, as did Lloyd. The Secretary General, while wanting enhanced support for UNOGIL, did not want a police action, whether or not US and British forces were involved.[15]

[15] Dulles-General Twining telephone conversation, 11 June 1958, *FRUS*, 1958–1960, XI, 68, p. 109; Eisenhower-Policy Group Meeting, 15 June, *FRUS*, 84, pp. 133–39; Dulles-

Dulles found a measure of relief from this uncertainty by telling Malik, on 30 June, that US intelligence tended to agree with Hammarskjöld's assessment that UNOGIL was effective, and that infiltration from Syria was considerably reduced or even terminated. US or Western military intervention at that time would be an error and would be at most the lesser of two evils. It would not have UN support given Hammarskjöld's judgment of UNOGIL's competence. As long as the Secretary General opposed military intervention, the United States could not muster seven votes in the Security Council for such an initiative.[16] Dulles made substantially the same case at his press conference on 1 July.

It took the revolution in Iraq to change Eisenhower's mind on 14 July. That unanticipated and shocking event seemed to mean that Iraq would now be too weak to restrain Syria from assaulting Lebanon directly or indirectly. Yet if it were a tool of Egypt and the Soviet Union, Iraq might be strong enough and determined to threaten a very fragile and isolated Jordan, now cast adrift from Iraq. The coup also made Iraqi and even Jordanian support at the United Nations, but not that of Turkey, Iran, and Pakistan, virtually irrelevant.

Yet in those tense, congested and difficult discussions on the need, seemingly unavoidable, to intervene in Lebanon, which involved Donald Quarles, Deputy Secretary of Defense, and William MacComber, Assistant Secretary of State for Congressional Affairs, the UN factor was a central consideration. Dulles agreed with Quarles that the United States must act under the cover of the UN umbrella. Activating UN procedures, under the "Essentials for Peace Resolution" of 1949 or Article 51 of the Charter, was necessary to convince a skeptical delegation of congressional leaders. True enough, Eisenhower was not prepared to wait on the Security Council and decided to intervene militarily and then to seek UN support. The situation required a carefully crafted strategy, which did not involve the Chamoun

---

Lodge conversation, 15 June, *FRUS*, 79, p. 124; Policy Community Meeting (Dulles, Allen Dulles, Donald Quarles), 17 June, *FRUS*, 92, pp. 148–49; Rountree to Dulles, 17 June, *FRUS*, 93, pp. 150–52; Dulles to McClintock, 16, 17 and 19 June, *FRUS*, 87, pp. 142, 90, pp. 145–46, and 97, p. 158–60; Hood (British Embassy)-Rockwell meeting, 20 June, *FRUS,* 100, pp. 164–65; Policy Community Meeting (Dulles, Allen Dulles, Quarles, Lodge) 22 June, *FRUS*, 102, pp. 166–68; Lodge to Dulles, 23 June 1958 and Dulles to Lodge, 25 June, *FRUS*, 103, pp. 186–69 and note 4; and Dulles-US Senators meeting, 23 June, *FRUS*, 105 pp. 171–75. See also Dulles press conference of 17 June and Eisenhower press conference of 18 June 1958, *FRUS*, 96, p. 156, note 4.

16 Dulles-Malik meeting, 30 June 1958, *FRUS*, 1958–1960, XI, 111, pp. 185–90.

government submitting a new complaint to the Security Council and waiting for a Security Council Resolution.

The preferred strategy would be to implement US military intervention, at Lebanon's request, covertly and in coordination only with Britain. The United States, diplomatically, would call and report to an emergency session of the Security Council, on 15 July. It would emphasize the evidence of continued UAR infiltration into Lebanon, along with the coup in Iraq and plots in Jordan, the invitation from the Lebanese government to intervene, the need to protect US lives and property, and regrettably, the understandably limited effectiveness of UNOGIL. US intervention was to be depicted as unavoidable and as providing the foundation for a most necessary UN police action. It would therefore claim the moral and legal standing provided by UN procedures. US forces would cooperate on the ground to that end with UNOGIL, and would be withdrawn when either the United Nations filled the void and defended Lebanon's integrity, or the government of Lebanon stood on its own feet. Soviet charges, it was hoped, would be countered and any resolution condemning the United States defeated. As for Hammarskjöld, Lodge reported that he was "not having as bad a reaction" as feared. "He is moved and thinks we are on weak legal ground. Chamoun will fall after we get out. The Syrians will counteract very vigorously."[17]

As July moved into August, and Jordan's vulnerability pushed aside the perceived threat to Lebanon's independence, Dulles found further reason to look to the United Nations. Chamoun and Malik pressed the United States almost immediately to stay on in Lebanon, and actually to increase its military presence there rather than hand over to the United Nations. Indeed, they argued, this was the opportunity to counter decisively, with military force, both Nasser's ambitions and the regional threat of Communism. It would, Chamoun suggested, have been better had the

[17] Policy Community Meeting (Dulles, Allen Dulles, Twining) 9:30 a.m., 14 July 1958, *FRUS*, 1958–1960, XI, 123, p. 209–11; Eisenhower-Policy Community Meeting, 10:50 a.m., 14 July *FRUS*, 124, pp. 211–15; Eisenhower-Policy Community-Congressional Leaders Meeting, 2:35 p.m., 14 July, *FRUS*, 127, pp. 218–26; Eisenhower-Policy Community Meeting, 14 July, *FRUS*, 128, pp. 226–28; Rountree meeting with Ambassadors of Iran, Turkey and Pakistan, 14 July 1958, *FRUS*, 129, pp. 228–30; and Dulles to Lodge, 9:22 p.m., 14 July, *FRUS*, 133, pp. 236–37. Eisenhower informed the Canadian Conservative government and thanked it for its support (Eisenhower to Prime Minister John Diefenbaker, 14 July, JFD, Chronological Series, Box 16). See also Dulles-Lodge and Dulles-Hammarskjöld telephone conversations, 14 and 15 July, JFD, Telephone Call Series, Box 8.

United States not intervened at all than to leave Lebanon to the United Nations with its "dubiously adequate ability." They were therefore critical of the Japanese resolution of 19 July, which handed a further initiative to Hammarskjöld.

Dulles saw things differently. This was not the occasion to attack either Nasserism or Communism. It was the time to help Hammarskjöld implement the Japanese resolution, fund expansion of UNOGIL, and put a stop to press stories that the Secretary General was less than cooperative. Indeed, Hammarskjöld was acting with the United States despite having grave doubts about US policy. Lebanon's independence, beyond the Presidential election, the creation of a new government and the restoration of order would come by way of an expanded UN presence and gradual US withdrawal, and through the United Nations crafting a political solution "creating a separate and independent status for the Lebanon, making it a ward of the United Nations and keeping it out of the United Arab Republic.... A UN mantle should be cast over the Lebanon." The United States was maintaining "good working relations with the Secretary General," but Eisenhower and the newly elected President, Fouad Chehab, not Hammarskjöld, would decide when US forces would hand over to an expanded UNOGIL. US forces would not leave Lebanon prematurely. Similar reasoning prevailed with respect to a British withdrawal from Jordan alongside Eisenhower's determination to extricate Britain without a regional war and without entangling the United States in Jordan.[18]

A Matter of Evidence

Permeating both the US decision to intervene militarily in Lebanon, and the debate over the withdrawal, lay the contested evidence of UAR indirect aggression against the Chamoun government and Lebanon's

---

[18] Dulles-Malik conversation, 19 July1958, *FRUS*, 1958–1960, XI, 198, pp. 334–36; Dulles-Lloyd, and others conversation, 19 July, *FRUS*, 202, pp. 340–43; McClintock to Dulles, 21 July, *FRUS*, 206, pp. 350–51, Eisenhower-Dulles conversation, 21 July 1958, 210, pp. 359–60, Dulles-Lodge telephone conversation and Lodge to Dulles, 22 July 1958, *FRUS*, 215, pp. 368–69 and note 6; Eisenhower-Congressional Leaders Meeting, 22 July, *FRUS*, 213, p. 365, note 2; Eisenhower-Dulles conversation, 23 July, *FRUS*, 221, pp. 376–77; National Security Council, 24 July, *FRUS*, 226, pp. 382–85; and Dulles to Murphy, 25 July, *FRUS*, 234, pp. 400–401.

integrity. The sources of evidence reflected, unavoidably, the roster of interested parties—the Lebanese government, Chehab, the opposition to Chamoun, the United States (the CIA, the Embassy in Beirut, G-2, and other unidentified intelligence sources), Britain, Israel, the UAR, and the United Nations. No one, including Nasser, disputed the veracity of Malik's fifth and sixth "facts" presented on 6 June to the Security Council. Omar Loufti, Nasser's representative at the United Nations, challenged Malik on other grounds—the civil war reflected an essentially domestic crisis; Malik's charges were a diversionary tactic; Chamoun, himself a traitor to Arab nationalism, the rejecter of the Arab League resolutions, was the problem; and Malik's evidence came purely from Lebanese police reports. Nasser himself admitted the obvious, and defended it, to Raymond Hare, the US Ambassador in Cairo, to Hammarskjöld, and to Robert Murphy, US Deputy Undersecretary of State for Political Affairs. Media aggression, electronic and print, with the Voice of the Arabs broadcasting from Cairo, was an act of self-defense against conspiratorial enemies in Iraq, Jordan, and Lebanon, by a weak UAR with an intelligence budget of one million pounds per annum—a veritable pittance.[19]

Beyond that, all was fact *and* perception, ideology *and* psychology, with the meeting of agendas, the serving of purposes, and the courting of constituencies by all the interested parties, raising unavoidably the issues of competence and credibility, not least for Chamoun and Malik. Chamoun, almost as bereft of political skill as he was of military solutions, and growing progressively Wagnerian in citadel Beirut, felt that personal and political vindication lay in wrapping his tribulations in external conspiracy and aggression. The devilish Nasser and the rampant UAR were the sources of Lebanon's turmoil. To build a case for UN support and US military intervention, Chamoun had to believe his own exaggerations—the rebels were armed to the teeth; UAR agents were everywhere; the revolt was Syrian engineered and led; an outright Syrian offensive was imminent; some five hundred or three thousand Palestinians were involved; Beirut was about to be attacked and Tripoli was to be leveled by artillery; massacres were imminent, and so on. To secure US military intervention, Chamoun must discredit UNOGIL when it failed him. He described its members as

---

19 Hare to Dulles, 31 May 1958, *FRUS*, 1958–1960, XI, 55, pp. 84–86; Hare to Dulles, 24 July *FRUS*, 1958–1960, XIII, 213, pp. 461–464; Hammarskjöld-Nasser conversation, 22 June, Urquhart, *Hammarskjold*, pp. 268–69; and Lufti statement, UN, Security Council, Official Records, 823rd meeting, 6 June.

tourists, spending their days on the beach and their nights in bars. They would not recognize a Syrian if they captured him. UNOGIL's limited competence in, for example, night-time surveillance, was beyond question, thereby destroying its credibility. Malik on 8 July, in an unimpressive response to UNOGIL's first report of 1 July, denounced it as "inconclusive, misleading, and unwarranted." Indeed, properly interpreted, Malik asserted, the evidence presented in the first UNOGIL report actually substantiated Lebanon's case. In fact, the proportions and impact of the infiltration from Syria, this "infernal work," grew on Malik's tongue and under his pen as he sensed victory in the Security Council before 11 June, and as he pressed for US military intervention before 14 July. He became caught up in rebuttal and in his own defense. Malik's position contrasted markedly with Chehab's assessment. Chehab admitted that his military forces could not prevent the ongoing infiltration of men and arms, and that "the country is now saturated with clandestine arms and threatened with civil war." UAR "commandos" were operating in the Basta. But Chehab, who rarely exaggerated the extent of that infiltration, corrected Chamoun's wilder estimates and never subscribed to Chamoun's analysis of an externally-inspired civil war. Chamoun's and Malik's judgments were essentially political and psychological, and never substantially credible.[20]

The relationship of intelligence to policy is that of the inductive to the deductive, of information to first principles.[21] When intelligence seems to confirm established policy, intelligence is influential; when information challenges first principles, information almost invariably loses. This thesis may seem stark, even pre-emptive, especially when policy is fluid. But it helps explain why policy communities lapse into cognitive dissonance,

---

[20] On Chamoun and Malik, see Malik rebuttal to 1st UNOGIL report, UN, Security Council, Official Records, 8 July 1958, S. 4043; R. Higgs (Deputy Chief of Mission) to Dulles, 9 January, *FRUS*, 1958–1960, XI, pp. 1–3; McClintock to Dulles, 30 January , 21 February, 23 April, 4, 11, 12, 13 and 25 May 1958, 15 and 19 June 1958, and 1 July, *FRUS*, 5, pp. 8–9, 7, pp. 10–13, 15, pp. 24–25, 18, pp. 28–29, 24, pp. 37–38, 26, pp. 40–41, 27, pp. 41–43, 52, pp. 77–79, 80, pp. 214–26, 96, pp. 156–58, and 112, pp. 190–93; Rountree-Malik conversations, 14 and 17 June, *FRUS*, 72, p. 115 and 78, pp. 122–23; Dulles-Malik conversation, 15 June, *FRUS*, 83, pp. 130–32; and Murphy to Dulles, 19 and 26 July, *FRUS*, 199, pp. 337–38 and 235, pp. 402–403. On Chehab see McClintock to Dulles, 11 May, 6 and 15 June and 15 August, *FRUS*, 22, pp. 35–37, 61, pp. 98–100, 80, pp. 124–26, and 74, pp. 476–79. See also Chamoun interview in the *Daily Mail*, 6 July, and Hammarskjöld to Lloyd, n.d., Urquhart, *Hammarskjöld*, p. 274.

[21] Michael Graham Fry and Miles Hochstein, "Epistemic Communities: Intelligence Studies and International Relations," *Intelligence and National Security* 8, 3 (July 1993), pp. 14–28.

into modes of reasoning whereby initial preferences are reinforced, established beliefs are buttressed and alluring analogies are confirmed, against evidence to the contrary.[22] For example, Dulles's ability to recreate productive relationships with Nasser, to secure UAR acquiescence in preserving Lebanon's independence, and always to leave Nasser a bridge by which he could cross back into the Western fold, were all wise and necessary policy steps that Nasser would have welcomed. Yet these moves were circumscribed by Dulles's intemperate, utterly negative convictions about Nasser and Pan-Arabism. When the Iraq crisis seemingly necessitated US military intervention in Lebanon, UNOGIL's reports "became" more suspect and UNOGIL itself less effective. A policy community, moreover, might instruct its intelligence sources to provide "confirming," "acceptable" information. Hammarskjöld may have indulged in such practices.

The US intelligence community, citing reports from Lebanon and Cairo, and Allen Dulles in, for example, briefings of the National Security Council, set out the basic case of massive infiltration and threatening subversion which pointed to a partition of Lebanon, and thus the UAR's primary responsibility for Lebanon's crisis.[23] Eisenhower and Dulles, both perhaps influenced by Malik, bought into the construct of indirect aggression and external conspiracy. If Nasser, moreover, continued to support the rebels after Chamoun gave up the pursuit of a second term, his actions would provide indisputable evidence of the external threat to Lebanon's independence. But, to be sure, Dulles acknowledged some of the nuances and fluctuations even as he used evidence to serve other purposes. He admitted that subversion could originate in the UAR independent of UAR policy, but also that Nasser could, if he wanted, prevent what was not originally his responsibility. He recognized that media aggression did outmatch all other forms of subversion and that Lebanese exiles acting from Syria were not Syrians. Dulles conceded: that Nasser was caught between preferring to halt the infiltration and wishing to see Chamoun fall; that Chamoun was a problem; that infiltration and subversion fluctuated in their intensity and impact rather than being sustained and ever increasing; and that much of the damage had

---

[22] Michael Fry, *Statesmen as Historians: History, The White House and the Kremlin* (London and New York, 1991).

[23] Special National Intelligence Estimates, 5 and 14 June 1958, *FRUS*, 1958–1960, XI, 60, pp. 93–98 and 77, pp. 120–22; and National Security Council, 8, 22 and 29 May and 3, 19 and 26 June, *FRUS*, 22, pp. 34–35, 46, pp. 71, 53, pp. 79–80, 57, pp. 89–90, 95, pp. 155–56 and 107, p. 18.

occurred before UNOGIL set foot in Lebanon. But the infiltration, tapering off by the end of June as Nasser honored his commitment to Hammarskjöld, reappeared, conveniently, at dangerous levels when US military intervention seemed necessary in mid-July. Dulles instructed Lodge on 16 July to tell Hammarskjöld that the UAR had ordered Lebanese irregulars to oppose US forces if they moved beyond their current positions, and had called for paramilitary activity on the West Bank so as to activate pro-UAR groups in Jordan. In addition, the UAR was seeking to undermine Chehab's army and to prevent a cease-fire in Lebanon.[24]

When Eisenhower and Dulles had preferred to avoid the need for US military intervention, and had sought to curb what enthusiasm there was for such a step in Washington and London, they had found ample reason to conclude both that Chehab's military forces, with US aid, could maintain civil order, and that UNOGIL was growing in effectiveness. Lodge, on the frontline at the United Nations, found it difficult to handle Hammarskjöld's convictions and UNOGIL's reports: "I was astounded at his picture of the situation which conflicted in so many ways with what we understood to be the case."[25] He was never quite sure that he had either an airtight case of external subversion or unambiguous evidence of a UAR threat to Lebanon supported by the USSR. In Beirut, McClintock, though failing to convince Dulles, reported that the civil war had plural origins but was essentially rooted in domestic soil. He did not blame Chamoun's predicament on Nasser and he uncovered no concerted UAR plan of subversion. The evidence of superbly organized external infiltration seemed weak and Malik's accounts were patently partisan. At most, McClintock saw external factors as contributory, not causal, in a highly complex series of events.[26]

Nasser, beyond conceding the fact of media aggression, mixed defiance with evasion and lapsed into self-incrimination. He had no role in starting

---

[24] Dulles to Hare, 15 May 1958 and 5 and 19 June 1958, *FRUS*, 1958–1960, XI, 36, pp. 54–55, 59, pp. 91–93 and 64, pp. 103–04; Herter to Hare, 27 May, *FRUS*, 51, pp. 76–77; Dulles-Malik conversation, 30 June, *FRUS*, 111, pp. 185–90; Dulles-Hammarskjöld-Lodge conversation, 7 July, *FRUS*, 116, pp. 200–01; Dulles-Congressional Leaders Meeting, 14 July 1958, *FRUS*, 127, p. 218; Dulles to Lodge, 16 July, *FRUS*, 150, p. 258; State Department-Joint Chiefs of Staff Meeting, 16 May, *FRUS*, 39, pp. 58–59; and Dulles-Allen Dulles-Admiral Burke Meeting, 19 May, *FRUS*, 42, pp. 63–66.

[25] Lodge to Dulles, 26 June 1958, *FRUS*, 1958–1960, XI, 106, pp. 175–80.

[26] McClintock to Dulles, 20 March 1958, 18 April 1958, 7 May 1958 and 8 June, *FRUS*, 1958–1960, XI, 11, pp. 18–19, 14, p. 23, 20, pp. 31–33, 56, pp. 86–89 and 76, pp. 119–20.

the civil war, no contacts with the rebels, and no way of ending the crisis, he insisted to Hare and Hammarskjöld. There were several possible explanations for the traffic in arms from Syria—out of control and over-zealous agents and Druze arms smuggling, for example—but the problem could not be placed at the door of the UAR. Yet, almost in the same breath, Nasser admitted that he had lifted the ban on infiltration from Syria in early June, in retaliation against Chamoun's rejection of the Arab League's resolutions and Malik's indicting of the UAR before the Security Council. Furthermore, in the face of Hammarskjöld's empathetic and precise language, Nasser undertook to give categorical orders in plain language to the Syrian Prime Minister to halt the supply of men and materiel entering Lebanon as of 24 June, and to inform the Lebanese rebels of that step.[27] Hammarskjöld, while attempting to hold Nasser to his undertaking, preferred to see the positive side of the situation, linked as it was to his efforts to settle the Lebanese crisis, demonstrate UNOGIL's effectiveness, and avoid the need for US military intervention.

That preference on Hammarskjöld's part caused others to question both the objectivity of his judgment and the wisdom of his policy. Having implemented the Security Council's resolution of 11 June personally, and believing in UNOGIL's mission, Hammarskjöld went to some lengths to demonstrate its effectiveness and validate its reports.[28] UNOGIL made five reports—on 1 and 25 July, 12 August, 25 September, and 14 November 1958, and two interim reports on 15 and 17 July 1958.[29] The

---

[27] Hare to Dulles, 20 and 31 May 1958, and 7 and 8 June 1958, *FRUS*, 1958–1960, XI, 44, pp. 67–70, 55, pp. 84–86, and 63, pp. 101–103; Lodge to Dulles, 26 June, *FRUS*, 106, p. 175–80 and Dulles-Hammarskjold-Lodge conversation, 7 July, *FRUS*, 116, pp. 200–01; Urquhart, *Hammarskjöld*, pp. 268–69; and Hare to Dulles, 27 June and 3 July, *FRUS*, 1958–1960, XIII, 211, pp. 458–59 and 212, pp. 460–61. The Egyptian and Syrian archives should help scholars across this contested ground.

[28] Hammarskjöld reports, 16 and 28 June 1958, and 15 and 16 July, UN, Security Council, Official Records, S/4029 and S/4038; Hammarskjöld to Bunche, 21 June, Urquhart, *Hammarskjöld*, p. 267; Hammarskjöld report to General Assembly, 29 September, Cordier and Foote, *Public Papers*, pp. 203–16; Hammarskjöld to President of Security Council, 17 November, *FRUS*, p. 220; and Hammarskjöld press conferences, 16, 17 and 28 June and 15 and 16 July, *FRUS*, pp. 107–10, 110–16, 117–19, 130–33 and 134.

[29] UNOGIL reports, 1 and 25 July 1958, 12 August, 25 September, and 14 November, and interim reports, 15 and 17 July, UN, Security Council, Official Records, S/4040, S/4069, S/4085, S/4100, S/4114, and S4051 and S/4052. The dates given here are those on UNOGIL reports and precede the dates of registry at the Security Council, e.g., 1 July was registered on 3 July, 25 July report on 30 July, 12 August report on 14 August, 25 September report on 29 September and 14 November report on 17 November. The interim report of 15 July was received on 16 July; that of 17 July was received the same day. Most authors use the date of registry with the Security Council.

reports had two essential themes: (1) to demonstrate that initial difficulties of access to the Lebanese-Syrian border—and of developing surveillance capability, day and night, on the ground and in the air, in rough terrain and difficult circumstances—were rapidly overcome, and (2) to rule on the issue of external infiltration and subversion.[30] These themes were both inextricably linked and controversial. UNOGIL's claim to competence was contested, then and since.

That was unavoidable because of UNOGIL's judgment, from its first report, that there was "no tangible evidence of mass infiltration of arms or of UAR nationals." The substantial movement of armed men occurred within Lebanon; the armed bands were Lebanese. The source of the plentiful supply of small arms, mostly of British, French and Italian make, could not be identified. The opposition's military forces were neither coordinated nor impressive. As a result of the presidential election in Lebanon on 31 July, the arms traffic, always quite limited, was further reduced considerably. What illegals there were had left Lebanese soil, though lawlessness continued. By early November, infiltration of any kind had ended, the opposition forces had disbanded and only sporadic disturbances occurred, an eminently gratifying outcome and surely a triumph for UNOGIL. It could now leave Lebanon, and it did, by 9 December 1958.

From one perspective, UNOGIL's reports were impressive because of their consistency and lack of ambiguity. But their categorical and unequivocal conclusions, resolutely maintained against all critics within and outside Lebanon, brought charges less of incompetence and more that they served other purposes—Hammarskjöld's purposes. After his first visit during the crisis to the Middle East, Hammarskjöld briefed Lodge.[31] Gallo Plaza, head of UNOGIL's triumvirate, had said it all: "the world is being taken for a ride." Chamoun's political and military incompetence had spawned and fed an opposition which was as determined to oust him as it was to avoid collaboration with Nasser. The evidence of collusion with the UAR evaporated under careful scrutiny. Syrian officers who had made damning con-

[30] In the two interim reports of 15 and 17 July 1958, UNOGIL recorded the presence of 113 UN observers on the ground, 20 air observers, 15 observation posts, 82 air missions flown, night photography capability and being fully operational on the whole border as a result of successful negotiations with opposition leaders. In its second and third reports, of 25 July and 12 August, UNOGIL noted a setback in its capability because of the opposition's negative reaction to US military intervention, but the prompt overcoming of that distrust. The decline in surveillance competence had thus been quite temporary. See also David W. Wainhouse, *International Peace Observation* (Baltimore, 1966), pp. 373–86.

[31] Lodge to Dulles, 26 June 1958, *FRUS*, 1958–1960, XI, 106, pp. 175–80.

fessions were illiterate minors; cases of ammunition were crates of meat; nighttime convoys carried fresh fruit and vegetables, not arms; and the massive arms traffic consisted of a single mortar, while other arms were merely personal weapons. The UAR had not staged the revolt, and while there probably had been active Syrian involvement from the outset, Nasser had not condoned it until Chamoun complained to the Arab League and the United Nations. The Druze were receiving aid from Syria, infiltration was occurring across the northern part of the border, and supplies were coming directly from Damascus, but Nasser's sins were largely ones of omission not commission, allowing things to continue rather than initiating action. In sum, "UN observers had uncovered practically no evidence of UAR involvement." Little wonder Lodge was "astounded." Selwyn Lloyd's doubts about Hammarskjöld promptly resurfaced.

These conclusions raised both a technical and a political issue, the effectiveness of air surveillance and the extent to which Nasser was honoring his commitment to Hammarskjöld. Given the difficult terrain and rebel control of sections of the Lebanon-Syrian border, UNOGIL's air reconnaissance capability, at night as well as during the day, seemed crucial, almost an acid test of UNOGIL. Its critics questioned its capability. The heads of UNOGIL insisted that such capability was rapidly and comprehensively achieved and rarely interrupted. While pressing Nasser on the issue before 15 July, Hammarskjöld continued to blame the Syrians, not Nasser, on the political point. He also went to some lengths to demonstrate that UNOGIL was free of his guiding hand, but the protestations were not entirely convincing. He could and did ask UNOGIL to provide information helpful to his viewpoint. In a memorandum on the need to expand UNOGIL, for example, Major-General Odd Bull, UNOGIL Chief of Staff, referred to infiltration routes, distribution centers, and headquarters used by the rebels, and the current inadequacies of UNOGIL, although his concern was more the frontier between government and rebel-held territory within Lebanon than the Lebanon-Syrian border.[32] Charges that UNOGIL, on Hammarskjöld's orders, also suppressed unwelcome evidence to the contrary cannot be dismissed.

---

[32] Rountree-Hood conversation, 3 July 1958, *FRUS*, 1958–1960, XI, 115, pp. 198–99, and Dulles-Hammarskjöld conversation, 7 July, *FRUS*, 117, p. 202. A UNOGIL official had told the British that the rebels had from 5,000 to 12,000 men under arms, of whom 300–1,000 were Syrian; Urquhart, *Hammarskjold*, pp. 275–77; and Bull memorandum, 25 July, UN archives (New York). Hammarskjöld, at his press conference on 3 July on the first UNOGIL report, said, "There is no editing here; it is their work down to the last comma." (Cordier and Foote, *Public Papers*, pp. 120–26).

The issue of external intervention was as political for Hammarskjöld as it was for Chamoun, Dulles, or Nasser. It served Hammarskjöld's six-point agenda for the United Nations, UNOGIL, and himself, before 15 July.[33] First, he did not want to explode Chamoun's case, his indictment of the UAR, prematurely. Second, he wanted to ensure that his personal triumph in Cairo, bringing Nasser to heel and persuading him to order Syria to stop the flow of arms and materials to the Lebanese rebels, would, for the foreseeable future, insulate Lebanon from UAR intervention. Third, Hammarskjöld hoped to save Nasser's face by not telling Chamoun or the British, as opposed to the United States, about Nasser's commitment, and, a matter of concern to Nasser, to ensure an amnesty for the rebels. Fourth, Hammarskjöld was determined to ensure Nasser's compliance by "engag[ing] myself personally," by "mak[ing] myself a hostage to the implementation from your side of the policy." Fifth, it seemed essential to confirm UNOGIL's limited but effective role as a deterrent and to remove the need for increased UN involvement, i.e., to the level of a peacekeeping force. Finally, Hammarskjöld wanted to eliminate the need for US intervention at Chamoun's or Macmillan's request.

These six stratagems fed on the epistemological and semantic debate which pervaded the issue of external intervention. Was the civil war in Lebanon rooted in a domestic political crisis or an external conspiracy? If both, which was causal and which was merely contributory, which provided the fuel and which was the triggering spark? Had Nasser gone to Moscow to demonstrate his noninvolvement, or was he genuinely uninvolved? Was the civil war organized internally or externally, or spontaneous? And did the UAR initiate it or support it only when it had a life of its own? Responding to those who termed the UAR's intervention "massive," critics countered with the words "limited," "legitimate," and "routine." They also ridiculed Chamoun, who, they charged, welcomed the arms traffic because Muslims sold the weapons to Christians. But that all missed the point. The issue was whether the infiltration of men and materiel, whatever its proportions, was decisive, was "scale-tipping" in favor of the opposition. That difficult calculation involved several factors. What was the military balance within Lebanon (Chehab commanded a 9,000-man army and a 2,500-man gendarmerie)? Were Chehab's forces loyal to the government and did Chehab use them effectively and appro-

[33] Dulles-Hammarskjöld-Lodge conversations, 7 July 1958, *FRUS*, 1958–1960, XI, 116, pp. 200–201 and 117, p. 202; Hammarskjöld to Fawzi, 25 June, Urquhart, *Hammarskjöld*, pp. 270–71; and Hammarskjöld to Dulles and Lloyd, n.d., *FRUS*, pp. 272–73.

priately? What was the extent and nature of US military assistance to Chamoun, assistance freely acknowledged by Dulles when countering Malik's pressure for military intervention. What was the value quantitatively and qualitatively of the arms and personnel supplied to the rebels from Syria?[34] It was a calculation wrapped in politics and psychology.

The fact that external intervention fluctuated over time both spoke to Nasser's role and fed into the issue of UNOGIL's competence and the justification for US military intervention. UNOGIL could not report authoritatively on what had occurred before it set foot in Lebanon—and before it became operationally effective. At what point in late June or early July it became effective was difficult to pinpoint and controversial. UNOGIL had a record of deterrence both before and after the US military intervention on 15 July, and once Chamoun had given way to Chehab following the presidential election of 31 July and the actual transfer of power on 23 September.

These issues reflected the uneasy relationship between UNOGIL and US forces on the ground, and Hammarskjöld's doubts about the wisdom and legality of Eisenhower's action. The latter theme found a place in the lingering contempt for US policy evident in the literature favorable to the United Nations and Hammarskjöld. Odd Bull, for example, viewed US military intervention as unnecessary, erroneous, destabilizing, and threatening to UNOGIL. Hammarskjöld instructed UNOGIL to keep its distance from the US forces, to emphasize its independence and to avoid either any hint of complicity or acts of cooperation with the US contingent. UNOGIL had its mandate from the Security Council and would observe it, strictly and independently. Urquhart, subsequently, depicted a poorly-informed US government, led on by the CIA, and misinterpreting both the reasons for and the nature of the Iraqi coup. US military intervention in Lebanon was, in consequence, an illegal, irrelevant, precipitate and naive act, even one of panic, which risked a Soviet response and injured the process of domestic reconciliation in Lebanon. It was unnecessary and unwise, an anachronistic act of gunboat diplomacy. Hammarskjöld was left to rescue the United States and Britain from their folly through face-saving devices that would allow them to evacuate from Lebanon and Jordan, by 25 October and 2 November 1958 respectively.[35]

---

[34] Dulles-Malik conversation, 30 June 1958, *FRUS*, 1958–1960, XI, 111, pp. 185–90.

[35] Odd Bull, *War and Peace in the Middle East* (London, 1976), pp. 10–20; Urquhart, *Hammarskjöld*, pp. 261, 273, 277–81 and 284–85; Brian Urquhart, *A Life in War and Peace*, (New York, 1987), pp. 142–43; and Cordier and Foote, *Public Papers*, pp. 5–6, 128–29, and 136.

UNOGIL remains controversial. Some point to its impressive leadership. Gallo Plaza, a former President of Ecuador, Rajeshwar Dayal, previously India's Ambassador to the United Nations, and the Norwegian air officer, Major-General Odd Bull, shared command. David Blickenstaff, Director of the UN office in Paris, and Shiv Shastri led a competent secretariat. An experienced and well-qualified group of military and civilian personnel, from UNTSO and UNRWA, were involved in what some claim was a large and well-financed operation. UNOGIL, from its own perspective, was organized promptly, and became operationally effective by the end of June 1958. Its Beirut headquarters staff developed an intelligence capability that underpinned investigatory and evaluative powers that were impressive and objective. In the field, UNOGIL, with ground and air capability, operating day and night, could observe carefully, respond promptly to incidents, and report thoroughly.[36] To the extent that it could detect, it could deter. UNOGIL, moreover, won and retained the cooperation of both the Lebanese authorities, even after its first report of 1 July, and the opposition leaders, even after the US military intervention on 15 July. Consequently, it is argued, UNOGIL, detecting what limited infiltration occurred and deterring large-scale intervention, had a stabilizing effect. It influenced the eminently satisfactory and reasonably prompt outcome in Lebanon, and ended the civil war. US military intervention was at most a complement.

Others, taking their lead perhaps from Chamoun, US intelligence agents on the ground, and the CIA, poured contempt on what they concluded was an ineffective UNOGIL.[37] Its build-up was slow; its capability unimpressive. It operated in very different terrain, on poor roads,

---

[36] Hammarskjöld reported on 28 June 1958 that UNOGIL had 94 observers in the field by 26 June at 6 observation posts, with 74 vehicles, 8 reconnaissance planes and 2 helicopters. By mid-August, it had 190 observers at 22 posts; by the end of September, it had 287 observers at 34 posts. At its full strength UNOGIL had 591 observers, 49 posts, 12 planes and 6 helicopters. It began to withdraw on 28 November and completed the operation by 9 December. See also Rosalyn Higgins *United Nations Peacekeeping, 1946–1967*, Vol. I, *The Middle East* (London, 1969), pp. 555–602.

[37] The two most quoted sources on US intelligence activities in the Middle East are Miles Copeland, *The Game of Nations* (New York, 1969), and Wilbur Crane Eveland, *Ropes of Sand: America's Failure in the Middle East* (London, 1980). Copeland, in effect, ignored UNOGIL (pp. 231–44). Eveland ridiculed UNOGIL leaders. Galo Plaza was a gambler, a USC football player, and irresponsible; Dayal was a squatting mystic who warmed to Kamal Jumblatt; and Odd Bull was "the Queer Steer." He questioned both the competence of UNOGIL and Hammarskjöld's objectivity and integrity (pp. 273–302).

observing an itinerant and shadowy population, initially on only the 18 miles of the border held by the government, while the rest of the 165 miles were in rebel hands and never fully accessible. UNOGIL had no access to the Syrian side of the border, surely a crucial impediment. The nationality of armed bands could not properly be identified. The source of the weapons, as opposed to their make, defied identification. US military intervention saved both Lebanon from its external enemies and UNOGIL from its incompetence. UNOGIL's ineffectiveness, in fact, necessitated US military intervention; that was the "Lebanese" as opposed to the "Iraqi" reason for Eisenhower's decision on 14 July.

The fact was, unavoidably, UNOGIL was less effective at the outset when its presence was needed most. It was more effective later, after the US military intervention and Lebanon's presidential election, when it was needed less. UNOGIL was less competent to report when its reports were critical. It was more competent to report on a decidedly improving situation in late July and early August, as it was expanded and when infiltration became even more an artifact of the beleaguered Chamoun's imagination.[38] But such conclusions rob neither UNOGIL of its deterrent value nor Hammarskjöld of his control of the situation and his influence with Nasser.

Hammarskjöld: Assumptions and Goals

Hammarskjöld was prominent in the Lebanon crisis in two ways—at the Security Council and in the General Assembly in New York, and because of his two sorties to the regional capitals (principally Beirut, Amman, and Cairo, and secondarily Jerusalem and Baghdad), from 19 to 25 June and from 26 August to 12 September. The first visit focused on UNOGIL and indirect aggression, the second on implementing the Arab Resolution, passed in the General Assembly on 21 August. Hammarskjöld's seven assumptions mixed vision with naiveté. He believed that Middle East security must, with UN assistance, come essentially from within the region rather than being imposed or provided from the outside, by either the

---

[38] Murphy to Dulles, 2 August 1958, *FRUS*, 1958–1960, XI, 249, pp. 423–26. Murphy reported an emerging cooperative atmosphere between UNOGIL and evacuating the US force, so as to increase Chehab's chance of pacifying the country. See also Wainhouse, *International Peacekeeping*, pp. 102–36.

United States or the Soviet Union. He was not, therefore, a devotee of the Eisenhower doctrine of assisting states to withstand the assault of "International Communism." Despite moments of despair with these "neurotic children," he regarded Arab nationalism as a spontaneous and authentic force which, with UN assistance, could be made positive, cooperative, problem-solving, forward-looking, and effective, rather than remaining negatively-based and finding vigor only in uniting against enemies, internal and external, real and imagined. The Arab Resolution of 21 August, with its emphasis on the principle of non-intervention in the internal affairs of other Arab states, a welcome and extraordinarily positive step in Hammarskjöld's view, demonstrated the validity of this second assumption. It was folly, surely, for the West to think that it could counter Arab nationalism through military intervention.

Hammarskjöld was convinced that Nasser and the UAR were the keys to Middle Eastern security, self-reliance, and stability. Nasser, bent on economic development rather than external adventures, a man who could be managed and trusted, fairly reflected the aspirations of all nationalists in the Arab world. The fact that Nasser, in his villainous moods, was difficult to manage and might one day, as Bunche forecast, "explode in some nervous paroxysm," did not undermine this assumption. Nor did US explorations of Saudi Arabian leadership of the Arab world. Hammarskjöld was equally convinced that the Lebanese crisis was, for the most part, the result of Chamoun's domestic problems with the opposition and not an outburst orchestrated from outside by the UAR in an act of indirect aggression. Infiltration and subversion from the UAR had occurred and must be stopped, but Chamoun, inept and isolated, not Nasser was the cause of the tragedy. Neither the United Nations nor the United States could save it; Lebanon, he was sure, must save itself. It must do so with UN assistance that temporarily might make Lebanon, and Jordan, wards of the United Nations.

More broadly, Hammarskjöld had come to the conclusion that they were facing, in 1958, a revolutionary situation in the Middle East and that the Lebanon crisis was significant, actually and symbolically, in ways that Eisenhower and Macmillan did not quite understand. It had to be given priority, over the Arab-Israeli and Palestinian questions, for example, and managed deftly and prudently so as to avoid unacceptable, radical outcomes. It followed, as the seventh assumption, that there was ample room for his own personal initiative and diplomacy, in New York and on the ground. Hammarskjöld, given his creativity, could improvise and help manage this dangerous crisis. Several of these assumptions left Israel on the sidelines, a situation that Hammarskjöld saw as positive.[39] He had no illusions about Ben-Gurion's preferences. Should the 1958 crisis bring on a regional war, Israel's expansionist policies, and its determination to seize the West Bank if and when Jordan collapsed, would provide the most likely spark.

Hammarskjöld's goals changed in emphasis after the US military intervention on 15 July. Before that point he had worked to recreate a neutral, independent, and peaceful Lebanon, free of both unwarranted Western and UAR influence, depriving Chamoun of US military intervention or aid, and the opposition of UAR assistance. An effective UNOGIL would help lock Lebanon into a political stalemate, forcing Chamoun and his opponents to mend their ways, behave responsibly, and solve the domestically-derived crisis. The inept Chamoun must give up his quest for political salvation by way either of US intervention or UN peacekeeping; the opposition must accept that it could not triumph from UAR support. All concerned, especially Chamoun, must accept the fact that domestic reconciliation and constitutionally correct behavior must take precedence over factional interests and personal ambition. The Lebanese, swimming around in their own "goldfish bowl," would elect a new President and rally around a reconstituted government. Order would follow. Building on that commitment, Hammarskjöld would then cement Lebanon's stability. He would bring Lebanon under UN protection by establishing, on an indefinite basis, a small group of UN observers in Beirut "to report any external interference in Lebanon's independence and integrity."[40] When Hammarskjöld's preference became clear, Chamoun, who had welcomed UNOGIL and looked to Hammarskjöld and the United Nations to "save" Lebanon by defeating his opposition, turned on UNOGIL and the Secretary General. But in early July, he gave up the idea of pursuing a second term as President.

It followed that Hammarskjöld would pursue three other interlocking goals. He wanted to bring Nasser into line, head off precipitate US military intervention and thus countervailing USSR action, and demonstrate

---

[39] Hammarskjöld statement, 11 August 1958, and report to the General Assembly, 29 September, Cordier and Foote, *Public Papers*, pp. 4, 165, and 203–216; Urquhart, *Hammarskjöld*, pp. 287–88; Wright (Amman) to Dulles, 28 August, *FRUS*, 1958–1960, XI, pp. 538–39; and McClintock to Dulles, 11 September, *FRUS*, 316, pp. 561–62.

[40] Hammarskjöld-Lodge conversations, 26 June 1958, *FRUS*, 1958–1960, XI, 106, p. 175–80; Dulles-Hammarskjöld-Lodge conversations, 26 June, *FRUS*, 116, pp. 200–201 and 117, p. 202; Hammarskjöld to Fawzi, 25 June, Urquhart, *Hammarskjöld*, pp. 270–71; and Hammarskjöld to Dulles and Lloyd, n.d., *FRUS*, pp. 272–73.

to both Nasser and Eisenhower that they were treading on a substantial amount of common ground. To bring Nasser into line, Hammarskjöld, in Cairo from 22 to 24 June, was very frank in his criticism of UAR policy toward Lebanon. Nasser had overplayed his hand badly; it was time to change course. If not, the General Assembly might indict the UAR as an aggressor. UNEF could be undermined; UNOGIL might not succeed. Britain and the United States and then the USSR might intervene, and the Middle East could erupt into war, a prospect that could not benefit the UAR. But Hammarskjöld mixed frankness and threat with a display of trust and understanding of Nasser, and a determination to help him save face. He was equally frank and conciliatory with Mahmoud Fawzi, Nasser's Foreign Minister.[41]

To wean the Eisenhower administration from military intervention in Lebanon, Hammarskjöld worked to counter pressure, principally from the British government and Chamoun. That was not an excessively formidable task unless influential members of the US policy community changed course, for Eisenhower and Dulles welcomed reasons to avoid military intervention. Hammarskjöld knew of Dulles's recognition that US military intervention would soil its image in the region, actually undermine Chamoun, provide ammunition for the region's radicals and a platform for the Soviet Union, and possibly compel Nasser, rather than deter him, actually to order increased subversive activities. That put the United States in Hammarskjöld's debt for what he had accomplished with Nasser. Dulles made what he could of Nasser's transgressions against Lebanon. He pointed to 125 acts of intervention by Syria in May and June 1958, UNOGIL reports reflecting its own modest capabilities, and intrigue originating in Cairo so that he could more easily absorb the embarrassment of having endorsed Chamoun's case against the UAR, which UNOGIL was beginning to undermine. He would settle for an independent Lebanon free of Nasser's influence. Whether Dulles bought into the idea of Lebanon as a Middle East Switzerland, with "guaranteed neutrality" and an element of regional stability, is impossible to say.[42]

---

41 Hammarskjöld-Lodge conversation, 26 June 1958, *FRUS*, 1958–1960, XI, 106, pp. 175–80 and Urquhart, *Hammarskjöld*, pp. 268–69.

42 Dulles-Hood conversation, 27 June 1958, *FRUS*, 1958–1960, XI, pp. 181–82 and Rountree-Hood conversation, 3 July, *FRUS*, 115, pp. 198–99; Hammarskjöld to Dulles and Lloyd, n.d., Cordier and Foote, *Public Papers*, p. 127; Dulles-Hammarskjöld-Lodge meeting, 7 July, JFD, Chronological Series, Box 16; Eisenhower cabinet meeting, 18 July, DDE Ann Whitman Files, Cabinet Series.

Unpredictable behavior and evidence of personal distrust, in private and public, bedeviled Hammarskjöld's attempts to demonstrate the common ground between US and UAR policies. Washington press conferences and Cairo radio advertised the lack of trust. Dulles's intemperate judgments, fed by the Shah of Iran and Ben-Gurion, which Eisenhower did not contradict—that Nasser's pan-Arabism was akin to Hitler's pan-Germanism, or that Nasser, a rampant threat, a tool of the Kremlin, was bent on reducing Israel and subverting every moderate pro-Western government in North Africa and the Middle East—were particularly damaging. So were Nasser's outbursts of complaint, seeing a US-inspired conspiracy against him at every turn. Together they hindered the achievement of what both parties preferred for their different reasons, i.e., the departure of Chamoun, a Lebanese compromise settlement, order in an independent Lebanon, continued influence on Lebanon's foreign policy, and a distinct improvement in US-UAR relations. That would free the UAR from dependence on the Soviet Union and the Middle East from Soviet mischief. Hammarskjöld's role, therefore, was to help Nasser, and Eisenhower to a much lesser extent, to follow the path they both preferred. Again, UNOGIL, kept to its mandate, was a vital part of Hammarskjöld's strategy of convincing Eisenhower and Nasser that UNOGIL was preferable either to UAR embroilment or US military intervention. Hammarskjöld, in fact, banked on Nassers rejecting schemes to bring Lebanon into the UAR, and seeing involvement in Lebanon's affairs as a dangerous complication, not a golden opportunity. It was sufficient for Egypt to digest Syria and turn to domestic economic development, and, from mid-July, to benefit from the Iraqi coup.[43]

After 15 July, Hammarskjöld first sought to distance UNOGIL from the US military intervention. The credibility and effectiveness of UNOGIL was at issue, instantaneously.[44] There must be no cooperation, no hint of UN complicity in US actions. But Hammarskjöld kept his dis-

---

[43] Hare to Dulles, 20 May 1958 and 7 June, *FRUS*, 1958–1960, XI, 44, pp. 67–70 and 63, pp. 101–103; Herter to Hare, 27 May, *FRUS*, 51, pp. 76–77; Dulles-Congressional Leaders Meeting, 23 June, *FRUS*, 105, pp. 171–75; Hare to Dulles, 27 June and 3 and 24 July, *FRUS*, 1958–1960, XIII, 211, pp. 458–59, 212, pp. 460–61 and 213, pp. 461–64; Dulles to Eisenhower, 25 July, *FRUS*, 214, pp. 464–65; Rountree-Mustapha Kemal (UAR Ambassador) conversations, 5 August, 4 September and 8 October, *FRUS*, 215, pp. 465–68, 218, pp. 473–77, and 221, pp. 481–84; and Dulles to Eisenhower, 20 July, JFD, Chronological Series, Box 16. The United States, Dulles concluded, could not support Nasser's brand of Arab nationalism. See also Eisenhower-Dulles-Shah of Iran meeting, 1 July, DDE, Ann Whitman Files, Staff Memoranda Files, Iran.

[44] Dulles to McClintock, 15 July 1958, *FRUS*, 1958–1960, XI, 143, pp. 250–51.

like of Eisenhower's initiative—which represented a setback to his own policy—in check so as not to prejudice other goals. US military intervention spawned intense diplomatic activity inside and beyond the Security Council from 15 to 22 July, necessitating the maintenance of a working understanding with the United States. Apart from the deviant Swedish resolution of 17 July calling for the suspension of UNOGIL, which Lodge attributed to fear of a confrontation with the Soviet Union, all other resolutions introduced into the Security Council—by the United States, the Soviet Union, and Japan—recommended for differing reasons or permitted an expansion of UNOGIL. The United States would support and, in effect, finance and equip a strengthened UNOGIL. As he told Selwyn Lloyd, Dulles saw merit in casting a "UN mantle" around Lebanon and developing a UN solution for Jordan, which could not expect to live off US subsidies. Hammarskjöld, for his part, worked out an arrangement with Lodge, which Lloyd endorsed, whereby he would implement the spirit of the Japanese resolution despite a Soviet veto. That ploy would keep the issue out of the General Assembly where the "Russians want to get the Afro-Asians to put on a show" to "get 25 votes for us [the United States] to withdraw." Hammarskjöld also agreed to "sit on" the next UNOGIL report until late on 21 July, after the anticipated vote on the Japanese resolution (in fact the vote took place on 22 July, but the UNOGIL report was not despatched until 25 July).

Hammarskjöld would not compromise the integrity of UNOGIL, however. He warned Lodge that its report would not substantiate the "extravagant claims" of the Lebanese, British and US governments. He dismissed as gossip reports of Dayal's unauthorized contacts with UAR representatives, and backed the UNOGIL triumvirate—"these three men who have to sign their names [to UNOGIL reports] and stake their honor on it."[45]

45 UN, Security Council, Official Records, meetings 827 to 838, 15, 16, 17, 18, 21, and 22 July 1958 and 7 August. The critical resolutions were introduced by the United States (S/4050 of 16 July, revised on 17 July), the vote on 18 July was 9 for and 1 against (the Soviet veto), and 1 abstention; by the Soviet Union (S/44047 of 15 July 1958, revised on 16 July); the vote on 18 July was 1 for, 8 against and 2 abstentions; by Sweden (S/4054 of 17 July); the vote on 18 July was 2 for and 9 against, and 1 abstention; by Japan (S/4055 of 19 July revised on 21 July); the vote on 22 July was 10 for and 1 against (the Soviet veto). The Soviet Union proposed two amendments to the revised Japanese resolution, both of which were defeated on 22 July. See also Dulles-Lodge telephone conversations, 15, 17, 18 and 19 July and Dulles to Lloyd, 22 July, JFD, Telephone Call Series, Box 8, and Chronological Series, Box 16. At this stage Dulles was still talking of a Soviet-Egyptian takeover of Iraq. He also saw plots against Saudi Arabia and the Yemen, masterminded by Nasser.

Hammarskjöld therefore confirmed the effective distance between UNOGIL and the US forces while cooperating with the United States in expanding UNOGIL in an attempt finally to seal Lebanon's borders. Moreover, he did so without transforming it into a police force and embarrassing US policy unduly. His initiatives in this regard, following the vote on 22 July on the revised Japanese Resolution of 21 July, were not challenged. That meant that UNOGIL would have enhanced capacity to monitor the rapidly improving situation in Lebanon following Chehab's election as President. UNOGIL's reputation, damaged by US military intervention, was poised for recovery. If that were accompanied by Nasser honoring his word to cease interfering in Lebanon, a US military withdrawal would follow. As Dulles told Fawzi, "Our purpose is to get out of it if it is your purpose to keep your hands off."[46]

Hammarskjöld participated prudently in the tedious but seemingly vital exchange of letters initiated by Khrushchev, seeking a summit, on 19 July.[47] He was able to ensure that the Lebanon crisis stayed within the jurisdiction of the Security Council until it seemed wise to transfer it to the General Assembly.[48] That step would entail risk for both the United States and Britain, because the General Assembly would demand their immediate withdrawal from Lebanon and Jordan. The risk became, however, less formidable. Eisenhower, at Hammarskjöld's suggestion, addressed the General Assembly on 13 August. Both Selwyn Lloyd and Dulles began to look to the General Assembly to authorize Hammarskjöld to help resolve the Jordanian crisis, by then clearly more menacing than the situation in Lebanon. Jordan's fragility produced a delicious irony.

[46] Dulles-Lodge conversation, 22 July 1958, *FRUS*, 1958–1960, XI, 215, pp. 368–69; Dulles and others-Fawzi meeting, 18 August, *FRUS*, 279, pp. 490–95; NSC meeting, 24 July, DDE, Ann Whitman Files, NSC Series, Box 9; and Hammarskjöld statements to Security Council, 15, 21 and 22 July, Cordier and Foote, *Public Papers*, pp. 130–33, 140–43 and 144–48.

[47] Hammarskjöld to Sobolev, 21 June 1958, *FRUS*, 1958–1960, XI, pp. 147–48; UN, Security Council, Official Records, Resolution S/4062; and Eisenhower-Policy Community Meetings, 20 and 21 July, *FRUS*, 1958–1960, XI, 205, pp. 347–50, and DDE, Ann Whitman Files, Staff Memoranda, July. Vice President Richard Nixon deplored Hammarskjöld's seeming preference for, and willingness to attend, a summit meeting.

[48] UN Security Council, Official Records, 838th meeting, 7 August 1958 and resolution S/4083; UN General Assembly, Official Records, Third Emergency Special Session, plenary meetings, 732–746, 8–21 August, and Cordier and Foote, *Public Papers*, pp. 165–70; and Hammarskjöld speech, General Assembly, 8 August, *FRUS*, 1958–1960, XI, pp. 161–64.

Lloyd, counting on the now "redoubtable" Hammarskjöld's ingenuity, saw the future of Jordan as a "ward of the UN," this being "one time we really do want something out of the UN." The irony matched that of Malik seeing as an insult the comparison made of Lebanon to Jordan, in its infirmity. The principal obstacle to such an outcome, predictably was Britain's client, King Hussein.[49]

The deliberations of the General Assembly, with Hammarskjöld's guiding hand subtly evident, produced the Arab Resolution (#1237 ES-111) on 21 August. The vote was unanimous, and thus included Israel. Hammarskjöld was almost euphoric.[50] Arab states would not interfere in the internal affairs of other Arab states, thus pointing to what was a globally desirable practice, and would begin to shoulder their regional responsibilities. Hammarskjöld, reasonably free of constraints, was asked to help create this state of affairs, specifically as it applied to Lebanon and Jordan. He set off almost immediately for the Middle East to implement the Arab Resolution, arriving in Beirut on 26 August, en route to Amman, Cairo, Jerusalem, and Baghdad, and returning to New York from Beirut on 13 September. Lebanon was by then an almost routine matter. Hammarskjöld must provide for an expanded UNOGIL and pave the way for a US withdrawal at the right time, and in the right sequence, under appropriate circumstances, with no loss of face for Eisenhower and to the benefit of the Chehab regime and Lebanon's independence. Jordan, "the febrile point" of the region, "fortress Jordan," was far more problematic. Indeed, its fragility presented the greatest threat to the spirit and letter of

---

[49] UN Security Council, Official Records, 838th meeting, 7 August 1958, and resolution S/4083; UN General Assembly, Official Records, Third Emergency Special Session, plenary meetings, 732–746, 8–21 August, and Cordier and Foote, *Public Papers*, pp. 165–70; and Hammarskjöld speech, General Assembly, 8 August, *FRUS*, pp. 161–64.

[50] Hammarskjöld press conference, 22 August 1958, Cordier and Foote, *Public Papers*, pp. 171–75; and Urquhart, *Hammarskjöld*, pp. 290–92. Loufti helped craft the resolution that could be seen, justifiably, as a constraint on UAR policy. But Nasser had every reason to support such a step. UAR sponsorship would enhance its standing in the Arab League, at the United Nations, and with Hammarskjöld. It signaled the probability of improved relations with the incoming Chehab regime. On 10 August, according to US intelligence sources, Chehab sent a secret envoy to Cairo to arrange a *modus vivendi* with Nasser. UAR military-type personnel would leave the Lebanon, which would adopt a more neutralist foreign policy (NSC meeting, 14 August, DDE, Ann Whitman files, NSC Series). The Arab Resolution left Israel on the sidelines and was likely to preface the withdrawal of the United States and Britain from the Lebanon and Jordan. Finally, the Arab resolution was a threat neither to what Nasser had accomplished nor to what he planned to seek in the immediate future.

the Arab Resolution. Hussein, neither trusted Hammarskjöld nor saw Jordan's future as a ward of the United Nations. He balked at every arrangement, be it an observation force or peacekeeping. Under siege, Hussein saw, in Anglo-American financial and military assistance, salvation from a menacing UAR and a treacherous Nasser, a rogue, thief, and liar; from Israel; and possibly from Iraq. Hussein wanted neither a prompt British military withdrawal nor abandonment by the United States. Cooperating with Hammarskjöld brought one advantage at least, beyond the breathing room of the "Arab honeymoon," by improving Jordan's standing with a skeptical Eisenhower administration.

There lay the task for Hammarskjöld. Part of the answer lay in his influence with Nasser, and Nasser's reluctance to challenge the United States. The prospects were mildly encouraging as Hammarskjöld confronted Nasser again in Cairo. Nasser had not overreacted either to the US military intervention in Lebanon or to the British intervention of 17 July in Jordan, despite an understandable fear that both steps were the preface to an attack on Iraq. Indeed, he was sobered and deterred by those military actions. Nasser had assured Murphy, on 8 August, that he had opposed Chamoun but not threatened Lebanon's independence, and wanted the admirable Chehab to succeed. He had no appetite for Lebanese stew. As he faced bankruptcy, Nasser would do nothing to exacerbate Hussein's problems with the Palestinians, the refugees, and Israel. There was no need. Jordan could not survive. Perhaps Iraq, Nasser speculated, would take it over. If Israel, the immediate threat to Jordan's independence, attacked Jordan to seize the West Bank and East Jerusalem, however, then the UAR would respond.

The situation was menacing, but there was fertile soil for Hammarskjöld to cultivate. An effective UNOGIL and a formidable Chehab were two of the clues to US withdrawal from Lebanon; a creative UN "presence" in Jordan might permit a British withdrawal. Israel would be denied its opportunity. Nasser had every reason not to obstruct Hammarskjöld, who was as firm and frank with him over Jordan as he had been over Lebanon on 22 June.

> [Hammarskjöld] had [a] stormy session [with] Nasser at which he presented evidence of vicious anti-Hashemite radio broadcasts calling on people [to] overthrow [the] Hussein regime. Ultimately Nasser in [Hammarskjöld's] presence directed Ali Sabri (close political advisor) [to] take necessary steps [to]...stop extremist type broadcasts, yet reserve rights

> [of] political coverage. [Hammarskjöld] specifically took Nasser to task for statement that Hussein['s] request [for] UN troops [was an] act [of] treason; said if Nasser belief he had no right to make public statements which caused repercussions beyond the UAR borders.

As a result, according to Hammarskjöld, Nasser accepted a six-point program which marked his agreement to help implement the Arab Resolution and promote inter-Arab cooperation. Like the Iraqis, however, Nasser would not accept a UN "presence" in his capital, Cairo. Hammarskjöld could not be sure, moreover, that what he had accomplished with respect to Lebanon and Jordan pointed to an immediate withdrawal by US and British forces. Eisenhower was determined to control the timing of the US withdrawal and Hammarskjöld was adept enough not to challenge him on that point. Indeed, the Secretary General conceded to Prime Minister Samir al-Rifai of Jordan that:

> [U]ntil Nasser demonstrates a willing[ness and ability]...to fulfill [the] spirit/letter [of the] GA [General Assembly] resolution, [his] demand [for] withdrawal [is] not valid.... [Hammarskjöld was] not optimistic Nasser will fulfill his promises. Therefore [the Secretary-General] will make no recommendations in his report to GA re troop withdrawal.

That was welcome news to Hussein, Chehab, and Eisenhower. If Hussein accepted a UN "presence" and Nasser behaved responsibly, then normal relations, economic, commercial and political, could be restored between the UAR and Jordan, and between Jordan and Iraq. Jordan, under UN quasi-protection, would thus have a further—and perhaps the final—opportunity to attempt to survive.[51]

---

[51] Murphy to Dulles, 8 August 1958, *FRUS*, 1958–1960, XI, 260, pp. 439–43, Dulles and others-Fawzi conversation, 21 August, *FRUS*, 285, pp. 507–09; Dulles-Hammarskjöld conversation, 16 September, *FRUS*, 320, pp. 568–69. The brothers Dulles continued to complain of Nasser's "vicious propaganda war" and his economic blockade of Jordan (NSC meeting, 2 October, DDE, Ann Whitman Files, NSC Series). They, and Eisenhower, found merit in dealing with Nasser on bi-lateral US-UAR issues and thus undercutting Soviet influence, but would not treat Nasser, the embodiment of radical pan-Arab nationalism, as the leader of the Arab world. Eisenhower, in fact, spoke of detaching Syria from Egypt, supporting Syria's union with Iraq, and denying Nasser access to the revenues of the oil producing states (NSC meeting, 16 October, *FRUS*).

Hammarskjöld's Accomplishments

On 29 September Hammarskjöld reported to the General Assembly on his efforts to implement the Arab Resolution of 21 August.[52] He was, justifiably, cautiously optimistic without drawing clear lines between what could not have happened without him and what he had assisted rather than initiated. An expanded UNOGIL had been kept to its original mandate, as Hammarskjöld preferred, avoiding peacekeeping responsibilities. UNOGIL's very creation had been a mark of the concern of the international community for Lebanon, and its determination to provide an impartial, objective moral force to help resolve the crisis. Hammarskjöld's implementation of the Security Council's resolution of 11 June had laid the foundation of what effectiveness and capability UNOGIL had mustered. UNOGIL's expanded presence, the re-emergence of a stable if more neutral Lebanon, and Nasser's cooperation provided the basis for a US withdrawal which both Eisenhower and Hammarskjöld wanted. The US withdrawal would be graceful, calibrated, prompt, and sufficiently face-saving to enable Eisenhower to claim victory, with scarcely a hint in public that US actions were due to UAR-USSR pressure. Nasser disclaimed any influence in Lebanese affairs, let alone a wish to fold Lebanon into the UAR. At the request of the Chehab government made on 16 November, the Lebanese crisis was taken off the Security Council's agenda on 25 November 1958.

Hussein had accepted a UN "presence" and Hammarskjöld had despatched Piero Spinelli to Amman on 27 September. He was the Secretary General's Special Representative, not to be replicated in Baghdad or Cairo, but to be augmented by a second roving UN envoy when necessary. The personification of the improvised, novel UN "presence in Jordan," Spinelli was Hammarskjöld's contribution to Jordan's stability. More generally, he was to report on inter-Arab cooperation. Should that cooperation falter, should Nasser defect and the regional situation deteriorate markedly, Hammarskjöld could put the matter either to the Security Council or the General Assembly.[53] This UN "presence" helped Hussein avoid a dangerous loss of prestige and gave credibility to his argument that he had faced an external rather than an internal threat, a con-

---

[52] Hammarskjöld report to General Assembly, 29 September 1958, Cordier and Foote, *Public Papers*, pp. 203–16.

[53] Wright (Amman) to Dulles, 9 September 1958, *FRUS*, 1958–1960, XI, 314, pp. 557–59; Whitney (London) to Dulles, 24 September 1958, 330, pp. 578–79; and Dulles to Wright, 2 October 1958, *FRUS*, 341, p. 592.

clusion Hammarskjöld had denied Chamoun. Britain could withdraw from Jordan after arranging diplomatic, financial, and military support for Jordan from the United States. Jordan's collapse was avoided although its long-term viability remained in doubt. Macmillan could claim the victory in Jordan that Eisenhower achieved in Lebanon—an orchestrated, timely, and justifiable withdrawal. Israel remained inactive; the UAR had reason neither to intervene nor react. The 1958 crisis, erupting in Lebanon and spreading to Jordan, had not produced a regional war.

In an important way, Hammarskjöld, acting on a fundamental assumption, had challenged the Arab League to begin, with UN assistance, to handle the region's problems, and to free the Middle East from external interference. He had not been able to prevent either US or British military intervention, and it was naive to think that he could rid the Middle East of Western or Soviet influence, or that the "Arab" honeymoon would last.[54] But he had helped formulate the General Assembly resolution of 21 August, and, in his second mission to the Middle East, from 26 August to 12 September, had attempted to implement its terms. The important work of implementation took place in Beirut, Amman, and Cairo. It reflected principally his relationship with Nasser, and his ability to reassure Chehab and, to a far lesser degree, Hussein. Securing Nasser's commitment to restraint was a considerable achievement. It should not, however, be exaggerated. Nasser had no grand design on Lebanon and he was willing to wait for what he regarded as inevitable, the fall of the regime in Jordan. Whether that would prompt an Israeli seizure of the West Bank remained to be seen. Eisenhower and Nasser, in any case, preferred to avoid conflict in Lebanon. Hammarskjöld was, therefore, moving people in the direction they preferred. He could well afford Chamoun's insults and contempt; indeed, they could be worn as a badge of prudence and realism. Ben-Gurion's hostility, as evident as ever, was tolerable, but less so.

Given wide discretionary powers by the Security Council after both the resolution of 11 June, and the vote on the Japanese resolution on 22 July, and by the General Assembly on 21 August, Hammarskjold took the initiative, improvised, and created opportunities. He found a path for the United Nations between being marginalized and accepting excessive tasks, on each occasion helping create and implement the spirit of the resolutions. In turn, the United Nations, in the Lebanon crisis, and as that challenge embraced Iraq and Jordan, was not "used" by any state or group of states in the inter-

[54] Nasser's lifting of the economic blockade on Jordan became the immediate issue (Dulles-Rifai conversation, 15 October 1958, *FRUS*, 1958–1960, XI, 354, pp. 611–12).

national system. Rather, the United Nations was an essential part of the diplomatic calculus, constraining unilateral behavior, enabling statesmen to accept risk. It provided avenues of response that led to effective management of, if not long-term solutions to, regional problems. In that process, the status of the Secretary General was enhanced. On most counts, in diagnosis and treatment, Hammarskjöld had outshone both Eisenhower and Macmillan, freer as he was of Cold War reasoning, and thoroughly unimpressed with Chamoun's "Communist onslaught on the Middle East."

That is a justifiable verdict, his critics notwithstanding. The CIA trusted neither Hammarskjöld nor Nasser, and did not welcome the former's initiatives in Beirut, Cairo, and Amman. US intelligence agents in Lebanon fed and shared Chamoun's contempt for the UN Secretary General. But the fact was that the CIA found itself competing with UN intelligence, independently gathered, provided by and through UNOGIL, and did not come through the competition unscathed. It was less a case of ill-conceived particularist interests challenged by detached globalist interests, of axe-grinders facing objectivity, although there was some of that. It was more a case of capability in changing circumstances, of greater reach and accuracy on the part of UNOGIL. UNOGIL provided Hammarskjöld with credible information; he made effective use of what he received, and what he learned as he toured the region's capitals.

Allen Dulles was an active and integral part of the policy community in Washington. Two issues were crucial. There was the issue of the validity of the allegation of infiltration and subversion from Syria, which spoke to the questions of the internal or external origins of the civil war and Nasser's responsibility. There was also the question of the effectiveness of UNOGIL. The basic case of the US intelligence community was deeply flawed, though it was a model of accuracy in comparison with estimates of the coup in Iraq. Eisenhower and Dulles bought into it. It reinforced some of Dulles's images of Nasser, for example, but, as they weighed the nuances and the competitive evidence, the CIA's case did not amend their set preferences until mid-July. Eisenhower and Dulles were determined to influence the course of Lebanese politics and, indeed, the politics of the region, while avoiding US military intervention. It was necessary to give UNOGIL a chance, wise not to challenge its effectiveness. Because of the coup in Iraq in mid-July, they reinvented the basic case to justify the change of policy they had already decided on—military intervention. It followed that UNOGIL must be judged ineffective. And thus the competition with the United Nations in the Middle East continued to unfold.

5

Perceptions and Reality: The Arab World and the West

RASHID KHALIDI

I

Historians reading contemporary sources on the Western and Arab sides of the great divide in the Middle East during the revolutionary year of 1958 might be forgiven for assuming that they were reading about two entirely different crises. Veteran observers of the Middle East will note how common is this phenomenon of two opposing parties existing side by side, but apparently operating in separate dimensions, drawing opposite historical conclusions from the past.

The revolutionary upsurge in the Middle East, which began in the early 1950s and peaked in the dramatic events of 1958 in Iraq, Lebanon, and Jordan, was one of those moments when this gap in perceptions was the widest. Views may differ as to when this upsurge began. Possibilities include the rise of the Mossadeq government in Iran in May 1951, the Egyptian revolution of July 1952, the Israeli raid on Gaza of February 1955, the Egyptian-Soviet arms deal of the same year, Egypt's nationalization of the Suez Canal in 1956, or the subsequent Anglo-French-Israeli attack on Egypt. And some historians have questioned the extent to which the events of 1958 were revolutionary.[1] But there is no question that these

[1] See the chapter by Irene L. Gendzier and her monograph, *Notes from the Minefield: United States Intervention in Lebanon and the Middle East, 1945–1958* (New York, 1997), for an examination of this question.

dramatic events provoked an unprecedented crisis in relations between the West and the peoples of the Middle East. In any case, the culmination of these events came in 1958.

In many British and American diplomatic despatches and press reports of the period, the predominant description of the Middle East is of a largely passive region that was prey to the subversive machinations of two monolithic and related entities, "international communism" and "Nasserism."[2] In the Arabic press and other sources, in contrast, the prevalent view, which most reflected and influenced Arab popular perceptions, was of a region victimized by a voracious Western imperialism, unified despite the differences between its American, British, and French facets. The West was generally seen as operating in close collaboration with its Israeli clients and conservative local elites. Thus the standard demonological trinity of *imbariyaliyya, sihyuniyya wa raj'iyya*—imperialism, Zionism, and reaction—was constantly evoked in the Arab nationalist discourse.

The above summary is of course an over-simplification. Western diplomats and journalists often wrote nuanced reports, or recognized in retrospect the faulty perceptions on both sides. Thus, Sir Charles Johnston, the British Ambassador in Amman from 1956 until 1960, wrote in his memoirs, "It is curious that just as Nasser looked everywhere for British influence operating against him, so we on our side were inclined for a time to find Nasser under every bed."[3]

Similarly, many in the Arab world saw the Western powers as differing among themselves and motivated by more than just predatory imperialism. Indeed numerous Arabs, particularly those among the traditional elites (the "reactionaries" of the nationalists' trinity), were deeply committed to alignment with the Western powers, as were several Arab regimes which these elites dominated. It nevertheless remains true that the way in which the revolutionary crisis of 1958 was seen from within the region differed fundamentally from the way it was seen from without.

---

[2] For an example of this rhetoric, see the recently declassified letter from Israeli Prime Minister David Ben-Gurion to President Dwight Eisenhower dated 24 July 1958, during the Iraqi revolution. In it, the Israeli leader adroitly tries to exploit American fears of these two bogeys to obtain US support for the Israeli policy of encircling the core Arab countries with a belt of mainly non-Arab allies: Iran, Turkey, Ethiopia, and the Sudan. It is impossible to discern whether Ben-Gurion fully believed in some of the lurid specters he conjured up for Eisenhower. I owe Dr. Ilan Pappé my thanks for this document.

[3] Charles Johnston, *The Brink of Jordan* (London, 1972), p. 20.

Arab politicians and journalists, including some of those most closely tied to the West, generally had a far more subtle view of regional events and of the role of the Soviet Union than did many Western observers. This is evident, for example, from articles in the Saudi-financed Beirut daily *al-Hayat,* written after Saudi Arabia had accepted the Eisenhower Doctrine in early 1957, and had taken a strongly anti-Soviet and anti-Egyptian line. It is true even of items in the Jordanian dailies *Filastin* and *al-Difa,'* published after King Hussein had removed the Arab nationalist al-Nabulsi government in April 1957 and re-imposed his direct rule, and with it, press censorship.

In spite of their strong pro-Western orientation, these newspapers offered portrayals of the Soviet Union, its local allies, and its influence which, although mostly hostile, were generally quite balanced.[4] Arab observers often noted how inaccurate much Western reporting was: in a press conference at the height of the Lebanese crisis in 1958, the Maronite Patriarch, Mar Boulos Meouschi, castigated British and American journalists for distorting the situation in Lebanon, advising them to "present correct information to their peoples."[5] Of course, with the benefit of hindsight, it is possible to see that much in the contemporary media, both Arab and Western sources, was profoundly mistaken.

Several chapters of this book, as well as other works, examine the contemporary British and American views of these years of crisis in the Arab world, whether in Iraq, Lebanon, Jordan, Syria, or elsewhere.[6] This chapter will contrast some of those perceptions with the current understanding of the causes of the instability that affected several different Middle

---

[4] For example, the coverage in *al-Hayat* of the Syrian domestic crises of August and September 1957 (when a "pro-Communist" officer, Col. Afif Bizri, became Syrian Army Chief of Staff), and that in *Filastin* and *al-Difa'* in July 1958 at the height of the Lebanese crisis, when the Iraqi coup took place, is full of references to the USSR, which, while sometimes sensational, are usually factual and often perceptive.

[5] This and other anti-Chamoun statements by the Patriarch are reported in banner front-page headlines in the Egyptian daily *al-Ahram*, 21 May 1958.

[6] The most attention in this regard has been devoted to the Suez crisis and the events surrounding it, notably in Herman Finer, *Dulles over Suez: The Theory and Practice of His Diplomacy* (Chicago, 1964); Diane B. Kunz, *The Economic Diplomacy of the Suez Crisis* (Chapel Hill, 1991); and Wm. Roger Louis and Roger Owen, eds., *Suez 1956: The Crisis and Its Consequences* (Oxford, 1989). More broadly, see the perceptive essays by Albert Hourani, "A Moment of Change: The Crisis of 1956," pp. 117–144, in his *A Vision of History: Near Eastern and Other Essays* (Beirut, 1961); and "A Note on Revolutions in the Arab World," in his *The Emergence of the Modern Middle East* (London, 1981). The memoirs of the British and American officials concerned are also revealing in this regard.

Eastern countries. Specifically, it will examine in turn the internal political crisis in Lebanon that ultimately developed in 1958 into what was variously called a civil war and an uprising; the unrest in Jordan during the same years over the country's internal governance and external orientation; and some of the events leading up to the Iraqi revolution of July 1958.

Although the simultaneous struggle for the control of Syria involved both domestic factions as well as foreign and Arab powers in the 1950s, and was directly related to all these events, it will be excluded from the purview of this chapter. The primary reason for this exclusion is that by the climactic year of 1958, Syria had already been absorbed in the United Arab Republic.[7] Throughout this chapter, in addition to the examination of different Western and Arab perspectives, it will be necessary to analyze the roles played by Egypt under President Gamal Abdel Nasser, the impact of Arab nationalism, and the policy of the Soviet Union and its local allies, the Communist movements, in these countries.

Among the central questions about the upheavals in the Arab world in the period leading up to 1958 are: What drove the opposition to the monarchy in Jordan and its Anglo-American connections, the growing resistance in Lebanon to President Camille Chamoun and his policies, and the revolution in Iraq? Were these events the outcome primarily of processes internal to the countries in question? Or of a wave of transnational anti-imperialist fervor under the banner of Arabism? Or of well-financed subversion by Egypt, Syria, and the Soviet Union? Or of some combination of the three?

There is little question where many contemporary Western observers placed the weight of their interpretations. Writing from Amman in 1958, Ambassador Johnston characterized "Jordanian Nasserists" as "100% venal," and as likely to be "bought by Russia in no time at all."[8] Johnston

---

[7] The Arabic newspapers reviewed for this chapter included the Damascus daily *al-Nasr*, as well as the pre-eminent Cairo paper *al-Ahram*, the Beirut daily *al-Hayat*, and the leading Jordanian newspapers, *Filastin* and *al-Difa'*, both published in Jerusalem. Developments in Syria have not been dealt with here partly because the interweaving of the different domestic, Arab, and foreign strands that influenced Syrian politics during these years has been masterfully analyzed by Patrick Seale in *The Struggle for Syria: A Study of Post-War Arab Politics,* 2nd ed. (New Haven, CT, 1987), a work whose scope and perceptiveness it would be difficult to surpass.

[8] Johnston to Foreign Office, no. 1341, telegram, 18 August 1958, PRO, PREM 11/2381.

made allegations of corruption by Suleiman al-Nabulsi, who as Prime Minister of Jordan in 1956–57 headed that country's first (and its last) democratically-elected, nationalist government. According to Johnston's account, al-Nabulshi shifted policy as the result of "a large bribe, perhaps as much as £100,000, from the Russians."[9] Johnston's views mellowed only slightly in retrospect. Although his memoirs occasionally give al-Nabulsi the benefit of the doubt, his portraits of nationalist politicians are scathing. Thus, al-Nabulsi's Foreign Minister, 'Abdullah al-Rimawi, "was far from incorruptible," he had "malicious eyes" and a "fanatical quality";[10] the "corruption of some leaders of the regime was on a scale which shocked even Arabs," and so forth.[11] Throughout his memoirs, Johnston stresses that "Nasser's propaganda was certainly responsible for the nationalist agitation in Jordan."[12] That Jordanians may have had their own reasons for hostility to Britain or the West, and did not need to be spoon-fed by Egyptian propaganda, does not appear to have occurred to him.

An inability to ascribe agency to local actors, and a belief in the power of external forces to manipulate them, was shared by the British Ambassador in Lebanon, Sir George Middleton. Writing to London in 1957, he saw "intrigue by Egypt and Syria" as the foundation of hostility to collaboration with the West.[13] In regard to the well-founded charges of massive covert American financing of Lebanese President Chamoun's rigged 1957 election,[14] Middleton, with masterful diplomatic understatement, was able to say no more than: "I am afraid that I have some doubt

---

9 Johnston to Foreign Office, no. 26, 8 May 1957, FO 371/127880. In a later dispatch the same month, Johnston described how a "nouveau riche revolutionary," Hikmat al-Masri, was preparing to distribute £50,000 to members of the Jordanian Parliament "in order to secure his election as President of a Jordanian Republic": no. 31, 29 May 1957, FO 371/127880. In his memoirs (*The Brink of Jordan,* p. 54), Johnston was more circumspect regarding al-Nabulsi; he states that "there was some reason to believe that about the middle of March he was in contact with the Soviet Government and that they were able to establish a considerable influence over him."

10 Johnston, *The Brink of Jordan*, p. 24.

11 Ibid., p. 164.

12 Ibid., p. 20.

13 Middleton to Foreign Office, no. 99, June 5, 1957, FO 371/127999.

14 These events are described in detail by the CIA agent Wilbur Crane Eveland, who was the bagman for the multi-million dollar operation. Eveland noted in his memoirs, *Ropes of Sand: America's Failure in the Middle East* (London, 1980), p. 252: "Throughout the elections I traveled regularly to the presidential palace with a briefcase full of Lebanese pounds, then returned late at night to the embassy with an empty twin case I'd carried away for Harvey Armada's CIA finance-office people to replenish."

in my own mind as to whether some of these allegations may not have had a basis of truth."[15]

Similarly, the American Ambassador to Iraq from 1954–58, Waldemar Gallman, described the 16 nationalist deputies (out of a total of 135) elected to the Iraqi Parliament in 1954 as having "the means for considerable trouble-making," as a "closely-knit and well-disciplined unit," and as a "small, determined minority."[16] To his evident satisfaction, most of these troublesome opposition deputies disappeared in the rigged elections ordered by the veteran pro-Western Prime Minister, Nuri al-Said, after his return to power in the same year.

Western diplomats were not always so categorical in denying agency to the local opposition politicians or to indigenous political forces in the countries where they were stationed. Nor did they always ascribe responsibility for the unpleasantness with which they had to deal to the Russians and Egyptians.[17] Some British diplomats, indeed, were capable of recognizing that the threats of Communism and Soviet infiltration in the region were occasionally exaggerated.[18] But this was certainly not the general trend in much Western diplomatic and journalistic reporting from these countries during this period. Sensationalist Western newspapers went even further in seeing Communist and Nasserist (the same for many of them) conspiracies everywhere.[19]

It was possible for exceptionally acute diplomats, and a few other competent Western observers, to accept that the region could be prey to an indige-

15 Middleton to Foreign Office, no. 100, 12 June 1957, FO 371/127999.

16 Waldemar Gallman, *Iraq under General Nuri: My Recollections of Nuri al-Said, 1954–1958* (Baltimore, MD, 1964), p. 4.

17 For example, the first Annual Report sent from Amman by Johnston in March 1957, and which he noted had been drafted by his Head of Chancery, Heath Mason, due to his own recent arrival in Amman, correctly described the powerful movement which brought the al-Nabulsi government to power as motivated firstly by "a genuine popular desire, not created, but certainly fostered, by Egyptian propaganda and example, to be free of western influence...": Johnston to Foreign Office, no. 20, 19 March 1957, FO 371/127876.

18 This was particularly the case if the exaggerations were the work of Americans, as with the "over-emphatic American statements about the Communist threat from Damascus" noted by Johnston, *Brink of Jordan*, p. 78. In a letter cited two pages earlier in his memoir, however, Johnston wrote that "Communist Syria is going all out to organize terrorism in Jordan."

19 Western intelligence services, whose primary mission during this phase of the Cold War was to combat Soviet influence the world over, were even more prone to see such conspiracies. The memoirs of two former American intelligence operatives in the region are replete with examples: Eveland, *Ropes of Sand*, and Miles Copeland, *The Game of Nations: The Amorality of Power Politics* (London, 1969).

nous trans-national wave of Arabism. Even if they accorded it some sympathy, however, they most frequently described this trend in terms of extremism or fanaticism. Indeed, the terms "extremism" and "fanaticism" are ubiquitous in British despatches from Baghdad, Beirut, and Amman from 1955 until 1959, where they are normally contrasted with the "moderation" of the Arab politicians most closely associated with Britain.[20] But it was much harder for such observers to accept that the opposition to Western policies was driven mainly by processes which were internal to the countries in which they were posted. The casual disrespect or even contempt of Western diplomats for their Middle Eastern interlocutors comes through in many of their despatches and memoirs. It is not hard to understand why such perceptions may have arisen. It is more interesting to attempt to discern the extent to which internal processes were actually the decisive factors in what transpired on a country-by-country basis in Lebanon, Jordan, and Iraq.

It is impossible to be as definite about the factors driving the opposition to President Chamoun and King Hussein as one can be with regard to Iraq. Popular opposition to the Western orientation of the Lebanese and Jordanian regimes was certainly deep-rooted. But it is necessary to be cautious in making any assessment because of the divided nature of the two polities. The Lebanese were split along sectarian lines, and the Jordanians between those of East and West Bank origins. Yet these major divisions, most conspicuous to Western observers, often obscured many other important divides in each population. There were factions among Christians of the same or different sects in Lebanon. There were divisions among East Bankers in Jordan between the settled village-dwellers of the north of the country and the semi-nomadic and nomadic tribal populations of other parts of Jordan. This schism between the settled and nomadic peoples, which comes out forcefully in the Arabic press reports of events in Jordan, is almost entirely absent from Western accounts, which tend to focus on fissures between the West Bank Palestinian majority and East Bank Jordanians.[21]

---

[20] Johnston's memoirs, *The Brink of Jordan*, are peppered with the words "fanatical," "rabidly," "agitators," and "mobs," which appear at least nine times.

[21] Reports of popular unrest in Jordan in the Damascus paper *al-Nasr* are particularly informative on divisions between the settled and nomadic populations, and are often sensational in stressing this topic, as can be seen from this front-page banner headline on 9 January 1956: "Has Glubb [Gen. Sir John Bagot Glubb: the British commander of the Jordanian Army] prepared a division of bedouins to be unleashed on Amman to pillage and shed blood?" Subsequent reports indicated that there was much resistance to attempts to restore order by mainly bedouin units of the Jordanian army from villagers and townspeople in Ramtha and other areas in the north of the country.

Another cause for caution in determining the reasons for opposition to Hussein and Chamoun is the much higher degree of vulnerability to external manipulation of both the Lebanese and Jordanian political systems in comparison with that of Iraq. Iraq also was divided, permeable, and fragile in the 1950s, but was considerably less so than Lebanon and Jordan. Moreover, these flaws were perhaps less evident before the 1958 revolution, when the old regime had so little credit with most politicized segments of Iraqi society and popular opinion seemed unified against it. In other words, the opposition appeared more "authentic," and more clearly and exclusively motivated by internal causes in Iraq than in Lebanon and Jordan, where the signs of some degree of external meddling were unmistakable.[22] Nevertheless, even allowing for some "external involvement," one can analyze the opposition to the regimes in power in Beirut and Amman without resorting to the oversimplifications and exaggeration which can be found in much of the Western reporting at the time. Needless to say, this reporting rarely emphasized Western interference in these countries.

While this line of inquiry is of relatively limited importance in and of itself, it has a certain resonance for understanding the Western views of unrest in the Middle East up to the present. Many Western observers in the 1950s, reporting in lurid language, saw the sinister hand of Moscow, Cairo, and Damascus at work every time anything unfavorable to the West happened in the region. We can see a similar stress on blaming the devil-of-the-moment in the Middle East in subsequent decades, whether it be the fingers pointed at designated pariah states such as Iran, Iraq, Libya, or the Sudan, or at Islamic movements like Hizballah, Hamas, or Islamic Jihad. While the bogey of choice in the Cold War was Communism, it later became terrorism, particularly "Islamic terrorism."

In some sense the more recent mode of analysis is worse than the earlier one, for it has spawned a ubiquitous and influential school of "terrorism" studies, invariably focusing on the Middle East. The distortion in reporting on the Middle East in the 1950s thus has a certain enduring relevance, as it forms the foundation for a structure of misunderstanding regarding the region which still prevails in some sectors of American government, the media, and public discourse.

---

[22] Ironically, the Iraqi Communist Party, which was certainly a vehicle for Soviet influence, even while representing important indigenous Iraqi social and political trends, was both far bigger and more influential than were the Communist parties of Lebanon and Jordan.

II

Even today, Lebanon is the site of much misunderstanding and distortion. Some of this goes back to the events of 1958, which are generally seen as a lead-up to the much more destructive and prolonged Lebanese conflict which began in the 1970s. This misunderstanding involves both the analysis of the internal situation in Lebanon, and the relative importance of external influences in the crisis. In Lebanon in 1958, the opposition to Camille Chamoun and to the Eisenhower Doctrine was not confined to Muslims, as was so often asserted by Western observers, nor were the issues raised by his opponents artificial or unique to the Chamoun presidency. Prominent and powerful Christian leaders like Hamid Frangié, the leading Maronite politician of the North of the country (and brother of Suleiman, who became President in 1970), former President Béchara el-Khoury, and the Maronite Patriarch, Mar Boulos Meouschi, were leading members of the opposition to Chamoun.[23] It included as well other influential Christian political figures like Philippe Takla and Henri Faroun. Allied with them were most of the country's paramount Sunni, Druze, and Shia political leaders (including Saeb Salam, Raschid Keramé, Hussein al-Uwaini, and Abdallah Yafi; Walid Jumblatt; and Sabri Hamadé, Ahmed and Kamil el-Assad, and many others), and members of many political parties which transcended confessional boundaries.

Far from being a foreign-inspired minority, the coalition of Chamoun's opponents, most of them organized into the United National Front together with others in the "Third Force" which opposed Chamoun's "domestic political ambitions,"[24] encompassed most of the Lebanese political spectrum. Moreover, if one were to look for external influences in the Lebanese crisis, it would be at least as important to look at American and British (and Iraqi and Saudi) intervention as at Egyptian and Soviet support for their protégés. Western support reinforced not only Chamoun, but also the Phalangist and Partie Populaire Syrienne (PPS) parties, whose

[23] For an indication of how fierce was the Patriarch's opposition to Chamoun, see his statements attacking him at the height of the crisis, for example at his press conference at Bkerki on 20 May reported in *al-Ahram* on the following day, pp. 1, 9, when he called the Chamoun regime "corrupt," and demanded that the President leave the country.

[24] Gendzier, *Notes from the Minefield*, p. 225.

militias were Chamoun's main armed allies, and the recipients of extensive covert support from both Western powers.[25]

Nor was the opposition to Chamoun driven only by anger at the President's stubbornness in bucking the regional trend towards neutralism and Arab nationalism by insisting on bringing Lebanon firmly into the Western orbit, galling as this was to many Lebanese.[26] It was Chamoun's domestic policies, notably his flagrant violations of the provisions of the unwritten and fragile basis of Lebanese unity, the National Pact of 1943, which most angered the opposition. These violations included his apparent disregard for the provisions which called for a balance between Lebanon's Arab and Western orientations. But what infuriated many of his political opponents more was his curbing the already circumscribed powers assigned to the Sunni Prime Minister. Chamoun's Prime Minister in 1957–58, Sami Solh,[27] was universally perceived as a weak and unrepresentative figure, completely under the influence of Chamoun, as was his leading Druze ally, Emir Majid Arslan.[28]

The simmering grievances over Chamoun's high-handed rule were compounded by the outrage of Muslims and Christians alike when the President blatantly rigged the 1957 elections with the help of generous CIA funding. The resulting parliament excluded dozens of popular opposition politicians. Yet those leaders, such as Raschid Keramé in Tripoli, Kamal Jumblatt in the Shuf, Saeb Salam in Beirut, and many others, were

---

[25] This was insinuated by the Maronite Patriarch at his press conference reported in Al-Ahram, 21 May 1958, when he stated that far from Egypt smuggling weapons into Lebanon via Syria, "the people" had obtained weapons from Chamoun's supporters. The clear implication was that these were supplied to them by foreign powers. In fact, although the UN Observer Group in Lebanon (UNOGIL) found no evidence of significant infiltration from Syria, the UAR's intelligence services did manage to smuggle some weapons into Lebanon for use by the opposition: personal communication with the author, Walid Khalidi, 7 August 1996.

[26] Earlier in his career, Chamoun himself had been considered something of a nationalist hero by Lebanese and other Arabs for his efforts to maintain Lebanon's independence from France from 1944 onwards when he was his country's representative in Cairo, London, and at the United Nations, where in addition he was known as a forceful advocate of the Palestinian cause; for details, see his own memoirs of this period, *Marahil al-istiqlal: Lubnan wa duwal al-ʾArab fil-mu'tamarat al-duwaliyya* [Stages of Independence: Lebanon and the Arab States in the International Conferences] (Beirut, 1949).

[27] Sami Solh was a cousin of Riyad Solh, one of the architects of Lebanon's independence and of the National Pact, and the first Prime Minister of independent Lebanon.

[28] This issue is analyzed in Wade Goria, *Sovereignty and Leadership in Lebanon, 1943–1976* (London, 1985). For more on the immediate background to this period, see Nicola A. Ziadeh, *Syria and Lebanon* (London, 1957).

strongly entrenched in their home districts and would have been difficult for any opponent to unseat electorally, except through under-handed methods.[29]

To ensure his own re-election to a second term in 1958, Chamoun resorted to these methods with the obvious objective of packing the parliament, which chose the President under the Lebanese system. This was seen as yet another attempt to circumvent the Lebanese constitution.[30] Chamoun's maneuvers were all the more outrageous in that he had been one of the Lebanese politicians who, in the name of freedom and the Constitution, had successfully opposed the autocratic tendencies of his predecessor. Lebanon's first President, Béchara el-Khoury, had directed Parliament, whose election in 1947 he was accused of having influenced, to amend the constitution in 1949 in order to enable him to serve another six-year term. These actions alienated many of his supporters and precipitated an erosion of his power, which ultimately led to his resignation in September 1952. His departure was forced by a political coalition of which Chamoun was a prominent member. Ironically, this broad coalition of traditional Lebanese political leaders resembled in many ways the one which six years later came to oppose Chamoun for many of the same reasons.

This summary of the opposition's grievances against Chamoun in 1957–58 illustrates that his pro-Western foreign policy was not the sole reason for the antagonism to him in many quarters. Rather, it was Chamoun's dictatorial domestic inclinations, his flouting of conventions regarding sectarian balance, and his willingness to trample on the Lebanese constitution to remain in power that understandably motivated the opposition. Moreover, while this opposition was undoubtedly supported from without, it was not externally instigated but had deep indigenous roots, amply watered by the President's indifference towards his fellow-citizens' sensibilities.

While Western observers focused on Egyptian and Soviet intervention in the Lebanese crisis, they tended to ignore that of France, Britain, and the United States. This included in particular the arming of the Lebanese gendarmerie by the latter and the covert arming of the pro-Chamoun

29 The results of the parliamentary elections of August–September 1996, in which a Keramé, a Jumblatt, and a Salam were elected nearly 40 years after the events we are discussing, show the enduring nature of some of these local leaderships, in spite of the massive changes which have taken place in Lebanon in the interim.

30 Lebanon's constitution specified a single six-year term for the President and four-year terms for members of parliament.

Phalangist and PPS militias by Western intelligence services. This support shored up the President's resistance to the opposition when the army refused to come to his aid. And even some acute Western observers who perceived the validity of opposition grievances against Chamoun undermined their analyses with demeaning comments about the venality, base personal motives, and frustrated ambitions of opposition politicians.

In comparing the complex picture we now have of events in Lebanon during this period (accurately reflected in most Arabic press accounts), with Western diplomatic and press reports on the Lebanese crisis, the discrepancies are striking.[31] In British despatches, many of the criticisms of Chamoun for his domestic misdeeds are overlooked. Instead, he is described as beleaguered by his external foes and their local allies mainly because of his pro-Western orientation and his refusal to bow to the wishes of the Egyptians.[32]

Even the account of the 1958 crisis in Lebanon by a relatively sophisticated participant such as former CIA officer Miles Copeland downplays the many domestic causes for discontent with Chamoun, although these are mentioned in passing. He stresses instead the role of Egypt in animating, instigating, financing, and arming the opposition.[33] Eveland is even more oblivious to Chamoun's failings in Lebanese domestic affairs, perhaps because he believed that maintaining Chamoun in power would measurably facilitate the major US intelligence presence in Lebanon for which Eveland was responsible during the crisis.[34]

The explanation for the Western inattention to violations of the democratic process, in contrast to the genuine outrage at Chamoun's behavior on the part of many Lebanese, may be simple. What seems to have been at work was no more than the casual, borderline-racist cynicism of Westerners who saw Arab politics as inevitably authoritarian and corrupt. The Western countries helped measurably to sustain this corruption by their subventions and bribes to local politicians, newspapers, political par-

---

[31] Even the unanimously anti-Chamoun Egyptian press, which contemporary Western observers universally castigated for its inflammatory and partisan tone, was reasonably factual in its descriptions of the acute phase of the crisis, which started with the assassination of the Lebanese opposition journalist Nasib al-Metni in May 1958. The front-page report on his killing in *al-Ahram* on 9 May 1958, is low-key and matter-of-fact. Even reporting in the Cairo press after the civil war had begun, while highly partisan and virulently opposed to Chamoun, conforms fairly well to much of what we now know about this conflict.

[32] See, e.g., Middleton to Foreign Office, no. 100, 12 June 1957, FO 371/127999.

[33] Copeland, *The Game of Nations*, pp. 191–207.

[34] Eveland, *Ropes of Sand*, relates not only his own direct involvement in Lebanese politics, but that of other American intelligence officers in operations directed against Syria.

ties, and trade unions. Given their cynical world-view, such observers could not credit the possibility that there was a widespread popular aspiration among influential segments of the Lebanese public for the democratic process and the rule of law. This bias seeps out of the pages of period memoirs such as Miles Copeland's. It is reflected in much of the British and American diplomatic reporting on this period in Lebanon.[35] We will see this cynical predisposition once again in Western reports on the struggles between the monarchy and the opposition in Jordan.

III

Many of these assessments of Lebanon apply to Jordan as well. Outside influences there were aplenty, but those of Britain and the United States and of the West's local allies such as Iraq and Saudi Arabia matched or exceeded those of Egypt, the Soviet Union, and their allies. It must be remembered that Jordan was unlike any of the other Arab states that emerged from the post-First World War settlements. It resembled others in that it was established as a state by British fiat, within borders drawn for the convenience of the imperial powers of the day. It differed from them, however, in having as its core a British-officered, -financed and -controlled military establishment, called, ironically, the Arab Legion. This was the preponderant institution in the state and society for nearly the first three decades of the nation's existence.[36] In a country which was long overwhelmingly dominated by Britain, and later, to a lesser degree, by the United States, it is highly misleading to focus exclusively on such "external influences" as those of Egypt and the USSR, as did many Western observers in the 1950s.

Transjordan, as it was originally known, began to change with a gradual growth in the population, which reached about half a million in the years after the Second World War. More rapid change came with the annexation of the West Bank to Jordan in 1949, which involved granting citizenship to a number of Palestinians, both refugees driven from their

[35] See the American diplomatic despatches cited by Irene Gendzier in her extensive analysis of US policy in Lebanon, *Notes from the Minefield*.

[36] The best sources on Jordan's early years and the preponderant role of the military are Naseer Aruri, *Jordan: A Study in Political Development, 1921–1965* (The Hague, 1971); P.J. Vatikiotis, *Politics and the Military in Jordan: A Study of the Arab Legion, 1921–1957* (New York, 1957); and the indispensable memoir of the architect of the Arab Legion, Sir John Bagot Glubb, *A Soldier with the Arabs* (London, 1957).

homes elsewhere in Palestine and residents of the West Bank. It was a larger polity, with a more educated, urban, and politicized population than the Transjordanian citizenry had been. This larger country, now called Jordan, was a far different entity to rule over than the old one, with much more complex requirements. Many observers have concluded that the failure of King Abdullah to reckon with these changes was among the reasons for the increasing difficulties he faced during the last years of his rule.[37]

In this more politicized Jordan, operating in the super-charged atmosphere of the Middle East after the Palestine war of 1948, there was much more scope for dissatisfaction with the orientation of the country towards Britain. By the early 1950s there were deep political divisions within the polity, with important segments of the public alienated from the monarchy, its British backers, and the West generally. The disaffected element included many East Bankers from the towns and villages of the northern parts of Jordan, who were generally less involved in military service. This was by design of the British, with their penchant for recruiting the more "martial" and "virile" nomadic and tribal populations into their native auxiliary forces.[38] The settled populace thus benefited less from the large share of the budget which was devoted to the military than did the country's less settled population.[39] Moreover, these town-dwellers and village residents were much more likely than their nomadic compatriots to be educated, exposed to the press, and influenced by regional trends such as Arab nationalism. Nearby Damascus, a center for these trends, was also the traditional market and social hub for much of northern Jordan. Damascus thus exerted a constant influence on these areas.[40]

---

[37] On this subject see Mary Wilson, *King Abdullah, Britain and the Making of Jordan* (Cambridge, 1987); and Avi Shlaim, *Collusion Across the Jordan: King Abdullah, the Zionist Movement, and the Partition of Palestine* (New York:, 1988), especially Wilson, pp. 165–67.

[38] This British approach to divide and rule derived from their lengthy Indian colonial experience, which left British colonial officials with firm views on which "races" and tribes could be relied upon to serve them militarily. For the ideology behind this policy as it worked itself out in the African case, see Victor Kiernan, "Colonial Africa and Its Armies," pp. 77–96, in *Imperialism and Its Contradictions* (London, 1995).

[39] In 1937–38, security absorbed £P159,000 of a total Tranjordan budget of £P463,000; in 1941–42, when Britain paid for the costs of the Jordanian military due to the outbreak of World War II, the former item alone took £P470,000 of a total budget of £P828,000: "Police and Prisons" and "Transjordan Frontier Force," Economic Research Institute, Jewish Agency for Palestine, *Statistical Handbook of Middle Eastern Countries* (Jerusalem, 1945).

[40] This influence was a constant source of concern to the Jordanian authorities, who in the late 1940s imposed a fine of £100 on those caught listening to Syrian radio broadcasts: Wilson, *King Abdullah,* p. 165. As late as the 1990s, over 70 years after the border between

The Palestine issue served to complicate further the political equation in Jordan, whether among East Bankers or the country's new Palestinian citizens, who after 1948 formed a discontented majority of its population. Embittered by the traumatic experience of the loss of their country, this community would have been a formidable challenge for any government to absorb. It was a particularly daunting challenge for Jordan, however, since most Palestinians were deeply opposed to the country's Hashemite regime and to its British patrons, for historical reasons. To nationalist Palestinians, King Abdullah had constantly and faithfully served the interest of the British imperial power which had brought the Palestinian people nothing but grief from the issuance of the Balfour Declaration until the end of the Mandate. They saw him as having pursued his own narrow ambitions, aggrandizing his Emirate by the annexation of the Arab parts of Palestine, at the expense of an independent Palestinian national movement and in collusion with the Zionists as well as the British. As a result of recent scholarship, we now know that these perceptions were not in the least fanciful.[41] Moreover, the facts regarding Palestinian attitudes were not unknown to Western observers. As Ambassador Johnston accurately wrote:

> If offered a plebiscite on Jordan's future...the refugees would almost certainly have voted against the Hashemite Kingdom at any time since 1948. They have no feeling of loyalty to Jordan as such, nor is there anything more which the Jordan Government could have done to give them such a feeling. They are an undigested foreign body...The truth is that they were "dumped" on Jordan as a result of previous Western policies....[42]

Syria and Jordan had been established, an anthropologist working in the villages of the Irbid region observed the degree to which this region of north Jordan looked to Damascus as a center, rather than Amman. This was often true of marriage connections, land ownership and economic relations, and politics: Julie Peteet, personal communication with author, Chicago, October 1992.

[41] The work of Wilson, *King Abdullah*, and Shlaim, *Collusion*, as well as Ilan Pappé's *The Making of the Arab-Israeli Conflict* (London, 1992), is conclusive in this regard. Readers of Arabic knew several decades earlier much of what these Western and Israeli historians have demonstrated with recently available documentary evidence regarding this subject: it was revealed in the memoirs of Col. 'Abdullah Tal, *Karithat Filastin* [The Disaster of Palestine] (Cairo, 1959), who after loyally serving 'Abdullah and his grandson Husayn, fled to Cairo and published his revelations about the 1948 war and crucial aspects of Transjordan's relations with the British and the Israelis.

[42] Johnston to Foreign Office, telegram no. 1341, 18 August 1958, PREM 11/2381.

The Hashemite regime had resources to deal with this unfavorable situation vis-à-vis its new Palestinian subjects. These included the long-standing alignment of a number of Palestinian politicians with Abdullah against the dominant faction of the traditional Palestinian leadership. Men such as Ragheb al-Nashashibi and Muhammad Ali al-Ja'bari, who had welcomed Abdullah's aspirations to expand west of the Jordan in the partition plans of 1937 and 1947, gave the Hashemite regime a natural base of support among elements of the Palestinian notable classes. The regime was able to broaden this base on the West Bank, as it had in some parts of the East Bank, through strategic use of patronage: the perks of office, salaries, sinecures, and pensions. While these means had sufficed to ensure domestic tranquillity before the era of mass politics, however, they were of little use in the towns and cities of Jordan of the 1950s, where public opinion was a powerful force, not easily bought off by the monarchy.

Against this background, the British presence in Jordan was extensive. Until he was dismissed by King Hussein in 1956, General Sir John Bagot Glubb was the commander of the Arab Legion. Most of the senior officers were British. Britain's pervasive influence over Jordan grated on the sensibilities of many Jordanians. Not surprisingly, the strong nationalist response to the domination of Britain and the West among broad sectors of the Jordanian public proved fertile ground for anti-British propaganda originating in Cairo, Damascus, and Moscow. Egypt, its allies, and the Soviets directed more than propaganda against the Jordanian regime. They also offered support, material and otherwise, for the opposition parties, many of which were local branches of trans-national organizations directed from elsewhere, such as the Communists and the Baath. Nevertheless, these parties, as well as other purely Jordanian groups, represented a broad majority of indigenous public opinion. This was true even by the admission of British diplomats, although they nonetheless tended to label this opposition to their policies as "extremist," or "rabidly anti-British."[43]

Even after Glubb and other British officers had been dismissed in 1956, Britain, the United States, and their local allies affected events in Jordan by means of their influence on the monarchy, the political class, and the army, not to speak of the covert CIA payments to the King, which began in early 1957. The best example of this process was the climactic crisis of

---

43 The words are those of the British Ambassador to Jordan describing the largest party in the Jordanian Parliament elected in October 1956: Johnston to Lloyd, no. 26, 8 May 1957, FO 371/127880.

April 1957, a political watershed in Jordanian history. This crisis ended with the dismissal of the democratically elected and popular al-Nabulsi government on the murky pretext that an anti-monarchical coup was brewing, and the appointment of a new one described by a British diplomat as "frankly authoritarian."[44]

The new government was nominally headed by Ibrahim al-Hashim, whom the British Ambassador patronizingly called "an elderly and enfeebled old gentleman,"[45] but in fact veteran Palace retainer Samir al-Rifai ran the country, together with the King and his generals, and their British and American advisors.[46] Samir al-Rifai was such a familiar figure to British diplomats that he was occasionally referred to by his first name in despatches.[47] This surprising habit connoted a degree of familiarity which, while faintly condescending, indicates the closeness of the political relationship involved. Clearly, the British considered "Samir" their man.

In a despatch reporting the onset of the crisis which led to the change of government, the British Ambassador, Charles Johnston, revealed how the King was brought to act against a government which had a clear majority in Parliament and strong popular support. He reported:

> For some time the Queen Mother, King Saud and President Chamoun, assisted within the limits of our ability by my U.S. colleague and myself, had been warning His Majesty of the danger which communism represented to his country and to his throne.... I ventured in my first audience to illustrate the Communist menace to monarchies by speaking about King Michael of Rumania and his fate.[48]

Soon afterwards, the prompting of these foreign advisors, and allegations of a military plot against him, encouraged King Hussein to end Jordan's first democratic experiment, dismiss the elected government, and impose martial law through the pliable al-Hashim government.

Queen Zayn, the Queen Mother, did more than give the King advice in concert with the British and American Ambassadors, and the Lebanese

---

44 Johnston to Lloyd, no. 64, 6 November 1957, FO 371/127882. There are differing views of the role of the Western powers in this crisis, and of the real nature of the military plots against the King. For a pro-Hashemite view, see Uriel Dann, *King Hussein and the Challenge of Arab Radicalism: Jordan 1955–67* (New York, 1989), pp. 55–67.

45 Charles Johnston, in his annual report for 1956, cited in n. 13.

46 Johnston to Lloyd, no. 31, 29 May 1957, FO 371/127880.

47 E.g., see ibid.

48 Johnston to Lloyd, no. 26, 8 May 1957, FO 371/127880.

and Saudi leaders. The way in which she browbeat Jordanian politicians into accepting participation in the new government at a late night meeting at the Royal Palace, in spite of the highly questionable circumstances of its formation, could stand as a classic tale in the annals of neo-colonial monarchies:

> The Ministers had been reluctant to assume the responsibilities of office, and had asked the King why a military Government could not be formed.... The Queen Mother was present at these discussions and pointed out forcibly that a military Government would make any other form of Government unnecessary. Finally Her Majesty told the Ministers designate that they would not be allowed to leave the Palace until they had taken the oath of office, and it was on this not altogether encouraging basis that the new Government was eventually formed.[49]

This description by the British Ambassador would read like farce were it not for the far-reaching consequences of the dismissal of Nabulsi and the formation of the al-Hashim-al-Rifai government. Johnston's relief at this turn of events was palpable: "Now, only just in time, His Majesty had struck a blow at the forces of extremism.... Jordan felt a firm hand which it had not known since the days of King Abdullah."[50]

It is worth noting that of forty seats in the Jordanian Parliament elected in October 1956 which had brought Sulayman al-Nabulsi to power, "the pro-Communists received only five" by the count of the British Ambassador, and some of these were only Communists by a stretch of the British diplomatic imagination.[51] Thus the real "danger" to the traditional authoritarian Hashemite regime came from another quarter entirely, from the parliamentary elections which, Johnston acknowledged, "were the first approximately free ones in the history of Jordan."[52] He later freely admitted to the Foreign Secretary that "nobody believes that by-elections held under the present conditions [of martial law] will genuinely reflect popular feeling." He called the result "a rump Parliament reinforced by rigged

49 Johnston to Lloyd, no. 31, 29 May 1957, FO 371/127880

50 Ibid.

51 Ibid. In fact, only two of the five, Fa'iq al-Warrad and Dr. Ya'qub al-Zayadin, were Party members, one was close to the Party, and the other two were members of groups which had joined together with it in the National Front: Hanna Batatu, *The Old Social Classes and the Revolutionary Movements of Iraq: A Study of Iraq's Old Landed and Commercial Classes and of Its Communists, Ba'thists and Free Officers* (Princeton, NJ, 1978), p. 758, n. 1.

52 Johnston to Lloyd, no. 26, 8 May 1957, FO 371/127880.

by-elections."[53] Nevertheless, the same British diplomat stated dismissively that "The short and wild career of the Nabulsi Government presents a disheartening spectacle to those who would like if they could to take an optimistic view of human, and Arab, nature."[54]

Such expressions of contempt for officials of the country to which he was accredited, and for its constitutional processes, were common in Johnston's despatches, and those of other British diplomats of this era. He reported in November 1957: "[members of] the present Government...are...simply a rather average lot of Arab politicians, with all the normal predatory and fratricidal instincts." He remarked of one minister that he was "no less corrupt than the average," and noted that "Six months of office have produced their inevitable results on an Arab government. Corruption and nepotism have flourished and personal rivalries...have produced obvious cracks in the regime."[55] The reasons which Johnston gave for the failures of the Nabulsi government were simple, and marked by the subtle racism so common in much of this reportage:

> These attempts at statesmanship proved too much of a strain for Nabulsi and his colleagues. In their last month of office...demagogy took charge and the Gadarene slope ahead became all too plain to the observer. It was clear that owing to the venality and irresponsibility of their elected representatives, the Jordanians were not qualified to run their own affairs in the face of Egyptian, Syrian and Soviet subversion, and that for the moment at least the country's best hope of salvation lay in a return to the Hashemite paternalism of King Abdullah.[56]

This same system of "a firm hand" was still in force in Jordan in July 1958, when its weaknesses were revealed by the need to bring in British troops out of fear that without them, the Western-oriented "Hashemite paternalism" in Jordan might go the way of that of Iraq.

---

[53] Johnston to Lloyd, no. 64, 6 November 1957, FO 371/127882.

[54] Johnston to Lloyd, no. 26, 8 May 1957, FO 371/127880.

[55] Johnston to Lloyd, no. 64, 6 November 1957, FO 371/127882.

[56] Johnston to Lloyd, no. 26, 8 May 1957, FO 371/127880. Johnston did not see fit to revise these words. They were repeated almost verbatim fifteen years later in his memoir, *Brink of Jordan*, p. 66.

IV

In view of what we now know about modern Iraqi history, there can be little question that the revolutionary upheaval which shook the country in July 1958 was driven almost entirely by powerful social and political forces internal to Iraqi society.[57] The monarchy and its supporters, as well as many British and American observers, claimed that the Soviet Union and Egypt (the United Arab Republic, or UAR, after that country's February 1958 union with Syria) were the instigators of unrest in Iraq in the years leading up to the revolution. Such analyses in effect denied independent agency to these powers' respective local surrogates, the Iraqi Communist Party, Iraqi Nasserists and Baathists, and to the Iraqi people themselves. While the Soviet Union and Egypt strongly opposed Iraqi policies such as support for the Baghdad Pact and the Eisenhower Doctrine, it is an exaggeration to say that they incited the domestic Iraqi opposition to the Hashemite regime, led by the unpopular Nuri al-Said and the Regent, Abdel Illah.

The Iraqi Free Officers who carried out the coup against the monarchy were indeed inspired by the Egyptian example, as their name, modeled on that of the Egyptian Free Officers, attests. They had in fact tried to contact Egypt's President Nasser through the Chief of Syrian Military Intelligence, Colonel Abdel Hamid Sarraj,[58] but he had not taken them seriously, and told their emissaries to return after they had successfully overthrown the monarchy. According to Muhammad Haikal, Nasser's close confidant, the two emissaries were Brigadier Abdel Karim Qasim and Colonel Abdel Salam Aref, the group's two most prominent leaders, and both future rulers of Iraq.[59] According to another version reported by Hanna Batatu, contacts with Egypt before the revolution took place through the intermediary of the Iraqi nationalist politician Seddeq Shanshal, who visited Cairo in February 1958.[60] Irrespective of which ver-

[57] See in particular Hanna Batatu, *The Old Social Classes*, pp. 709 ff.; Marion Farouk Sluglett and Peter Sluglett, *Iraq since 1958: From Revolution to Dictatorship* (London, 1987); and Robert Fernea and Wm. Roger Louis, eds., *The Iraqi Revolution of 1958: The Old Social Classes Revisited* (London, 1991).

[58] He later became Minister of the Interior of the Syrian Region of the UAR, and ultimately UAR Vice President.

[59] Muhammad Haikal, *Nasser: The Cairo Documents: The Private Papers of Nasser* (London, 1972), p. 126.

[60] *The Old Social Classes*, p. 795.

sion is correct, what clearly emerges from both accounts is that the Iraqi Free Officers were determined to go ahead with the coup, and were not in any sense acting at the behest of the Egyptians.[61]

As for the Iraqi branch of the Baath Party, it played only a very small role in the 1958 revolution, and had always been largely independent of the Baath Party headquartered in Damascus. The party in any case was formally dissolved early in 1958, and was ignored by the Egyptian leaders who controlled the UAR.[62] The Iraqi Communist Party was clearly influenced by the Soviet Union, as is indicated by its otherwise inexplicable and highly unpopular endorsement in June 1948 of the Soviet position in favor of the partition of Palestine.[63] But it was certainly not controlled by Moscow, and its leadership was often completely out of touch for lengthy periods with representatives of the Soviet Union and other Arab Communist parties.[64] These and other Iraqi parties were essentially responding to Iraqi events and reflected the Iraqi social strata from which they were drawn. The external links of both the Baath and the Communists were at times a source of strength, but also a source of vulnerability, opening them to the accusation of being pawns of external powers.

Two other points are important to stress in this regard. The first is the fact that although what took place in Baghdad in July 1958 was a military coup, it was one which met with enthusiastic popular support once it had taken place. The Iraqi regime was deeply unpopular with broad sections of the public, at least those whose attitudes we can assess. Contrary to British and American observers' assertions that the opposition represented only a few isolated extremists, it was the supporters of the regime and the British connection who were almost totally isolated in Iraqi society, and the gov-

[61] Typically, Copeland, *The Game of Nations*, p. 175, claims that "they almost certainly would not have launched their coup without Egyptian encouragement and assurances," a statement for which there is little evidence, and indeed much to contradict it. It was not only American observers who entertained mistaken ideas as to Egyptian influence over the architects of the coup: Soviet Premier Nikita Khrushchev was reported by Haikal as telling 'Abd al-Nasir in Moscow three days after the coup: "They are your men in Iraq": *Nasser, The Cairo Documents*, p. 126.

[62] This is summed up by Malcolm Kerr, who covers this topic brilliantly in *The Arab Cold War: Gamal 'Abd al-Nasir and his Rivals, 1958–1970* (Oxford, 1971), pp. 7–16, with the words: "The Ba'th had expected Nasir to sense a need for their services, whereas in fact, rightly or wrongly, he did not."

[63] Batatu, *Old Social Classes*, pp. 597–603. It nevertheless took the Iraqi Communists from November 1947, when the USSR surprised its supporters by shifting to a position of support for partition, until mid-1948, to swallow this unpalatable idea.

[64] Ibid., pp. 574–596 includes a detailed discussion of this question.

ernment's overthrow met with great public approval. The acknowledged authority on the subject, Hanna Batatu, is unequivocal on this matter. He gives a "conservative estimate" of the revolutionary crowds which came out to support the military coup on the morning of July 14, 1958, as numbering "at least one hundred thousand people in Baghdad alone." He adds that these crowds "must have had a greater weight in determining the historical outcome of that fateful day than one may at first glance be disposed to admit."[65] Batatu is scornful of the dismissive comments made in the memoirs of the American Ambassador, Waldemar Gallman, who called the demonstrations "not representative." This remark, in fact, came from the same observer who had called the 1954 Iraqi Parliament, whose election he acknowledged was rigged by Nuri al-Said, "a fairly representative group."[66]

The second point worth stressing is the diversity among the opponents of the regime, which was mirrored in the composition of the Free Officers. This diversity, hardly reflected in the early reporting on the Iraqi revolution by outsiders, is one of the most striking features of Iraqi, and indeed of Arab, politics during this period. It was illustrated soon after the revolution, when the victorious anti-regime coalition composed of Nasserists, Baathists, Communists, and Iraqi nationalists fell apart at the seams. The divisions between these political forces, during the five years of Qasim's rule and afterwards, had a huge and enduring impact on the course of relations between Egypt and the Soviet Union; between those powers and Iraq; and between those powers and much of the Arab world.[67]

For some Western observers, all of these forces in Iraq before July 1958 were opposed not only to the existing regime but to the West itself, as were the opposition movements in Lebanon and Jordan. Moreover, the Egyptian and other Arab regimes which grew out of the revolutions of the 1950s and 1960s were all non-aligned in the broadest sense, and were generally unwilling to follow American policy leads. And all established relations with the Soviet Union, which extended arms and economic aid to them. By these indices, and these alone, all could be placed into a single

---

[65] Ibid., p. 805.

[66] Gallman, *Iraq under General Nuri*, pp. 6–7.

[67] Chapters 41–59 of Batatu, *Old Social Classes*, and Kerr, *The Arab Cold War*, are particularly illuminating on these differences within Iraq and their broader ramifications. See also Malik Mufti, *Sovereign Creations: Pan-Arabism and Political Order in Syria and Iraq* (Ithaca, NY, 1996), which underlines the elements of American-British rivalry which were implicit in the conflict between Nasser and Qasim.

analytical category. But the differences between the Qasim and Nasser regimes grew into perhaps the most savage inter-Arab conflict of the modern era, severely straining Soviet-Egyptian relations. The simplistic approach of many Western observers and their preconceived notions of Arab politics could not explain such phenomena. Nor could they account for the peaceful resolution of the Lebanese crisis through Egyptian-American collaboration in the wake of the American intervention. Whether in Lebanon, Jordan, or Iraq, reality was clearly more complex and less susceptible to reduction into the black-and-white categories of analysis employed in London and Washington at the height of the Cold War.

The question of why the diversity of the Arab polities escaped the notice of Western observers of the region is impossible to answer conclusively. It made possible, however, far-fetched depictions of Nasserism and Communism working hand-in-glove, and Egypt and the Soviet Union collaborating in subversion. We now know that much of the time nothing could have been further from the truth. But such a view produced British analyses such as the following, which described the apocalyptic consequences of following American advice in Jordanian affairs: "The result would be not only that Jordan would promptly join the UAR, but that its accession would give the whole UAR a sharp twist to the left and indeed might replace Cairo's influence by Moscow's throughout Greater Syria. [It] would, in my view, lead straight to the establishment of Communist control over the Levant."[68]

While such hyperbolic comments could frequently be found in Western despatches from the region and in the pronouncements of policy-makers like John Foster Dulles, over time realism and pragmatism appeared in some Western analyses. By the end of the 1950s, for example, British diplomatic observers had developed a nuanced view of the Qasim regime. They came to understand the delicate balance which the Iraqi leader had to maintain between the country's fiercely competing political forces, although they continued to demonize the Egyptian regime, seeing it as working with the Soviets. American observers, by contrast, especially those in the region or involved with intelligence, realized that the Nasser regime had major differences with the Soviet Union and with Iraq under Qasim. Unlike his Iraqi counterpart, the Egyptian leader firmly suppressed

68 Johnston to Foreign Office, no. 1341, telegram, 18 August 1958, PRO, PREM 11/2381.

local Communists, banning the Communist party both in Egypt and in Syria. Americans thus came to perceive Egypt under Nasser as the main regional bulwark against Communism, returning to the initial view of many Americans involved in policy-making just before and after the 1952 revolution. At the same time, they perceived Qasim as a stooge of the large and powerful Iraqi Communist Party.[69]

In the case of the British, this evolution certainly had to do with the extremely friendly attitude which the new Iraqi regime took towards British oil interests. For example, it dropped the insistence on revisions in the fifty-fifty profit-sharing arrangement which the Nuri al-Said government had urged before its overthrow. The change was related as well to the fact that Egypt under Nasser was seen in London as an old and hated antagonist whose regional interests were opposed to those of Britain. By contrast, the Qasim government, although it had overthrown a British client regime and murdered several of its faithful servants, had limited regional ambitions, and indeed dropped the old Iraqi claim to Kuwait which Nuri al-Said had revived just before his death.[70]

On the American side, a continuing obsession with Soviet influence, which Nasser seemed at times to further, did not blind policy-makers to the fact that "the prevention of further Soviet penetration of the Near East...depends on the degree to which the United States is able to work more closely with Arab nationalism" in the words of a National Security Council report in November 1958.[71] Since American officials closely identified Arab nationalism with Nasser, an alignment with him was advisable despite the objectionable policies of his regime, and became a feature of American policy for several years after 1958.[72] The increasingly weak Qasim regime, largely dependent on the Iraqi Communist Party for popular sup-

---

[69] See Mufti, *Sovereign Creations*, pp. 117–120, 129–132. See also Fawaz A. Gerges, *The Superpowers and the Middle East: Regional and International Politics, 1955–1967* (Boulder, CO, 1994).

[70] Johnston, *Brink of Jordan*, p. 98, reports Nuri al-Said's diatribe on the subject at a joint session with King Hussein in Amman in June 1958. Qasim made the fatal mistake of reviving the Iraqi claim to Kuwait in 1961, compromising the heretofore consistent support he had enjoyed from Britain, provoking the formation of a formidable regional coalition against him, and setting the stage for the humiliation of his regime when he had to back down.

[71] "NSC 5820/1: U.S. Policy toward the Near East," 4 November 1958, US Diplomatic Documents, 1980, 386B, pp. 2,10, cited in Mufti, *Sovereign Creations*, p. 130.

[72] For a book based on the proceedings of a Council on Foreign Relations study group which met in 1960–61 and which captures this American orientation, see Charles D. Cremeans, *The Arabs and the World: Nasser's Arab Nationalist Policy* (New York, 1963).

port, and perceived as a Soviet pawn, benefited from no such charitable interpretations of its actions or potential in Washington. As a result, until its bloody collapse, it remained the object of unremitting American hostility.

V

In view of the pan-Arab fervor they demonstrated, it is ironic that the Iraqi revolution of July 1958, the Syrian-Egyptian union of February 1958, and the crises of that year in Lebanon and Jordan did not result in any lasting movement towards Arab unity. To understand this paradoxical outcome, we must know what pan-Arabism meant in the context of the domestic policies of each specific country concerned, and what it meant in the Egyptian context in particular. In fact, pan-Arabism frequently was all things to all men. Among Palestinians in Jordan, for example, the unification of Egypt and Syria meant a potential resolution of their problems resulting from the creation of Israel and their expulsion from their homeland in 1948. A British report from Jerusalem illustrates this, contrasting the apathy of Jerusalemites at the proclamation of a federation between Iraq and Jordan in February with their hearty support for the idea of union with the UAR. This was entirely for reasons having to do with the Palestinian conflict with Israel rather than the dogma of pan-Arabism.[73] Similarly, in Lebanon, Syria, and Iraq, support for Nasser and Arab nationalism was largely utilitarian, and a function of each country's internal politics.[74]

Pan-Arabism can be shown to have operated in this instrumental way in Egypt, with the difference that Egypt was a major player in the rest of the region, and Egyptian domestic politics were considerably more stable than those of any of the other countries we have examined. While Western diplomatic reports and memoirs by Egyptian and foreign statesmen, diplomats, and intelligence officers can help explain the role of pan-Arabism in Egyptian foreign policy, they are much less useful in showing its domestic aspect. For this, it is necessary to examine the Egyptian press, which provides a rich source for understanding what pan-Arabism meant in practical terms to the Nasser regime.

[73] Charles Stewart to E.M. Rose, 19 February 1958, FO 371/134025.

[74] Mufti, *Sovereign Creations*, Kerr, *The Arab Cold War*, and Seale, *The Struggle for Syria*, all illustrate different aspects of the way in which this process worked.

The front page of the leading Cairo daily, *al-Ahram,* edited by Nasser's close friend and advisor, Mohammed Heikal, was a mirror of the outlook and concerns of the Egyptian government, particularly in regard to domestic politics. Its article on the Iraqi elections organized by the Nuri al-Said regime in May 1958 is framed by a banner headline which stresses that the Iraqi people are opposed to their beleaguered government. Egypt, on the other hand, is depicted in headlines on the same page as progressing from triumph to triumph, as President Nasser continued a successful trip to the Soviet Union.[75] Its conclusion is summed up by a huge two-word headline, "Intasarat siyasatuna" (Our Policy Has Triumphed), and sub-heads proclaiming that all countries, including the United States, have recognized Egypt's neutrality and value its friendship, and that "the whole world regards our people with respect, admiration and esteem."[76] The message is clear: Egypt's regime has restored international respect for the Egyptian people, after years of international humiliation.

In other cases, more subtle messages are being transmitted to readers of *al-Ahram.* A front page story on the outbreak of civil war in Lebanon in May 1958 features a photograph of an insurrectionary street scene in which can be discerned a large poster of a smiling Nasser. This is presumably meant to show that, even in far-away Lebanon, "the people" revere Egypt's leader.[77] In the period leading up to the Iraqi revolution and the Anglo-American interventions in Jordan and Lebanon, there are frequent stories and headlines illustrating the concatenation of forces opposing Egypt's pan-Arab policies. "Nuri al-Said Leads the Battle in Lebanon" reads one headline, while another speaks darkly of "A Baghdad-Amman-Beirut-Tel Aviv Axis"; both front pages refer to the possibilities of Anglo-American intervention in Lebanon.[78] Western intervention is a constant theme in the following weeks.[79]

When the Iraqi revolution finally broke out, under the bold headline "Revolution in Iraq," *al-Ahram* stressed familiar themes of Egyptian pan-Arab leadership and Western opposition in its sub-headlines. One declared that the new Iraqi government's first decisions were to recognize the

---

[75] *al-Ahram*, 6 May 1958.

[76] *al-Ahram*, 17 May 1958.

[77] *al-Ahram*, 18 May 1958. The same people were now in control: "The people have established a local government in Tripoli," a sub-headline on the same page reads.

[78] *al-Ahram*, 8 June 1958, 10 June 1958.

[79] E.g. "Dulles States: America Will Send Forces to Lebanon If This Is the Only Solution!" *al-Ahram*, 2 July 1958, p. 1.

UAR, affirm Arab unity, and respect the Bandung non-aligned principles. Another screamed: "London: The Revolution a Mortal Blow to the Eisenhower Plan and the Baghdad Pact; Washington: The Revolution is the most Dangerous Blow to the West since the Suez Canal Nationalization."[80] The Iraqi revolution, in other words, validated the policy choices of the Egyptian leadership, and reaffirmed the centrality of Egypt in the Arab world as well as in the world at large. These were potent messages for Egyptian readers, but it is worth noting that notwithstanding their apparent radicalism, they were essentially conservative, confirming and legitimizing the internal Egyptian status quo.

In the end, this chapter must ask a basic question: to what extent were the events occurring in the Arab world in 1958 truly revolutionary? In Lebanon, prosperous establishment politicians challenged others of the same class, aided and abetted on both sides by ideological parties which at no stage were able to dictate the course of events. There was popular involvement, but ultimately events in 1958 produced a new government but not a change of regime, a shift in orientation in keeping with the National Pact, but no revision of the Pact itself. It was left to a later civil war in Lebanon to challenge the fundamental basis of the Lebanese system, a challenge which was ultimately repulsed, notwithstanding massive levels of external intervention. These levels make Chamoun's charges of foreign interference in Lebanon in 1958 seem derisory.

In Jordan, what was at issue was the alignment of Jordan with Britain and the West, and the institution of a constitutional monarchy, not the fundamental nature of the regime. The fact that both challenges were turned back, leaving Jordan under authoritarian Hashemite rule and aligned with the United States, obscures the fact that Sulayman al-Nabulsi and his allies, who won the largest number of seats in the parliament elected in 1956, were basically traditional politicians.[81] This was true even though they were more consistent nationalists than had ever been allowed into previous Jordanian governments. The idea of a republic in Jordan, or of a fundamental restructuring of the country's social relations, was never part of their government's program, although it may have figured in the aspirations of some of their supporters.

---

[80] *al-Ahram*, 15 July 1958.

[81] Batatu, *Old Social Classes*, p. 758, notes that al-Nabulsi's National Socialists got 72,000 votes, or 19% of the vote, the Communists and their allies 51,000, or 12.7%, and the Baath 34,000 or 8%.

It was in Iraq that the changes which took place in 1958 most closely approximate a real revolution, in the sense of fundamental change and profound social transformation. But even there, what was in question in 1958 was the existence of a regime established by the hated colonial power, and it was only on this question that there was unanimity among the Iraqi opposition. The collapse of the apparently unified opposition into the political factionalism which thereafter characterized Iraqi politics reveals the true state of affairs. And although there was a change of regime in Iraq, and a major shift in the country's external orientation, as well as important social changes thereafter, these reforms went no further than those undertaken in Egypt and Syria during this period. From the vantage point of several decades, these appear to be relatively limited gains.

This raises the final question of whether what was happening in the Arab world in the years leading up to and following 1958 was in fact only seen as threatening by Western observers because of its geopolitical implications. In other words, was the fact that the Soviet Union appeared to benefit from these events the main reason they were viewed with such alarm by American and British observers, or was it a more prosaic set of challenges to Western business, personal, and other interests which was at work? US policy-makers, at least, were preoccupied with the activities of the Soviet Union, and often paid little attention to local factors except insofar as they were relevant to Soviet influence. Now that the Cold War is over and the Soviet Union is no longer with us, there is perhaps hope for deeper understanding of events in this region today. Or perhaps a new bogey-man will take Moscow's place, manipulated by those with interests in the Middle East to scare the public into supporting their course of action.

6

The Pan-Arab Movement and the Influence of Cairo and Moscow

PETER SLUGLETT

This chapter is an attempt to set in context the part played by Nasser's Egypt and the Soviet Union in the Iraqi revolution of 1958, and, more generally, in the region as a whole. On 14 July, the Iraqi military staged a classic coup in which the commanders of a number of disaffected units took advantage of a combination of favorable circumstances to capture various key military and civilian installations and imprisoned or executed leading members of the *ancien regime*.[1] Given the suddenness of events, there was no direct involvement on the part of either Egypt or the Soviet Union. At least by implication, however, it was clear that the two countries would welcome a change of regime in Baghdad which would probably tilt Iraq in the direction of greater sympathy towards "Arabism," "positive neutralism," or perhaps both. Indeed some general assurances of Egyptian and Soviet support had apparently been given in February 1958.[2] Both Egypt and the

[1] See Hanna Batatu, *The Old Social Classes and the Revolutionary Movements of Iraq; a Study of Iraq's Old Landed Classes and Its Communists, Ba'thists and Free Officers* (Princeton, NJ, 1978), pp. 800–807; Uriel Dann, *Iraq under Qassem: A Political History* (London, 1969), pp. 28–32.

[2] Seddiq Shanshal of the Hizb al-Istiqlal met Nasser in Cairo in February 1958 on behalf of the Front of National Union "and received definite assurances from him that the United Arab Republic would back the revolution without reserve." Shanshal was apparently given a similar pledge by the Soviet ambassador to Egypt. It is difficult to imagine what cash value either of these promises may have had, or their effect upon Shanshal and his colleagues. See Batatu, *Old Social Classes*, p. 795.

Soviet Union had exercised important influence on Iraqi politics since the early 1950s, developments which had been viewed with increasing alarm both by the old guard in Iraq and by Western diplomats. Given the geopolitical realities of the day, however, it is hard to imagine that anything more concrete was, or could have been, involved.

The Beginnings of Soviet Interest in the Middle East

The Soviet Union had only very limited interests in the "Third World" in the immediate post-war years, 1945–1953.[3] Under Khrushchev, however, a new policy was adopted beginning in 1955, under which the Soviet Union sought to extend its influence in the political and economic sphere in the Third World, particularly in the Middle East, where a series of alliances and defensive arrangements had resulted in the Soviets' virtual encirclement on their southwestern border by Western missiles. The Soviets reacted to developments in the Middle East in the belief that they could not "remain indifferent to events creating a grave menace in an area adjacent to [their] frontiers...."[4]

Greater Soviet activism in the region was also encouraged by the apparently relentless forward march of decolonization, and by the general deterioration of relations between the West and much of the Arab world after the creation of Israel in 1948.[5] As far as Britain and France were concerned, relations with Egypt had deteriorated further as a result of Nasser's seizure of power in 1952–1953 and of his government's opposition to the Baghdad Pact in 1954–1955.

The fortuitous coincidence of Egypt's reorientation with the major changes in Soviet foreign policy under Khrushchev culminated most visibly in the Czech arms deal of September 1955, which itself took place partly as a reaction against the United States' refusal to supply arms to Egypt. The Czech arms deal also took place in the wake of an audacious Israeli raid on Gaza a few months earlier and against the background of

---

[3] Oles Smolansky, *The Soviet Union and the Arab East under Khrushchev* (Cranbury, NJ, 1974), especially pp. 15–122.

[4] See the chapter by Carol R. Saivetz, which quotes a statement from Tass reported in the *New York Times* of 17 July 1958. It is worth stressing this point, particularly in view of Turkey's membership of NATO and the very close relations between Iran and the West until 1979. The US-Cuba parallel is also obvious.

[5] See the chapter by Michael Graham Fry.

the formulation of the doctrine of positive neutralism symbolized by the Bandung conference of April-May 1955. Various economic and cultural agreements preceded or followed the arms deal, which was a further trigger for the worsening of Egypt's relations with the European colonial powers.

At the end of July 1956, following Egypt's recognition of mainland China, Britain and the United States announced that they were no longer prepared to assist in the financing of the Aswan Dam, a project long regarded as essential to Egypt's future economic development. Nasser riposted a few days later by nationalizing the Suez Canal, declaring that the revenues from it would be used to pay for the construction of the dam. In retaliation, Britain, France, and Israel initiated military action against Egypt in October and early November.

The Baghdad Pact, Suez, and Iraq

The far-reaching consequences of the extraordinarily foolhardy Suez operation caused sea changes in the internal and international politics of the region, and, to a large extent, of world international relations, which have been amply described elsewhere.[6] As far as Iraq was concerned, Suez was particularly damaging for the credibility of a regime whose continuing close association with Britain had already brought it considerable obloquy. The violence surrounding efforts to renegotiate the Anglo-Iraqi Treaty of Alliance with Britain early in 1948, followed by the Arab defeat in Palestine a few months later, had been major causes of the government's unpopularity. This was compounded by the Baghdad Pact, which pushed the regime even further into the arms of the West at a time when public opinion in Iraq was very much influenced by the essentially anti-Western actions and attitudes of Egypt and the Soviet Union.

Hence, Suez and its aftermath, and the enormous and growing prestige which Nasser enjoyed for the rest of the 1950s, helped to create a situation in which dissatisfaction with the Baghdad government rose to unprecedented heights. Put simply, the question was not if, but when, it was likely to fall, since the passage of time served only to increase its isolation. The situation is well described by an official of the British Council,

---

[6] See the relevant chapters in Wm. Roger Louis and Roger Owen, eds., *Suez 1956 : The Crisis and Its Consequences* (Oxford, 1989).

writing under the pseudonym "Caractacus."[7] Caractacus was a rather more acute observer than the British Ambassador, Sir Michael Wright, who was still sending reassuring despatches to London as late as April 1958.[8] Probably because of the rather limited milieu in which he moved, Wright seems to have taken the affluent lifestyle of upper-class Baghdadis and the generally sensible but long-term schemes for economic development being put in place by the Development Board as indications of a level of satisfaction and contentment which bore little relation to reality. An almost willful blindness to the genuine concerns of local and regional opposition politicians characterized British and American diplomatic despatches from Amman, Baghdad, Beirut, Cairo, and Damascus for most of the period under consideration, as did an almost axiomatic belief in the ubiquity of the evil machinations of Cairo and Moscow and of their local supporters and sympathizers.[9]

Politics in Iraq—beyond the debate of the officially permitted political parties—was dominated by the desire to attain two objectives: independence from Britain, and the establishment of a generally statist or interventionist model of economic development which would pursue such goals as land reform, industrialization, and some degree of economic autarky.[10] Of course, more defined ideologies, including Nasserist pan-Arabism, Baathist Arab Socialism, and, though it was imperfectly understood, Communism, were influential, but it is sensible to resist the temptation to categorize the trends too sharply. This is the case especially since information gathered by police informers is so scanty about groups other than the Communists, and the informers were not above telling their employers exactly what they wanted to hear. As in many situations of long-standing political discontent under authoritarian regimes—one has only to think of the situation in Eastern Europe in the late 1980s—there was a general con-

---

[7] Caractacus [Norman Daniel], *Revolution in Iraq: An Essay in Comparative Public Opinion* (London, 1959).

[8] See Wm. Roger Louis, "The British and the Origins of the Iraqi Revolution," in Robert A. Fernea and Wm. Roger Louis, eds., *The Iraqi Revolution of 1958 : The Old Social Classes Revisited* (London, 1991), pp. 31–61.

[9] See the chapter by Rashid Khalidi. Khalidi also manages to capture the widespread belief among Western intelligence agencies and operatives of the period that covert activity undertaken by "our side"—ballot-rigging, disseminating false information—was perfectly legitimate, whether or not there was any evidence of actual or intended subversion on the part of the opposition.

[10] See Marion Farouk-Sluglett and Peter Sluglett, *Iraq since 1958: From Revolution to Dictatorship,* 3rd ed. (London, 2001), pp. 35–45.

sensus on what was *not* wanted (the continuation of the regime), and some consensus on what was wanted (independence and social justice), but, almost inevitably, little consensus on how this might be achieved. For the time being, however, the main parties and unofficial political coalitions were prepared to sink their differences and, for electoral purposes, formed "Fronts of National Union" in 1954 and 1957.[11] At this stage, the inherent contradictions between pan-Arabism and socialism or Communism do not seem to have been widely apparent in Iraq outside relatively small circles of committed intellectuals.

The Appeal of Nasserist Pan-Arabism in Iraq

The phenomenon of pan-Arabism had relatively little echo in Iraq, compared with other Arab states. In this context "pan-Arabism" means the notion that the regeneration of the Arab world can only occur through taking steps to create a united or unified Arab state from the Atlantic to the Gulf, though opinions differ on the precise form such a political entity might take. Through Arab unity, the Arab world would revert to the allegedly natural order of things which had been distorted, first by four centuries of Ottoman rule and second by the European colonial division of the region in the years after 1918.

This particular invention of tradition was especially, though not only, appealing to Sunni Muslim and Orthodox Christian Arabs. Roughly half the population of Iraq is Shia Arab, and between a fifth and a quarter is Kurdish; at various times since the creation of modern Iraq in 1920, both Shias and Kurds had implicitly or explicitly resisted what they regarded as built-in Sunni Arab dominance and discrimination within the Iraqi state structure. Thus they were unlikely to be seduced by an ideology which would make them a tiny minority in an overwhelmingly Sunni Arab mega-state.[12]

On the other hand—and this is why definitions are best kept loose—there is no doubt that the appeal of Nasser throughout the Middle East,

---

[11] There was no Nasserist "party" in Iraq. In Egypt, political parties had been abolished in 1953, and the official one-party national rally, the Arab Socialist Union, was created only after the secession of Syria from the United Arab Republic in 1961.

[12] See Farouk-Sluglett and Sluglett, *Iraq since 1958*, pp. 1–45, and, by the same authors, "The Historiography of Modern Iraq," *American Historical Review* 96, 5 (1991), pp. 1408–1421.

even in Iran, was almost irresistible, especially after the Suez crisis. Nasser had succeeded in challenging the West, in part because of the realignment of forces in the West. When the Americans opposed traditional gun-boat diplomacy in the Middle East, Britain and France were forced into what could only be described as an ignominious defeat in November 1956, and Nasser emerged as the man of the hour. It is a sad comment on the warping of values and the sheer desperation of ordinary people in the Middle East in 1990–91, more than thirty years after these events, that the actions of a vicious mass murderer, Saddam Hussein, in invading Kuwait, should awaken delirious enthusiasm for much the same reason, his apparent defiance of the West in the name of the Arab world.

Nasser's appeal was based more on his youth, his defeat of Britain and France, and his personal magnetism than on pan-Arab ideology. If examined in detail by some of his Iraqi admirers, that ideology may well have raised awkward questions.[13] With hindsight, given the nature and course of the dictatorships which subsequently came into existence in Iraq, Libya, and Syria, the era which the Egyptian revolution in some sense ushered in seems infinitely more dreadful than anything which preceded it.

For all his talk of Arab unity, Nasser seems to have been quite cautious about extending himself in any formal sense across the Middle East. The much-vaunted union with Syria, certainly in the form which it took in February 1958, was far more a Syrian Baathist-inspired creation than an Egyptian one. The United Arab Republic (UAR) would have been inconceivable had Akram al-Hawrani and Salah al-Din Bitar not realized late in 1957 that they would not, at least in the climate of the day, be able to gain power through the electoral process, and focused on the Egyptian connection in order to save themselves politically and to avoid what seemed their almost inevitable eclipse by the Communists.[14]

Though it is difficult to speculate on Nasser's understanding of the situation in Iraq before July 1958, and thus the extent to which he might have wished a newly-oriented Iraq to join the UAR, it is also clear that he was unprepared for the Iraqi revolution and was anxious to see what line

[13] See Marlène Nasr, "L'univers national arabe nasserien," in Dominique Chevallier, ed., *Renouvellements du Monde Arabe 1952–1982* (Paris, 1987), pp. 17–46, which contains a number of extracts from Nasser's writings and addresses.

[14] See Malik Mufti, *Sovereign Creations: Pan-Arabism and Political Order in Syria and Iraq* (Ithaca, 1996).

Moscow would take before committing himself to anything.[15] Again, almost all the pressure for Iraq to join the UAR after the July revolution came from the Iraqi side, from Abdel Salam Aref and the Baath asserting themselves against Abdel Karim Qasim and the Communists, rather than from Cairo.

Communism, the Soviet Union, and the Arab States

To many ordinary people in the Middle East in the 1950s, and of course to many intellectuals, the apparent achievements of the Soviet Union exemplified economic and social progress and aspirations towards a better life. For some intellectuals, the Marxist-Leninist analysis of capitalism and imperialism and the revolutionary imperative of Communism provided both a convincing description of the present and an attractive prescription for the future.[16] In Iraq, a potentially prosperous country where average life expectancy in 1953 still hovered around 38 years, the appeal was probably more practical than theoretical, and reflected widespread disillusionment in the face of an oligarchic regime composed of rich landowners and corrupt pro-British politicians.[17] The excesses of Stalinism could be dismissed as Western propaganda, and the prospect of a regime that offered the possibility of economic and social development without political liberty seemed preferable to one that apparently offered neither.

The fear of the potentially dangerous combination of "Arab-Nationalism-and-Communism" looms large in the Western diplomatic despatches of the period. Here again, there is a significant gap between perception and reality. While it is quite clear that the governments of Iraq and Jordan in many ways owed their continued existence to the British government, and that Camille Chamoun and his supporters were funded by the United States, the relations between Egypt and the Soviet Union were of a very different order. Egypt was not, and could not be, another satellite such as the German Democratic Republic or Bulgaria, although this prospect seems to be an underlying assumption of a classic Cold War

[15] See the chapter by Carol R. Saivetz.

[16] On a more mundane level, only a handful of Iraqis in the 1950s would have had the slightest idea of the realities of life in the Soviet Union; the enrollment of relatively large numbers of Iraqi students in Soviet and Eastern Europe was a phenomenon of the 1960s and 1970s.

[17] According to Professor Michael Critchley, quoted in Rony Gabbay, *Communism and Agrarian Reform in Iraq* (London, 1978), p. 29.

study like Walter Laqueur's *The Soviet Union and the Middle East*, which first appeared in 1959.[18]

Although more obviously characteristic of Nasser's middle years than of those immediately after the Egyptian revolution, relations between the Egyptian Communists and the post-revolutionary nationalist regime were, to say the least, far from cordial.[19] The intense antagonism harbored by Arab nationalists against Communists (at least when the former were in power), which reached its temporary apogee in the Iraqi Baathist-nationalist massacre of Communists following the counter-revolution of February 1963, demonstrated, perhaps more clearly than anything else, the complex nature of the links between the Soviet Union and its Arab allies. The fact that first Egypt, and subsequently Syria and Iraq, became dependent on the acquisition of Soviet arms "purchases" for much of their basic weaponry did not mean that Moscow could dictate policy in Baghdad, Cairo, or Damascus.

For its part, beginning with the Twentieth Party Congress in 1956, the Soviet Union seems to have understood the pragmatic necessity of accommodating itself to the political realities of the post–Second World War colonial and post-colonial world. Gandhi and other "national" figures were rehabilitated, and the notion of "revolutionary democracy" was formulated to permit national liberation movements pursuing the "non-capitalist path" to be deemed worthy ideological allies and political partners.[20] It was thought that by encouraging non-alignment and planned development in Third World countries where national liberation movements had seized or been given power, the resultant friendship with the Soviet Union would cause the strength of the United States and its allies to be correspondingly reduced.

---

[18] This kind of thinking persisted well into the 1970s, in spite of the appearance of more thoughtful and balanced studies by that time. The "Reds under the Middle Eastern bed" trend is exemplified in a Hoover Institution publication, *The Soviet Union and the Middle East: The Post-World War II Era* (Stanford, CA, 1974), edited by Ivo J. Lederer and Wayne S. Vucinich; a more balanced and analytical approach can be found in Hélène Carrère d'Encausse, *La Politique Soviétique au Moyen Orient 1955–1975* (Paris, 1975), and in Smolansky, *Soviet Union and the Arab East*.

[19] Especially after the Egyptian-Syrian Union of February 1958. See Joel Beinin, "The Communist Movement and Nationalist Political Discourse in Nasirist Egypt," *Middle East Journal* 41, 4 (1987), pp. 568–584.

[20] Although the doctrine was not fully articulated until the 1960s. See the discussion in Jaan Pennar, *The USSR and the Arabs: The Ideological Dimension* (New York, 1972), pp. 1–28; for its application in Iraq in the late 1960s and early 1970s see Farouk-Sluglett and Sluglett, *Iraq since 1958*, pp. 140–43, and note 99 on p. 306.

At the same time, and it is not always easy to assess cause and effect, there were clear limits to the extent to which the Soviet Union would commit itself to nationalist allies such as Egypt, a limitation which emerged fairly early on in that particular relationship. According to a senior Egyptian naval officer: "[Nasser] had expected that Egypt would be able to rely on the USSR in the event of a crisis with Western countries, but he was soon disappointed during the Suez crisis. The Soviet Union's behaviour left Nasser in no doubt that [it] was unable to play any effective military role in the region. Apart from psychological and moral support, the USSR could not challenge American superiority and influence in the Eastern Mediterranean."[21]

The inherent economic and military weakness of the Soviet Union, and its evident reluctance to expose itself to direct confrontation with the West, are constants in the period from the mid-1950s until the late 1980s. These continuities were reflected in the circumscribed nature of the commitments which the Soviets made to the various Arab states. In spite of the alarmist assessments of Western intelligence agencies, it is extremely difficult to point to a moment at which the Soviet Union posed a serious threat to the West in the Middle East, or indeed anywhere in the Third World.

Again, even the revolutionary Arab states would have purchased superior Western weapons, particularly aircraft, if the West had been prepared to sell such weapons to them, and proved eager to do so when restrictions were eased in the 1980s. The West's unwillingness to sell to these states effectively drove them to buy arms from the Soviet Union, although the relationships thus created were far more strained than the cozy ties between Jordan or Saudi Arabia and the United States. Though this became clearer in the later 1950s and 1960s, the fundamentally anti-Communist character of all the regimes in the region was in many important ways the United States' inadvertent trump card. Arab anti-Communism was probably the main reason for Washington's support for Nasser until 1967, for his successor Sadat, and for the regimes of Iraq in 1968 and Syria since 1970.[22]

---

[21] Mohrez Mahmoud El Hussini, *Soviet-Egyptian Relations, 1945–1985* (New York and Basingstoke, England, 1987), p. 67. See also Saivetz, "The Soviet Union."

[22] See the memoirs of Wilbur Eveland, a leading CIA agent in the Middle East describing the situation seen from Beirut in the summer of 1956: "I said that although the Syrian Ba'ath was dedicated to Socialism, it was basically a party of Syrian nationalists who could be expected to oppose Communist domination as well as Western colonialism." Wilbur Eveland, *Ropes of Sand: America's Failure in the Middle East* (London, 1980), p. 185.

Nasser was particularly adept at managing Egypt's relationship with the Soviet Union, as Malik Mufti notes, "frightening the Americans by flirting with Moscow, while at the same time assuring them that he and only he stood between the Middle East and a Soviet takeover."[23] Moscow's irruption into the region provided the Middle Eastern states which it was anxious to champion, especially Egypt, with golden opportunities for manipulation, and Nasser's great skill lay in his ability to steer between the two rival power blocs to Egypt's maximum advantage. In the 1950s and 1960s, it was Nasser, rather than the Soviet Union, who determined and defined the relationship between them. That connection was as close or distant as Nasser required, depending on his perceptions of geo-political realities both inside and outside the region.[24]

To give an adequate answer to the question of the actual extent of the Soviet and Egyptian contribution to the events of 1958, the historian would need access to Egyptian, Iraqi, and Soviet archives which may never become fully available. Other colleagues have made extremely skillful use of American, British, and Arab diplomatic documents and memoirs to explore American, British, and Arab perceptions of the revolutionary Middle East in 1958. It seems most unlikely that we shall ever be in a position to be able to pinpoint the perceptions of Egypt or the Soviet Union with as much accuracy.

It is clear that Egypt and the Soviet Union played a vital role in the events of 1958, although this was more symbolic than substantial. Nasser may have been the prime cause of Britain and France being chased out of most of the Middle East, but this was more because of what he represented, and because the United States supported him, than because of anything he did. Similarly, the US landings in Lebanon and the British landings in Jordan, which took place within days of the overthrow of the *ancien régime* in Iraq, were preemptive strikes to give public support to faithful clients rather than because of any real danger of intervention on the part of Egypt or its minions—let alone of the Soviet Union.

---

[23] Mufti, *Sovereign Creations*, p. 75.

[24] This has been well-documented for a later period: "Gratitude for Soviet support has not carried with it any willingness to tolerate Soviet interference in Egyptian decision-making on key issues.... Throughout much of the period examined [1967–1975], Egypt was not strong enough to stand on its own, but it was strong enough to refuse to take orders. On no major occasion in Soviet-Egyptian relations was Moscow able to make Egypt do something against its will...." Alvin Z. Rubenstein, *Red Star on the Nile: The Soviet-Egyptian Influence Relationship since the June War* (Princeton, NJ, 1977), p. 334.

Both Egypt and the Soviet Union provided inspirational models for the generation of Middle Easterners that came of age politically in the 1940s and 1950s, however tarnished these models may seem at the beginning of the new millennium. Both represented anti-imperialism, anti-colonialism, independence, and economic and social development, together with the sense, however misplaced in reality, that the citizens of a country might have a say in its destiny. Such notions were almost bound to appeal to ordinary people who felt that they were ruled by Western puppets and that they were trapped in an apparently endless cycle of social and political deprivation.

As is well known, the Iraqi revolution was the end result of a long period of simmering discontent, and was almost entirely the product of forces and tendencies within the country. Its causes were essentially socio-economic and political: the overwhelming inequalities caused by the formation of large landed estates in the late nineteenth and twentieth centuries; the extraordinary concentration of wealth in a very few hands; the nature and extent of the influence of Britain and its supporters; the limitations which this imposed on political discussion and debate; and, in general, widely-shared aspirations, however vaguely and loosely conceived, for political independence and economic development.

When it actually took place, the Iraqi revolution—or more accurately the coup that made the revolution possible—was the work of a tightly-knit group of military officers, who represented a wide variety of anti-status quo political viewpoints, but whose actions clearly resonated with the majority of the public. In its form, the revolution closely followed the Egyptian model, and would most probably not have happened if Nasser had not seized power in a similar fashion in Egypt in 1952, and perhaps also if the Soviet Union had not "discovered" the Arab world a few years later. The tactless and overbearing British presence in Iraq, together with the extreme unpopularity of Britain's principal Iraqi supporters (among whom Abd al-Ilah was thought particularly odious) ensured that few would mourn the passing of the Hashemite regime, still less man any barricades to defend it.

In the event, at least during its first years, the Iraqi revolution turned out to be something of a paper tiger. Apart from withdrawing from the Baghdad Pact and the rather Gilbert-and-Sullivan union with Jordan which the previous regime had entered into in February 1958, Qasim's government generally respected its predecessors' international commitments, and was not in favor of nationalizing the Iraq Petroleum Company.

In December 1958, Sir Michael Wright reported that the new government did not seem to wish to burn "all or even many" bridges with the British, and that since no better government was in sight, Britain would have to accommodate itself to the new regime.[25]

For much of the Qasim period (1958–1963), the nationalist-Communist divide effectively paralyzed the regime. The fate of their comrades in Syria provided a dramatic cautionary tale to the Communists, whose distaste for the United Arab Republic dovetailed neatly with Qasim's evident disinclination to be subordinate to Nasser. Qasim only became dangerous to the West when he quixotically attempted to annex Kuwait in June-July 1961, and again a few months later, after he sponsored the passage of Law 80 which constituted a serious challenge to the authority of the Iraq Petroleum Company.[26]

In the 1960s and 1970s, Qasim and his successors as rulers of Iraq aligned themselves more closely with the Soviet Union. They pursued generally isolationist policies. But while the lack of cooperation with the rest of the Arab world was real enough, the alliance with the Soviet Union was a chimera, a tactical maneuver for a number of pragmatic purposes, such as the nationalization of the Iraq Petroleum Company in June 1972, which could not have been done without previous assurances on oil purchases and some significant technical assistance.

Ironically, therefore, it is difficult to point to a time when either pan-Arabism or the Soviet Union played a decisive or dominant role in either pre- or post-revolutionary Iraq, or at least a role which significantly threatened the West, in spite of the fears and expectations of those most influential in formulating policy in Britain and the United States. The principal effect of the Soviet presence was that the West ceased to wield the unfettered influence in the Middle East that it had exercised before the Egyptian revolution. Nevertheless, there were limitations on what the Soviet Union could or would provide, and Moscow hesitated to expose itself to the West for fear of reprisals in other theaters. After the revolutions of the 1950s, the Arab states, for all their posturing, generally had a shrewd idea of where real power in manipulating the region actually lay, and made their calculations accordingly.

---

[25] Wright to Lloyd, 7 December 1958, FO 371/133075 (Public Record Office).

[26] This is discussed at length in Edith and E.F. Penrose, *Iraq: International Relations and National Development* (London, 1978), pp. 257–73.

7

The Soviet Union and the Middle East, 1956–1958

CAROL R. SAIVETZ

> Father on that day brought up more than once the Suez Crisis. Then, his appeal to interested governments facilitated dotting the "i." Now he decided to repeat that maneuver.
>
> Sergei Khrushchev, *Nikita Khrushchev: krizisy i rakety*
> (Nikita Khrushchev: Crises and Rockets)

Andrei Gromyko, the former Soviet Foreign Minister, was fond of saying that there was not a crisis anywhere in the world that could be resolved without Soviet involvement. But, while that claim may have been apt from the late sixties until the collapse of the Soviet Union, it had not always been the case. The simultaneous crises that erupted in the Middle East in the summer of 1958—civil war in Lebanon; serious political instability in Jordan; and the military coup, or revolution, in Iraq—offered the Soviet Union a second chance both to play a major role in a region deemed vital to its interests and to diminish still further Western influence there. The first opportunity had come two years earlier with the Suez Canal crisis.

These early forays into Middle East politics raise a number of important questions. First, what were Soviet objectives in backing Egypt in its confrontation with the West in 1956, in trying to force the evacuation of the British troops from Jordan and the US marines from Lebanon, and in offering support to the Iraqi coup leaders, or revolutionaries, in 1958?

Second, what methods did the USSR leadership employ in attempting to achieve those goals? And, third, what lessons did Moscow, as a relative newcomer to the Middle East, learn in 1956 that it applied to the crises in 1958?

In order to answer these questions, this chapter will first analyze Soviet objectives in the region, and then go on to examine the Suez crisis and its lessons for the USSR. It will next focus on the crises of 1958: what were Soviet reactions and how did the Soviet leadership attempt to influence the outcomes? It will conclude by looking at the Soviet position in the Middle East at the end of the 1950s, with a view to offering an assessment of both the constants of Soviet behavior in the region and the problems that repeatedly presented obstacles to the achievement of Moscow's objectives.

Soviet Objectives in the Middle East

Although the Soviet Union, and Tzarist Russia before it, had a history of interest and involvement in the Middle East—particularly the areas contiguous to its borders—it was not until the mid-1950s that the USSR became actively and consistently involved in Middle Eastern affairs. In the early post-World War II period, the central focus of Kremlin policy was the consolidation of the Soviet empire in Eastern Europe. This European focus was reinforced by Josef Stalin's suspicion of Third World national liberation movements because they were not Marxist-Leninist. Stalin's death in 1953 initiated a general rethinking of Soviet foreign policy.

In the course of the power struggle that ultimately brought Nikita S. Khrushchev to power, the issue of how to handle ties with the West was one of the most contentious. As Khrushchev maneuvered among his rivals, he rejected the Stalinist line that war with the West was inevitable and promoted the concept "peaceful coexistence," which he interpreted to mean a sharp ideological, rather than military, struggle between East and West. The new party secretary firmly believed that military confrontation was useless in the nuclear age. He concluded, however, that he could mobilize so-called "progressive" forces both in the West and in the Third World to bolster the Soviet cause. It was in the name of this ideological struggle that he reached out to the decolonizing states of Africa and Asia.

In the Middle East, this took the form of opposition—cloaked in lofty phrases about protecting the freedom of the newly independent states of the region—to the British-sponsored Baghdad Pact. In a far-reaching statement, the Soviet Foreign Ministry definitively criticized Western schemes for the so-called Northern Tier. Issued on 16 April 1955, the statement read as follows:

> As has frequently happened in the past, now, too, efforts are being made to cloak the aggressive nature of the Near and Middle Eastern plans of the United States and Britain with ridiculous fabrications about a "Soviet menace" to the countries of that area.
>
> Of course, the Soviet Union cannot remain indifferent to the situation arising in the region of the Near and Middle East, since the formation of these blocs and the establishment of foreign military bases on the territory of the countries of the Near and Middle East have a direct bearing on the security of the USSR...since the USSR is situated very close to these countries....
>
> Upholding the cause of peace, the Soviet government will defend the freedom and independence of the countries of the Near and Middle East and will oppose interference in their domestic affairs.[1]

In his speech to the Twentieth Congress of the Communist Party of the Soviet Union (CPSU) in February 1956, Khrushchev described the new world situation as one in which nuclear confrontation was no longer inevitable, but one in which a "zone of peace" had emerged in the Third World. It seemed to Khrushchev that the several varieties of home-grown socialism and vehement anti-Westernism espoused by many Third World leaders confirmed the trend that the balance of power was shifting in favor of socialism.[2] Khrushchev thus added to his speech: "[We intend] to work untiringly to strengthen the bonds of friendship and cooperation with the Republic of India, Burma, Afghanistan, Egypt, Syria, and other countries which stand for peace; to support countries which refuse to be involved in military blocs...."[3]

Khrushchev, in effect, laid out three essential foreign policy goals. The first was to avoid face-to-face nuclear confrontation with the West, although this did not mean forgoing opportunities to challenge the West in non-military ways. The second, put simply, was to establish the USSR

---

[1] Documents on International Affairs, 1955, pp. 300–304, in Yaakov Ro'i, *From Encroachment to Involvement* (New Brunswick, NJ, 1979).

[2] For a detailed analysis of changing Soviet views of the Third World see Carol R. Saivetz and Sylvia Woodby, *Soviet-Third World Relations* (Boulder, CO, 1985).

[3] Khrushchev's "open" speech, as translated by *Current Digest of the Soviet Press* (hereafter *CDSP*) l, VIII, 4 (March 7, 1956), p. 12.

as a major player in the Third World. The third was to foster those Third World forces whose goal was the elimination of Western influence. The pursuit of a Soviet presence in the Middle East began tentatively by providing weapons to Syria as early as 1954 and arms to Egypt in 1955.[4] Although these goals were clearly interrelated, and in many respects reinforced one another, Khrushchev and future Soviet leaders were to find these aims difficult to achieve and frequently contradictory. For example, while professing the desire to avoid a superpower standoff, the Soviet Union was simultaneously supporting precisely those forces which openly challenged the Western presence in the Middle East. As the Suez and later Middle East crises were to reveal, Soviet pronouncements left unanswered the question of what would happen when support for decolonization directly contradicted the dictate to avoid a nuclear showdown with the West.

Suez and Its Lessons[5]

When less than a year after the Czech arms deal Nasser announced the nationalization of the Suez Canal Company,[6] Moscow waited a full twenty-four hours before responding. According to Sergei Khrushchev, his father proceeded carefully.

> At first father was cautious. To my question about why we were not undertaking anything, not helping the oppressed peoples in the fight with the imperialists, he answered that we were not able to show direct military

---

[4] There are varying versions and disagreements as to how, when, and with whom the so-called Egyptian-Czech arms deal was negotiated. Haikal offers one chronology which is disputed by Uri Ra'anan and Rami Ginat. See Muhammad Hasanayn Haikal, *The Sphinx and the Commissar* (New York, 1978). See also Uri Ra'anan, *The USSR Arms the Third World: Case Studies in Soviet Foreign Policy* (Cambridge, 1969) and Rami Ginat, *The Soviet Union and Egypt 1945–1955* (London, 1993). Ginat draws some of his chronology from the Ra'anan case study, but argues convincingly that there were indeed two separate deals.

[5] The materials on Suez are drawn from a larger study on Soviet policy during the crisis sponsored by the Kennedy School of Government's Case Study Project. See the three Soviet cases done by the author, forthcoming.

[6] He claimed that shareholders in the company would be compensated and that income generated from tolls would be used to finance the Aswan Dam. In the same speech, Nasser acknowledged what everyone had long suspected, that the September 1955 arms deal had in fact been concluded with the Soviet Union and not with Czechoslovakia. See report, for example, in *Washington Post*, 27 July 1956, p. 1.

> help, we didn't have a common border [with Egypt] and it was necessary to understand what the true position of the Egyptian government [was]. It was possible that they were only playing, trying to extract from the West a larger sum [of money].[7]

At the end of July, Khrushchev, in a major speech at Lenin Stadium, offered the first official pronouncement on the developing crisis. He declared Soviet support for Nasser and the nationalization and hinted that the situation would not become tense unless inflamed from outside the region.[8] Khrushchev next had to decide whether or not the USSR would participate in the London conference convened by the Western powers to discuss Suez. Still undecided on 7 August, Soviet Premier Nikolai Bulganin met with US Ambassador to Moscow Charles E. Bohlen. The latter offered the following description of his conversation with the Soviet Premier:

> Bulganin...said that in general the position of the Soviet government had been set forth in Khrushchev's speech at Lenin Stadium, that they had not yet reached a final decision as to the reply to the British invitation.... He said, however, [the] Soviet government had been giving careful consideration to the matter and he would like first of all to say that there seemed to be between the United States and the Soviet Union a common position in that both felt this matter must be settled by peaceful means. As to the conference itself, after repeating that no final decision had been made, he said nevertheless that they had doubts 1) as to the aims of the conference and 2) as to the composition.[9]

Bulganin's conversation with Bohlen clearly demonstrates Soviet backing for Egypt and the desire to be a major force in the region. It also implicitly raises the possibility of joint US-Soviet action.

In the end, the Soviet leadership sent Foreign Minister Dmitry Shepilov to London. (It should be noted that Shepilov, as editor and chief of *Pravda,* had been to Cairo in the summer of 1955 and had been instrumental in the negotiations of the arms deal.) The London Conference left

---

[7] Sergei Khrushchev, *Nikita Khrushchev*, p. 217.

[8] *Pravda*, 1 August 1956, in David J. Dallin, *Soviet Foreign Policy After Stalin* (New York, 1961), p. 401.

[9] Memorandum from Charles Bohlen to the Secretary of State, dated 1 August 1956. The quotation is from pages 2–3.

the issue unresolved and the Soviet Union still in the position of having to forestall any British or French use of force against its new Egyptian ally. In letters to British Prime Minister Anthony Eden and French Prime Minister Guy Mollet, the USSR warned of "severe consequences" and indicated that it would stand "on Egypt's side."[10]

In addition to the rhetorical support provided for Nasser, and the verbal threats issued against France and Great Britain, the USSR leadership sought for other means not only to back the Nasser government, but also to deter an attack on the canal. When the Suez Canal Company attempted to pressure Egypt by withdrawing pilots from the canal, Moscow sent Soviet pilots. Sergei Khrushchev quotes his father as saying: "Our pilots...would show that our country had no intention of retiring into its shell. The Soviet Union would, this way, make a claim for active participation in world politics. Yet, with caution."[11]

Discussions continued during October at the UN, where the Soviet Union used the Security Council meetings to bolster ties with Egypt, to blast Western imperialism, and to propose a six-power summit to resolve the issue. When the final resolutions came to a vote, the USSR supported the so-called six principles of future negotiations that would respect Egyptian sovereignty, but vetoed a French motion that would have forced Egypt to accept the earlier majority report of the London conference. The veto possessed tremendous political value. According to some observers, Moscow felt that the veto was a firm reminder that the USSR had a role to play in the resolution of the crisis.[12]

Soviet Behavior During the Crisis

Moscow could continue to play this game until the Israeli, British, and French invasion of Egypt. The outbreak of the 1956 war forced

---

[10] To Eden, he wrote, "It is not Egypt who concentrates forces and threatens military action against anyone.... How in such a situation and guided by the noble principles of the United Nations, can one help standing on Egypt's side?" And in his letter to Mollet, Bulganin warned "of severe consequences." Cited in Kennett Love, *Suez, the Twice Fought War* (New York, 1969), p. 428.

[11] Sergei Khrushchev, *Nikita Khrushchev*, p. 219.

[12] Comments of former Soviet Deputy Foreign Minister Sergei Tarasenko made at the Ditchley Conference on the Suez Canal Crisis, December 1996.

Khrushchev to choose between the contradictory tenets of Soviet policy. Soviet action was, of course, constrained by the crisis which had erupted in Hungary, where Soviet military force was used to put down an anti-Communist revolution. Maintenance of the East European empire was the first priority, but even in the midst of the Hungarian crisis, the Soviet leadership kept an eye on the Middle East.

In a Politburo meeting on 28 October 1956, convened to discuss the Hungarian situation, Khrushchev, almost as an afterthought, added, "The English and the French are in a real mess in Egypt. We shouldn't get caught in the same company. But we must not foster illusions. We are saving face."[13] Then, in a meeting on 30 October, Khrushchev and the others seemed to decide on a peaceful resolution of the Hungarian crisis. Almost simultaneously, Britain and France issued their ultimatum to Israel and Egypt. On the thirty-first, the British and French invaded Egypt. The altered circumstances in the Middle East seem to have had an impact on the deliberations in Moscow. During a meeting on the same day, Khrushchev said: "If we leave Hungary, that would encourage the American, British, and French imperialists. They would understand this as our weakness and would be on the offensive. Our party wouldn't understand us. Besides Egypt, [they] would add Hungary.[14]"

The summary notes clearly show that Khrushchev abruptly reversed the decision of the previous day: the Politburo decided to use Soviet troops in a massive intervention in Hungary. It is also evident that Suez played a role in Khrushchev's reversal. In effect, he was arguing that the USSR could not give up Hungary, when the imperialists were on the advance in the Middle East. Given that Moscow had openly backed Nasser, the loss of Hungary would have portended a dual defeat. The impact of the Suez situation on decision-making about Hungary may be seen as well in comments made by Bulganin in a meeting on 1 November. He said then, "the international situation has changed. If we don't take measures—Hungary

[13] Malin notes, 28 October 1956, APRF, F.3, Op. 12, D. 1005, L1 54–63, as translated by Mark Kramer. V. M. Malin, the head of the general department of the CPSU, did not take down a stenographic record, but kept summary notes of meetings. Only those on Hungary are available. Additional notes on Egypt have not been declassified.

[14] "Working Notes of the session of 31 October 1956," as contained in "Kak Reshalis' Voprosy Vengrii" [How the Hungarian Question Was Decided], *Istoricheskii Arkhiv*, 3 (1996), p. 87.

will be lost."[15] It is fair to infer that Bulganin referred both to the presumed need to respond to the dramatic deterioration in Hungary as well as to the attack on Egypt.

On 2 November, Khrushchev flew off to the Yugoslav island of Brioni where he meet with Josef Broz Tito, who played a crucial role in the Hungarian deliberations. According to Veljko Micunovic, then the Yugoslav Ambassador to Moscow, Khrushchev did discuss Suez, at least indirectly, with Tito. In the course of explaining that the Soviet Politburo had decided to intervene again in Hungary, Khrushchev reportedly told Tito that the British and French pressure on Egypt "provided a favorable moment for a further intervention by Soviet troops. It would help the Russians." He added, "They are bogged down there, and we are stuck in Hungary."[16]

It was only on 4 November, after the military situation in Budapest was under control, that the Politburo began to turn its attention to the Middle East. The third item on the agenda for that day was to "more actively take part in help for Egypt...to think up a series of measures." And in parentheses it was noted: "a demonstration at British embassy in Moscow and wide newspaper coverage."[17] Then, on 5 November, when the Budapest uprising had been suppressed, Moscow acted on Suez. It was then that the famous Bulganin letters were sent to President Eisenhower and to Prime Ministers Eden, Mollet, and Ben Gurion. Each of the notes contained an implicit threat of nuclear retaliation. To Eden, Bulganin wrote:

> What kind of position would Britain be in if she had been attacked by stronger powers with all kinds of modern offensive weapons at their disposal? Yet at the present time such countries would not even need to send their naval and air forces to British shores, but could use other means, such as rockets. If rocket weapons were used against Britain and France, you would doubtless call that a barbarous act....[18]

And to Mollet, Bulganin issued a similar threat. He wrote, "What kind of position would France be in if she were subjected to an attack by other

---

[15] "Working Notes from the Session of 1 November 1956," *Istoricheskii Arkhiv*, 3 (1996), p. 85.

[16] Veljko Micunovic, *Moscow Diary* (London, 1980), p. 134.

[17] "Working Notes of the Session of 4 November 1956," *Istoricheskii Arkhiv*, 3 (1996), p. 111.

[18] The letters have been reprinted and extracted in many sources. They were also published in both *Pravda* and *Izvestiia* in the 6 November editions. This translation is from the *CDSP*, VIII (1956), 45, pp. 23–24.

states possessing terrible modern devices of destruction?"[19] Finally, in the letter to Ben Gurion, Bulganin openly questioned Israel's future existence: "It is sowing hatred for the state of Israel among the peoples of the East; this cannot fail to have an effect on the future of Israel and *jeopardize its very existence as a state*."[20]

A second component of Khrushchev's strategy was a proposal for joint action with the United States to counter the tripartite attack on Egypt. In a letter to Eisenhower—also sent on 5 November—Bulganin invited the United States to join with the Soviet Union to "guarantee peace" and "condemn aggression." The letter read in part:

> Soviet Union and US are permanent members of Security Council and are two great powers possessing all contemporary forms of armaments, including atom and hydrogen weapons. On us lies special responsibility to put stop to war, and to restore peace and tranquility to area of Near and Middle East.
>
> US has in area of Mediterranean Sea a strong naval fleet. Soviet Union also has strong naval fleet and powerful aviation. United and urgent use of these means on part of US and Soviet Union in accordance with decision of UN would be reliable guarantee of termination of aggression against Egyptian people....
>
> Soviet govt. appeals to govt. of US to unite their efforts in UN for adopting decisive measures to terminate aggression.
>
> Soviet govt. is prepared to enter into immediate negotiations with govt. US on practical aspects of execution of proposals presented above.[21]

When asked if the USSR expected the US to take up arms against Britain and France, Shepilov stated that it would not be necessary "if the US and the USSR would make plain their 'determination' to see that the fighting come to a halt in the Middle East."[22]

[19] *Pravda* and *Izvestiia*, 6 November 1956, p. 1 in *CDSP*, VIII (1956), 45, p. 24.

[20] *Pravda* and *Izvestiia* 6 November 1956, p. 1, in *CDSP*, VIII (1956), 45, p. 25. Emphasis added.

[21] As contained in telegram sent from US Ambassador in Moscow Charles Bohlen to Washington, declassified 1977, 344A. Also printed in *Pravda* and *Izvestiia*, 6 November 1956.

[22] Telegram from Embassy in the Soviet Union to the Department of State, *Foreign Relations of the United States*, 1955–1957, XVI, p. 993.

The Lessons of Suez

What were the lessons learned from the Suez crisis that were subsequently applied in 1958? It seems evident that Soviet experience during the crisis convinced the leadership that, within certain limits, the three basic Soviet foreign policy goals could be juggled successfully. First, despite the inflammatory rhetoric and the nuclear threats against Britain and France, Moscow apparently understood that any *real* confrontation had to be avoided. Sergei Khrushchev, in his memoir of his father, offers some insight into the thinking behind the despatch of the notes. He states that the USSR did not want to get involved in the war, but clearly wanted to frighten the "aggressors." According to the younger Khrushchev, the Soviet leader figured:

> It wouldn't be so bad to threaten Eden and Guy Mollet with rockets, about which [Khrushchev] had regaled them the previous spring in London....
>
> Father knew well that not only did we not have the rockets, deployed in position, but they really didn't exist in the numbers about which the discussion had gone.... Neither the French nor the British knew how many we had.[23]

Shepilov, in an interview conducted shortly before his death, added further dramatic detail. He claimed that from the beginning, he was opposed to the USSR becoming involved militarily. He went on:

> There was a firm decision not to bring the matter to the point of an armed conflict. However, I devised some measures of a psychological nature and carried them out. Let's say, I summoned the French, British, and Israeli ambassadors at night. Just think of it: it's night-time, their eyes are red because they're having a sleepless night, the situation is very unusual....[24]

In an interesting touch, he explained to his interviewer that the threats were predicated both on the calculation that the United States would not risk superpower war and on perceptions of Khrushchev's unpredictability. "I also went ahead on the basis that there were grounds for believing that

---

23 Sergei Khrushchev, *Nikita Khrushchev*, p.266.

24 Alexei Vassiliev, *Russian Policy in the Middle East: From Messianism to Pragmatism* (Reading, 1993), p. 40.

the USSR would be ready to interfere because of the apparently unbalanced personality of Khrushchev and a seeming lack of responsibility for every single word that he said."[25]

Throughout the Suez crisis, the Soviet Union searched for ways to demonstrate its staunch support for Egypt and for national liberation movements more generally. Every Soviet statement throughout the crisis underscored the legitimacy of the nationalization and warned the British and the French against any precipitous military activity. That this was Moscow's goal is manifest in a number of additional ways. Following the delivery of the 5 November letters, the Egyptian Ambassador to Moscow was called to the Soviet Ministry of Foreign Affairs on 6 November. As Nasser confidant Muhammad Haikal recounts, in Shepilov's office the ambassador was handed copies of the notes to Eden and Mollet and was told, "We have taken a very firm position, Mr. Ambassador...and we shall stand beside you to defeat aggression."[26] In the period following the cease-fire, when British, French, and Israelis seemed to be delaying the withdrawal of their troops, the Soviets began to talk of sending volunteers to assist Egypt. According to Yugoslav Ambassador Micunovic, Khrushchev gave some thought to giving truth to the propaganda. Micunovic recounted a conversation with Khrushchev on 12 November:

> Khrushchev said they had finally threatened the West with a statement about sending volunteers, but he didn't think it would come to that. He said in conclusion that the Soviet Union was not thinking of going to war, but that the Soviet Union's latest threats of war had been necessary and correct."[27]

Two days later, on 14 November, it was reported from Moscow that Muhammad al-Koni, the Egyptian Ambassador in Moscow, had been ordered by Cairo to ask the Kremlin to expedite the transference of Soviet "volunteers."[28] Yet the next day, other accounts indicated that Egypt would accept no volunteers from the Soviet Union. An embassy spokesman in Moscow claimed that Egypt wanted volunteers only if Britain, France, and Israel failed to withdraw.[29]

---

[25] Vassiliev, *Russian Policy in the Middle East*, p. 40.
[26] Haikal, *The Sphinx*, p. 72.
[27] Micunovic, *Moscow Diary*, p. 157.
[28] "Egypt's Call for Russians Is Reported," *Washington Post*, 15 November 1956, p. 1.
[29] "Arab States Reject Foreign 'Volunteers'," *Washington Post*, 16 November 1956, p. 1.

Although no volunteers were known to have been sent to Egypt, there were Soviet military advisors there at the time. Khrushchev admitted to Micunovic that advisors had been sent to Egypt during the 1956 war, at Nasser's request.[30] Years later during the Cuban Missile Crisis, a Senior State Department Official, Raymond Garthoff, affirmed that Soviet military advisors in Egypt were removed from conflict areas during the war.[31]

Nonetheless, Moscow also very clearly understood the limitations of that support. In 1956, there would have been no way to offer any more extensive support to the Egyptian cause. At the height of the crisis, on 31 October, Syrian President Shukri al-Quwatli arrived in Moscow. According to Haikal, he immediately demanded an audience with Khrushchev, Bulganin, and Marshal Georgi M. Zhukov. When he questioned what the Soviet Union was prepared to do to help Egypt, Khrushchev responded, "We'll see what we can do. At present we don't know how to help Egypt, but we are having continuous meetings to discuss the problem."[32] Again, on 2 November, Khrushchev reiterated the Soviet Union's inability to help the Egyptians. At a diplomatic reception in Moscow, Khrushchev is reported to have told the Egyptian Ambassador to Moscow, "We are full of admiration for the way in which you are resisting aggression...but unfortunately there is no way in which we can help you militarily. But we are going to mobilize world public opinion."[33] This was perhaps the first hint of exactly what the Soviet leadership was contemplating.[34]

Khrushchev and successive Soviet leaders found this combination of tactics successful. Through bluff and bravado, the Soviet Union had assured itself a future role in the region. Moreover, the Soviets repeatedly

---

30 Micunovic, *Moscow Diary*, p. 157, 12 November 1956.

31 Declassified Memo to Deputy Undersecretary U. Alexis Johnon included in Raymond Garthoff, *Reflections on the Cuban Missile Crisis* (Washington DC, Brookings, 1987), p. 147.

32 Haikal, *The Sphinx*, p. 71.

33 Haikal, *The Sphinx*, p. 71.

34 These stories are corroborated, in large measure, by Kennett Love in *Suez*, p. 610. He writes:

> When I asked Nasser whether the Russians had offered help, he said: "President Quwwatly [of Syria] was in Moscow at that time [from 31 October to 3 November]. So the contacts were with President Quwwatly, not with Kissilev.... And President Quwwatly sent to me and said he had asked for a meeting with Bulganin, Khrushchev, and Zhukov. He discussed the question with them. And they said that they were ready to send us arms and technicians [not volunteers]. And we were not in need of arms because by that time we had 150 aeroplanes, for instance, fighters, but only forty trained pilots. And some of our pilots were in Moscow. So we were not in need of aeroplanes at all."

The brackets are in the original text.

took credit for saving the Nasser regime. In several statements and in his memoirs, Khrushchev claimed that Soviet policy had forced Britain and France to back down. Mikoyan seconded this assessment:

> The British and the French decided that the Russians had gotten stuck in Hungary. So, [they reasoned,] let us strike Egypt, [the Soviets] will not be able to come to its assistance, they cannot fight on two front[s]. We will splash the Russians with mud, knock Egypt out, and undermine the influence of the USSR in the Middle East. [But] we found resources both to keep troops in Hungary and to warn the imperialists that, if they would not stop the war in Egypt, we might use missile armaments. Everyone admits that with this we decided the fate of Egypt.[35]

The Soviet Stakes in 1957–58

Egyptian President Nasser emerged victorious from the Suez crisis, and the Soviet Union profited as well. It had not only established itself as a major outside actor in the Middle East, but it laid the foundation for a series of new alliances. Between 1956 and the revolutionary summer of 1958, the USSR repeatedly condemned imperialist intrigues in the region while working to solidify relations with Egypt and with Syria. The immediate issue was the US promulgation of the Eisenhower Doctrine in January 1957. Soviet media labeled the doctrine "aggressive" and "colonial," and TASS claimed that the new US policy was contrary to the principles and goals of the United Nations.[36] Moscow's rhetorical opposition to the Eisenhower Doctrine was complemented by diplomatic efforts. In a drive that paralleled the 1956 proposal to coordinate action with the United States, the Kremlin sent notes to Washington, London, and Paris suggesting a joint declaration on principles of non-intervention in the Middle East. The proposal would have excluded unilateral actions on the part of any one power and forestalled the Western attempt to enlist the Middle East states in the Baghdad Pact or any future similar pacts.[37] The Soviet Union also attempted to push the United Nations to condemn

[35] Vladislav Zubok and Constantine Pleshakov, *Inside the Kremlin's Cold War* (Cambridge, 1996), pp. 191–192.

[36] "TASS announcement in Connection with the so-called 'Eisenhower Doctrine,'" in *SSSR i Arabskie strany, 1917–1960*, published by the Ministry of Foreign Affairs (Moscow, 1961), pp. 288–94.

[37] Letter, 11 February 1957, in *SSSR i Arabskie strany*, p. 308.

what it called "US aggressive measures."[38] The Western powers rejected these Soviet initiatives.

Within the region itself, debates over whether or not to endorse the Eisenhower Doctrine not only engendered major political turmoil, but also exacerbated preexisting conflicts within many Middle Eastern states. The specifics of the domestic politics in the key states of the region are discussed in other chapters in this volume, but it is important to note how the USSR responded to this round of instability.

In Jordan, the government, which favored neutrality and the establishment of diplomatic relations with the USSR, confronted the King, who welcomed the Eisenhower Doctrine and opposed ties to Moscow. In the face of growing anti-Americanism, the King asked for help. The Eisenhower administration responded by deploying units of the US Sixth Fleet in the Mediterranean and offering $10 million in aid.[39] On 29 April, the Soviet Foreign Ministry issued a statement condemning US interference in Jordan's internal affairs: "Events in Jordan...are [an example of] the 'Dulles-Eisenhower Doctrine' in reality...[one can see] whom this doctrine serves."[40] In Lebanon, attitudes toward the Eisenhower Doctrine inflamed an already tense situation.[41] There, the government accepted the Eisenhower Doctrine while the opposition, supportive of Egypt, organized large-scale demonstrations and strikes. The USSR quickly condemned US military assistance to Lebanon, but because Beirut had established diplomatic relations with Moscow, the criticism was more measured.

The nature of the growing Soviet relationship with Syria was quite different. Syria was the first Arab country to purchase Soviet arms, and it moved rapidly to expand political and economic ties with other Warsaw Pact states. When the Syrian Communist Party was included in the ruling coalition, the Kremlin was obviously pleased. According to one insider, the Syrian communists were the "darlings" of the CPSU's International Department, whose mandate was to promote relations with non-ruling communist parties.[42] In August 1957, Soviet and Syrian officials con-

---

[38] As cited in Yaacov Ro'i, *From Encroachment to Involvement* (New Brunswick, NJ, 1974), p. 215.

[39] See the chapter by Rashid Khalidi.

[40] "Announcement of the USSR Ministry of Foreign Affairs Regarding Imperialist Intrigues in Jordan," 29 April 1957, *SSSR I Arabskie strany*, p. 336.

[41] See the chapter by Irene L. Gendzier.

[42] Georgi Mirskii, "Nasser, Moscow, and the Model of Socialist Orientation," unpublished paper.

cluded a far-reaching agreement that included credits and Soviet assistance for a wide variety of infrastructure projects. According to the final communiqué, the discussions in Moscow were conducted in "friendship" and "cordiality" and in "conformity with the aspirations of the two countries for the reinforcement of peace and security in the Near East."[43] In the early fall of 1957, when Turkey seemingly threatened Syria with military activity on the border, the Soviet Union moved to protect its new ally. In a letter addressed to Turkish Prime Minister Adnan Menderes, Bulganin wrote:

> We cannot conceal the fact that we have received with great concern the report about Turkish troop concentrations on Syria's frontiers and also about shipments of American arms to Turkey to carry out an attack on Syria.
>
> It is our deep-seated conviction that Turkey could only bring upon herself great calamities.... We are convinced that should military action against Syria be started and a war begun in the Middle East, Turkey would undoubtedly only suffer.... The geographical conditions in which such a conflict would develop with Turkish participation, should also be taken into account.[44]

The not-so-veiled threat to Turkey was given substance by Soviet troop maneuvers in the Caucasus and the arrival of two Soviet warships in the Syrian port of Latakia.[45] The crisis was ultimately diffused.

In this same period, links between Moscow and Cairo were strengthened. In November 1957, Egyptian Field Marshal Abdel Hakim Amer, in Moscow to attend the fortieth anniversary celebrations of the Bolshevik revolution, met with Khrushchev, Bulganin, and other Soviet civilian and military leaders. During these sessions, Egypt secured some $200 million in Soviet assistance.[46] But this was only after serious negotiations. According to declassified Soviet documents, Amer explained Egypt's development plans to Mikoyan and to Khrushchev. The latter, in a separate meeting, promised 600 million rubles to pay for the deliveries of machinery and equipment. Khrushchev went on to state that the terms would be the same as those offered to Syria and did *not* include military assistance.

---

43 Joint communiqué, published on 6 August 1957, as cited in Ro'i, *From Encroachment*, pp. 229–233.

44 As cited in Ro'i, *From Encroachment*, p. 243.

45 Ro'i, *From Encroachment*, p. 241.

46 Haikal, *The Sphinx*, p. 82.

The Soviet leader added: "If you wish to receive any advice from us on the matter [of restructuring the armed forces], we will readily give it to you. The question of military aid does not depend on the structure of your armed forces." Amer then pushed for military assistance in addition to the economic assistance discussed.[47] Perhaps the most telling sign of the Soviet desire to court Nasser was the agreement, announced in January 1958, to fund the construction of the first stage of the Aswan Dam.

Soviet-Egyptian relations were informed as well by questions regarding Arab unification schemes. Prior to 1958, Soviet international and Middle East affairs specialists viewed all such proposals with disdain. Academics and politicians alike seemingly feared that the spread of Nasser's brand of nationalism would present an insurmountable obstacle to further Soviet influence in the region. Their tone changed, however, with the February 1958 proclamation of the merger of Syria and Egypt into the United Arab Republic (UAR). Nasser, as president of the newly created UAR, moved quickly to disband all political parties and the Syrian communist leader, Khalid Bakdash, fled to the USSR. Thus Nasser not only cracked down on communists in Egypt itself but also marginalized the Syrian Communist Party. This left the USSR to decide between supporting local communists or anti-Western nationalists. The diminution of communist strength in Syria disappointed the CPSU International Department, but Nasser's growing leadership in the Arab world was viewed far more favorably by the Foreign Ministry.[48] In an authoritative Soviet commentary in *International Affairs,* published by the Foreign Ministry, the merger was seen as giving "patriotic forces of the new state every chance to...[rally] the Arab people...in the struggle against colonialism, for economic development, and general progress."[49]

Despite the misgivings and conflicting opinions in Moscow, Soviet officials extended an especially warm welcome to Nasser when he visited the USSR in April 1958. According to Nasser confidante Haikal, they pressed Nasser about plans for economic and social development, but skirted the question of the ban on Communist activities.[50] At the end of the two-week trip, Nasser and Khrushchev signed a joint communiqué which

---

[47] See the documents included in "USSR/Russia-Egypt: 50 Years of Cooperation," *International Affairs* 10 (1993), pp. 93–94.

[48] Mirskii, "Nasser."

[49] K. Ivanov, "A New Arab State," *International Affairs* 3 (1958), pp. 56–57. It should be noted that Ivanov is a pseudonym used for authoritative Soviet statements in the media.

[50] See the varying descriptions of Nasser's trip in Haikal, *The Sphinx*, and *The Cairo Documents*.

expressed the "profound satisfaction with the development of the close and steadily expanding relations."[51] The communiqué carefully ignored the issue that would prove to be a major stumbling block to Egyptian-Soviet relations, Nasser's treatment of the local communist party.

Finally, the military coup which overthrew the Iraqi monarchy presented the USSR with one more opportunity to pursue its objectives. Relations between the USSR and Iraq had been severed in 1955, when Prime Minister Nuri al-Said led his government into the Baghdad Pact. The new Qasim regime, however, almost immediately reestablished ties with the Soviet Union and initiated arms purchases from Moscow. It seemed to Moscow at the time that Iraq's new policies were, in many ways, congruent with Soviet foreign policy goals.[52]

Thus the simultaneous crises of July 1958 in Lebanon, Jordan, and Iraq were a true challenge to the Soviet Union. At stake were Moscow's anti-imperialist credentials, its role as supporter of so-called progressive forces, its ties to Nasser, and its nascent links to the new Iraqi government. In the words of one Russian academic expert on the Middle East, from Moscow's perspective, the year 1958 was seen as a worse threat than 1956—precisely because two years of efforts had been made on behalf of Nasser and the new Soviet investment in the Middle East.[53]

How Moscow Played the Triple Crises

When the Iraqi coup occurred, followed in quick succession by the US Marine landing in Beirut and the British deployment in Jordan, Soviet statements both condemned what was labeled as "aggression" and offered immediate recognition to the new Iraqi regime. In language that would be repeated throughout the years, the Soviet leadership, through the TASS news agency, declared "that the Soviet Union cannot remain indifferent to events creating a grave menace in an area *adjacent* to its frontiers, and reserves the right to take the necessary measures dictated by the interests of peace and security."[54] Moscow also claimed that British military support for King Hussein was not only aimed at crushing the Jordanian national liberation movement, but also was designed to establish a military base

51 As cited in Ro'i, *From Encroachment*, p. 253.
52 For the Iraqi perspective, see Peter Sluglett's chapter.
53 Mirskii, "Nasser," p. 5.
54 *New York Times*, 17 July 1958, p. 7.

from which to attack Iraq in conjunction with the US.[55] Simultaneously, the Soviet representative at the United Nations sponsored a Security Council resolution that called upon the United States to cease its armed intervention in the domestic affairs of the Arab states and to remove its troops from Lebanon.[56]

Nasser, who was in Yugoslavia when the Iraqi revolution occurred, decided to proceed to Moscow to confer with Soviet officials. Haikal offers two slightly varying accounts of these meetings. In his book *The Cairo Documents*, he first notes that Khrushchev had assumed that Nasser's men were behind the coup.[57] He then quotes the Soviet leader as follows: "Frankly, we are not ready for a confrontation. We are not ready for World War III." Khrushchev continued that "Nasser would have to bend with the storm, there was no other way because Dulles could blow the whole world to pieces."[58] More details are offered in Haikal's book *The Sphinx and the Commissar*. In this version, Khrushchev supposedly told Nasser that the USSR was strong enough to inflict serious damage on the US Sixth Fleet, but that the real issue was war or peace.[59] Nasser reportedly asked Khrushchev if he would be willing to issue a statement declaring that the Soviet Union was prepared to intervene in the region if the West attacked. The Soviet party chairman answered, "That would complicate matters...because it would raise the temperature, and at this point suddenly raising it could produce unforeseeable consequences.... We shouldn't do anything to aggravate it [the temperature]."[60] In contrast, Western reports about the visit indicated that Nasser asked that nothing precipitous be done,[61] although these same reports allege that Nasser was told that "volunteers" were waiting at Soviet airports to fly to the Middle East, should the Arabs request help.[62] Khrushchev, in a later conversation at a Polish Embassy reception, told US Ambassador Lwellyn Thompson that he and Nasser had "reached an identity of views...though I am a communist and he is not."[63]

---

[55] "Russians Assert 'Security' Will Guide Policy in Crisis," *New York Times*, 19 July 1958, p. 2.

[56] Text of Soviet Resolution at the United Nations, *New York Times*, 16 July 1958, p. 4.

[57] Haikal, *The Cairo Documents*, p. 130.

[58] Ibid., p. 131.

[59] Haikal, *The Sphinx*, p. 97.

[60] Ibid., p. 99.

[61] See front page report, *New York Times*, 19 July 1958.

[62] "Russian Said to Tell Nasser 'Volunteers' Are Available," *New York Times*, 21 July 1958, p. 1.

[63] "Moscow Is Cool to West's Offer," *New York Times*, 23 July 1958, pp. 1, 8.

The several reports of the conversations with Nasser reveal that as in 1956, the Soviet leader recognized that events in the Middle East could escalate. Yet, as during Suez, the USSR wanted both to present itself as the savior of Arab nationalism and to ensure a role for itself in the resolution of the crisis, firstly by attempting to use the weapon of public opinion. On 16 July well-organized demonstrators gathered outside the US embassy in Moscow. In all, some two thousand participants protested the US intervention in Lebanon. Equally as important, many of the demonstrators threw stones at the building. This mirrored the demonstrations in front of the British Embassy mentioned in the 1956 Politburo notes.

A second tool was military in nature, although calculated to be understood as a signal and not an overt threat. All accounts of the Nasser-Khrushchev meeting indicate that, following consultations with the Politburo, Khrushchev told Nasser that the USSR would hold general maneuvers on the Bulgarian-Turkish border.[64] Widespread publicity was given to the maneuvers which were staged both in the Turkestan military district and in the Transcausasus. According to Yugoslav Ambassador Micunovic, Khrushchev reiterated that "In order to reduce pressure from the West [he had] given orders for troop movements and military maneuvers to take place in the area of the Caucasus, close to Turkey, which will be directed by Marshal Grachko, as well as in Turkmenia opposite Iran, to be directed by Marshal Meretskov. They have arranged for similar maneuvers by Bulgarian forces with the participation of the Soviet Air Force close to the Turkish-Bulgarian frontier." Micunovic continued: "I asked him what he thought the prospects were of the conflict reaching dangerous dimensions. He did not give me a direct answer, but I had the impression that he does not foresee the worst happening."[65]

These moves were complemented by political activity. Because the Lebanese question had already been referred to the Security Council, one obvious tool was the international forum provided by the United Nations.[66] Yet, simultaneously, the USSR tried to work outside of the United Nations by proposing a five-power summit to include itself, the US, Britain, France, and India. After vetoing a US-sponsored resolution that would have sent UN troops to Lebanon, Khrushchev himself sent letters to the Western powers and to India underlining the need to act

[64] Haikal, *The Cairo Documents*, p. 132.

[65] Micunovic, *Moscow Diary*, pp. 409–10.

[66] For details about UN Secretary-General Dag Hammarskjöld's handling of the crises, see the chapter by Michael Graham Fry.

quickly to avert war and suggesting a summit conference in Geneva. In a letter to Eisenhower on 19 July, Khrushchev alleged that the UN had been pushed aside by "bayonets of US and British troops." Echoing Bulganin's 1956 letters, the Soviet leader continued, "We know that the USA has atomic and hydrogen bombs, we know that you have an air force and a navy, but you well know that the USSR also has atom and hydrogen bombs, an air force and a navy and ballistic rockets of all types, including intercontinental ones."[67]

In response, the United States denied blame for the crisis and accused the Soviet Union of inflaming the situation. Eisenhower recommended that a Security Council meeting be convened at which heads of state or prime ministers would represent their countries. The initial Soviet response was unenthusiastic. The leadership apparently felt that the USSR would be outnumbered in any Security Council meeting. Nonetheless, in a letter of 23 July, Khrushchev provisionally accepted the idea of a Security Council meeting. He added, however, that he wanted India (then not a member of the council) and the Arab countries to be included. Two days later, Eisenhower answered Khrushchev, saying that only those states that were then members of the council should participate. The debate, conducted through official letters, continued for several days. Finally, on 1 August, the Eisenhower administration proposed that on 12 August the Security Council facilitate a meeting of heads of governments or prime ministers in New York or elsewhere, but not Moscow.[68]

Before Khrushchev responded to Eisenhower's proposals, he traveled to Beijing for a meeting with Chinese Communist leaders. With hindsight, and in light of the soon-to-erupt Sino-Soviet dispute, we may infer that the Chinese urged a tougher line on the Soviet leader. The joint communiqué issued on 3 August sternly denounced "the flagrant aggression carried out by the United States and Britain in the Near and Middle East," and called for a big power summit to settle the situation. The document ended with a demand for withdrawal of British and US troops.[69] This tone was reflected in Khrushchev's 5 August rejection of the US suggestion; he asked instead for a General Assembly meeting. Moreover, in his letter, he claimed that the very proposal for a summit had deterred Britain and the

---

[67] Khrushchev to Eisenhower, *New York Times*, 20 July 1958, p. 2.
[68] Eisenhower to Khrushchev, 1 August 1958, in *American Foreign Policy, 1958*, p. 1018.
[69] *New York Times*, 4 August 1958, p. 3.

US from attacking either Iraq or Egypt.[70] In the end, Eisenhower accepted this proposal.

By the fall, the multiple crises were defused. The Lebanese civil war was ended for the time being when General Fouad Chehab, the Commander-in-Chief of the army, was elected, thus preventing Camille Chamoun from succeeding himself. The latter's attempt to alter the Lebanese constitution so that he could remain in power had been one of the major focal points of the opposition. The new government conducted a more moderate and less pro-American foreign policy; nonetheless, with the restoration of political order, the United States withdrew its forces. In addition, the British withdrew from Jordan once the situation there was stabilized and it became clear that the new Iraqi government enjoyed widespread public support. Any thoughts of a potential British attack on Iraq disappeared when the Qasim government made clear its determination to abide by previously negotiated oil agreements with Great Britain.[71]

Objectives, Tools, and Future Problems

It should be clear from this analysis of the years 1956 and 1958 that Moscow's objectives remained unchanged. In each instance, the opportunities presented by Middle Eastern events were seized with a view to maximizing Soviet prestige and influence and securing new allies while limiting the escalatory potential of any crisis. These goals remained constant even after Khrushchev was ousted in 1964. In fact, one could argue that Khrushchev introduced the concept of "Third World opportunism," but Leonid Brezhnev developed it to an art form. That said, however, it should also be evident that the situation in 1956 was different from that of 1958. The Suez crisis of 1956 saw the birth of Nasserism as a force, but in the aftermath of that crisis and particularly in the 1958 crises, it was viewed in the West as a force linked to Soviet expansionism. A second difference to be noted is that in 1956, the United States was not involved militarily, as it was in 1958. Moreover, if the USSR used 1956 to insinuate itself into regional politics, by 1958, it too was more involved. This difference in context meant that the USSR needed a slightly different mix of tools to attain its goals.

70 Khrushchev to Eisenhower, 5 August 1958, *New York Times*, 6 August 1958, p. 6.

71 See the chapter by Roger Owen.

During the 1958 crises, Moscow refined the tactics it had used in 1956. First, the rhetoric chosen in both crises is significant. Moscow time and again selected its words to convey what it deemed to be the acceptable policy agenda. There were several notable themes: that the USSR was protecting the disadvantaged, that the West was holding back progress, and that Moscow had every right to be involved in the Middle East given its geographic proximity to the Soviet Union. Khrushchev reportedly told Micunovic that "the West's hostile attitude toward the Arab nationalists who had carried out the coup in Iraq and toward the Arab countries where the Arab nationalists were in power would serve only further to compromise Western policy in the Near and Middle East."[72]

One of the most interesting features of Soviet rhetoric in both crises is the overt mention of Soviet nuclear weapons capabilities. Although Khrushchev did not threaten war, he sought to establish the USSR's superpower credentials. Hence he repeatedly and pointedly noted that Moscow possessed sophisticated military technology. This rhetorical device was abandoned after the Cuban Missile Crisis. Later statements about the Middle East repeat most, if not all, of the classic themes, but after 1962, the USSR's nuclear parity had been demonstrated.

Second, in both 1956 and 1958, the USSR expressed clear preferences on the international forums which were most appropriate for discussing the crises. In both cases, however, there was debate not only on venue, but also on which countries would be considered acceptable participants in the discussions. This maneuvering demonstrated, first of all, the Soviet demand for a "say" in the politics of the region. Moreover, it reflected a desire to "stack the deck," and a fear of being left out, even if Soviet objections were not met.

Third, the tactic of issuing threats after-the-fact became a frequently-used tool. It was clearly safer to threaten *after* the crisis had abated. Fourth, proposals for joint action were to become a hallmark of Soviet Middle East policy. Perhaps the most famous example was Soviet Premier Leonid Brezhnev's letter to President Richard Nixon in October 1973. These proposals served multiple purposes. They ensured a Soviet role in the resolution of any crisis and, one can argue, they facilitated superpower communication in order to forestall any particular situation getting out of hand.

Finally, in 1958, the Soviet Union did introduce one new tactic—military maneuvers within the Soviet Union. Whereas in 1956 the Soviet

[72] Micunovic, *Moscow Diary*, p. 409.

Union was preoccupied with events in Hungary, there was no comparable crisis to deflect Soviet attention or manpower in 1958. And, as with the proposals for joint intervention, this tactic was used again to illustrate Soviet determination to protect its clients in 1973.[73]

Ironically, while the Soviet Union did employ these tactics to protect its new-found stake in the Middle East, it retained doubts about the reliability of its allies in the region. This was first evident in 1956, when, as Sergei Khrushchev describes, his father questioned Nasser's objectives in nationalizing the canal. As the Soviet-Egyptian relationship evolved, the treatment of local Communist parties by Arab nationalists was a repeated irritant. Soviet disappointment with and caution among some circles about the creation of the UAR has been noted. In mid-fall of 1958 Khrushchev articulated his disappointment with some aspects of Nasser's policies. In response to a question about Communist subversion in the Middle East, the Soviet leader told visiting US State Department envoy Eric Johnston:

> We are not doing that.... Do you think Nasser is a communist? Communism is outlawed in Egypt and I understand there are 5,000 or more communists under arrest.... Take Iraq, there the leaders are not communists. In fact, they are anti-communists. The revolt was against a feudal system.... But in your case you support these feudalistic regimes with troops. If it had not been for British troops in Jordan, Hussein would have been murdered long ago by his people, not by communists.[74]

The Egyptian treatment of communists later burgeoned into a bitter dispute between Egypt and its USSR patron. As Nasser arrested communists, the Soviet press defended the prisoners, calling them part of the progressive intelligentsia. One *Pravda* correspondent charged that unless the communists were included in the Egyptian government, it ran the "danger of becoming merely a revival of the old colonialist order under a new guise."[75]

---

[73] For a further discussion of 1973, see Carol R. Saivetz, "Superpower Competition in the Middle East and the Collapse of Détente," in Odd Arne Westad, *The Fall of Detente, Soviet-American Relations during the Carter Years,* Nobel Symposium 95 (Boston, 1997); and Georgi Kornienko, *Kholodnaia voina: svidetel'stvo ee uchastnika* [The Cold War: Testimony of a Participant] (Moscow, 1994).

[74] Report of meeting between Eric Johnston and N. Khrushchev, on 6 October 1958 (dated 10 October 1958). Declassified 1983.

[75] V. Mayevskii, "Hassanein Haykal's Sortie," *Pravda*, 19 February 1959, p. 4, in *CDSP* XI, 6–7 (18 March 1959), p. 27.

History would show that many of Khrushchev's reservations about his Arab nationalist allies were well-founded. As the Soviet leadership was to find out both with Iraq and Egypt, congruence in foreign policy objectives did not necessarily denote that either Middle Eastern state was going to follow what Soviet scholars called the non-capitalist path of development. And the role of the local communist parties was merely one issue. Others included land reform and nationalization of key industries, just to name a few.

Even the identity of foreign policy interests between the Soviets and the Egyptians was to prove short-lived. Moscow was wary of Nasser's designs for Arab unification. When pressure was applied on Iraq to join the nascent UAR, Qasim resisted and enlisted Soviet support in his efforts. As relations deteriorated between Iraq and Egypt, Khrushchev and the Soviet leadership openly sided with Iraq. This led to open polemics between Moscow and Cairo over not only intra-Arab diplomacy but also the treatment of local Communists.

Projecting beyond the timeframe of this chapter, it should be noted that Moscow's relations with Baghdad were also uneasy. The issues that divided them were the role of the local communist party, the Kurds, and later Iraq's tense relations with Iran. The more difficult Iraq's relations with the Soviet Union, the closer Cairo and Moscow drew together. By the mid-sixties, Nasser and the new Soviet leadership had overcome their ideological and tactical disputes. But even with Egypt, the USSR eventually confronted the limits of its ability to influence the course of Middle East events. While clearly supportive of Egypt during the 1967 Middle East war, Moscow was only a reluctant supporter of Nasser's adventures in Yemen. And of course, ultimately, Nasser's successor Anwar Sadat shifted Egypt's orientation toward the US.

In the late 1950s, however, Moscow had yet to learn these lessons or to discover the immense difficulties complicating its long-term relationships with Arab states. Khrushchev gained from Suez the tools that could cultivate such relations. He refined those implements in 1958. But the maintenance of these relationships proved to be far more problematic.

8

The Junior Partner: Israel's Role in the 1958 Crisis

ILAN PAPPÉ

Israel's role in the 1958 crisis was quite limited and marginal. But nonetheless it becomes an intriguing historiographical subject if it is analyzed within an overall assessment of Israeli policy towards the Arab world between the Suez 1956 crisis and the June war of 1967. There have been two distinct periods of academic interest in the era. In the early period, from the 1950s through most of the 1980s, research was done by political scientists and historians who based their work on accounts of the principal policy-makers at the time—some of these scholars and officials were close friends—as well as on a vast array of secondary sources. In these studies, Israel in the 1950s is a country preoccupied with containing the expansionist tendencies of its Arab neighbors.[1]

The second period of historiographical significance began after 1988 with the declassification of voluminous documents in the Israeli, British, and American archives. Some subsequent works dealt specifically with the 1958 crisis. The new material, so it seems, did little to transform the initial historical portrayal: Israel in and around the 1958 crisis is still depicted by most Israeli historians as a passive actor whose policies were of a defensive and reactive nature only, and always in the face of a hostile Arab

[1] See for example Dan Horowitz, *The Israeli Concept of National Security* (Jerusalem, 1973) (Hebrew), pp. 1–50, and Michael Breecher, *Israel's Foreign Policy: The First Twenty Years in the Foreign Policy System of Israel* (Oxford, 1972), pp. 557–62.

world.[2] This historiographical interpretation represents faithfully the public mood and discourse of the time, that is, a public obsessed with the "Arab Threat." The discussion of, and preoccupation with, the "Threat" overshadowed all other issues before the Israeli public and dominated the policy-makers' agenda as well.

This chapter challenges the historiographical image of a passive and defensive Israel. It forms part of the on-going historiographical debate in Israel about the country's past and present realties. The previous decade in the country's history, 1948–1956, has become a topic for a heated historiographical debate in Israel, as revisionist local historians, usually referred to as the "new historians," have begun rewriting the history of early statehood, describing Israel of the early 1950s as quite often an aggressive and bellicose neighbor in the midst of the Arab world. The participants in the debate—be they defenders of the national narrative or its opponents—all rely on the same archival material. In other words, the basis for the historiographical discord is not just factual but also ideological.[3]

This chapter is also based on the same material other Israeli historians have used or are using on the 1958 crisis. But it is one of the few attempts starting from a more revisionist point of view. The merit of this approach lies not so much in a readiness to adopt a critical stance, but more in the willingness to view Israel in the 1950s as an active player in the area's politics. In fact, I argue that throughout its history Zionism should be seen as an active player not only in Palestine, but in the neighboring Arab countries as well. This forward policy was pursued with ever-greater force, especially since the 1930s. Zionist leaders, and after 1948, Israeli politicians, actively intervened in Arab politics, and quite often this intervention took the form of direct military operations on Arab territory. On several occasions in the 1950s, Israeli leaders even considered wide-scale invasions of other countries. In the 1960s, this policy was then translated into unilateral annexations and sheer expansionism. The measures taken were always presented as defensive to justify them.

---

[2] Three of them should be mentioned here: Zach Levey, *Israel and the Western Powers, 1952–1960* (Chapel Hill, 1998); Michael Oren, "Israel and the Question of Overflights to Jordan, 1958," *Iyunim Bitkumat Israel* (*Studies in Zionism: The Yishuv and the State of Israel*) (Hebrew) 1, pp. 262–275; and Mordechai Bar-On, "Status Quo—Before or After: Commentary Notes on Israel's Defense Policy, 1949–1958," *Iyunim Bitkumat Israel* (*Studies in Zionism: The Yishuv and the State of Israel*) (Hebrew) 5, pp. 65–111.

[3] See Ilan Pappé, "Critique and Agenda: The Post-Zionist Scholars in Israel," *History and Memory* 7, 1 (Spring–Summer 1995), pp. 66–91.

Most scholars in Israel have found it difficult to accept such a revisionist analysis. Scholarship in Israel has been closely linked with ideology and thus it was deemed necessary, as part of the overall struggle with the Arab world, to highlight only the aggressiveness—which of course there was—on the Arab side, and to describe it as uncompromising and total. Admittedly, once the Jewish state had become a reality, few in the Arab world were willing to accept it or to acknowledge Israel's right to exist. And yet, there were Arab leaders willing to make peace with Israel if they were given assurance that Zionist expansionism would be checked and some of the principal demands of the Palestinians met. Moreover, it has to be recognized that the aggressive Israeli policy, even if seen as generated by Arab hostility, left little hope for any reconciliation and strengthened already-existing negative stereotypes on the Arab side.

I am emphasizing the historiographical dimension of the issue in order to highlight the novelty of the more critical assessment of Israel's role in the 1958 crisis. This approach challenges the tendency of many Israeli academics to accept obediently the leaders' "discourse of defense" when analyzing Israel's role in the Middle East or position in the Arab world. For many Israelis, "offense" and "defense" are synonyms for "Arab" and "Israeli" policies: everything Israel has ever done is defensive and everything the Arabs have done is offensive. One cannot help but notice how often the adjective "defensive" appears in the documents. Since there was an Arab threat, Israeli politicians formulated what they termed a "defense doctrine" in response to that threat. This doctrine was to be executed by the Israeli Defence Forces (IDF); it also prepared the way, in the name of self-defense of course, for the military operations of the June 1967 war.

The defense doctrine does not appear in any official document. Israeli scholars speculate about it through references in diaries and autobiographies, thus completing a jigsaw puzzle that presents a coherent strategy. By far the favorite source is Yigal Alon's autobiography *Masch Hol* (A Curtain of Sand), a book published in 1959.[4] In this book, Alon, a revered hero of the 1948 war, lists a set of contingencies, each of which constituted a cause of war for Israel. The most singular among them, not least for an analysis of the 1958 crisis, was the downfall of the Hashemite monarchy in Jordan resulting from a radical Arab takeover. In such an event, according to Alon, Israel should occupy the West Bank and possibly parts of the East Bank of

[4] Yigal Alon, *A Curtain of Sand* (Tel-Aviv, 1959) (Hebrew), pp. 344–48.

the Jordan River. The other scenarios related to aggressive Arab actions such as the closure of the Tiran straits or the conversion of the estuaries in Arab countries of the Jordan River in such a way that would endanger Israel's water supply.

Alon was quite specific on the contingency of a Hashemite collapse. Israel's need to act owed nothing to past alliances with King Abdullah or his grandson, King Hussein. Alon, and other Israeli leaders, claimed that a radical takeover in Jordan constituted a grave danger to Israel's security, indeed to Israel's very existence. Alon does not explain why. He took it for granted that his Israeli readers would understand that radical regimes would naturally be obsessed by the wish to eliminate the state of Israel.

Alon may have had other reasons for describing domestic changes in Jordan as a *casus belli* scenario. He was one of the leaders of *Ahdut Ha-avoda,* a political party that represented a mixture of socialism and romantic nationalism. For its members Israel's borders of 1967 were unacceptable. In their hearts they found it hard to forgive the political leaders of the 1948 war for allowing Jordan to annex the West Bank and for not exploiting the war to occupy what they regarded as the heart of the Jewish homeland—the towns of Hebron, Nablus, and of course the whole of Jerusalem.

Israel's hidden agenda during the 1958 crisis was thus motivated by a desire finally to capture what should already have been taken in 1948 and to consolidate the Zionist presence in post-mandatory Palestine. Or, to put it differently, the year 1958 offered an opportunity to create a "Greater Israel." Publicly, however, Israeli leaders explained their actions and policies during the crisis in language similar to that employed by those in the West, a language displaying strong animosity to, and deep fear of, the forces of Arab radicalism. For the Israeli Prime Minister and his Cabinet, as well as for many American and British observers, the demon at that time, as in 1956, was Gamal Abdel Nasser, a Nasser who wished to control Jordan as well as the rest of the Arab world. Nasser represented not only Arab nationalism but also world Communism. Hence, his expansionist policy meant only one thing—a Communist, or a Soviet, rule over most of the Arab Middle East.

Thus the key element in the 1958 crisis, as far as the Israelis were concerned, was Jordan. While sharing with the West the strong opposition to the establishment of a pro-Nasser regime there, the Israelis had their own ideas on how to proceed in the eventuality of such a coup. The West planned a military operation that would help to reinstall the Hashemite dynasty in Jordan. At worst, the Western governments were willing, perhaps, to consider the annexation of Jordan to Hashemite Iraq. The Israeli government, and particularly the IDF, preferred to exploit such a situation for expanding Israel's eastern border as far as the Jordan river. For this purpose, Israel was willing to divide Jordan between Israel and Iraq, Israel annexing the West Bank, Iraq the East Bank.

The Israelis failed in their attempt to exploit the crisis. They were frustrated, as they would be again many years later during the 1991 Gulf War, by the subordinate role the West had allocated to them. Israel was a "junior partner" on the scene, unable to pursue its own policy. Hence it was the Western solution to the threat of radicalism that was eventually implemented—keeping a Hashemite kingdom intact at any cost. The Israeli solutions were not welcomed by the West, and the split between Britain and the United States prevented Israel from immediately reaping the only feasible and potentially attainable fruit of the 1958 crisis—a closer alliance with the West. On the other hand, it was in 1958 that the seeds for a special relationship with the United States were planted, the sprouts of which would become the delayed reward for Israeli restraint and obedience in the general policy as formulated by the Americans.[5]

The analysis of Israel's role in the 1958 crisis is perhaps best pursued by concentrating on three issues, or rather three motives, of Israeli policy-makers: the desire to create a Greater Israel; the aspiration to become a Western ally; and the wish to make the IDF the most powerful army in the region. All three were long-term ambitions. The crisis also brought to the surface the need to confront a more concrete problem—the rise of Arab radicalism. In fact, the emergence of Arab radicalism was used to justify the need to pursue these three objectives. This chapter will not deal separately with each of these three goals or with the danger of Arab radicalism, but will maintain a chronological structure in which these issues can be examined. For the sake of clarity, this chronology must begin in the early 1950s.

Arab Radicalism and the Lost Dream of Greater Israel, 1953–1956

Before the 1948 war ended, an important group of Israeli politicians and generals continued to feel that Israel had missed an opportunity to take

[5] Irene Gendzier in fact argues that already during the 1958 crisis American relations with Israel vastly improved. See Irene L. Gendzier, *Notes from the Minefield; United States Intervention in Lebanon and the Middle East, 1945–1958* (New York, 1997), pp. 254–55.

over the whole of western Palestine. The part Israel did not possess in the west was the geopolitical area known, since 1949, as the West Bank, which became part of Jordan.[6] Those in Israel who regarded the agreement as a mistake kept up their efforts to prove to the Israeli government that the Jordanians were violating the armistice agreement of 1949 so that Israeli annexation of at least parts of the West Bank was fully justified. They did not have an easy task because the Jordanians adhered faithfully to the agreement's principal points. The activist group was headed by David Ben-Gurion, Israel's Prime Minister. In the last years of Abdullah's life (1948–1951), Ben-Gurion's government considered three different plans to justify the incorporation of the West Bank into Israel, but it was mainly fear of a strong British reaction that caused Israel to abandon these expansionist plans.[7]

Abdullah's assassination in 1951 provided a more solid opportunity to contemplate annexation. The difference this time was that in order to fulfill the dream of a Greater Israel the experts on the Israeli side suggested a collusion with Hashemite Iraq. The two banks would be divided between the two countries. This concept of an Israeli-Iraqi partitioning of Jordan, should the Hashemites fall in Jordan, crops up again and again between 1951 and 1958. Alternatively, should Iraq refuse to take part in such a scheme, the Israelis were ready to annex the West Bank unilaterally. Israel chose this unilateral option in 1967, the Jordanians providing the ultimate pretext by bombing western Jerusalem on the first day of the June 1967 war.

Israeli interest in the political affairs of Jordan grew quickly after Arab radicalism began to appear. The emergence of this new brand of Arab nationalism, with branches in Jordan, generated a more active, and at times aggressive, Israeli involvement in the politics of the neighboring states. The policy and orientation of those who were regarded as the leaders or spokesmen of Arab radicalism, however, never warranted such a combative Israeli attitude. In the early 1950s, the acknowledged leader of Arab radicalism, Nasser, was willing to probe the possibilities of peace with Israel. Whether the chances for peace were real depended in part on Israeli domestic politics, more specifically on the outcome of the political

---

[6] Ilan Pappé, "The Making of the West Bank, 1948–1951," *Orient* 34, 4 (1993), pp. 553–62.

[7] I have discussed these points in my book *The Making of the Arab-Israeli Conflict, 1947–1951* (London, 1992), pp. 180–91.

rivalry between David Ben-Gurion and Moshe Sharett, the two leaders of the ruling MAPAI party, which represented the Zionist labor movement.[8]

On the face of it, both men should have had at least an ideological affinity with the rise of a more radical trend in Arab politics: Sharett had a traditionally moderate and empathic view towards the Arab struggle for independence, and Ben-Gurion had been inclined towards radical socialism in his early years. There had been times when both leaders had viewed themselves as radicals and Zionism as a revolutionary movement. But this experiment with radicalism on the left was short-lived. In 1948, Ben-Gurion led his country into what he termed "statism"—moving the nation progressively towards state-formation. Out went revolutionary ideas and anarchy and in came "loyalty to the state" and "conformity." Radicalism became a pejorative term in Israeli political and cultural discourse. Political invective was increasingly reserved for anti-Zionist Jews and, of course, the Palestinian citizens of Israel, the majority of whom never succumbed to co-optive and coercive policies of the government and retained a pan-Arabist or Palestinian identity.

In 1952 there was still a residue of respect for radicalism in the attitude of both Ben-Gurion and Sharett. Their initial reaction to the news of the Egyptian revolution was quite enthusiastic and positive. Moshe Sharett, Israel's Foreign Minister until the late 1950s, and briefly also its Prime Minister, favorably regarded the rise of Nasser. Sharett saw Arab radicalism as a political movement determined to improve the social and economic state of affairs in the Middle East and hence, in the long run, one that might recognize Israel's positive role in the area—provided the Jewish state would be willing to compromise on such issues as territory and refugees. This is why, during his term in office as Prime Minister (1953–1955), he looked for ways to establish a substantial dialogue with the Egyptian leader.

In mid May 1953, Nasser sent a letter to Abdel-Rahman Sadeq, the Press Attaché at the Egyptian embassy in Paris, indicating that he was willing to reach an agreement with the Jewish state. Sadeq had conducted secret talks with his counterpart in the Israeli embassy over the previous two years. Nasser addressed his letter to Sadeq but directed it to the Israeli government. In it he asked for Israeli understanding of his position in the area as a whole but particularly in Egypt. He stressed his commitment to

[8] MAPAI was later called the Labour Party, which dominated Israeli politics until 1977 and is still in power today.

peace negotiations between the two countries, but he asked for time. As a first step he was willing to refrain from making any aggressive declarations, and he asked the Israeli government to exercise its influence in Washington in Egypt's favor, particularly to persuade Washington to support the Egyptian demand for a total British withdrawal from his country.[9] Whereas Sharett, as Foreign Minister, was willing to use the new channel, Ben-Gurion, the Prime Minister, as before in such historical junctures, showed no enthusiasm, and nothing came of this episode.

It seems that during those same months, Ben-Gurion formulated his uncompromising attitude towards Arab radicalism, which he now saw as Communism in disguise, or in other words, an anti-Israeli and anti-Western Arab version of Communism. He feared its ideological orientation, but, more importantly, he was alarmed by the military capability that the USSR could offer the radical regimes. In early 1953, he was in favor of a pre-emptive Israeli action against radical regimes. He regarded them as more committed to the armed struggle against Israel than the "inefficient" traditional regimes, and believed the former would perform better on the battlefield, unless defeated by a preemptive Israeli attack.[10]

Unexpectedly Sharett became Prime Minister in December 1953. He resumed the negotiations with Nasser. Talks progressed from vague promises to concrete details. Egypt wanted part of the Negev in return for peace and asked Israel to acknowledge its principal role in creating the Palestinian refugee problem. But at this stage the peace movement bogged down. In the midst of these negotiations, in February 1955, the Israeli army struck an Egyptian base at Gaza. Sharett was led by the generals of the army to believe that this would be a limited retaliatory action against continued Palestinian *Fedayeen* infiltration from the Egyptian-controlled Gaza Strip. In the event, it proved to be devised in such a manner that it could only harm Nasser's prestige and lessen the Palestinian guerrilla effort. Not surprisingly, Nasser abandoned his peaceful intentions and moved to a more aggressive policy towards the Jewish state.[11]

While Sharett was Prime Minister, Ben-Gurion conducted an "alternative" government from what he called "voluntary exile" in his Kibbutz in

---

[9] Divon (Paris) to Shiloah, 12 May 1953, Israel State Archives 2453/20.

[10] Moshe Sharett, *A Personal Diary*, 6, (1955–1956), (Hebrew) (Tel-Aviv, 1978), 27 July 1956.

[11] See Ilan Asia, *The Core of the Conflict: The Struggle for the Negev, 1947–1956* (Hebrew) (Jerusalem, 1994), pp. 126–27.

Sede Boker. Ben-Gurion used his influence to boycott any attempt at reconciliation with Egypt. By adopting this position he not only undermined the chances for peace with Egypt, but also strained Israel's relations with the United States because the Americans had succeeded in establishing a working relationship with Nasser that enabled them to assume the role of mediators in the Palestine conflict.

From his desert resort, Ben-Gurion called for an active Israeli policy against the improvement of the Egyptian-American relationship which he saw as a most harmful development. It might impair Israel's ability to influence American politics. No less ominous in his eyes were Secretary of State John Foster Dulles's efforts to establish a regional defense pact without Israel, which was an initiative at first welcomed by Nasser. One American official in particular, the Ambassador to Cairo, Henry Byroade, was branded as anti-Israeli because of his efforts to strengthen America's position in the Arab world. All in all, the Eisenhower administration seemed to be hostile to Israel. When the Americans and the British jointly launched the "Alpha Plan"—yet another Western peace initiative—Ben-Gurion regarded it as a unacceptable.

The Alpha Plan should be seen in the context of NATO's efforts to organize a Middle Eastern network of pro-Western alliances and political settlements. The first major effort, the Baghdad Pact, was launched in January 1955 by Turkey, Iraq, and Britain. In March 1955 the Alpha plan was considered by policy-makers both in Washington and in London. As a comprehensive proposal for ending the Arab-Israeli conflict, it had solutions for the problems of the Palestinian refugees, the fate of Jerusalem, and the territorial division of post-Mandatory Palestine. It had little to offer to Palestinian nationalism, though this is not surprising in view of the weakness of the Palestinian movement in those years. On the other hand, the Alpha plan provided for the Israeli repatriation of refugees and concession of territory in exchange for the normalization of Israeli diplomatic relations with the Arab world. There were lengthy and enervating attempts made to persuade both sides to accept the plan as a basis for negotiations and in a sense it formed a prelude to the 1958 crisis. But Israel continued to pursue an uncompromising policy towards its Arab neighbors, particularly its radical neighbors. This was at a time when Nasser welcomed the Alpha plan as the first step toward peace.[12]

[12] Three sources provide a succinct analysis of the plan: David Carlton, *Anthony Eden: A Biography* (London, 1981), pp. 382–83 (although Carlton was not aware of the name,

It is difficult to assess how far Nasser would have gone. The American and British plan was actually quite ambiguous. Nasser was invited to conclude peace with Israel and at the same time, to accept the Baghdad Pact, which according to its critics sought to undermine radical, or even reformist, Arab regimes. But Nasser's ambition was to be one of the leaders of the Third World, an equal to Tito and Nehru. His objective was to face the West with a new global power, and confronting Israel was only one step on the way to achieving this goal. Thus, more important for Nasser than the Negev was the meeting of neutral or non-aligned countries of Asia and Africa at Bandung, which represented the high-priority struggle with the West.

Sharett, who by then must had grown used to Ben-Gurion's uncompromising line, was nonetheless bewildered by the Prime Minister's reluctance even to examine the Alpha plan.[13] He regarded Ben-Gurion's aggressive behavior as unnecessarily heightening the already tense Arab-Israeli relationship. But since Ben-Gurion represented faithfully the mood of most politicians and generals in Israel, Sharett acquiesced. The commanders of the Israeli army, under the energetic guidance of Moshe Dayan, were already designing plans in May 1955 to go to war against Egypt. Nasser became a target not only because of his support for Palestinian guerrilla warfare or his arms deal with the Eastern Bloc, but because he was an enemy of the West. He had to be toppled by Israel and the Western Powers. Six years after the victory of 1948, an intoxicating sense of Israeli invincibility still lingered on. Dayan, like other Israeli generals, confidently contemplated a re-drawing of the Middle Eastern map by dint of Israeli military power. He initiated a series of provocative actions that buried the Alpha plan for good, and prepared the ground for Israel's attack on Egypt in 1956.[14]

Peace negotiations failed only in part because of Ben-Gurion's intransigence. Nasser was willing to accept Israel as an accomplished fact only if certain conditions and qualifications were met to contain Israel's expansionist tendencies. Nasser demanded that the negotiations be secretive and gradual. He would continue his anti-Israeli public rhetoric and betray no change of official policy. In contrast, the Israeli government of Moshe

---

"Alpha," given to the plan); Michael Oren, "The Diplomatic Struggle for the Negev, 1946–1955," *Studies in Zionism* 10, 2 (1989), pp. 197–215; and Shimon Shamir, "The Collapse of Project Alpha," in W. R. Louis and Roger Owen, eds., *Suez 1956: The Crisis and Its Consequences* (Oxford, 1989), pp. 73–102.

13 Asia, *The Core,* p.166.

14 This is the main thesis in Motti Golani, *Israel in Search of War* (Brighton, 1998).

Sharett demanded publicity because it could not keep secrets for too long and needed fast results. Sharett was suspicious of what he saw as a "double play" on the part of Arab leaders.

Sharett emerged from this episode with his reputation and standing badly damaged for conceding too much to Arab and international demands. He was depicted by the army as a leader who, in the face of Arab radicalism and Palestinian terrorism, proved to be inadequate and irresolute. Most of those who influenced public opinion shared Ben-Gurion's total mistrust of Arab radicalism. They believed it to be an extreme and escalated form of Arab hostility towards Israel. For them Nasser became Israel's number one enemy.[15] Sharett consequently had to go.

The Suez campaign ended Sharett's political career for good. His short term in office, his weakness as a politician, and his lack of public courage limit our ability to assess the realism of his plans for peace. After 1956, in any case, he no longer played a significant role in shaping the policy of the government or the views of the public on Arab radicalism. From then on, and well into the mid-1960s, Ben-Gurion's star was in the ascendancy.

Formulating a Defense Doctrine, 1956–1958

In the aftermath of the Suez crisis, Ben-Gurion, together with several ministers and the Chiefs of Staff, devoted more time contemplating how to deal with the threat of Arab radicalism. Ben-Gurion, however, never seemed to be interested in long-term planning. Most Israeli historians speak of a defense "concept," but probably it is merely the best term for what remained primarily an ad-hoc policy.

There were four major components to this concept. The first was the need to ally Israel as closely as possible to the West, and particularly to the United States. This was the inevitable lesson Israel had learned from Suez. If an official alliance with the United States proved unattainable, Israel would at least seek closer cooperation with NATO as a whole, not merely with France or Britain. The second complementary component of this concept, which could only have been achieved through a good relationship with the West, was the need to arm the Jewish state to the teeth with sophisticated weapons including nuclear arms.

[15] Avi Shlaim, "Conflicting Approaches to Israel's Relations with the Arabs: Ben-Gurion and Moshe Sharett, 1953–1956," *The Middle East Journal* 37, 2 (1983), pp. 180–201.

The third component was the need to pursue an active "involvement" in the affairs of neighboring Arab states. This involvement began immediately after 1948, and continued in various forms of intervention thereafter: from wide-scale commando raids as part of a retaliation policy against Palestinian infiltration, to clandestine espionage and terrorist activities in the Arab capitals, to attempts to bribe and influence leading politicians in the Arab world. A few lessons were learned from the *Parasha* or "the affair," the name given by the Israeli press to the abortive attempt in 1954 by the Israeli Mossad whereby Egyptian Jews would be enlisted to plant bombs in a number of Western buildings in Egypt and thus strain Egypt's relations with the West.[16] After 1956 more subtle and cautious means were used to meddle in Arab affairs.

The fourth and final component was probably formulated just before or during the 1958 crisis. This was the idea of establishing, preferably as part of NATO, a peripheral pact in the Middle East consisting of Turkey, Ethiopia, Iran, and Israel. In his negotiations with the Americans, Ben-Gurion referred to it as the "outer perimeter." It was mainly the American support for Iran and Turkey that led him to believe that a united non-Arab bloc in the Middle East was not just an Israeli but an American vision as well.

This defense concept also influenced Ben-Gurion's attitude towards the Israeli Arabs, whom he regarded as radical. This is why he insisted on the continued imposition of a military regime on the country's Arab citizens. Created in October 1948, this oppressive system was the target of growing opposition in Israel in the 1950s. Even the Secret Service in 1955 advised the Prime Minister that there was no security advantage in maintaining a draconian rule. But Ben-Gurion was adamant in his refusal to abolish it.[17]

Aligning Israel to the United States, arming it heavily, and seeking new allies in the periphery would be the main guidelines under which Ben-Gurion's government acted during the evolving crisis of 1957–1958.

---

16 It is noteworthy that mainstream Israeli historians such as Zaki Shalom, *Policy in the Shadow of Controversy* (Hebrew) (Tel-Aviv, 1996), and Ilan Asia, do not connect the "Parasha" to their assessment of Israel policy in those years, while Benny Morris in his *Israel's Border Wars, 1948–1956* (Oxford, 1995) integrates a discussion of it in an overall assessment of Israel's policy.

17 Ilan Pappé, "An Uneasy Co-Existence: Arabs and Jews in the First Decade of Statehood," in I. Troen and N. Lucas, eds., *Israel: The First Decade of Independence* (New York, 1995), pp. 617–58.

The Syrian Crisis—1957–1958

The emergence of the Baath as the main radical force within geographical or "Greater Syria" riveted the attention of policy-makers in Israel. The political upheavals in Syria which ended with the formation of the United Arab Republic (UAR) in early 1958, on the one hand, and the Socialist and Marxist orientation of Palestinian politics in Jordan, on the other, stimulated extensive intelligence assessments and reports in the Israeli Foreign and Defense Ministries.

The IDF itself, especially its commanders, were less interested in the internal affairs of Syria than in the deteriorating situation on the Israeli-Syrian border. In 1957, this border was still highly unstable with Israelis and Syrians alternately violating the shaky armistice between them. The Israeli press was particularly anti-Syrian, and depicted Damascus as an anti-Israeli base from which only the worst could be expected. There were few voices to point out to readers that many of the clashes on the border were ignited by a provocative Israeli policy, in which the army encouraged Israeli farmers to encroach on territory designated as either Syrian or no man's land, knowing that this would trigger a Syrian response. Martin Buber and Ernest Simon were among the solitary critics within Ben-Gurion's own party who strongly criticized him, accusing him of acting against peace in the Middle East.[18]

The demonization of Syria in the Israeli media becomes evident when reading Ben-Gurion's diary from that period. The diary is not a particularly reliable source for the diplomatic history of Israel or the conflict, quite the opposite. One should be wary of the inclination of a growing number of Israeli historians to accept the diary at face value, as though it tells us what really happened. Quite often Ben-Gurion obviously wrote with a view to the future and did not reflect contemporary views. Yet in what may be seen as an interesting insight into the leader's perceptions and attitudes, Ben-Gurion reveals that in 1957 he felt there was an opportunity for an Israeli alliance with the West against the growing power of radicalism and Communism in Syria. He then, quite surprisingly if only for a brief moment, ponders the possibility of reaching some sort of understanding about Syria with the Soviet Union, but he quickly retreats from this line of thinking.[19]

18 Meetings of MAPAI Secretariat, 4 March 1957, Labour Movement Archives.

19 Ben-Gurion's diary, for instance 16 October 1957, Ben-Gurion Archives, Sdeh Boker.

The natural ally for joint action on Syria was France. Here the diary reads like the testimony of a genuine Francophile. In a conversation with General Maurice Challe, the French Deputy to the Chief of Staff of the Air Force, Ben-Gurion depicts Syria as "the problem of the world, not just of Israel."[20] The danger was so acute, explains the Israeli Prime Minster, that France should urgently work to include Israel in NATO officially, or at least encourage the Alliance to accept it as a privileged ally. France, of course, could not do this, but it delivered arms in large quantities. Moreover, in 1957 France provided Israel with its nuclear infrastructure.[21] But not everyone in Paris was pro-Israeli. The Quai d'Orsay, the French Foreign Ministry, balanced French government support to the Jewish state with a pro-Arab policy and encouraged the French military industry to supply weapons to Arab countries as well. It was the French Defense Ministry that safeguarded Israel's interest in those years, even after a more neutral French government came to power in May 1957.[22] One result of the French aid in building a strong Israel and instilling Israeli self-confidence was an even more uncompromising mood in Tel-Aviv.

On Syria, in any case, the Israelis and the French had a common language and purpose. Syria continued to be in the eyes of many Frenchmen a country that supported the Algerian revolution, like Egypt. Not surprisingly, these were favorable days for Israelis in Paris. In the Israeli collective national memory this period is recalled as the "Israeli-French honeymoon." April 1957 was a particularly good month. The press repeatedly remarked on the excellent Israeli-French relationship of a kind that Israel had never experienced before with any country. In its commentaries the Israeli press singled out the wave of French sympathy for the people of Israel as the only benefit Israel had reaped from the Suez war. France granted Israel a $30 million credit and helped to lay an oil pipeline from Eilat to the refineries in Haifa. The oil tankers reaching Eilat were mostly American, or American-registered, but France was seen as the principal benefactor. Israel's alliance with France was further strengthened by full-fledged French support for an Israeli attempt to send a ship through the Suez canal.[23]

---

[20] Ibid.

[21] See Zach Levey, "Israel's Pursuit of French Arms, 1952–1958," *Studies in Zionism* 14, 2, pp. 207–09.

[22] Ibid.

[23] A leased Danish ship entered the canal in July 1957 and was allowed to continue after the only Israeli on it, Rafi Eilon, had been arrested. At first, Eilon, who was a photographer for *Ha-Olam Ha-Zeh*, a Hebrew anti-establishment paper in Israel, received extensive

Ben-Gurion had already noted that however strong the alliance with France might be, it would not suffice in the long run. Appearing in front of his party's Members of the Knesset, Ben-Gurion declared: "the most popular people in Israel are now the French. But this is not good enough. We need the Americans. We cannot rely on Britain, since unlike in the United States, the Jews have no political influence [there]. Thus, for instance, the Labour Party are purely "*Goyim* [Gentiles]."[24] It is thus somewhat misleading to assume, as Michael Brecher does, that the basic aim of Israeli foreign policy between 1955 and 1966 was to sustain vital diplomatic and military assistance from France in the form of a de facto alliance.[25]

A first opportunity to elicit a stronger American commitment to Israel emerged in the summer of 1957. By then, despite extensive American clandestine operations—or perhaps because of them—it became clear that Damascus was "lost" to the West and was now leaning strongly towards Moscow. In August, the CIA plotted, not for the first time, to overthrow the Syrian government but was thwarted by the Syrians. The ensuing deterioration in the relationship between Washington and Damascus led Ben-Gurion to issue a firm statement of support for the American action in Syria.[26] This was done by devising a new terminology which portrayed Israel as the major anti-Soviet bastion in the area.[27]

Greater Israel Lost Again: Israel and the Jordanian Crisis, 1957–1958

The unification of Syria with Egypt in February 1958, the civil war that erupted in Lebanon in May and, finally, the revolution in Baghdad in July, were events that concentrated Israel's attention on its eastern border. By

---

hospitality from the Egyptians, though the rest of his stay was less pleasant. This did not lead him to portray Egypt in a negative way. He was the first Israeli to provide a first-hand report on Israel's southern neighbor, but his positive attitude was a far cry from the generally hostile mood of Israelis to Egypt.

[24] David Ben-Gurion, *The First Prime Minster: Selected Documents, 1947–1963*, Doc. 106, a speech to the parliamentary party, 19 September 1957, Israel State Archives.

[25] Michael Breecher, *Israel's Foreign Policy: The First Twenty Years in the Foreign Policy System of Israel* (Oxford, 1972), pp. 557–62.

[26] Letter to John Foster Dulles, 22 August 1957, Ben-Gurion, *Selected Documents,* Doc. 107.

[27] Ben-Gurion's diary, 16 October 1957.

now, the "defense doctrine" was firmly in place and it defined clearly where and how Israel should act. For most Israeli policy-makers it was clear that Israel was unable to interfere directly in Damascus and Beirut. Obviously the same was true in Baghdad. The State Department and the CIA nevertheless alerted the White House to possible Israeli intervention in Syria. But the potential ability of Israel to carry out such activity was doubted.[28] There is nothing in the Israeli documents that shows any such intention with regard to Syria.

Nor in Lebanon did the Israelis contemplate any active part in the crisis. The United States received, for what it was worth, a guarantee of unconditional Israeli support for the American intervention on behalf of Camille Chamoun in Lebanon. This is not to say that the Israelis were not concerned about the possible radicalization of Lebanon. The Israeli government saw Lebanon mainly in terms of a domino theory, as another pawn that could fall into the hands of Nasser or the Soviet Union. The Israeli government declared that a tough position on Lebanon was the last chance the United States had to avoid a total collapse of Western interests in the area. But Israel left it to the United States to cope with the situation.[29]

Jordan was a different story. As pointed out previously, any radicalization of that country would be interpreted by the Israeli leadership as a cause for war. Indeed, for Israel the 1958 crisis was essentially a Jordanian crisis. The Egyptian-Syrian merger was less important to the Israelis than the Iraqi-Jordanian counter federation in the same month, just as street riots in Lebanon were of less interest than the possible Iraqi intervention in Jordan in the wake of the July revolution in Baghdad.

In the case of Jordan, potential Israeli action was hampered by questions of timing and capabilities. Any intervention before a total radical takeover had occurred was a delicate matter for most Israeli leaders in view of the Jewish-Hashemite understanding that went back to the 1920s. After all, this special relationship carried much weight in Israeli political life, as it still does today in certain political circles. The radicalization of the political scene in the Hashemite kingdom was a process that was closely watched by the Israeli intelligence and by the Research Department of the Foreign Ministry. Accounts were written daily and assessments were handed over monthly to the policy-makers, in all of which Israeli experts strongly recommended keeping intact the de facto alliance with the

[28] Gendzier, *Notes From the Minefield*, p. 254.
[29] Ibid., p. 255, note 68.

Jordanians. The problem for Israeli policy-makers was that as the crisis became more serious, or in other words, when the ability of the Hashemites to stay in power appeared less convincing, Western involvement become deeper. The more the West was directly involved, the less Israelis were able to pursue an independent policy.

The alarm bells had begun ringing in October 1956 in Israel when the Left in Jordan won the parliamentary elections. It seems that contingency plans were immediately formulated as to the benefits that Israel might reap from the radicalization of Jordan. The main option considered was a unilateral Israeli annexation of the West Bank. Ben-Gurion discussed this possibility quite openly with the French Prime Minster, Guy Mollet, as part of the overall Israeli-French collusion against Arab Radicalism in 1956. He did not disclose to his French interlocutor the wish for unilateral Israeli action but proposed the division of Jordan between Israel (the West Bank) and Iraq (the East Bank).[30] The Americans somehow got wind of this exchange and explicitly warned Ben-Gurion against such action.[31]

Anxiety in Jerusalem grew in the winter of 1956–57 after the abolition of the Anglo-Jordanian defense treaty and its substitution by an Arab defense pact and a promise for a Saudi subsidy to Jordan. There followed the establishment of diplomatic relations between Jordan and the Soviet Union and tension on Israel's eastern border rose, with warlike rhetoric heard publicly in Israel.

The despatch of Iraqi forces to help Hussein to save his country from the "Left" evoked statements by Israeli leaders on the political right to assume "freedom of action" on Jordanian territory, which meant mainly to reserve the right to occupy the West Bank. Ben-Gurion, who was then Defense Minister as well as Prime Minster, put the Israeli army on the alert to prepare for such an operation in April 1957. The moment a pro-Nasserite regime toppled Hussein, the IDF would enter the West Bank.

At the time, the Israeli public was well aware of the high alert in the army and the possibility of a military operation. The press was consequently told that any such operation had been averted because the United States had sent the Sixth Fleet to the eastern Mediterranean to deter Israel from taking aggressive action. Commentators in the local press (and also in the United States) called the United States' effort to curb Israel the

[30] Ben-Gurion's diary, 22 October 1956.

[31] Robert H. Ferrell, ed., *The Eisenhower Diaries* (New York, 1981), 15 October 1956, p. 333.

"boldest American move since Korea." The culprit in the Israeli press was Dulles, who, it was reported, had personally dispatched the Fleet. But in fact, according to American documents, the Fleet was sent to counter the anti-American developments in Syria, not to check Israeli expansionist policies.[32] Israel at the time played a minor role in the overall American strategy. In any event Washington employed different means to deter Israel, as it does to this day.

In the unfolding of events after April 1957, Israel's main effort was twofold: to exploit the crisis for territorial expansion and to consolidate a strategic alliance with the West. On both accounts its plans came to naught because of the marginal role Israel was allocated by the Americans, who ruled the game. Under the circumstances, getting more territory and retaining American sympathy were contradictory aims.

American policy had the full support of the United Nations, and particularly of its Secretary General, Dag Hammarskjöld, who even more than the Americans wanted to relegate Israel to the sidelines in the 1958 crisis. His position derived from a conviction that the Israeli Prime Minister had only one aim in mind, the annexation of the West Bank. It is no wonder then that Israel's relations with the United Nations in the 1958 crisis sank to an unprecedented low.[33]

The intricacy of American policy was revealed to the Israelis during the mission of James F. Richards, President Eisenhower's Special Assistant for Near Eastern affairs, who arrived in Israel at the beginning of May 1957. Richards' task was to discuss how Israel could be integrated into the scheme of the Eisenhower Doctrine. The American thinking on Israel's role in American defense plans had not changed much since 1951, when the United States for the first time tried to link Arab-Israeli peace negotiations and the establishment of a pro-Western alliance in the area. The underlying assumption was that, in the face of the looming Soviet danger, Israel and at least some of the Arab countries would settle most of their differences and conflicts. In reality, both Israel and the Arab states saw the Cold War as offering a variety of opportunities that could help them strengthen their positions with respect to each other. Richards, however, showed up unexpectedly, and without the usual preparation such a visit should have demanded. It is no surprise therefore that the two sides failed

---

32 See Bonnie F. Saunders, *The United States and Arab Nationalism: The Syrian Case, 1953–1960* (Westport, 1996), pp. 80–86.

33 See the chapter by Michael Graham Fry.

even to publish a joint press release. The Israelis initially refused to officially endorse the Eisenhower Doctrine, claiming that they did not wish to alienate the Russians. But after Richards left, Ben-Gurion gave full-fledged Israeli support for the Doctrine in the Knesset.[34]

Not everyone in Israeli politics shared the idea of supporting the Eisenhower Doctrine. The Zionist Left, in other words parties such as MAPAM (the United Workers Party), was still loyal to Moscow and they thus rejected the doctrine. The Right wing accepted only the anti-Communist parts of it and objected to the part that called upon the parties of conflict to reach a compromise over historic Palestine. In this context, it is worthwhile to note that in the years 1957 and 1958 Ben-Gurion headed a minority government enjoying only the support of the nationalist sister party of MAPAI, *Ahdut Ha-avoda,* and MAPAM. It is quite possible that the domestic situation in Israel, more than the fear of a Russian response, lay behind the reserved attitude towards the Americans.

The text of Ben-Gurion's statement in the Knesset demonstrates MAPAI's image of Israel as a superior and self-contained entity in the midst of a "wild Middle East." Ben-Gurion stressed the uniqueness of Israeli's positive response to the Eisenhower Doctrine and pointed to the total rejection of it throughout the Arab world.

After officially committing his government to the Doctrine, Ben-Gurion sensed he could turn over a new leaf in Israel's strategic relationship with the United States. In September 1957, he sent messages to the CIA, and he offered grandiose schemes such as the establishment of a joint intelligence agency and a tacit anti-Russian alliance with Israel at its center. The rejection of these plans did not deter the Israeli Prime Minister. The July 1958 crisis seemed to him a good opportunity to impress upon the Americans the value of having a strategic ally such as Israel. "There was something pathetic and humiliating in the repeated efforts of Israel to cling to the US," wrote Ben-Gurion's biographer, Michael Bar-Zohar.[35] Ben-Gurion seemed driven by a sense of urgency, believing that without an official alliance the United States would refrain from coming to Israel's aid in case of a conflict.[36]

Ben-Gurion was not alone. Abba Eban, Israel's Ambassador to the United Nations at the time, felt like Ben-Gurion that the crisis was an

34 See Zach Levey, *Israel and the Western Powers*, p. 178.

35 Michael Bar-Zohar, *David Ben-Gurion* (Hebrew), (Tel-Aviv, 1978), 3, p. 1320.

36 In a speech to the Knesset, 3 June 1957.

opportunity to prove to the Americans the need to have an official strategic relationship with Israel. In May 1958, while on a mission to the State Department, Eban tried to convince the Americans that Israel had a superior position in the Arab world. The Israelis could interpret Arab politics, history, and culture as well as intervene decisively. Eban suggested basing the construction of US regional policy on the Israeli projection of the Middle Eastern reality.[37]

On the other hand, among those who felt that self-respect and *realpolitik* should lead Israel to be content with de facto alliances with the West was Moshe Dayan. Dayan on the whole preferred unofficial treaties. He saw the Arab-Israeli conflict as a given variable in Israel's future. He held it to be insoluble. It was thus the dominant factor according to which Israel's policy should be shaped. Everything else, such as questions of alliances and allies, would have to be frequently reviewed afresh according to new circumstances.[38]

In any case, it was Ben-Gurion who dictated the political line. He initiated a series of actions aimed at changing the low-profile American commitment by sparking a crisis that would force the US to exert pressure on Egypt. Among these actions were the despatch of a growing number of ships with cargo destined for Israel through the Suez Canal and the provocative laying of an oil pipeline between Eilat and Ashkelon. On 11 November 1957 the Israeli government put in an official request to have a strategic alliance with NATO, only to see it rejected out of hand by the Council of Ministers.

The "Junior Partner," July 1958

During the dramatic events of 1958, after the creation of the United Arab Republic, the pro-Nasserite rebellion against Camille Chamoun in Lebanon, and the Iraqi revolution, Israel offered much rhetoric but little action. Until Britain approached Israel in July 1958 with the request to allow British aircraft to fly over Israel to Jordan, Israel played no role in the crisis.

The tension on the Israeli side between verbal saber-rattling on the one hand, and paralysis and inaction on the other, may explain Ben-Gurion's

[37] Gendezier, *Notes from the Minefield*, p. 255.

[38] Dan Horowitz, *The Israeli Concept of National Security* (Hebrew), (Jerusalem, 1973), pp. 1–7, 23–41.

eccentric and bizarre behavior during the crisis. One can only speculate as to what exactly the British Ambassador to Israel, Sir Frances Rundall, must have felt when he was presented with Ben-Gurion's list of requests in return for Israeli consent to let the British fly over Israel. It was headed by the demand that Israel be included in the British Commonwealth.[39] Rundall summarized the other requests: "the integration of Israel into the Western Defense System. A tacit guarantee of Israeli present frontiers and the supply of armaments she needs."[40]

Some of these requests were not so far-fetched. At the time, of course, none of these "gifts" came Israel's way, but later some of these same conditions became the basis for the American commitment to Israel. In any event, Ben-Gurion was more specific about the conditions for Israeli assistance to the Western operation in 1958. There had to be a firm American commitment to conclude an official alliance with Israel. He told Rundall that Israeli consent depended on American approval for the British act, something which was of course more than procedural.[41]

Requesting the flight over Israel was at variance with normal Anglo-Israeli relations, which were already disturbed because of developments in Jordan. The British wished to keep the Hashemites intact at virtually any price while, as noted above, at least some of the Israelis were eager to annex the West Bank. It seems that the organizers of Operation Valour, the combined rescue operation for Jordan, Lebanon, Kuwait, and the Persian Gulf in general, had very little choice other than to make the request of Israel. Young King Hussein could not afford, given his tenuous position, to ask openly and directly for British or American assistance. The pro-Nasserite forces in the area had cut the main logistic air and land routes to Jordan and there was only one way left, via Israel.[42]

Although the British Ambassador came away from the conversation with the sense that approval had been granted, Ben-Gurion delayed his government's official response. In his public appearances and his conversations with other diplomats, Ben-Gurion presented Israel as a country torn between its wish to join NATO and also remain on good terms with

[39] The idea was first mentioned by Ben-Gurion in 1950, when Britain had sent its commanding officer in the Middle East, General Brian Robertson, on an unofficial visit to Israel. Ilan Pappé, "From an Open Conflict to a Tacit Alliance: Anglo-Israeli Relations, 1948–1951," *Middle East Studies* 26, 4, pp. 420–39.

[40] Tel-Aviv to London, 19 July 1958 FO 371/134284, VR 1015/12.

[41] Ben-Gurion's diary, 18 July 1958.

[42] Memoranda 6 June 1958 and 15 July 1958, CAB 128/32.

the Third World. Israeli leaders were worried particularly about the country's image in Asia and Africa, two continents in which decolonization brought with it a considerable share of goodwill towards the Jewish state. But the priorities of Israel at the time were clear enough. The desire to become a Western ally overshadowed any other foreign policy objectives.

Ben-Gurion told Rundall of a further reason for hesitation, which was the position of the British Labour party.[43] More than two hundred Members of Parliament voted on 17 July 1958 against the decision to intervene in Jordan. Rundall responded to Ben-Gurion by doubting whether Labour's objection was genuine. This is mentioned here only anecdotally because it is doubtful whether Ben-Gurion was at all affected by the position of the Labour party. He was merely showing off how well-informed and sophisticated he was. More to the point was Ben-Gurion's apprehension of a tough Soviet reaction. Ultimately, however, his concrete and relevant worries were domestic ones. Three of his partners in his minority coalition criticized his alliance with Britain.

The deterioration of Hussein's position led Britain to act in an uncharacteristic way. British aircraft flew through Israeli air space without waiting for Israel's official consent (although it should be mentioned that there was an element of confusion and the British believed that the authorization had been granted). Ben-Gurion was furious. He feared that his ability to uphold Israel's independence had been severely undermined. That indeed was the charge of the Revisionist opposition, who sharply criticized the government's approval of the overflight. Ben-Gurion wanted of course to appear as patriotic as the Right, and he was always attentive to criticism that he had failed to endorse Israel's proud sense of self-reliance and independence. He openly condemned the unauthorized flights but led Rundall to understand that the Israeli Air Force would not intercept any British flights over the country.

The airlift to Jordan lasted for about fifteen days, until 2 August 1958, when Israel officially asked them to be stopped. Ben-Gurion explained to the Americans and the British that he had received word of a direct Soviet threat. In London and Washington this threat, if indeed it had been made at all, was not taken too seriously, and Foreign Office and State Department experts analyzed Ben-Gurion's action as generated by domestic considerations.[44] It is also possible that the Israeli Prime Minister

---

43 Ben-Gurion's diary, 18 July 1958

44 Tel-Aviv to London, 3 and 4 August 1958 FO 371/134347/52.

expected a *quid pro quo* in the form of commitments and arms supplies. He learned, however, that the United States government did not regard it as necessary to reward Israel for an act fully in accordance with Israel's own interests.

The Soviet involvement was actually more positive than historians have tended to believe. The Russians exploited the tension by suggesting the convening of an international forum to solve the Arab-Israeli conflict. Ever since 1949, however, Ben-Gurion had been wary of international conferences as a means for other powers to exert international pressure on Israel and make it concede territory in return for peace. He flatly rejected the offer, as did the Americans.

This was all done in typical Ben-Gurion style. Until 2 August 1958, the Americans were led to understand that "the Prime Minister would know about the flights but not endorse them."[45] It was made easier for Ben-Gurion when the West decided now to use American aircraft instead of British. American airplanes now flew twice a week over Israel, well into September. These included two flights by members of the Royal Hashemite family.

During that period Israeli policy-makers began to press vociferously for a "peripheral treaty" with Iran, Turkey, and Ethiopia.[46] It was not only the attraction of a non-Arab alliance that led Ben-Gurion to pursue this option energetically, but it was also, especially in the case of Turkey, an indirect way of aligning Israel with NATO and the Eisenhower Doctrine.[47]

The first time this option had been seriously raised was in the beginning of 1958 following the creation of the UAR. The plan appears obsessively in Ben-Gurion's diary after the July revolution in Iraq. This line of thinking was widespread in his own party and it had the full endorsement of the party's leading members and newspapers. It is noteworthy that these ambitions were reciprocated by the countries concerned. But it seems that each preferred bilateral cooperation, rather than a multilateral treaty that would be conspicuously anti-Arab. Little ultimately came of these efforts, except for the establishment of an intelligence coordinating network between Israel and Turkey code-named "Trident."

The Turks were more forthcoming towards the Israelis than others, though positive signals came also from Adis Ababa and Teheran. The

[45] Oren, *Iyunim,* pp. 266–67 and Bar-Zohar, *Ben-Gurion*, p. 1341.

[46] Bar-On, *Iyunim*, p. 103.

[47] Avner Yaniv, *Politics and Strategy in Israel* (Tel-Aviv, 1994) (Hebrew).

Turkish Foreign Minister, Fatin Zorlu, was instrumental in cementing this Turco-Israeli connection. The new relationship reached its zenith with Ben-Gurion's visit to Ankara in August 1958. Unfortunately for the Israelis, the Turks insisted that the visit be kept secret, which meant that the public remained unaware of the Israeli diplomatic success.[48]

Ethiopia and Iran had to be seduced. Emperor Haile Sellassie was promised widespread assistance in the development of his country in return for participation in the peripheral treaty. In a personal letter Ben-Gurion warned the Emperor about the "military junta" in Cairo,[49] depicting Nasser as an agent of international Communism who had set his eyes on Ethiopia. Ben-Gurion hoped to cajole the Emperor by describing the Nile as mainly an Ethiopian river—or, as Ben-Gurion put it, "it is foremost a Sudanese and Ethiopian river. I have instructed our representatives abroad to stress this vital geographical fact in public."[50] Ben-Gurion also sent a letter to Said Abdullah Halil, the Sudanese Prime Minster and the head of the anti-Egyptian Umma party. Ultimately however the alliance with Ethiopia did not amount to much. In essence the Emperor did little more than send a number of commandos to be trained by the IDF.

While the Ethiopians were given minor military support, the Shah of Iran was promised scientific investments. In the case of both Ethiopia and Iran, Israeli leaders invoked ancient historical allegiances to accentuate how "natural" the contemporary alliances were between them by referring to Cyrus and the Jews in the case of the Iranians and Solomon and Sheba in the case of the Ethiopians. In the decolonized world of Asia and Africa, however, ancient ties counted for little. Among the Asian and African radicals, some of whom became leaders themselves, Israel was seen not only as fighting against Arab radicalism, but also as aligning itself with old world Asian and African despotism, thus becoming, in the jargon of the day, a neo-colonialist state.

Above all, the peripheral pacts needed the blessing of the United States. The Americans were notified about these proposed ties in a comprehensive letter that Ben-Gurion sent to President Eisenhower. Washington responded quite politely, welcoming the idea in general, but reluctant to be involved in the venture either directly or indirectly. Though Dulles had

---

[48] Ibid., p. 167.

[49] Letter to Haile Sellassie, 6 November 1958, Ben-Gurion, *Selected Documents,* Doc. 113, Letter to Haile Sellassie, 6 November 1958.

[50] Ibid.

initially favored the idea, he increasingly viewed it as dangerous. Both he and the President ultimately saw no alternative to the Eisenhower Doctrine to curb both the Soviet Union and Arab radicalism, an attitude which the Israeli Foreign Minister, Golda Meir, saw as "annoying." Moshe Dayan tried to enlist the services of British Field Marshal Bernard Montgomery, who at the time was the Deputy Commander in Chief of NATO Forces and a frequent visitor to Eisenhower. Although on friendly terms with Dayan, Montgomery did not act as Israel's advocate in the White House. He instead told Dayan that what Israel needed was not participation in a peripheral pact or more weapons but a sensible policy of peace.[51]

Dayan did not believe in the need of an official alliance with NATO. Convinced that the West would be relatively indifferent to Israel's needs, Dayan was confirmed in this view during the July 1958 crisis. Throughout those tense days, Dayan was as combative as ever. For him the crucial moment was the July Revolution in Iraq. When the news reached Israel, he warned the Israeli government that the country now faced the danger of another war, adding that Israel should be ready to repel a two-front attack in the near future. The Chief of the Air Force was more specific—an Arab offensive would take place, he predicted, in the end of 1959 or the beginning of 1960. The army demanded a pre-emptive strike.

Ben-Gurion briefly hesitated but then rejected jingoistic demands. Haim Laskov, the designate Chief of the General Staff who replaced Dayan in 1959, proposed to occupy most of the West Bank. Ben-Gurion again hesitated. He told his generals to wait until diplomatic efforts were exhausted.[52] The historian Mordechai Bar-On believes, in hindsight, that the Prime Minister feared a fierce and angry American response, and furthermore, that Ben-Gurion had not lost hope that the Americans themselves would take a military initiative against radical Arab regimes. Unlike the crisis in October 1956, this time Washington was more receptive. Although the United States reverted to a more cautious and neutral policy once the crisis was over, during the crisis itself the Americans were willing to consider anti-radical options. This more aggressive mood was

[51] Moshe Dayan, *Story of My Life* (Tel-Aviv, 1976) (Hebrew), pp. 367–70. Irene Gendzier has a different point of view and argues that there was American support for the peripheral treaty and a particular American interest in an Israeli-Turkish alliance. See Gendzier, *Notes from the Minefield*, p. 255, note 67.

[52] Mordechai Naor, *Haim Laskov* (Tel-Aviv, 1988) (Hebrew), p. 279.

revealed to the Israelis when two of Ben-Gurion's emissaries, Abba Eban and Reuven Shiloah, were sent to Washington to discuss with Dulles the possibility of dividing Jordan between Israel and Iraq.[53] General Nathan Twining, the Chairman of the Joint Chiefs of Staff, strongly recommended such a line of action in a meeting with Allen Dulles, the head of the CIA.[54] When the crisis came to an end in November 1958, though, Twining changed his mind. For the first time the possibility of American support for the creation of a Palestinian entity in the West Bank was mentioned.[55]

Ben-Gurion may also have feared a harsh British response to his maneuvers and schemes. But if he had any such apprehensions, there is no evidence that they played an important role in his decisions. His main inhibition from realizing the Greater Israel project may well have derived from demographic considerations. In his diary he wrote that annexation of the West Bank was impossible because "regrettably this time the Palestinians would not flee," and Israel would be left with the necessity to rule over a large number of Palestinians. Ever since the 1930s, he had been aware of the dilemma incurred in "expanding" Israeli rule over areas populated by Palestinians. He had always stressed the need for Israel to remain predominantly a Jewish state. Every measure to achieve that end was justified: in 1937 he had suggested expulsion, provided Britain would help; in 1948 he implemented it. In 1958, he saw no practical way of doing the same, and in 1968 he even recommended that the Israeli government immediately withdraw from the occupied territories.

In 1958 Ben-Gurion's demographic considerations led him to limit his directives to the army. He authorized only the occupation of the Arab neighborhoods connecting Mount Scopus with Western Jerusalem. But even this limited operation would be acceptable only if the Western operations failed.

Unlike the faulty reporting in 1957, in 1958 the Israeli press was full of accurate information and analysis of the pros and cons of the situation. The relatively unscrupulous and open way in which the Israeli press and political system dealt with the option of Greater Israel can be explained by the assessment of the leaders of the country that world public opinion

[53] Minutes Meeting with Shiloah and Eban, 27 July 1958, *Foreign Relations of the United States Series 1958–1960* (hereafter *FRUS*), XIII, pp. 74–76.

[54] This is mentioned in William Quandt, "Lebanon 1958, and Jordan 1970," in B. Bleichman and S. Kaplan, eds., *Force Without War* (Washington, 1978), p. 232.

[55] Memorandum by George Allen to the NSC, 1 November 1958, *FRUS*, 1958–1960, XII, p. 161.

would tolerate such an expansion. A similar and more blunt attitude would be displayed after Israel's occupation of the West Bank and the Gaza Strip in the 1967 war. Indeed, the Israeli intellectual elite of the country could not resist the temptation—the chance to create "Greater Eretz Israel" (the Greater Land of Israel) was suddenly there. The Committee for Defense and Foreign Affairs of the Knesset listened to coalition members urging the government to seize the historic opportunity while Menachem Begin, the leader of Herut, and his colleagues went so far as to suggest the occupation of both banks of the river Jordan. But Ben-Gurion wanted as "pure" a Jewish state as possible and maybe for the first time in his life he was willing to endorse an alliance with the Hashemites to maintain the status quo, if it was feasible, on Israel's eastern border. He differed from others in Israeli policy-making circles on the question of tactics, not strategy. He regarded the West Bank as part of Greater Israel, but could not envisage another transfer of Palestinians. Nor did he deem it necessary to achieve a greater Israel as long as Britain played a dominant role in Jordan.

Matters did not end here. The sense of a crisis lingered on until the end of 1958. Throughout these months the option of taking over part of the West Bank or reaching an agreement over its fate continued to be seriously considered by Israeli politicians and generals. The Arab world was alerted to the possibility of an Israeli military operation, perhaps supported by the West. During the first days of August 1958, despite a severe illness Foreign Minister Golda Meir embarked on a trip reminiscent of those taken by Israeli leaders during the days of the Suez plot in 1956. She visited Paris and London and the Arab capitals. A second collusion seemed on its way—this time targeting the West Bank.[56] The British Foreign Minister was forced to issue a declaration refuting the rumors that any such plan was being discussed, adding that Britain knew Israel did not have any aggressive plans towards the West Bank. And in fact, Meir in her talks faithfully represented Ben-Gurion's anti-annexationist position. She pointed out above all the demographic difficulties for Israel. Perhaps she pleased her British interlocutors when she emphasized that a British presence in Jordan would be the best solution.[57]

[56] See chapter by Fry. The UN Secretary General in fact believed that the UAR would go to war against Israel, should the latter annex the West Bank.

[57] Gendzier, *Notes from the Minefield*, p. 356.

In December 1958, Ben-Gurion contributed to the tension by airing new ideas about the West Bank in a revealing interview with the *Sunday Times* of London. He talked about the need to demilitarize the West Bank, and about the possibility of allowing the United Nations to take control. The Soviet Union and Egypt were quick to respond, each claiming in an official communiqué that such a proposal constituted a direct pressure on Jordan and indicated an Israeli wish to forcibly occupy the West Bank.[58] Ben-Gurion spoke as if the July crisis were over. He saw demilitarization as a means of helping Hussein consolidate his rule on the West Bank. This, at least, is how his position was understood by Arabists in the State Department, who discerned a genuine Israeli concern for Hussein's future. Ben-Gurion had in fact begun to develop high hopes for a future Israeli-Jordanian alliance. The problem, as far as he was concerned, was how to convince the young King to dissociate himself from the rest of the Arab world. It was this aspiration that the experts on Arab affairs in the State Department judged to be disastrous, as did the CIA.[59] Allen Dulles, when asked to clarify the situation to President Eisenhower, provided a complicated and confused overview on how far a would-be anti-Arab Jordanian-Israeli alliance had proceeded. He wrote that there "was no evidence of conniving between the two states [Israel and Jordan against the Arab world], but the action of the one might trigger the actions of the other and they might move then along parallel lines."[60]

Israel, throughout 1957 and 1958, was a more self-confident geo-political entity than it had ever been before in the ten years of its existence. It had absorbed a new wave of immigrants and it felt resilient in consequence of its demographic growth. It enjoyed a respectable position within the international community, so that, for example, the Third International Convention for Nuclear Research chose Israel as its venue. The first substantial private American investments began to arrive during the first half of 1958.

But these achievements did little to change the country's siege mentality, and its isolationist tendencies continued to crop up. This was the case, for example, when the Shell and BP oil companies decided to cease their activities in Israel as a result of the Arab boycott. This anti-Israeli act, as it was interpreted, was unexpected and it contributed to a sense of strangulation. It helped set the belligerent tone of public discourse and eventually

---

58 11 December 1958.

59 NSC session no. 390, on 11 December 1958, *FRUS*, 1958–1960, XI, p. 671.

60 Ibid.

the policies that Israel pursued towards its neighboring countries. The result was a vicious circle that, for some bizarre reason, Israelis quite often seemed to relish. One example may suffice: at the end of July 1957, Israel was condemned by the United Nations for a series of aggressive violations against the armistice agreement with Syria. The Israeli government branded the United Nations and the international community as anti-Zionist. The press used melodramatic language to describe the global hostility toward the very idea of a Jewish state. For many years such hysterical exaggerations prevented the emergence of any serious and concrete reassessment of Israel's policy towards the Arab world.

But Israelis found it difficult to maintain an attitude of alienation towards the world at large. After all, in the elite's self-image, Israel was in the West—culturally, financially, and militarily. Israel was willing to commit itself to the NATO alliance. The West, however, was ambivalent in its attitude to the Jewish state and it was this ambivalence that led Israel to the search for non-Arab allies in the area. Any ideas, such as those suggested by Sharett up to 1956, of a need for a more empathetic attitude towards the Arab world at large, were silenced after his withdrawal from politics. There was only one image which, in the eyes of Israelis, policy-makers and citizens alike, reflected Arab politics: it was that of Arab radicalism, which in its fanatical and uncompromising nature could only be defeated by aligning Israel as closely as possible to the West and by building a formidable conventional and potentially a non-conventional military capability. The United States was still—and this is important to note—reserved in its attitude towards Israel, especially in the immediate aftermath of the 1958 crisis. That is, Israel's mission was not fulfilled. Ben-Gurion found this difficult to understand. On the one hand, the United States was willing to plot an overthrow of the Syrian government, an operation fully endorsed by Israel; and on the other, the Americans refused to allocate Israel a strategic role in the Eisenhower Doctrine.

This all changed in the early 1960s. By supplying highly advanced arms to its ally, a prelude to subsequent American military support, France widened the qualitative military gap between Israel and its Arab neighbors before Charles de Gaulle re-oriented France's pro-Israeli Middle Eastern policy. There were also signs of a new American policy in the late 1950s. As a token of appreciation, after the crisis the Israeli military staff was invited on board one of the US Sixth Fleet ships, the same fleet which Israelis believed had been sent in 1957 to deter Israel from undertaking aggressive actions.

More substantially, at the end of 1958 one thousand American field artillery weapons were supplied to the Israelis, the first combat equipment ever to be shipped officially from the United States to Israel. In 1958 Washington also financed the purchase of arms by Israel in Britain. When Golda Meir met Dulles in October 1958 it was agreed that the Development Lending Fund would increase its credit to Israel by $10 million. It was understood that development meant further armament of the IDF, and more specifically the purchase of Centurion tanks in Britain. Symbolic gestures followed less easily. Although Ben-Gurion eagerly wanted to be invited to Washington, he had to wait until February 1960.

It is significant that, as American support for Israel grew, so did the expansionist tendencies in Israel. The July crisis brought to the center of Israeli politics secular nationalist Labour movement activists who wished to create a Jewish state stretching from the Jordan river to the Mediterranean sea. They may be called the "Redeemers," those who wanted to redeem the lost land of Greater Israel that had not been claimed in the 1948 war. Unlike the right-wing revisionists, they were part of the intellectual elite and, more importantly, they were considered to be among the builders of the state. They were thus people with a particular standing in Israeli society. The 1967 crisis would bring them to the government. They quickly drove out anyone who might still be as pragmatic as Ben-Gurion had been. They made sure that this time, in a coalition with the revisionists, they would implement their vision of Greater Israel.[61]

Israel's participation in the 1958 crisis was limited to the permission granted British aircraft to fly over its territory—for which Israel got nothing in return: no Greater Israel, no peripheral pacts, and no alliance with the West. Many generals and politicians spoke of missed opportunities, but not for long. In 1967, these generals would be there to make sure these goals would be successfully realized.

[61] Douglas Little, "The Making of a Special Relationship: The United States and Israel, 1957–68," *International Journal of Middle Eastern Studies* 25 (1993), pp. 565–85.

9

The Dog That Neither Barked Nor Bit: The Fear of Oil Shortages

ROGER OWEN

Oil, and Western worries about the security of oil supplies, have been a feature of every Middle East crisis since 1956. They were certainly very much present in July 1958 and led to the serious consideration of urgent emergency measures in both Britain and the United States. Yet, oil continued to flow smoothly through the Suez Canal and across the various trans-desert pipelines in 1958, leaving only the West's ally, Jordan, exposed to a brief, though serious, shortage. If a desire to preserve unrestricted access to Middle Eastern supply was a major factor in animating British and American policy toward the crises of 1958, as Irene Gendzier argues elsewhere in this book, this policy can be described as having been a success. Indeed, it can also be argued that one of the most significant aspects of this success is that it rarely needed to be referred to in public as a central Western interest. Hence in President Dwight D. Eisenhower's own retrospective summary of the main themes addressed during that tense and difficult summer, that of oil is nowhere to be found.[1]

This chapter briefly examines the world oil situation in the first half of 1958. It will then discuss the contingency measures designed to protect Western oil supplies in general and the particular measures taken in the

[1] See Alan Doughty, *Middle East Crisis: US Decision-Making in 1958, 1970 and 1973* (Berkeley, 1984), pp. 58ff and 85.

case of Jordan. The chapter will conclude with some comments on the major differences in the role of oil in the two crises of 1956 and 1958, and on the lessons that were drawn at the time.

The World Oil Situation in the First Half of 1958

What was known as the Free World's consumption of oil and oil products grew by only two percent in 1957, the smallest rise in any year since the Second World War.[2] More significantly, Western European consumption had grown by only one percent (1.5 million tons) while that of the United States had declined in the same proportion (one percent = 3.5 million tons). One important factor was the American economic recession of that same year with its considerable impact on the United States' economic partners such as Britain, where industrial production remained static throughout 1957. Another was the lingering effects of the 1956 crisis, during which supply chains were seriously interrupted by the blowing up of a section of the Iraqi-Syrian pipeline, repairs to which were finally completed in March 1957. Indeed, it was only in April 1958 that Iraqi oil production was able to return to its pre-Suez levels.[3]

Most forecasters expected only another small increase in world consumption to take place in 1958, citing the continued impact of the US recession. This is what happened in Western Europe, but demand in the Americas remained sluggish while oil output in the United States, Canada, and Venezuela continued to fall.[4] One result was the renewed salience of Middle Eastern supplies, which had risen from 20 percent of Free World production in January–June 1956 to 26 percent in July–December 1957 and 28 percent in the first six months of 1958.[5] Such was the general picture in July 1958: a slack oil market but one which provided some ammunition for those like Secretary of State John Foster Dulles or Sir Michael Wright, the British Ambassador in Baghdad, to argue that the series of Middle Eastern political crises in the early months of 1958, beginning

[2] These and all other figures for oil production and consumption from "Slower Growth of World Consumption," *Petroleum Press Service* XXV, 7 (July 1958), pp. 242–45. Free World production had previously been rising at an average of some six percent a year, "Ups and Downs in Crude Production," *Petroleum Press Service* XXV, 8 (August 1958), p. 285.

[3] R. S. Crawford, "Annual Report for 1958: Iraq," FO 371/140986.

[4] "Ups and Downs in Crude Production," p. 283.

[5] Ibid.

with the creation of the United Arab Republic, did indeed pose a renewed threat to Western Europe's oil supply.

Trying to Learn from the Last Crisis

By an unusual coincidence, the July phase of the 1958 crisis broke out at more or less the same moment that an Anglo-American report on measures to safeguard European oil supplies was under discussion in Washington. This report originated in the Bermuda meeting of March 1957 between Eisenhower and Prime Minister Harold Macmillan, at which they agreed to recommend an urgent study of the present situation and possible future developments in the Middle East, first addressing questions concerning access to the region's oil. The report was finally completed in May 1958 and then sent for government approval in a memorandum from the Deputy Undersecretary of State, Douglas Dillon, to the Acting Secretary of State, Christian Herter, on 30 June 1958. Dillon also noted that it was to be returned to the Anglo-American study group for further discussion at its next meeting, to be held in Washington on 9 July.[6] The report itself recommended such measures as the creation of additional stocks and storage capacity in Europe, the development of oil fields outside the Middle East, and changes in the pattern of transportation in order to reduce dependence on tankers transiting the Suez Canal.[7] None of these recommendations were close to implementation by the time the new crisis broke out.[8]

The studies conducted in Europe brought no concrete action apart from the establishment of committees to coordinate matters in the event of a second emergency. Hence the new Organization for European Economic Cooperation (OEEC) Oil Committee was still discussing what measures

---

[6] *Foreign Relations of the United States, 1958–1960* [FRUS] XII, "Near East Region, January-July 1958," pp. 64–65.

[7] "Transport of Oil from the Middle East," Joint Report by US-UK Officials, Washington, 12 May 1958, ibid., pp. 66–71.

[8] Compare Dillon to Herter, ibid., with the gloomy conclusion of Harold Lubell, a Rand expert on the Middle East, that since the Suez "shutdown," "no apparent steps have been taken to carry out any sort of program of increasing transport facilities as a means of insurance against possible future interruption by the transit countries of the flow of Middle East oil supplies...," "Middle East Crises and World Petroleum Movements," USAF Project Rand, Research Memorandum, RM-2185, AD 15018, "Conclusion," pp. 30–31.

to take, as was Britain's Oil Energy Committee, formed in November 1957 to assist the Ministry of Fuel and Power with future planning.[9] As the reports issued by such bodies clearly indicate, it was difficult to urge either governments or oil companies to expend money on extra capacity at a time when demand for oil was slack, when there was already a glut of tankers, and when the high cost of additional storage was such that Western Europe would have to spend $20 million to create just one extra day's reserve.[10] In the event of a new crisis, the United States and its allies would have to rely on the same ad hoc approach followed in 1956–57, notably fuel rationing and increasing output from North America's own fields. By the same token, lack of progress on the question of oil security was bound to put a greater premium on the continuing political and military effort needed to keep the oil producers in the Western camp. This was a matter that rose quickly to the top of the agenda in the crisis year of 1958.

The First Response to the July Crisis

Both the British and the US governments responded to the news of the overthrow of the Iraqi monarchy by developing contingency measures to protect Western Europe's supply of oil. The disruptions of late 1956 were obviously on everyone's mind. Moreover, the July Revolution in Baghdad took place after months of tension in the Middle East, during which many feared that a combination of Nasserite and Soviet ambitions might seriously damage Western interests, including, perhaps, an attempt to starve the West of oil. To make matters worse, there had been a significant change of leadership in Saudi Arabia in March, which aroused momentary concern that Prince Faisal might be less accommodating to the West than King Saud. In May, anxiety over Western vulnerability was briefly revived by the cutting of the Iraq Petroleum Company's pipeline near Tripoli in Lebanon.

These events were at the fore during the early Anglo-American discussions between the British Ambassador, Lord Hood, and those in the American administration, and then between Foreign Secretary Selwyn

[9] See, for example, OEEC, *Europe's Need for Oil: Implications and Lessons of the Suez Crisis*, (Paris, January 1958), pp. 43–46 and 78.

[10] Ibid., p. 44. See also, Lubell, "Middle East Crises," p. 30.

Lloyd, Eisenhower, and Dulles. One possibility—on which Dulles thought there was agreement—was the use of force, if necessary, to preserve access to Middle Eastern oil.[11] Other measures included Secretary of the Interior Fred Seaton's summons of 19 July 1958 to representatives of 16 oil companies to meet him four days later in Washington to prepare plans for an airlift of oil to Western Europe in case Middle Eastern supplies were blocked. Shortly thereafter it was announced in Washington that the US oil industry was prepared to increase production by three million barrels a day. And on 23 July, Dulles presented the oil company representatives, now known as the Foreign Petroleum Supply or "Suez" Committee, with his contingency plan. According to a correspondent of the *New York Times,* this plan was originally completed in October 1957 after members of the Senate's Anti-Trust and Monopoly Committee expressed their concerns. The main consequence of the plan was the creation of a Middle East Emergency Committee that included representatives of the major oil companies whose purpose was to gather information on the world's supply and demand for oil, and then to coordinate the necessary shipments.[12]

Meanwhile, in London, the Minister of Power persuaded the oil companies in Britain to hold substantially larger reserves than they had done two years earlier at the time of the Suez crisis, which would increase the level to fourteen weeks' supply. As an official report was later to show, this had the effect of raising average stocks to 9.4 million tons in 1958, as opposed to 5.8 million tons in the early part of 1956 and 8.4 million tons in June 1957.[13]

As it happened, none of these emergency measures were required. In a surprisingly short period of time the British and Americans were satisfied that the new Iraqi regime saw it in its self-interest to continue to export oil. At the beginning of the Iraqi Revolution an Iraq Petroleum Company (IPC) spokesman reported that oil was flowing along the Kirkuk to Tripoli and Banyas pipeline without interruption.[14] The next day the US

[11] "Memorandum of a Conference with President Eisenhower," 20 July 1958, *FRUS,* 1958–60, XII, pp. 81–87.

[12] Richard Mooney, "U.S. Revised Plan on Oil Emergency," *New York Times*, 24 July 1958, p. 3.

[13] "Oil supplies," Memorandum by Minister of Fuel and Power, 30 Sept. 1958, Cab Office/C (58), no. 198 and Appendix A.

[14] *Middle East Economic Survey* (Research and Translation Office, Beirut) X, 36 (18 July 1958), p. 1.

Ambassador to Iraq, Waldemar Gallman, had a friendly interview with the new Iraqi leader, Abdel Karim Qasim.[15] Then came Qasim's proclamation on Baghdad Radio on the evening of July 18: "In view of the importance of oil to the world economy, the government of the Iraqi Republic wishes to declare its anxiety to see the continuation of the production and flow of oil to the markets where it is sold because of its importance to national wealth and international economic and industrial interests."[16]

Other encouraging signs followed: the Iraqi broadcast of a statement by the Basra Oil Company to Prime Minister Qasim that oil operations were continuing normally (22 July) and a statement by the IPC's manager at Kirkuk that oil production was at a maximum and that families which had been on leave in Britain at the time of the coup were about to return (23 July).[17] Meanwhile, Qasim informed Eisenhower's special envoy, Robert Murphy, on a visit to Baghdad, that he himself had assured President Nasser that there would be no disturbance to the Mediterranean pipeline inside Iraq.[18]

There was also welcome evidence that the thrust of Iraq's pre-revolutionary oil policy would remain unchanged. The government was anxious to produce, and to sell, as much oil as possible in order, as the regime's new Ambassador to the United Nations put it, to "attain the standard of living that the new government had promised its people."[19] This in turn led the Qasim regime to stress the importance of cooperation with Western oil interests. There was just one complication when, on 30 July, an oil storage tank exploded on the outskirts of Baghdad. This event may well have been a rare example of sabotage. But by this time, the Western allies were sufficiently confident in the goodwill of the new regime for the British to grant it recognition on 1 August and the United States the next day.

The Iraq Petroleum Company also demonstrated its confidence in Iraqi intentions by resuming the negotiations which had been in progress before

[15] "Embassy in Iraq to the State Department," tel., 15 July 1958, *Foreign Relations, 1958–60*, XII, pp. 318–19. Gallman also reported that he learned of the death of Nuri al-Said immediately on his return from seeing Qasim.

[16] BBC, *Summary of World Broadcasts (SWB)*, 19 July 1958, p. 13. *Middle East Economic Survey* X, 37 (25 July 1958), p. 1, gives a slightly different version of this same speech.

[17] *SWB*, 23 July, p. 6, and 24 July, p. 15.

[18] Robert Murphy, *Diplomat Among Warriors* (London, 1964), p. 504.

[19] Speech by Hashim Jawad at Berkeley, California, 1 August 1958, quoted in *Middle East Economic Survey* X, 39 (8 August 1958), p.1.

14 July.[20] New talks began during a secret visit to Baghdad by the company's co-managing director on 20–21 August. He was surprised to learn that the new regime had simply dusted off its predecessor's demands, including those for an immediate increase in production accompanied by a four million Iraqi Dinar loan (ID1 = £1 sterling).[21] Negotiations went smoothly enough to allow the IPC to inform the Qasim regime in September of its readiness to supply such a sum in final discharge of its 1953 account. This step was widely interpreted as stemming from the IPC's desire to be as helpful as possible towards the Iraqi government at what was obviously a difficult time.[22] The gloss put on it by the British Ambassador in Iraq's end-of-the-year report is also significant. After noting the extreme financial difficulties experienced by the Iraqi government in the first few months after the July coup, he argued: "If the [Iraqi] government had not given every help to the Iraq Petroleum Company to conduct business as usual and in consequence received from the company oil royalties at a record level, as well as an advance of ID 4 million for their budget, the economy would have been seriously disrupted."[23]

Oil Crisis Averted in Jordan

Jordan was the one country that experienced serious difficulties with oil supplies after 14 July. By immediately closing its frontiers with Iraq, Syria, and Saudi Arabia, Jordan not only deprived itself of its main source of supply—road tankers from the Iraqi fields—but also of any prospect of compensating for this by other land routes.[24] To make matters worse the country contained no significant storage facilities and had extremely poor road communications between Aqaba, its only port, and the capital city of

20 For varying views about the state which these talks had reached by 14 July 1958, ibid., X, 36 (18 July 1958), p. 2, and "Review of GIO-IPC Relations," John Miles, US Embassy, Baghdad, to State Department, 25 August 1958, pp. 1–3 (US National Archives, Record Group 59, Jordan, Political Affairs, 1956–59).

21 Ibid., pp. 3–5.

22 Crawford, "Annual Report for 1958: Iraq."

23 Ibid. Crawford's definition of the July events was also incisive: he called it a coup which "quickly assumed the appearance of a popular revolution."

24 *The Economist* (19 July 1958), p. 230. Previous to the union between Egypt and Syria in February 1958, Jordan had received most of its oil by tanker, overland, from Beirut. But once this route was interrupted by the Syrians in March, the Iraqi government offered to make up the loss. See Wright (Baghdad) to Foreign Office, 6 March 1958, FO 371/134082.

Amman, while the nearest railhead to Aqaba was 83 miles to the north. It also lacked its own refinery, although a contract to build one had recently been signed with an Italian company in June.[25] Jordan's exact fuel requirement was difficult to calculate, but early estimates by the British and American Embassies in Amman estimated it at somewhere between 15,000 and 17,000 tons of gasoline, kerosene, and diesel fuel a month.[26] The British Embassy believed that the maximum that could brought in via Aqaba was some 8,000 tons a month.[27] In addition, there was the question of supplies for the British force insecurely established at Amman airport with six Hunter aircraft that needed 35 tons of aviation fuel a day to conduct operations.[28]

Fortunately for the Macmillan government, the United States, in the person of John Foster Dulles, was quick to offer "moral and logistical support" to the British troops.[29] Eisenhower was similarly appreciative of the danger and ordered an airlift of POL (petrol, oil, and lubricants) by Globemaster Aircraft beginning on 19 July.[30] There followed the despatch of engineers to Aqaba to examine the possibilities of bringing in more supplies by sea. The result was a flurry of British and American activity coordinated for the most part by a series of committees established in Amman, London, and Washington, as well as an agreement that the United States would pay for all of Jordan's emergency supplies.[31]

The two main methods for sending oil and other refined products to Jordan were by air and sea. Given the fact that the first tanker was only

---

[25] Bullard (Amman) to Foreign Office, 10 June 1958, FO 371/134081.

[26] "Oil supplies for Jordan," Ministry of Fuel and Power to Washington, 24 July 1958. Joint State-ICA-Defense Message, Washington, 25 July 1958. See also the estimate of Jordan's monthly demand as 105,000 barrels in Dwight D. Eisenhower, *Waging Peace 1956–1960* (London, 1966), p. 281.

[27] Joint State-ICA-Defense Message, State Department, Washington, DC, 25 July 1958, p. 1. S. A. MacCaffray, the American expert, was a little more optimistic and believed Aqaba could handle a few thousand tons more. See US Embassy (Amman), to State Department, tel., 30 July 1958 (Jordan, Political Affairs, 1956–59).

[28] Shattuck, Political Office of Middle East Forces (POMEF) to Foreign Office, (tel.), 18 July 1958, FO 371/134082.

[29] Alistair Horne, *Macmillan 1957–1986* (London, 1989), p. 94.

[30] *Keesing's Contemporary Archives* 26 July-2 August 1958); Eisenhower, *Waging Peace*, pp. 281–82.

[31] As far as the coordinating committees were concerned, these included an Anglo-American group in Washington, the London Committee of Supplies for Jordan and, in Amman, the Fuel Board (chaired by the American, Commander S. A. MacCaffray) and the Amman Coordinating Committee (sometimes known as the Amman Petroleum Committee).

predicted to reach Aqaba some ten days after the beginning of the crisis, initial efforts were focused mainly on air delivery. There were a number of obstacles to overcome before a satisfactory airlift became viable. Plans to fly oil from Bahrain were quickly abandoned on the twin grounds that the Bahraini workers involved in loading the oil were open to Nasserite Arab nationalist propaganda and might go on strike, and that the Saudis might not give permission to overfly their territory.[32] Beirut was the next best option. Here again, however, there was a momentary worry about a possible Israeli refusal to allow an overflight, especially because the Israeli government had initially denied permission to the first British planes carrying military detachments from Cyprus to Amman. Fortunately, it rapidly became clear that, although the Israeli government would not give its official consent, it would allow the American flights to go ahead without authorization, a stratagem dictated by worries about possible retaliation from either Nasser or the Soviet Union.[33] Given the political sensitivities involved, the first US flight which took off on 19 July was instructed to give its official destination as Nicosia, not Amman.[34] But thereafter there were no more political problems and by 21 July the C124 aircraft had already delivered 260 tons of fuel.[35]

The problems of bringing oil in by sea were considerably more daunting. As the early Anglo-American surveys showed, the port was poorly managed and lacked moorings for off-loading even medium-sized tankers. It was also needed as a point of entry for other equally necessary imports such as wheat. Hence, when the first tanker, the *Clyde Explorer,* arrived in late July with an accompanying barge it took about a week to unload a cargo of ten days' supply of gas and diesel fuel and one week's supply of kerosene. This required a number of barges, which transferred the oil from the ship to the four small storage tanks on shore. Worse was to follow: a

[32] See Hood (Washington), to Foreign Office (tel.), 19 July 1958, FO 371/134082 and FO to Amman (tel.), 19 July 1958, FO 371/134082. Given the secrecy which the Americans insisted on maintaining at this time, it is difficult to know whether the Saudis actually refused permission or not. Equally, there may have been one single flight from Bahrain on 18 July. It was President Eisenhower himself who expressed concern about the labor situation in Bahrain at a meeting held on 20 July. "He felt that the facilities could not operate in case of a general strike." "Memorandum of a Conference with President Eisenhower," p. 84.

[33] Hood (Washington) to Foreign Office (tel.), 19 July 1958 and FO to Amman (tel.), 19 July 1958,

[34] Ibid.

[35] Johnston (Amman), to Foreign Office (tel.), 21 July 1958, FO 371/134082.

tanker, the *Coe Victory,* subsequently took almost a month to off-load.[36] To make matters more difficult, the Jordanian contractor employed to upgrade the desert road north to Amman was at least a year behind schedule, having completed only 12 percent of the work by the time of the crisis. Transport by rail gave rise to other problems because the ancient engines of the trains required imported fuel oil.[37]

Nevertheless, after six weeks of intense shortage the fuel supply position had much improved by the end of August.[38] The country's reserves had been built up to two or three months' supply while the British forces at Amman had forty days' worth of stocks of their own.[39] Furthermore, the emergency short-term improvements to the Aqaba off-loading facility were almost complete, while Jordan's truck tanker fleet was reinforced by forty or more vehicles that had been briefly impounded in Iraq. A month later the railway was also in use and connected to a better-organized shuttle service between Aqaba and its southern terminus at Ras al-Naqb.

The question arose about how much more time and money should be expended on improvements at Aqaba in order to turn it into a major terminal. This was something King Hussein was anxious to pursue as a way of reducing his country's dependence on transit through Syria.[40] The British, on the other hand, were eager to use the passage of the Arab States' United Nations resolution of 21 August to persuade the Jordanians to test whether the government of the United Arab Republic was willing to permit resumption of the transit trade across Syria to Lebanon.[41] In the event, the Syrian authorities decided the matter by first allowing some Jordanian tankers through and then, on 12 September, holding up several

---

36 "US Gives Jordan $5 million; UK Promises $1 million," US Embassy (Amman), to Secretary of State, Weekly Economic Report, 16 September 1958, p. 2. See also "US and UK Increase Aid Commitments to Jordan," US Embassy (Amman), to Secretary of State; Washington, Weekly Economic Report, 3 September 1958, p. 3, where the *Coe Victory* is described as being unloaded at a "snail's pace" of just 50 to 60 tons per day.

37 Wright, US Embassy (Amman) to Secretary of State, Washington, 30 July 1958.

38 Foreign Service Despatch, Weekly Economic Review, "US financed Emergency Petroleum Supply Operation Continues," US Embassy (Amman) to State Department, Washington, 27 August 1958, p. 1.

39 *SWB*, 1 August 1958, p. 17; minute by R. M. Hadow, FO, Confidential, "Oil in Jordan" (Levant Department), FO 371/134084

40 Johnston (Amman) to Foreign Office (tel.), 25 August 1958, FO 371/134083.

41 Hadow, "Oil in Jordan." This view was subsequently modified to include a continuing British interest in improving the Aqaba route, FO to Washington (tel.), 28 August 1958, FO 371/134083. The Arab States' resolution was designed as a way of creating the conditions thought necessary for the withdrawal of British and American troops from the region.

others at the Syrian-Jordanian border.[42] This was enough to persuade the British to join the Americans and the Jordanians in a concerted effort to build up Aqaba. A new terminal company was formed and the oil storage capacity was expanded from 2,000 to 14,000 tons with the help of additional tanks provided by the United States.

The oil crisis itself was pronounced over in early December when the British troops were withdrawn and the United States ended its emergency delivery of supplies, and handed over responsibility for future imports to the Jordanian government. According to an American spokesman, the total value of the oil paid for by the United States was $5 million.[43]

Conclusion: The Role of Oil in 1956 and 1958

Questions of Western access to Arab and Iranian oil were a recurrent feature of every Middle Eastern crisis from 1956 to 1990–91. Inevitably, such access depended not only on the political situation in the major producing countries themselves but also in those along the major transit routes of the Gulf, the trans-desert pipelines, and the Suez Canal. Indeed, such was the geographical spread of the factors involved that the planners and politicians were forced to base their policy on considerations that embraced present and future trends throughout the entire region. One implication is that, for all the desire to depend on market forces alone to assure supply, there was always a possibility that either military force or powerful diplomatic intervention might have to be used as well. A second implication, well illustrated by the comparison of 1956 and 1958, is that no two political crises would ever be quite the same as far as the role of oil was concerned.

What were the major differences between the Suez crisis and that of July 1958? There is the obvious fact that, on the latter occasion, Britain and the United States remained firm allies. All sources testify to the need to cooperate as closely as possible in all aspects of the crisis. A second major difference was that the crisis itself was triggered by events in a country, Iraq, which was not only an important oil producer but overwhelmingly dependent on its oil revenues to overcome the economic difficulties experienced immediately after 14 July and to finance its ambitious investment

42 Johnston (Amman) to Foreign Office (tel.), 16 September 1958, FO 371/134084.

43 Reuters (Amman), 4 December 1958, FO 371/134085.

programs. It should be added that, on this occasion, both of the Middle East's two main transit routes, the Suez Canal and the Syrian pipelines, were controlled by President Nasser, who now had his own reasons for preventing any disruption in supply.

As a result there was no pressure on Western governments to change existing arrangements regarding Middle Eastern oil. Indeed, it may be noted how the peaceful resolution of the crisis provided useful ammunition for those who, like the editor of the *Petroleum Press Service*, took comfort from the fact that, while the Soviet Union did not need this oil for its own use, the West could rely on its position as "the Middle East's indispensable partner in its social advance, providing not only the financial and technical means for producing [its] oil, but also the no less important marketing outlets."[44] Nevertheless, as even this same editor was forced to acknowledge: "in recent weeks," Western governments "had been driven by fear of uncertainty and by fear of the subversive influences of the USSR to adopt [political and military] measures which may seem at variance with their role of partnership in the Middle East." Of course, he was most obviously thinking of the American landings in Lebanon. But he could also have been thinking of Jordan where both Britain and the United States had come to the aid of a state readily identified as "the last remaining pro-Western government in the Arab world."[45] This clearly made the British Foreign Office somewhat uneasy about appearing to support Jordan as what it termed a "pro-Western outpost."[46] And yet, for all the desire to see the return to normal relations between Jordan and its Arab neighbors such as Syria, the fact that both the British and the Americans became so heavily involved in the Aqaba project pushed them further toward a position as protectors of what everyone then regarded as a beleaguered country surrounded by potentially hostile forces. It also accelerated those tendencies by which the United States was to replace Britain as Jordan's main provider of military as well as of economic and financial assistance.[47]

---

[44] "The Middle East Tangle," *Petroleum Press Service*, XXV, 8 (August 1958), pp. 281–82.

[45] This is actually the phrase used by the Turkish Prime Minister in a meeting with a US Embassy representative in Ankara, 18 September 1958. Hall (Ankara), to Secretary of State, (tel.), 19 September 1958.

[46] The phrase can be found in FO, British Embassy, Washington (tel.), 28 August 1958, FO 371/134083.

[47] For example, for the Jordanian fiscal year which began in March 1958, the United States was providing $42 million in budgetary support and another $12 million in project

The debate on how best to ensure the security of Middle Eastern oil supplies for Western Europe in the future continued without ever reaching a consensus. In a meeting of the National Security Council to discuss a report on "Western European Dependence on Middle East Petroleum" held in Washington in May 1959, a spectrum of different views persisted. In the opinion of the Departments of Defense, Interior, and Commerce, the objective of US policy should be to *reduce* European dependence on the region. In contrast, the Departments of State, Treasury, and Budget preferred to try to *retard* its growth. There was also the question of the relationship between seeking out alternative, non-Middle Eastern supplies as opposed to inducing the Middle Eastern countries themselves not to deny oil to Europe. And, finally, there was the question of the degree of direct US intervention that might be involved if supplies should actually be put at risk.[48]

Of all the participants in these inconclusive discussions, Eisenhower was the most realistic. He had learned the most valuable lesson about oil supplies from the two crises. As the minutes of the meeting of 13 May 1959 record:

> The President said another factor should be taken into consideration, namely, that under a system of free enterprise Western Europe would follow economic rather than political impulses and would obtain oil from the Middle East as long as such oil was cheaper than other oil. He thought the reduction of Western European dependence on Middle East oil was an unrealistic objective. We should make certain that there are no obstacles to the development by private companies of petroleum resources world wide without, however, urging private crash programs for oil development.... As long as Middle Eastern oil continues to be as cheap as it is, there is probably little we can do to reduce the dependence of Western Europe on the Middle East.... He was not aware of any practicable thing we could do we were not already doing in connection with Western European dependence on Middle East oil.[49]

---

aid and technical assistance, as opposed to Britain's $2.8 million in budgetary support and loans of just over $3 million. See "US and UK Increase Aid Commitments to Jordan," US Embassy, Amman, p. 1.

48 "Memorandum of Discussion at the 406th Meeting of the National Security Council," 13 May 1959.

49 Ibid.

10

Conclusion

ROGER OWEN

The crisis year of 1958 involved a series of shocks to the old Middle Eastern order which, for a while, seemed set to produce an entirely new political landscape in the region. Coming so soon after the defeat of the Anglo-French and Israeli invasion of Egypt in late 1956 they suggested a revolutionary overthrow of many existing regimes as well as the re-drawing of old boundaries to create new configurations of united or closely allied Arab states. What made it even more exciting—or alarming, according to your point of view—was the fact that the three major events of that year, the formation of the United Arab Republic, the Lebanese crisis beginning in May, and the overthrow of the Iraqi monarchy in July all seemed linked together as though driven on by some malign or irresistible force characteristic of the new post-colonial, early Cold War age. For a few short months it looked as though every Arab regime from North Africa to the Gulf would be caught up in the turmoil of events which posed great threats for some, and significant opportunities for others.

Seen from the perspective of the year itself it was the overthrow of the *ancien régime* in Baghdad that seemed to be the culmination of a series of events beginning with the union of Syria and Egypt. The creation of the UAR had brought the destabilizing force of Nasserism into the heart of the Arab world, threatening each of the surrounding regimes in Lebanon, Jordan, Saudi Arabia, and Iraq. Then, when the first feeble countermove—the Arab Federation of Jordan and Iraq—was swept away in July, the threat of instability reached the Gulf itself with worries about a domino effect that menaced Kuwait and the British-protected states of Bahrain and the lower Gulf. What seemed to make the situation even more explosive was the fact that it involved a *terra incognita* for all concerned. Following soon after the independence of so many Arab states, and only three years after Egypt's Czech arms deal had paved the way for the build-up of Soviet influence in the region, the crisis created a sense of confusion and uncertainty among the leaders not only of the Arab states but also Israel and Iran, on the one hand, and Britain, France, and the United States, on the other. Almost all felt their interests threatened. None knew quite how to profit from the new possibilities on the distant horizon.

All of the chapters in this volume re-examine how the chain of crises was perceived at the time. They highlight the connections that were made and underline the perceptions and misperceptions that informed the always hasty response to fast-breaking events. They also suggest a more basic structure in which the forces for change—nationalism and Arab unity, popular discontent, and new forms of government—came into conflict with a counter-attempt by the British and the Americans to hold the line and to create new mechanisms for preserving their own influence while denying more power either to Nasserism or the Soviet Union. This analysis also explains the presence of a mix of policies: from the introduction of major initiatives such as the Baghdad Pact, the Eisenhower Doctrine, and the appeal to Arab unity, through one of the early experiments with United Nations intervention, to the more subversive attempts to overthrow governments, fix elections, and infiltrate arms. Such an analysis moreover explains the shrillness of much contemporary rhetoric, a great deal of which tended to exaggerate the threat to stability or the menace of outside intervention, whether Soviet, Egyptian, or good old-fashioned Anglo-American imperialism. Most of all, this shared interpretation helps us to understand the day-to-day uncertainty about what was actually going on and what might reasonably be expected to happen next.

It is a more complex task to disentangle contemporary perceptions from the underlying realities of those times to arrive at some better sense of their historical meaning. This process is not greatly helped by the search for new sources which generally tend simply to tell one what decision-makers knew, or thought they knew at the time, but which was not revealed to a larger public. Rather than summarize what has already been said in the previous pages of this volume, it is more useful to turn to an alternative approach based on three new perspectives. One is to compare the different views of the crisis at the time. A second is to say something about the way in which the crises of 1958 were brought to a more or less mutually satisfactory conclusion. Finally, a third is to look at the year 1958 in terms of the much longer period from 1945 to 1967, which marks the first phase of Arab independence, of Cold War rivalries for position, and of belligerent relations between the Arabs and the new state of Israel, as well as the almost total replacement of British by American power and influence in the region.

By and large there are three pairs of contested views to be found in the chapters of this book. These are the ones explored by Rashid Khalidi between what is basically an Arab versus a Western perception of events, by Carol Saivetz between the Soviet leadership and its Cold War rivals, and by Michael Fry between the United Nation's Dag Hammarskjöld and both his local and his great power partners. All are important but also, in some sense, partial and misleading. Or, to put it in more simple terms, we cannot assume that the truth necessarily lies somewhere between their two extremes. There were always other factors at work as well.

In Khalidi's argument, the view of the crisis from within the Arab world was generally more subtle than that of many Western observers. This was certainly true of Lebanon where newspapers were concerned mostly with the genuine domestic opposition to President Camille Chamoun and his policies. This opposition had deep local roots and needed no particular encouragement from the United Arab Republic. Nor, contrary to the prevalent British and American point of view, were Chamoun's pro-Western policies the sole reason for his unpopularity with a wide spectrum of Lebanese political opinion, Christian as well as Muslim. Rather, it was his "dictatorial domestic inclinations, his flouting of conventions regarding sectarian balance, and his willingness to trample on the Lebanese constitution to remain in power." There was also, Khalidi suggests, the obvious one-sidedness characteristic of Western reporting with its concentration on Soviet and Egyptian interference in Lebanon and Jordan to the almost total neglect of that other interference by the intelligence services of Britain and America.

The view from Moscow was also much occupied with Western attempts to thwart Arab independence by reasserting British and American influence, either directly by military force or, indirectly, by a new system of pacts, treaties, and alliances. It was these attempts which, in both 1956 and 1958, persuaded the Soviet leadership under Nikita Khrushchev that it had been presented with a golden opportunity to ally itself with those local regimes whose goal was the elimination of Western influence in the Middle East. As a general perception this was undoubtedly correct. But, as

Carol Saivetz makes clear, the initial belief that the Arab regimes would, unequivocally, welcome Soviet support was somewhat naive, the more so when it became clear that there were definite limits as to how far the Soviet Union was prepared to go in using military force to confront the West in the region.

Of the three-counter views on display it was undoubtedly UN Secretary General Hammarskjöld's which was the most perceptive and the one based on the deepest understanding not only of the general developments in the area but also of the principal actors involved. He regarded Arab nationalism, correctly, as what Michael Fry describes as a "spontaneous and authentic force." He was convinced that Nasser and the UAR were the keys to Middle East "security, self-reliance and stability." And, privy as Hammarskjöld was to the reports of the United Nations' own observer force, he was aware not only of infiltration across the Syrian-Lebanese border but also of its limited importance and the fact that, by and large, it could be turned on and off at Nasser's command. But, most of all, in Fry's argument, Hammarskjöld was aware of the intensity of the 1958 crisis, its revolutionary potential and the need to manage and contain it lest it develop in too radical a way. For this reason he was prepared to work with the United States even though his longer term goal seems to have been a Middle East (and, indeed, a Third World) free of American, European, and Soviet political influence.

Lastly, let us turn to the resolution of the crisis. As the chapters make clear, for all the alarm and confusion that reached fever pitch in July 1958, only six months later things had calmed down to a most remarkable extent. Brigadier Qasim was beginning to reveal himself as an Iraqi nationalist with little interest in confrontation with the West over oil and the deepest suspicions of Nasser and his local Iraqi acolytes. In Jordan King Hussein had not only survived the crisis but also used it to cement his relations with the United States. In Lebanon the new President, Fouad Chehab, was set for a remarkable six years of state building, economic prosperity and moves towards a new balance between rich and poor, Muslim and Christian, and those who naturally looked east for comfort and those who looked west. And all the while the oil had continued to flow without interruption.

To the West this might have looked like a major victory. Moreover, it had been achieved in Lebanon under the cover of the United Nations and, as Irene Gendzier notes, presented as though it was merely a counter to Egyptian-Syrian intervention rather than a move to protect a basic

American interest, which it really was. Nevertheless, this was only the case if one allowed oneself to believe that what had been achieved was not only a more successful version of the 1956 crisis, in which Britain and the United States had re-learned how to cooperate and to pull together, but also the rolling-back of the tide of rampant Arab nationalism backed by the Soviet Union. A more sober assessment would note that Qasim's coup had put an end to any significant Arab involvement in the Baghdad Pact, that British influence was almost totally eliminated in Iraq, and that new ways must be found to preserve Western interests throughout the Arab East. Within a few years Britain found itself under further attack as the creation of a republican regime in Sanaa, North Yemen, assisted by the Egyptians, began to put pressure on the British position in South Yemen in and around the colony of Aden. As far as the United States was concerned, post-crisis policy took the form, first of a short-lived attempt to rebuild its bridges with Egypt during the Kennedy presidency, and then, when this broke down in mutual hostility in 1963–66, to a growing reliance on both Israel and Saudi Arabia as a balance to Nasserite influence. The Soviets, too, could take some comfort in the fact that they had emerged from the crisis with their reputation for being a strong supporter of Arab independence more or less intact. But, like the British and the Americans, they were soon to face significant new challenges, notably the outbreak of bitter disputes with both Nasser and Qasim as these leaders turned against the Communist parties in Egypt, Syria, and Iraq in 1959.

There is also the question of what lessons there were to be learned. The apparent success of Western intervention in thwarting Nasserite and Soviet influence masked the fact that this was only a rather insignificant episode in the political development of all the Arab countries concerned. What had actually happened was that, for all the presence of outside forces and influences, the Lebanese political establishment had found its own way to deal with a second version of a crisis that it had already experienced in 1952, which had been triggered by a sitting President suddenly deciding to seek an unconstitutional second term. In this it was helped considerably by the supposedly dangerous President Nasser who, as both Louis and Fry show, was at least one of the backers of the key formula that had President Chamoun replaced by his Defense Minister, General Fouad Chehab. The United Nations under Hammarskjöld also played a key role. And it must remain an open historical question whether the US landings added anything extra to the solution or were simply an historical irrelevance to all but the Lebanese ice-cream sellers who met the troops on the beach.

Similarly, in Iraq, there was a perfectly understandable local process, in which internal opposition to Nuri al-Said and the Monarchy had built up to such an extent that, sooner or later, something had to give. This, as Peter Sluglett maintains, had little to do with Arab unity, which the bulk of the population opposed, and not much more to do with Nasserism except as an example of what an Arab military regime could achieve by way of dissolving its links with Britain and then setting out on the path of economic and social development. The British were certainly right to worry about the possibility of Iraqi pressure on Kuwait. But when this did occur, after Kuwait's independence in 1961, it was not strongly carried through and was quite easily contained by a mixture of British, and then Arab, forces on the ground.

As for Jordan, it was King Hussein himself who exacerbated the crisis brought about by the change of regime in Baghdad by immediately closing his borders to all traffic, including the vital oil tankers. He may even have played a role in encouraging British military intervention by circulating rumors of an Egyptian assassination plot against him in mid-July. Like all such talk of similar conspiracies, this will almost certainly remain hidden in mystery as even the intelligence sources concerned are unlikely to reveal whether mere rumor was behind it or hard evidence to indicate that something serious was afoot. Whatever private fears and misgivings he may have had, the King himself played his hand well enough to obtain a permanent US commitment both to finance and arm Jordan, in spite of British fears that this might simply increase Arab nationalist pressure on him as just another stooge of the West.

We may conclude that there was a crisis in 1958 but not quite the type of crisis that many believed at the time. More importantly, we may also conclude that whatever was going on was actually more significant than what was either supposed or, more cynically, proposed in the over-heated atmosphere of those few summer months. By shifting our attention to the internal dynamics of each country we can see how the events of 1958 were part of a larger and more general process of regime change or regime accommodation that began with the creation of the new states of Jordan, Lebanon, and Iraq after the end of the First World War and which has yet to produce anything that looks like the final answer to all these particular countries' particular economic, social, political, ethnic, and religious problems. This is the more understandable given the demographic complexity of both Jordan and Lebanon, the weakness of their institutions (apart from the Jordanian army), their proximity to Israel, their large Palestinian populations, and the general temptation that this has provided for outsiders to meddle in their politics. As for Iraq, the attempt to build up a strong, oil-financed state that could protect itself from outside interference, and the Ba'ath regime's wars not only against its neighbors but also large parts of its own domestic population, have only produced another, more vicious, type of instability.

These remarks about the twentieth-century trajectories of the three Arab countries most closely involved in the critical events of 1958 lead naturally towards some more general considerations as to where that particular year fits into the larger narrative of modern Middle Eastern history. What is needed, *par excellence,* is some means of telling the story in a way that meshes the concerns of both insiders (including Israel and Iran) and outsiders (including the United Nations). It must also try to combine a sense of the panic atmosphere of 1958 itself with the insight that this particular year, like any other, cannot be totally isolated from what went before or what came after. Finally, it must suggest the possibility of links between discrete events more various than the simplistic belief that they were all part of a plot or, just as problematic, all determined by some large general force like independence, nationalism, imperialism at bay, or the sudden unfolding of the Cold War.

For me, and it is probably best to put forward an entirely personal point of view, the immediate train of events begins with the creation of the Baghdad Pact, the Czech arms deal, and the nationalization of the Suez Canal Company together with the Anglo-French-Israeli response in the form of the botched attempt to over-turn both the nationalization and, almost certainly, the Nasser regime itself. This then produced a mixed Western counter-offensive in the shape of a combination of covert action—for example, the plot or plots in Syria in 1957 and the interference in the Lebanese elections in the same year—as well as the attempt to supplement the Baghdad Pact with the Eisenhower Doctrine. The result was to bring Syria firmly into the emerging Cold War struggle with Premier Nikolai Bulganin triggering a particularly bitter exchange of letters in September 1957 as a result of his comments on the dangers posed by Turkish troop concentrations along Syria's northern border. Egypt, in turn, sent some troops of its own, an act which soon led to a full military union between the two countries. All these events served only to intensify the political confusion in Syria. There the pressure of competing forces and ideologies, together with persistent outside interference from all sides, Western, Soviet, and Arab, led some officers and the leaders of the fledgling Ba'ath Party to use and appeal to Nasser's Egypt as what Malik Mufti has termed a species of "defensive union" designed primarily to bolster their own power base in Damascus.[1]

That this plan was immediately aborted by Nasser and the new government he set up in Syria is well known. A united Egyptian leadership based on a much larger economy and a much stronger army was no match for Syria's weak and divided politicians. The outcome, not surprisingly, was the perception of an immediate sense of the threat posed by the UAR to the regimes in Lebanon, Jordan, Saudi Arabia, and Iraq, leading, first to the formation of the Iraqi-Jordanian Union, then to the much murkier attempt by King Saud to engineer the assassination of President Nasser early in 1958. All this was to have a significant consequence. It was King Saud's incompetence, and the subsequent humiliation felt by his politically active brothers, which played an important role in his eventual replacement by King Faisal. His succession led to the possibility, first canvassed in 1958, that Saudi Arabia might take the lead in organizing a counter-Arab, or even Arab-Islamic, alliance to the United Arab Republic. It was the movement of Iraqi troops to defend Jordan in July 1958 which gave Qasim—just one of the various military plotters in Iraq at the time—the opportunity to lead his troops not to the border but into Baghdad. And it may be that it was the threat apparently provided by the UAR, as well as the encouragement that it gave to Arab nationalist forces in Lebanon itself, that emboldened Chamoun to seek a second term based on an appeal to the Eisenhower Doctrine. Perhaps he was even encouraged directly by officials from the United States. Certainly the words of the Doctrine, drafted, as Diane Kunz observes, mainly for domestic American consumption, provided a standing temptation for local elites to magnify, or sometimes simply to invent, a local Communist threat to obtain Washington's support.

Observed from this point of view there is no need for the historian to look for a *deus ex machina* in the form of an aggressively expansionist Nasserism, acting perhaps on orders from Moscow. From what little evidence there is about Egyptian policy-making at the time, it seems reasonable to conclude that Nasser himself had little interest in stirring things up beyond a certain point in Lebanon, particularly if this led to US military intervention. The recent union with Syria presented him with far too

[1] Malik Mufti. *Sovereign Creations: Pan-Arabism and Political Order in Syria and Iraq* (Ithaca, 1996), Chapter 1.

many problems of institution-building and coordination to encourage unnecessary adventurism. It may also be that actions interpreted in Lebanon and Jordan as hostile acts (the infiltration of armed groups into the former, the closure of the border to tankers in September in the latter) were the work of groups in Syria that had not yet been brought fully under Egyptian control. It seems from Michael's Fry's evidence that Nasser himself was for the most part willing to go along with Hammarskjöld's advice that conciliation in Lebanon was in Egypt's interest.

Fears of Egyptian and then, after July 1958, of Iraqi expansion, were cited by all concerned to justify the particular policies that they wanted to pursue. This was true of members of the weak Arab regimes, even the one in Kuwait, although they had to be careful that too much emphasis on an Iraqi threat might encourage a reassertion of the British influence that the Ruler himself had been successful in either resisting or cutting down to size. It was also true of the Shah of Iran, who used the events in Baghdad to press the United States, unsuccessfully as it turned out, for more weapons to protect his country from what he claimed to be a serious threat from his Iraqi neighbor. The Soviet Union was quick to take advantage of the Shah's rebuff by offering him a non-aggression pact in December. It was only when Soviet-Iranian discussions broke down in Moscow the following February that Washington was finally persuaded to offer more aid.

As for the Israeli government, Ilan Pappé has charted the particular balance of aggressiveness and caution which always characterized Ben-Gurion's own thinking. Sensing that the collapse of King Hussein's regime might offer an opportunity for territorial expansion on the West Bank, he was also worried, as he was to be again in 1967, by the demographic consequences of bringing such a large Palestinian-Arab population under Israeli control. In the end nothing happened. But the crisis year does seem to have paved the way for closer military cooperation with the United States, even if a large part of it had to be camouflaged by means of financing weapons-purchases from Britain (and Germany) with American money. As Kunz notes, there was a symbolic victory in Washington's inclusion of Israel in the Eisenhower Doctrine, from which it had been previously excluded.

Israel was able to benefit from the crisis in another, more indirect way as well. British politicians criticized the advice of the Foreign Office's leading experts on Arab affairs, further discrediting a generally pro-Arab policy. This gave more room for Harold Wilson (as Prime Minister) and Denis Healey (as Foreign Minister) to push Britain's Middle Eastern policy in a more pro-Israeli direction following Labour's return to power in 1964. One of the first fruits of this new direction was the sale to Israel of Centurion tanks, which played an important role in the ground war in 1967.

Looking at the period of relative peace from 1958 to 1967, one might be tempted to think that the swift resolution of the crisis was itself largely responsible for this apparently happy state of affairs. Certainly these were mainly good years for the regimes in Jordan, Lebanon, Kuwait, and Saudi Arabia. Nevertheless, this was in large part due to the fact that the energies of politicians in the larger Arab states were engaged elsewhere, notably in the long and often bloody search for a new equilibrium in Syria after the break-up of the United Arab Republic in 1961 and in Iraq following the overthrow of the Qasim regime in 1963. Egypt also turned inward, with Nasser attempting to use his defeat in Syria as the justification for the introduction of a new economic and political order based on an appeal to his own Egyptian version of "Arab Socialism." As for the United States, it made its own contribution to the short period of calm, as Kunz notes, by superseding the Eisenhower Doctrine with policies designed to come to terms with Nasserism both in Egypt and its neighboring Arab states. If there was one lesson which Eisenhower and Dulles learned from the crisis, it was that the Middle East was only on the "periphery" of the Cold War, a belief which, in Kunz's formulation, gave them greater freedom to form policies for that part of the world, and the chance to do little or nothing at all if they so chose.

It was only with the arrival to power of the Ba'ath regimes in Syria and Iraq in 1963 that Nasser turned once again to the political architecture of the Middle East. He tried first to build a progressive alliance against the so-called reactionary Arab regimes and then used the series of summit meetings from 1964 onward to champion a new version of Egyptian leadership in the Arab world. It was Nasser's actions, combined with the intra-Arab competition to encourage and support the newly created Palestine Liberation Organization (PLO), that introduced another period of instability in the Middle East and played a major role in the short crisis which preceded the 1967 Israeli-Arab war.

This analysis allows us to answer the question of how "revolutionary" the Middle East was in 1958. It is an interesting and intriguing subject, not only because it goes to the heart of the different perceptions of these events held at the time, but also because the interlocking crises of that year involved a mix of issues which were not to be found anywhere else in the non-European world. Most notable were the influence of oil, the unresolved dispute with Israel, and an Arab nationalism which, at this stage in its development, had taken a strong unionist turn under President Nasser's general direction. We must also note that we are dealing with a year in which the real and apparent linkages between the various forces at work in the Arab Middle East were first on view. The year 1958 came just at the time when the struggle between the West and the Soviet Union for influence coincided with and contributed to the creation of the United Arab Republic. Thereafter, Arab nationalism, Nasserism, oil, Israel, and the fear of either Western or Communist influence became mixed up together in people's minds. As a result, clear-sighted analysis of Middle Eastern realities became more problematic than in, say, sub-Saharan Africa where Pan-Africanism was not identified with any one powerful and charismatic leader except Nkrumah, and was politically and militarily very much weaker. With any number of dangerously unresolved domestic and cross-border conflicts, no one could reasonably predict whether the oil would keep flowing, whether war might not break out between Israel and its neighbors, or whether one of the many weak Middle Eastern regimes might not suddenly be swept away.

This was a combustible mixture believed by the British and the Americans, quite correctly, to pose a menace to their interests. Israel and the Soviet Union saw a possible opportunity for furthering some of their basic goals. Dag Hammarskjöld and Nasser saw such a threat to the stability and putative independence of the region as to require concerted and careful management. Furthermore, it was this particular mix of hopes, fears, and expectations that united all the participants, both local and foreign, in a shared sense of the interconnectedness of otherwise discrete national developments and of the need to address the situation with measures that took these larger relationships into account. It is in this sense that Hammarskjöld was also correct in his evaluation of the general situation as "revolutionary." It was not so much the threat of political and social revolution in any one Arab country, although this was certainly present, but that violent events in any one place had the potential to upset existing arrangements everywhere and might set off a chain reaction of moves and counter-moves without an obvious end.

Viewed from this perspective it is difficult to fault the statesmen and politicians trying to deal with the situation. They shared a deep concern even if, as events turned out, the problems of revolutionary interconnectedness were not as great as they seemed at the time. For example, Nasser's

Arab nationalism can now best be seen as Egyptian nationalism writ large, a conclusion which was quickly drawn by most members of the Syrian elite, and acted upon by the Syrian Ba'ath members of the United Arab Republic's cabinet when they resigned *en bloc* in December 1959. Although divided by many social and ideological differences, the one thing which almost all Syria's politicians agreed upon after the break-up of the UAR in 1961 was that they were never again going to enter a union with Egypt on Egypt's own terms. Nor was Nasser himself much more enthusiastic about a repeat of the experiment, as his behavior during the "unity" talks in Cairo in 1963 amply demonstrate. Thereafter, Arab nationalism returned largely to the formula enshrined in the creation of the League of Arab States in 1945, that is, of separate and sovereign entities seeking, where possible, common forms of action and cooperation.

Another concluding point concerns the relative ease with which even the weaker Arab regimes were able to resist Soviet attempts to influence their policies. They put Communists in jail with impunity, stood up well to Khrushchev's often bullying tactics and were able, on the whole, to obtain large quantities of Soviet military and developmental aid without any major surrender of sovereignty and independence. In the end it was the Soviet Union, and not the progressive Arab regimes, that had to yield on the question of the correct path toward "Socialism."

Finally, the survival of family-ruled regimes was much less problematic than it appeared in 1958. Over time, the Kings of Jordan and Saudi Arabia not only beat back their domestic opposition but also managed to create relatively stable, and, in Saudi Arabia's case, highly prosperous states. In the Gulf the British micro-managed the situation to ensure that those few individual rulers whose failure to modernize threatened widespread popular discontent were replaced by more progressive members of their own family, as in Abu Dhabi and then Oman. Only the Yemeni Imamate was forcefully overthrown by elements of its own population in the period between 1958 and the June war of 1967. Only the ruling house of Libya was overthrown thereafter.

Perhaps because of these underlying factors, the words "revolution" or "revolutionary" became less important after 1958 either as descriptions of events or of the policies that particular regimes pursued. And where they continued to be used it was usually with reference to some previous revolutionary event, as in the notion of a "corrective revolution" frequently employed in Ba'athist Syria. As a result, appeal to the notion of the need for yet further "revolution" remained largely a rhetorical device until the violent eruption of what was certainly a genuine political, economic, social, and, most important of all, religious revolution in Iran in the years around 1979. It spawned many would-be imitators and so created a new set of pan-Middle Eastern connections which, for good or ill, recreated some of the major problems of management and opportunity, analysis, definition, and prediction to be found two decades earlier in 1958.

Select Bibliography

HOWARD J. DOOLEY

Documents

Ba'th Party, *Nidal hizb al-Ba'th al-arabi al-istiraki 'abr bayanat qiyadatih al-qaumiya, 1955–1962* [The Struggle of the Arab Socialist Ba'th Party Through the Declarations of Its Nationalist Leadership, 1955–1962] (Beirut, 1971).

British Broadcasting Corporation, *Summary of World Broadcasts* (London, 1958).

Cordier, Andrew W., and Wilder Foote, eds., *Public Papers of the Secretaries-General of the United Nations*, vol. iv: *Dag Hammarskjöld, 1958–1960* (New York, 1974).

Egypt. Ministry of Information, *Majmu'at Khutab wa tasrihat wa bayanat al-ra'is Gamal Abdel-Nasser, 23 Yulio 1952–1958* [The Collected Speeches, Declarations, and Statements of President Nasser, 23 July 1952–1958], vol. i (Cairo, n.d.).

———, *President Gamal Abdel-Nasser's Speeches and Press Interviews* (Cairo, 1959).

Hoskins, Halford, "United States Interests and Policy Relative to the Middle East," January 30, 1959. Legislative Reference Service, Library of Congress (Washington, DC).

Kesaris, Paul, ed., *CIA Research Reports: The Middle East, 1946–1976* (microfilm) (Frederick, MD, 1981).

King, Gillian, ed., *Documents on International Affairs, 1958* (New York, 1962).

Middle East Economic Survey X (Beirut, 1958).

Minutes and Documents of the Cabinet Meetings of President Eisenhower (microfilm) (Washington, DC, 1980).

Minutes of Telephone Conversations of John Foster Dulles and of Christian Herter (microfilm) (Washington, DC, 1980).

Nasser Speaks: Basic Documents (London,1972).

Petroleum Press Service, XXV (Petroleum Press Bureau, London, 1958).

Ro'i, Yaacov, *From Encroachment to Involvement: A Documentary Study of Soviet Policy in the Middle East, 1945–1973* (Jerusalem and New York, 1974).
United Nations, Security Council, *Complaint of Lebanon: Resolution of the Security Council*, 11 June 1958, S/4023 (New York, 1958).
———, *First Report of the United Nations Observation Group in Lebanon*, 3 July 1958, S/4040.
———, *Official Comments of the Government of Lebanon on the First Report of the United Nations Observation Group in Lebanon*, 8 July 1958, S/4043.
———, *Security Council Official Records, Thirteenth Year, Supplement for July, August, and September 1958* (New York, 1958).
———, *Official Records of the General Assembly, Third Emergency Special Session 8–21 August 1958. Plenary Meetings and Annexes* (New York, 1958).
———, *Yearbook of the United Nations, 1958* (New York, 1959).
United States, Congress, *Congressional Record,* 104 (11), 85th Congress, Second Session (Washington, DC, 1958.)
———, Department of State, *Department of State Bulletin* (Washington, DC, 1958).
———, Bureau of Intelligence and Research, *World Strength of the Communist Party Organizations. Annual Report No. 10* (Washington, DC, 1958).
———, Bureau of Public Affairs, Office of the Historian, *American Foreign Policy Current Documents 1958* (Washington, DC, 1962).
———, *Foreign Relations of the United States, 1955–1957,* xvi, *Suez Crisis, July 26–December 31, 1956* (Washington, DC, 1990).
———, *Foreign Relations of the United States, 1958–1960,* xi, *Lebanon and Jordan* (Washington, DC, 1992).
———, *Foreign Relations of the United States, 1958–1960,* xii, *Near East Region; Iraq; Iran; Arabian Peninsula* (Washington, DC, 1993).
———, *Foreign Relations of the United States, 1958–1960*, xiii, *Arab-Israeli Dispute; United Arab Republic; North Africa* (Washington, DC, 1992).
United States, National Archives and Records Administration, *Public Papers of the Presidents of the United States: Dwight D. Eisenhower, 1958* (Washington, DC, 1959).
United States, President, *Public Papers of the Presidents of the United States: Dwight D. Eisenhower, 1958* (Washington, DC, 1958).
United States, Senate, *Hearings Before the Committee on Foreign Relations and the Committee on Armed Services on Senate Joint Resolution 19 and House Resolution 117. Part I, January-February 1957* (Washington, DC, 1957).
———, *Executive Sessions of the Senate Foreign Relations Committee, 85th Congress, 2nd Session, 1958*, Historical Series, 10 (Washington, DC, 1980).
United States, Treaty, *Status of United States Forces in Lebanon, Agreement Between the United States of America and Lebanon, Effected by Exchange of Notes Dated at Beirut July 31 and August 6, 1958.* Treaties and Other International Acts Series 4387 (Washington DC, 1958).
University Publications of America, *Confidential U.S. State Department Central Files. Lebanon: Internal Affairs and Foreign Affairs, 1955–1959* (microfilm) (Bethesda, MD, 1991).

———, Confidential U.S. State Department Central Files. Iraq, 1955–1959 (microfilm) (Bethesda, MD, 1991).

Primary Sources

Adams, Sherman, *Firsthand Report: The Story of the Eisenhower Administration* (New York, 1961).

al-Arif, Ismail, *Iraq Reborn: A Firsthand Account of the July 1958 Revolution and After* (New York, 1982).

al-Baghdadi, Abdel-Latif, *Mudhakkirat* [Memoirs], vol. ii (Cairo, 1977).

Birdwood, Lord, *Nuri al-Said: A Study in Arab Leadership* (London, 1959).

Bull, Odd, *War and Peace in the Middle East* (London, 1976).

Burke, Arleigh, "The Lebanon Crisis," in Arnold R. Shapack, ed., *The Navy in an Age of Change and Crisis: Some Challenges and Responses of the Twentieth Century*, Proceedings, Naval History Symposium (Annapolis, MD, 1973), 70–80.

Caractacus, [pseud. of Norman Daniel], *Revolution in Iraq: An Essay in Comparative Public Opinion* (London, 1959).

Chamoun, Camille, *Crise au Moyen-Orient* (Paris, 1963).

Copeland, Miles, *The Game of Nations: The Amorality of Power Politics* (London, 1969).

Cutler, Robert, *No Time for Rest* (Boston, 1966).

Daniel, Norman, "Contemporary Perceptions of the Revolution in Iraq on 14 July 1958," in Robert A. Fernea and Wm. Roger Louis, eds., *The Iraqi Revolution of 1958: The Old Social Classes Revisited* (London, 1991), 1–30.

Dayan, Moshe, *Story of My Life: An Autobiography* (New York, 1976).

Eban, Abba, *Abba Eban: An Autobiography* (New York, 1977).

———, *Personal Witness: Israel Through My Eyes* (New York, 1992).

Eisenhower, Dwight D., "Radio-television message, July 15, 1958," *Department of State Bulletin*, 39 (4 August 1958), 183–186.

———, *The White House Years. II. Waging Peace, 1956–1961* (Garden City, NY, 1965).

Eveland, Wilbur Crane, *Ropes of Sand: America's Failure in the Middle East* (New York, 1980).

Gallman, Waldemar J., *Iraq Under General Nuri: My Recollections of Nuri al-Said, 1954–1958* (Baltimore, 1964).

Heikal, Mohammed, *The Cairo Documents* (New York, 1973).

———, *The Sphinx and the Commissar: The Rise and Fall of Soviet Influence in the Middle East* (New York,1978).

Holloway Jr., James L., "The American Landing in Lebanon: Orders Firm but Flexible," *U.S. Naval Institute Proceedings* 89 (September 1963), 96–99.

———, "Rapid Deployment, 1958: A Personal Memoir of the Lebanon Landings," *Shipmate* 45 (January–February 1982), 24–27.

von Horn, Carl, *Soldiering for Peace: The Experiences and Views of a U.N. Observer* (New York, 1967).

Hughes, Emmet John. *The Ordeal of Power: A Political Memoir of the Eisenhower Years* (New York, 1963).
Hussein, King of Jordan. *Uneasy Lies the Head: An Autobiography* (London, 1962).
al-Jamali, Mohamed Fadil, *Al-'Iraq al-hadit: Ara'wa mutala'at fi su'unihi al-masiriya* [The New Iraq: Opinions and Readings in its Fateful Affairs] (Beirut, n.d.).
Johnston, Charles Hepburn, *The Brink of Jordan* (London, 1972).
Junblat, Kamal, *Haqiqat al-Thawrah al-Lubnaniyah* [The Truth About the Lebanese Revolution] (Beirut, 1959).
———, *Fi Majra al-siyasa al-Lubnaniyah* [In the Course of Lebanese Politics] (Beirut, n.d.).
Karami, Nadia, and Nawaf Karami, *Waqi' al-Thawrah al-Lubnaniyah* [The Reality of the Lebanese Revolution] (Beirut, 1959).
Khruschchev, Sergei, *Khrushchev on Khrushchev: An Inside Account of the Man and His Era* (Boston, 1990).
———, *Nikita Khrushchev: krizisy i rakety* [Nikita Khrushchev: Crises and Rockets] (Moscow, 1994).
Kubba, Mohamed Mehdi, *Mudhakkirati fi samin al-ahdat, 1918–1958* [My Memoirs in the Thick of Events, 1918–1958] (Beirut, 1965).
Kuneralp, Zeki, "Gunugunune (Temmuz–Agustos 1958)" [Day by Day, July–August 1958], *Tarih ve Toplum* [History and Society] 10 (1988), 15–19.
Lodge, Henry Cabot. *As It Was: An Inside View of Politics and Power in the '50's and '60's* (New York, 1976).
Macmillan, Harold. *Riding the Storm, 1956–1959* (London, 1971).
McClintock, Robert T. *The Meaning of Limited War* (Boston, 1967).
———, "The American Landing in Lebanon," *U.S. Naval Institute Proceedings,* 88 (October, 1962), 65–69.
Micanovic, Veljko, *Moscow Diary* (London, 1980).
Murphy, Robert. *Diplomat Among Warriors* (Garden City, NY, 1964).
Nasser, Gamal Abdel, *The Philosophy of the Revolution* (Buffalo, NY, 1959).
———, *Nahnu wa al-Iraq wa al-suyu'iyu* [We, Iraq, and Communism] (Beirut, n.d.).
Riad, Mahmoud, *Mudhakkirat: Al-amn al-qaumi al-arabi...baina al-injaz wa- al-fasal* [Memoirs: Arab National Security Between Realization and Failure], ii (Cairo, 1986).
Stewart, Desmond, *Turmoil in Beirut: A Personal Account* (London, 1958).
al-Sulh, Sami, *Moudhakkarat Sami al-Sulh* [The Memoirs of Sami al-Sulh] (Beirut, 1960).
Taylor, Maxwell D., *The Uncertain Trumpet* (New York, 1960).
Thayer, Charles W., *Diplomat* (New York, 1959).
Trevelyan, Henry, *The Middle East in Revolution* (London, 1970).
Twinning, Nathan, *Neither Liberty nor Safety: A Hard Look at U.S. Military Policy and Strategy* (New York, 1966).
Urquhart, Brian, *A Life in War and Peace* (New York, 1987).

Books and Articles

The Middle East: History and Politics

Abu Jaber, Kamal S., *The Arab Ba'th Socialist Party: History, Ideology, and Organization* (Syracuse, NY, 1966).

Barnett, Michael, "Institutions, Roles, and Disorder: The Case of the Arab States System," *International Studies Quarterly* 37 (1993), 271–296.

Devlin, J. F., *The Ba'th Party: A History from its Origins to 1966* (Stanford, CA, 1976).

Hourani, Albert, *The Emergence of the Modern Middle East* (London, 1981)

———, *A History of the Arab Peoples* (Cambridge, MA, 1991).

Hurewitz, J. C., *Middle East Politics: The Military Dimension* (New York, 1969).

Ionides, Michael, *Divide and Lose: The Arab Revolt: 1955–1958* (London, 1958).

Khalidi, Rashid, "Consequences of the Suez Crisis in the Arab World," in William Roger Louis and Roger Owen, eds., *Suez 1956: The Crisis and its Consequences* (Oxford, 1989), 377–392.

Khashan, Hilal, *Arabs at the Crossroads: Political Identity and Nationalism* (Gainesville, FL, 2000).

Korany, Baghat, and Ali E. Hillal Dessouki, eds., *The Foreign Policies of the Arab States* (Boulder, CO, 1984).

Laqueur, Walter Ze'ev, ed., *The Middle East in Transition* (New York, 1958).

Marlowe, John, *Arab Nationalism and British Imperialism: A Study in Power Politics* (London, 1961).

Mufti, Malik, *Sovereign Creations: Pan-Arabism and Political Order in Syria and Iraq* (Ithaca, NY, 1996).

Naveh, Hanan, and Michael Brecher, "Patterns of International Crises in the Middle East, 1938–1975," *Jerusalem Journal of International Relations* 2–3 (Winter–Spring 1978), 277–315.

Podeh, Elie, "The Struggle over Arab Hegemony after the Suez Crisis," *Middle Eastern Studies* 29 (January 1993), 91–110.

Rondot, Pierre, *The Changing Patterns of the Middle East* (London, 1961).

Sayegh, Fayez A., *Arab Unity: Hope and Fulfillment* (New York, 1958).

Segev, Samuel, *The Iranian Triangle* (New York, 1988).

Vatikiotis, P. J., *The Middle East: From the End of Empire to the End of the Cold War* (London, 1997).

Yergin, Daniel, *The Prize. The Epic Quest for Oil, Money, and Power* (New York, 1992)

The Cold War and the Middle East

Abu Jaber, Kamal S., *Communism in the Arab East* (New York, 1969).

DeLuca, Daniele, "Gli Stati Uniti e i Nuovi Rapporti di Forza in Medio Oriente: La Dottrina Eisenhower, 1957–1958" [The United States and the New Power Relations in the Middle East: The Eisenhower Doctrine, 1957–1958], *Storia della Relazioni Internazionali* 10–11 (1994–1995), 117–146.

Donno, Antonio, ed., *Ombre di guerra fredda. Gli State Uniti nel Medio Oriente durante gli anni di Eisenhower, 1953–1961* [Cold War Shadows: The United States in the Middle East during the Eisenhower Years, 1953–1961] (Naples, 1998).

Donovan, John, ed., *U.S. and Soviet Policy in the Middle East, 1957–1966* (New York, 1974).

Gaddis, John Lewis, *We Now Know: Rethinking Cold War History* (Oxford, 1997).

Genco, Stephen J., "The Eisenhower Doctrine: Deterrence in the Middle East, 1957–1958," in Alexander George and R. Smoke, eds., *Deterrence in American Foreign Policy* (New York, 1974), 309–362.

Gendzier, Irene L., "The United States, the USSR, and the Arab World in the NSC Reports of the 1950s," *American-Arab Affairs* 28 (Spring 1989), 22–29.

George, Alexander, and R. Smoke, *Deterrence in American Foreign Policy: Theory and Practice* (New York, 1974).

Gerges, Fawaz A., *The Superpowers and the Middle East: Regional and International Politics, 1955–1967* (Boulder, CO, 1994).

Karabell, Zachary, *Architects of Intervention: The United States, the Third World, and the Cold War, 1948–1962* (Baton Rouge, LA: 1999).

Kaufman, Burton L., *The Arab Middle East and the United States: Inter-Arab Rivalry and Superpower Diplomacy* (New York, 1996).

MacMahon, Robert, "Eisenhower and Third World Nationalism: A Critique of the Revisionists," *Political Science Quarterly* 101, no. 3 (1986), 453–473.

———, *The Cold War on the Periphery: The United States, India, and Pakistan* (New York, 1994).

McIntosh, David, "In the Shadow of Giants: U.S. Policy Toward Small Nations: The Cases of Lebanon, Costa Rica, and Austria in the Eisenhower Years," *Contemporary Austrian Studies* 4 (1996), 222–279.

Paterson, Thomas G., *Meeting the Communist Threat: Truman to Reagan* (New York, 1988).

Sayigh, Yezid and Avi Shlaim, eds., *The Cold War and the Middle East* (Oxford, 1997).

Soulié, G. Jean-Louis, "Confrontations Étrangeres au Proche-Orient" [Confrontations between Foreign Powers in the Near East], *Revue de Défense Nationale* 24 (1968), 1245–1254.

Stivers, William, *America's Confrontation with Revolutionary Change in the Middle East, 1948–1983* (New York, 1986).

———, "Eisenhower and the Middle East," in Richard A. Melanson and David Meyers, eds., *Reevaluating Eisenhower: American Foreign Policy in the 1950s* (Urbana, IL, 1987), 192–219.

Stookey, Robert W., *America and the Arab States: An Uneasy Encounter* (New York, 1975).

Takeyh, Ray, *The Origins of the Eisenhower Doctrine: The U.S., Britain, and Nasser's Egypt, 1953–57* (London, 2000).

Egypt and Gamal Abdel Nasser

Beinin, Joel, "The Communist Movement and Nationalist Political Discourse in Nasirist Egypt," *Middle East Journal*, 41 (1987), 568–584.

Cremeans, Charles D., *The Arabs and the World: Nasser's Arab Nationalist Policy* (New York, 1963).
Dawisha, A. I., *Egypt and the Arab World: The Elements of Foreign Policy* (London, 1976).
al-Dib, Mohamad Fathi, *Abdel Nasser et la Révolution algérienne* (Paris, 1985).
Hasou, Tawfiq Y., *The Struggle for the Arab World: Egypt's Nasser and the Arab League* (London, 1985).
Kerr, Malcolm H., *The Arab Cold War: Gamal Abd al-Nasir and His Rivals, 1958–1970* (London, 1970).
Khadduri, Majid, *Arab Contemporaries: The Role of Personalities in Politics* (Baltimore, MD, 1973).
Lacouture, Jean, *The Demigods: Charistmatic Leadership in the Third World* (New York, 1970).
———, *Nasser: A Biography* (New York, 1973).
Lesch, David W., "Gamal Abd al-Nasser and an Example of Diplomatic Acumen," *Middle Eastern Studies* 31 (April 1995), 362–374.
Mansfield, Peter, *Nasser's Egypt* (London, 1969).
Nasr, Marlene, "L'univers national arabe nasserien," in Dominique Chevallier, ed., *Renóuvellements du Monde Arabe, 1952–1982* (Paris, 1987).
Nutting, Anthony, *Nasser* (New York, 1972).
Rejwan, Nissim, *Nasserite Ideology: Its Exponents and Critics* (New York, 1974).
St. John, Robert, *The Boss* (London, 1961).
Stephens, Robert, *Nasser: A Political Biography* (London, 1971).
Vatikiotis, P. J., *Nasser and His Generation* (London, 1978).
Keith Wheelock, *Nasser's New Egypt: A Critical Analysis* (New York, 1960).
Woodward, Peter, *Nasser* (London, 1992).

Great Britain

Aldous, Richard, and Sabine Lee, *Harold Macmillan and Britain's World Role* (London, 1996).
Almog, Orna, "An End of an Era: The Crisis of 1958 and the Anglo-Israeli Relationship," *Contemporary Record* 8 (1994), 49–76.
Ashton, Nigel John, "'A Great New Venture'? Anglo-American Cooperation in the Middle East and the Response to the Iraqi Revolution, July 1958," *Diplomacy and Statecraft* 4/1 (March 1993), 62–67.
———, *Eisenhower, Macmillan, and the Problem of Nasser: Anglo-American Relations and Arab Nationalism, 1955–1959* (London, 1996).
———, "Macmillan and the Middle East," in Richard Aldous and Sabine Lee, eds., *Harold Macmillan and Britain's World Role* (London, 1996).
———, "A Microcosm of Decline: British Loss of Nerve and Military Intervention in Jordan and Kuwait, 1958 and 1961," *Historical Journal* 40 (1997), 1069–1083.
Balfour-Paul, Glen, "Britain's Informal Empire in the Middle East," in Judith M. Brown and Wm. Roger Louis, eds., *The Oxford History of the British Empire,* iv, *The Twentieth Century* (Oxford, 1999), 490–514.
Baylis, John, *Anglo-American Defence Relations, 1939–1984*, 2nd edition (London, 1984).

Clayton, Anthony, "'Deceptive Might': Imperial Defence and Security, 1900–1968," in Judith M. Brown and Wm. Roger Louis, eds., *The Oxford History of the British Empire,* iv, *The Twentieth Century* (Oxford, 1999), 280–305.

DeLee, Nigel, "'More Like Korea Than Suez': British and American Intervention in the Levant in 1958," *Small Wars and Insurgencies* 8 (1997), 1–24.

Fitzsimons, Matthew, *Empire by Treaty: Britain and the Middle East in the Twentieth Century* (Notre Dame, 1964).

Holland, Robert, *Britain and the Revolt in Cyprus, 1954–1959* (Oxford, 1998).

Horne, Alistair, *Macmillan: 1957–1986* (London, 1989).

Lamb, Richard, *The Macmillan Years, 1957–1963: The Emerging Truth* (London, 1995).

Louis, Wm. Roger, and Hedley Bull, eds., *The Special Relationship* (Oxford, 1986).

———, and Roger Owen, eds., *Suez 1956: The Crisis and Its Consequences* (Oxford, 1989).

———, "The British and the Origins of the Iraqi Revolution," in Robert A. Fernea and Wm. Roger Louis, eds., *The Iraqi Revolution of 1958: The Old Social Classes Revisited* (London, 1991), 31–61.

———, "Harold Macmillian and the Middle East Crisis of 1958," *Proceedings of the British Academy* 94 (1997), 207–228.

———, "The Dissolution of the British Empire," in Judith M. Brown and Wm. Roger Louis, eds., *The Oxford History of the British Empire,* iv, *The Twentieth Century* (Oxford, 1999), 329–356.

Monroe, Elizabeth, *Britain's Moment in the Middle East, 1914–1971* (London, 1981).

Ovendale, Ritchie, "Great Britain and the Anglo-American Invasion of Jordan and Lebanon in 1958," *International History Review* 16 (May 1994), 284–303.

———, *Britain, the United States, and the Transfer of Power in the Middle East, 1945–1962* (London, 1996).

Robinson, Francis, "The British Empire and the Muslim World," in Judith M. Brown and Wm. Roger Louis, eds., *The Oxford History of the British Empire,* iv, *The Twentieth Century* (Oxford, 1999), 398–420.

Royal Institute of International Affairs, *Survey of International Affairs, 1956–1958* (London, 1962).

———, *British Interests in the Mediterranean and the Middle East: A Report by a Chatham House Study Group* (London, 1958).

Sluglett, Peter, "Formal and Informal Empire in the Middle East," in Robin W. Winks, ed., *The Oxford History of the British Empire,* v, *Historiography* (Oxford, 1999), 416–436.

Tal, Lawrence, "Britain and the Jordan Crisis of 1958," *Middle Eastern Studies* 31 (January 1995), 39–57.

Turner, John, *Macmillan* (London, 1994).

Watt, Donald Cameron, *Succeeding John Bull: America in Britain's Place, 1900–1975* (New York, 1984).

France and the Algerian War

Fluery, Georges, *La Guerre en Algérie* (Paris, 1993).

Horne, Alistair, *A Savage War of Peace: Algeria, 1954–1962* (London, 1977, rev. ed. 1987).

Talbott, John, *The War Without a Name: France in Algeria, 1954–1962* (New York, 1980).

Iraq

Batutu, Hanna, *The Old Social Classes and the Revolutionary Movements of Iraq: A Study of Iraq's Old Landed and Commercial Classes and of Its Communists, Ba'thists, and Free Officers* (Princeton, NJ, 1978).

———, *The Egyptian, Syrian, and Iraqi Revolutions: Some Observations on Their Underlying Causes and Social Character*. Inaugural Lecture of the Shaykh Sabah al-Salem al-Sabah Chair in Contemporary Arab Studies, Center for Contemporary Arab Studies, Georgetown University, 25 January 1983 (Washington, DC, 1984).

———, "The Old Social Classes Revisited," in Robert A. Fernea and Wm. Roger Louis, eds., *The Iraqi Revolution of 1958: The Old Social Classes Revisited* (London, 1991), 211–222.

Dann, Uriel, *Iraq Under Qassem: A Political History, 1958–1963* (New York, 1969).

De Gaury, Gerald, *Three Kings in Baghdad, 1921–1958* (London, 1961).

Elliot, Matthew, *"Independent Iraq": The Monarchy and British Influence, 1941–1958* (London, 1996).

Farouk-Sluglett, Marion, and Peter Sluglett, "The Transformation of Land Tenure and Rural Social Structure in Central and Southern Iraq, 1870–1958," *International Journal of Middle East Studies* 15 (1983), 491–505.

———, "Labor and National Liberation: The Trade Union Movement in Iraq, 1920–1958," *Arab Studies Quarterly* 5 (1983), 139–154.

———, *Iraq Since 1958: From Revolution to Dictatorship* (London, 1987).

———, "The Historiography of Modern Iraq," *American Historical Review* 96 (1991), 1408–1421.

———, "The Social Classes and the Origins of the Revolution," in Robert A. Fernea and Wm. Roger Louis, eds., *The Iraqi Revolution of 1958: The Old Social Classes Revisited* (London, 1991), 118–142.

Fernea, Robert A., "State and Tribe in Southern Iraq: the Struggle for Hegemony before the 1958 Revolution," in Robert A. Fernea and Wm. Roger Louis, eds., *The Iraqi Revolution of 1958: The Old Social Classes Revisited* (London, 1991), 142–153.

Gabbay, Rony, *Communism and Agrarian Reform in Iraq* (London, 1978).

Hopwood, Derek, with Habib Ishow, Thomas Koszinowski, eds., *Iraq: Power and Society* (Reading, UK, 1993).

Khadduri, Majid, *Independent Iraq, 1932–1958: A Study in Iraqi Politics* (London, 1960).

———, *Republican Iraq: A Study in Iraqi Politics since the Revolution of 1958* (London, 1969).

———, *Arab Contemporaries: The Role of Personalities in Politics* (Baltimore, MD, 1973).

———, "Nuri al-Sa'id's Disenchantment with Britain in His Last Years," *Middle East Journal* 54 (2000), 83–96.

Khalidi, Rashid, "The Impact of the Iraq Revolution on the Arab World," in Robert A. Fernea and Wm. Roger Louis, eds., *The Iraqi Revolution of 1958: The Old Social Classes Revisited* (London, 1991), 106–117.

Marr, Phebe, *The Modern History of Iraq* (London, 1985).

Owen, Roger, "Class and Class Politics in Iraq before 1958: the 'Colonial' and 'Post-Colonial State,'" in Robert A. Fernea and Wm. Roger Louis, eds., *The Iraqi Revolution of 1958: The Old Social Classes Revisited* (London, 1991), 154–171.

Penrose, Edith and E. F., *Iraq: International Relations and National Development* (London, 1978).

Simons, Geoff, *Iraq: From Sumer to Saddam* (New York, 1994).

Tahir, Alaa, *Irak: aux origines d'un régime militaire* (Paris, 1989).

Thatcher, Nicolas G., "Reflections on U.S. Foreign Policy toward Iraq in the 1950s," in Robert A. Fernea and Wm. Roger Louis, eds., *The Iraqi Revolution of 1958: The Old Social Classes Revisited* (London, 1991), 62–76.

Tripp, Charles, *A History of Iraq* (Cambridge, UK, 2000).

Yousif, Abdul-Salaam, "The Struggle for Cultural Hegemony during the Iraq Revolution," in Robert A. Fernea and Wm. Roger Louis, eds., *The Iraqi Revolution of 1958: The Old Social Classes Revisited* (London, 1991), 172–196.

Zubaida, Sami, "Community, Class and Minorities in Iraqi Politics," in Robert A. Fernea and Wm. Roger Louis, eds., *The Iraqi Revolution of 1958: The Old Social Classes Revisited* (London, 1991), 197–210.

Israel

Allon, Yigal, *Masakh Shel Hol* [Sand Curtain] (Tel Aviv, 1959).

Bar-On, Mordechai, "Status Quo—Before and After: Commentary Notes on Israel's Defense Policy, 1949–1958," *Iyunim Bitkumat Israel* [Studies in Zionism, the Yishuv and the State of Israel] 5 (1995), 65–111.

Bar-Zohar, Michel, *Ben-Gurion: The Armed Prophet* (New York, 1968).

———, *Ben-Gurion: A Biography* (New York, 1978).

Brecher, Michael, *Israel's Foreign Policy: The First Twenty Years in the Foreign Policy System of Israel* (Oxford, 1972).

Derogy, Jacques, and Hesi Carmel, *The Untold Story of Israel* (New York, 1979).

Horowitz, Dan, *Israel's Concept of Defensible Borders* (Jerusalem, 1975)

Levey, Zach, "Israel's Pursuit of French Arms, 1952–1958," *Studies in Zionism* 14, no. 2 (1993), 183–210.

———, *Israel and the Western Powers, 1952–1960* (Chapel Hill, NC, 1998).

Naor, Mordechai, *Haim Laskov* (Tel Aviv, 1988).

Oren, Michael B., "The Test of Suez: Israel and the Middle East Crisis of 1958," *Studies in Zionism*, 12, (1991), 55–83.

———, "Israel and the Question of Overflights to Jordan, 1958," *Iyunim Bitkumat Israel* [Studies in Zionism, the Yishuv and the State of Israel] 1 (1991), 262–275.

Pappé, Ilan, "Critique and Agenda: The Post-Zionist Scholars in Israel," *History and Memory* 7 (Spring/Summer 1995), 66–91.

Schultze, Kirsten E., *Israel's Covert Diplomacy in Lebanon* (London, 1998).

Shlaim, Avi, *The Iron Wall: Israel and the Arab World* (New York, 2000).

———, "Israel, the Great Powers, and the Middle East Crisis of 1958," *Journal of Imperial and Commonwealth History* 27 (1999), 177–192.

Tal, David, "Seizing Opportunities: Israel and the 1958 Crisis in the Middle East," *Middle Eastern Studies* 37 (2001) 142–158.

Yaniv, Avner, *Politikah ve-astrategyah be-Yisflra'el* [Politics and Strategy in Israel] (Tel Aviv, 1994).

Yizhar, Michael, "Israel and the Eisenhower Doctrine," *Wiener Library Bulletin* 28 (1978), 58–64.

Jordan

Abidi, Aqil Hyder Hasan, *Jordan: A Political Study, 1948–1957* (New York, 1965).

Aruri, Naseer Hasan, *Jordan: A Study in Political Development, 1921–1965* (The Hague, 1972).

Dann, Uriel, *King Hussein and the Challenge of Arab Radicalism, Jordan, 1955–1967* (New York, 1989).

De Luca, Daniele, "La diplomazia armata. Gli Stati Uniti e le crisis giordana e libanese, 1957–1958" [Armed Diplomacy: The United States and the Jordanian and Lebanese Crises, 1957–1958], in Antonio Donno, ed., *Ombre di guerra fredda. Gli State Uniti nel Medio Oriente durante gli anni di Eisenhower, 1953–1961* [Cold War Shadows: The United States in the Middle East During the Eisenhower Years, 1953–1961] (Naples, 1998), 651–686.

Faddah, Mohammad Ibrahim, *The Middle East in Transition: A Study of Jordan's Foreign Policy* (London, 1974).

Kaplan, Steven S., "United States Aid and Regime Maintenance in Jordan, 1957–1973," *Public Policy* 23 (1975), 189–217.

Lunt, James, *Hussein of Jordan: A Political Biography* (London, 1989).

Maddy-Weitzman, Bruce, "Jordan and Iraq: Efforts at Intra-Hashemite Unity," *Middle Eastern Studies* 26 (1990), 65–75.

Parker, Richard B., "The United States and King Hussein," in David W. Lesch, ed., *The Middle East and the United States: A Historical and Political Reassessment*, 2nd. ed. (Boulder, CO, 1999).

Salibi, Kamal Suleiman, *The Modern History of Jordan* (London, 1993).

Satloff, Robert B., *From Abdullah to Hussein: Jordan in Transition* (New York, 1994).

———, "The Jekyll-and-Hyde Origins of the U.S.-Jordanian Strategic Relationship," in David W. Lesch, ed., *The Middle East and the United States: A Historical and Political Reassessment,* 2nd. ed. (Boulder, CO, 1999), 114–127.

Simon, Reeva S., "The Hashemite 'Conspiracy': Hashemite Unity Attempts, 1921–1958," *International Journal of Middle East Studies* 5 (1974), 314–327.

Snow, Peter John, *Hussein: A Biography* (London, 1972).

Vatikiotis, P.J., *Politics and the Military in Jordan: A Study of the Arab Legion, 1921–1957* (London, 1972).

Kuwait

Alani, Mustafa M., *Operation Vantage: British Military Intervention in Kuwait, 1961* (Old Woking, Surrey, UK, 1990).

Joyce, Mariam, "Preserving the Sheikhdom: London, Washington, Iraq and Kuwait, 1958–1961," *Middle Eastern Studies* 31 (April 1995), 281–292.

Lebanon: History, Politics, and Crisis

Abercrombie, Thomas J., "Young-old Lebanon Lives by Trade," *National Geographic Magazine* 113 (April 1958), 479–523.

Agwani, Mohammed Shafi, "The Lebanese Crisis of 1958 in Retrospect," *International Studies* 4 (April 1963), 329–348.

———, ed., *The Lebanese Crisis, 1958: A Documentary Study* (New York, 1965).

Asmar, Michel, *Ba'd al-Mihnah wa Qablha* [After and Before the Crisis] (Beirut, 1959).

"Austrian Role for Lebanon," *Foreign Report* 581 (July 24, 1958).

Binder, Leonard, ed., *Politics in Lebanon* (New York, 1966).

Choueiri, Youssef, ed., *State and Society in Syria and Lebanon, 1919–1991* (New York, 1994).

Cobban, Helena, *The Making of Modern Lebanon* (London, 1985).

Deen, Said Taky, *Bridge Under the Water: This Is How We Chased Eisenhower Out of La République Libanaise* (n.p., 1958).

Faris, Nabih Amin, "Reflections on the Lebanon Crisis," *SAIS Review* 3 (Autumn 1958), 9–14.

Frankel, Ephraim A., "The Maronite Patriarch: An Historical View of a Religious Za'im in the 1958 Lebanese Crisis," *Muslim World* 66 (1976), 213–225, 245–258.

Frye, William R., "Lebanon: Story Behind the Headlines," *Foreign Policy Bulletin* 38 (1 November 1958), 25–26.

Gerges, Fawaz A., "The Lebanese Crisis of 1958: The Risks of Inflated Self-Importance," *The Beirut Review* 5 (1993), 83–113.

Gordon, David C., *The Republic of Lebanon: Nation in Jeopardy* (Boulder, CO, 1983).

Goria, Wade R., *Sovereignty and Leadership in Lebanon, 1941–1976* (London,1985).

Gilmour, David, *Lebanon: The Fractured Country* (New York, 1983).

Hanf, Theodor, *Co-Existence in Wartime Lebanon: Decline of a State and Rise of a Nation* (London, 1993).

Hitti, Philip, *Lebanon in History* (London, 1962).

Hudson, Michael, *The Precarious Republic: Political Modernization in Lebanon* (New York, 1968).

Hurewitz, J. C., "Lebanese Democracy in Its International Setting," *The Middle East Journal* 17 (Autumn 1963), 487–506.

Kalawoun, Nasser, *The Struggle for Lebanon: A Modern History of Lebanese-Egyptian Relations* (London, 2000).

Kerr, Malcolm H., "The Lebanese Civil War," in Evan Luard, ed., *The International Regulation of Civil Wars* (New York,1972), 65–90.

———, "Lebanese Views of the 1958 Crisis," *Middle East Journal* 15 (Spring 1961), 211–217.

al-Khazen, Farid, "Kamal Jumblatt: The Uncrowned Druze Prince of the Left," *Middle Eastern Studies* 24 (1988), 178–205.

Majzoub, Mohammad, and Ma'rouf Saad, *Indima qawamna* [When We Resisted] (Beirut, 1959).

Meo, Leila M. T., *Lebanon, Improbable Nation: A Study in Political Development* (Bloomington, IN, 1965).

Nour, Francis, "Particularisme Libanais et Nationalisme Arabe," *Orient* 7 (1958), 29–42.

Odeh, B. J., *Lebanon: Dynamics of Conflict, a Modern Political History* (London, 1985).

Petran, Tabitha, *The Struggle Over Lebanon* (New York, 1987).

Qubain, Fahim, *Crisis in Lebanon* (Washington, DC,1961).

Salam, Nawaf, *L'Insurrection de 1958 au Liban*. 5 vols. (Paris, 1979).

Salibi, Kamal Suleiman, "Lebanon Since the Crisis of 1958," *World Today* 17 (January 1961), 32–42.

———, "The Lebanese Crisis in Perspective," *World Today* 14 (September 1958), 369–380.

———, *The Modern History of Lebanon* (New York, 1965).

———, "Lebanon Under Fuad Chehab, 1958–1964," *Middle Eastern Studies* 2 (April, 1966), 211–226.

———, *Crossroads to Civil War: Lebanon, 1958–1976* (London, 1976).

———, "Recollections of the 1940s and 1950s." Paper given at the University of Texas Conference on Lebanon in the 1950s, 10–13 September 1992.

Sulemain, Michael W., *Political Parties in Lebanon: The Challenge of a Fragmented Political Culture* (Ithaca, NY, 1967).

Tuwayni [Tueni], Ghassan, *Al-Ayyam al-Asibah* [Days of Crisis] (Beirut, 1958).

Ziadeh, Nicola A., *Syria and Lebanon* (London, 1957).

American Intervention in Lebanon, 1958

Alin, Erika, "U.S. Policy and Military Intervention in the 1958 Lebanon Crisis," in David W. Lesch, ed., *The Middle East and the United States: A Historical and Political Reassessment,* 2nd. ed. (Boulder, CO, 1999), 144–162.

———, *The United States and the 1958 Lebanon Crisis: American Intervention in the Middle East* (Lanham, MD, 1994).

Bishku, Michael B., "The 1958 American Intervention in Lebanon: A Historical Assessment," *American-Arab Affairs* 31 (Winter 1989–1990), 106–119.

Bodron, Margaret M., "U.S. Intervention in Lebanon—1958," *Military Review* 56 (February 1976), 66–76

Bradshaw, K. A., "1958 and the First Beirut Peacekeeping Mission," *Profile* 26 (December 1982), 18–19.

Brands Jr., Henry W., "Decisions on American Armed Intervention: Lebanon, Dominican Republic, Grenada," *Political Science Quarterly* 102 (1987–1988), 607–624.

Braestrup, Peter, "Limited War and the Lessons of Lebanon," *The Reporter* 20 (30 April 1959), 25–27.

Brunnhunber, Ulrich H., *Die Libanonkrise 1958: U.S. Intervention im Zeichen der Eisenhower Doktrin?* (Hamburg, 1997).

Calhoun, Christopher, "Lebanon: That Was Then," *U.S. Naval Institute Proceedings* 111 (September 1985), 74–80.

Cooper, Bert, "The Undenounced Intervention," in Robert De McLaurin, ed., *The Art and Science of Psychological Operations: Case Studies of Military Application*, vol. i (Washington, DC, 1976), 241–246.

DeLuca, Daniele, "La diplomazia armata. Gli Stati Uniti e le crisis giordana e libanese, 1957–1958" [Armed Diplomacy: The United States and the Jordanian and Lebanese Crises, 1957–1958], in Antonio Donno, ed., *Ombre di guerra fredda. Gli State Uniti nel Medio Oriente durante gli anni di Eisenhower, 1953–1961* [Cold War Shadows: The United States in the Middle East During the Eisenhower Years, 1953–1961] (Naples, 1998), 651–686.

Dimekchie, Nadim, "The United States Intervened Militarily by Sending the Marines to Lebanon in 1958: Why Did This Happen," Paper given at the University of Texas Conference on Lebanon in the 1950s, 10–13 September 1992.

Dowty, Alan, "United States Decision-Making in Middle East Crises: 1958, 1970, 1973," *Middle East Review* 12 (Spring 1980), 23–30.

———, *Middle East Crises: U.S. Decision-Making in 1958, 1970, and 1973* (Berkeley, 1984).

Gendzier, Irene L., "The Declassified Lebanon, 1948–1958: Elements of Continuity and Contrast in U.S. Policy Toward Lebanon," in Halim Barakat, ed., *Toward a Viable Lebanon* (London, 1988), 187–209.

———, "'No Forum for the Lebanese People': U.S. Perceptions from Lebanon, 1945–1947," *Middle East Report* (January/February 1990), 34–36.

———, "The U.S. Perception of the Lebanese Civil War According to Declassified Documents: A Preliminary Assessment," in Reeva S. Simon, ed., *The Middle East and North Africa: Essays in Honor of J.C. Hurewitz* (New York, 1990), 332–348.

———, "Presidential Leadership in Foreign Policy: The Case of Lebanon, 1958," Paper presented at SHAFR [Society for the History of American Foreign Relations] (June 1992).

———, *Development Against Democracy* (Hampton, CN, 1995).

———, *Notes From the Minefield: United States Intervention in Lebanon and the Middle East, 1945–1958* (New York, 1998; paperback ed., Boulder, CO, 1999)

Godwin, Paul H. B., and Lewis B. Ware, "Linkage Politics and Coercive Diplomacy: A Comparative Analysis of Two Lebanese Crises," *Air University Review* 28 (1976), 80–89.

Hadd, Harry A., "Who's a Rebel: The Lesson Lebanon Taught," *Marine Corps Gazette* 46 (March 1962), 50–54.

———, "Orders Firm but Flexible," *U.S. Naval Institute Proceedings* 88 (October 1962), 80–89.

Hussain, Syed Rifaat, "American Intervention in the Middle East: A Case Study of Lebanon, 1958," *Strategic Studies* 13 (1990), 39–60.

Knebel, Fletcher, "Day of Decision," *Look* 22 (16 September 1958), 17–19.

Korbani, Agnes G., *U.S. Intervention in Lebanon, 1958 and 1982: Presidential Decisionmaking* (New York, 1991).

Lerner, Max, "American Views on Lebanon," *Foreign Policy Bulletin* 37 (15 August 1958), 180–182.

Little, Douglas, "His Finest Hour? Eisenhower, Lebanon, and the 1958 Middle East Crisis," *Diplomatic History* 20 (Winter 1996), 27–54.

Nadaner, Jeffrey M., "Strife Among Friends and Foes: The 1958 Anglo-American Military Interventions in the Middle East," *UCLA Historical Journal* 17 (1997), 82–123.

O'Donnell, James P., "Operation Double Trouble," *Saturday Evening Post* 231 (20 September 1958), 42ff.

Potter, Elmer Belmont, *Admiral Arleigh Burke: A Biography* (New York, 1990).

Potter, Pitman B., "Legal Aspects of the Beirut Landing," *American Journal of International Law* 52 (October 1958), 727–730.

Quandt, William B., "U.S. Intervention in Lebanon, 1958 and Jordan, 1970," in Barry M. Blechman and Stephen S. Kaplan, eds., *Force Without War: U.S. Armed Forces as a Political Instrument* (Washington, DC, 1977), 222–288.

Shulimson, Jack, *Marines in Lebanon, 1958* (Washington, DC, 1966).

Sights Jr., Albert P., "Lessons of Lebanon: A Study in Air Strategy," *Air University Review* 16 (July/August 1965), 28–43.

Spiller, Roger J., *"Not War but Like War": The American Intervention in Lebanon* (Fort Leavenworth, KS, 1961).

Steeves Jr., W. D., "Crisis in Retrospect," *Marine Corps Gazette* 57 (December 1973), 31–34.

Steward, Hal D., "The U.S. Army and Public Relations in Lebanon," *Irish Defense Journal* 18 (October 1958), 490–493.

"Story of a Decision," *U.S. News and World Report* (25 July 1958), 68–70.

Viccello, Henry, "The Composite Air Strike Force 1958," *Air University Review* 11 (Summer 1958), 3–17.

Wade, Gary H., *Rapid Deployment Logistics: Lebanon, 1958* (Fort Leavenworth, KS, 1985).

Wade, Sydney S., "Operation Bluebat," *Marine Corps Gazette* 43 (July 1959), 10–25.

———, "Lebanon," *Marine Corps Gazette* 49 (November 1965), 86.

"Washington's Heap of Trouble," *Foreign Report* 579 (10 July 1958), 1–2.

Wright, Quincy, "United States Intervention in Lebanon," *American Journal of International Law* 53 (January 1959), 112–125.

Wylie, J. C., "The Sixth Fleet and American Diplomacy," *Proceedings of the Academy of Political Science* 29 (1969), 55–60.

Saudi Arabia

Bligh, Alexander, *From Prince to King: Royal Succession in the House of Saud in the Twentieth Century* (London, 1984).

Long, David E., *The United States and Saudi Arabia: Ambivalent Allies* (Boulder, CO, 1985).

Soviet Union

Carrère d'Encausse, Hélène , *La Politique Sovietique au Moyen Orient 1955–1975* (Paris, 1975).

Dallin, David. J., *Soviet Foreign Policy After Stalin* (New York, 1961).
Denkos, Helen, *Al-siyasa al-Sufyatiya fi sharq al-awsat, 1955–1975* [Soviet Foreign Policy in the Middle East, 1955–1975] (Beirut, 1983).
Donovan, John, ed., *U.S. and Soviet Policy in the Middle East, 1957–1966* (New York, 1974).
Golan, Galia, *Soviet Policies in the Middle East: From World War Two to Gorbachev* (Cambridge, UK, 1990).
el-Hussini, Mohrez Mahmoud, *Soviet-Egyptian Relations, 1945–85* (New York, 1987).
Laqueur, Walter Ze'ev, *The Soviet Union in the Middle East* (New York, 1959)
Lederer, Ivo J., and Wayne S. Vucinich, *The Soviet Union and the Middle East: The Post World War Two Era* (Stanford, CA, 1974).
Mirsky, Georgyi, "The Soviet Perception of the U.S. Threat," in David W. Lesch, ed., *The Middle East and the United States: A Historical and Political Reassessment*, 2nd. ed. (Boulder, CO, 1999), 395–403.
Rainow, Peter, "La percezionne sovietica della politica americana e dei rapporti tra le superpotenze nel Medio Oriente durante gli anni '50" [Soviet Perceptions of American Middle East Policy and Superpower Relations in the Middle East during the 1950's], in Antonio Donno, ed., *Ombre di guerra fredda. Gli State Uniti nel Medio Oriente durante gli anni di Eisenhower, 1953–1961* [Cold War Shadows: The United States in the Middle East During the Eisenhower Years, 1953–1961] (Naples, 1998), 687–716.
Ro'i, Yaacov, *From Encroachment to Involvement: A Documentary Study of Soviet Policy in the Middle East, 1945–1973* (New Brunswick, NJ, 1974).
Saivetz, Carol R., and Sylvia Woodby, *Soviet-Third World Relations* (Boulder, CO, 1985).
Smolanksy, Oles M., *The Soviet Union and the Arab East under Khrushchev* (Lewisburg, PA, 1974).
———, *The USSR and Iraq: The Soviet Quest for Influence* (Durham, NC., 1991).
Stork, Joe, "The Soviet Union, the Great Powers, and Iraq," in Robert A. Fernea and Wm. Roger Louis, eds., *The Iraqi Revolution of 1958: The Old Social Classes Revisited* (London, 1991), 95–105.
Vassiliev, Alexei, *Russian Policy in the Middle East: From Messianism to Pragmatism* (Reading, UK, 1993).
Zubok, Vladislav, and Constantine Pleshakov, *Inside the Kremlin's Cold War* (Cambridge, MA, 1996).

Syria

Heydemann, Steven, *Authoritarianism in Syria: Institutions and Social Conflict, 1946–1970* (Ithaca, NY, 1999).
Hopwood, Derek, *Syria: Politics and Society, 1945–1986* (London, 1988).
Lesch, David W., *Syria and the United States: Eisenhower's Cold War in the Middle East* (Boulder, CO, 1992).
———, "Prelude to American Intervention in Lebanon: The 1957 American-Syrian Crisis," Paper given at the University of Texas Conference on Lebanon in the 1950s, 10–13 September 1992.

———, "The 1957 American-Syrian Crisis: Globalist Policy in a Regional Reality," in David W. Lesch, ed., *The Middle East and the United States: A Historical and Political Reassessment*, 2nd. ed. (Boulder, CO, 1999), 128–143.

Olson, Robert W., *The Ba'th and Syria, 1947 to 1982: The Evolution of Ideology, Party, and State* (Princeton, NJ, 1982).

Pipes, Daniel, *Greater Syria: The History of an Ambition* (New York, 1990).

Rathmeil, Andrew, *Secret War in the Middle East: The Covert Struggle for Syria, 1949–1961* (New York, 1995).

———, "Brotherly Enemies: The Rise and Fall of the Syrian-Egyptian Intelligence Axis, 1954–1967," *Intelligence and National Security* 13 (1998), 230–253.

Roberts, David, *The Ba'th and the Creation of Modern Syria* (London, 1987).

Saunders, Bonnie F., *The United States and Arab Nationalism: The Syrian Case, 1953–1960* (Westport, CT, 1996).

Seale, Patrick, *The Struggle for Syria: A Study of Postwar Arab Politics*, 2nd ed. (London, 1986).

Torrey, G. H., *Syrian Politics and the Military. 1945–58* (Columbus, OH, 1964).

Yamak, Labib Zuwiyya, *The Syrian Social Nationalist Party: An Ideological Analysis* (Cambridge, MA., 1966).

Ziadeh, Nicola A., *Syria and Lebanon* (London, 1957).

United Nations

Curtis, Gerald L., "The United Nations Observation Group in Lebanon," *International Organization*, 18 (Autumn 1964), 738–765.

Dayal, Rajeshwar, "The 1958 Crisis in Lebanon—the Role of the U.N. and the Great Powers," *India Quarterly* 26 (April/June, 1970), 123–133.

Doyle, Colm, "UN Observer Missions in the Middle East and Central America," *Irish Sword* 20 (1996), 32–36.

Franck, Thomas, "Who Killed Article 2(4)? or: Changing Norms Governing the Use of Force by States," *American Journal of International Law* 64 (October 1970), 809–837.

Fry, Michael Graham, and Miles Hochstein, "Epistemic Communities; Intelligence Studies and International Relations," *Intelligence and National Security* 8 (July 1993), 14–28.

———, The Uses of Intelligence: the United Nations Confronts the United States in the Lebanon, 1958," *Intelligence and National Security* 10 (January 1995), 59–91.

Ghali, Mona, "United Nations Observation Group in Lebanon: 1958," in William J. Durch, ed., *The Evolution of UN Peacekeeping: Case Studies and Comparative Analysis* (New York, 1993), 163–180.

Higgins, Rosalyn, *United Nations Peacekeeping, 1946–1967: Documents and Commentary*, vol. i., *The Middle East* (London, 1969).

James, Alan, *Peacekeeping in International Politics* (London, 1990).

Lash, Joseph P., *Dag Hammarskjöld: Custodian of the Brushfire Peace* (New York, 1961).

Levine, Israel E., *Champion of World Peace: Dag Hammarskjöld* (New York, 1962).

United Nations, *The Blue Helmets: A Review of United Nations Peacekeeping* (New York, 1990).

Wainhouse, David W., *International Peace Observation* (Baltimore, MD, 1966).
———, *International Peacekeeping at the Crossroads: National Support—Experience and Prospects* (Baltimore, MD, 1973).
Weiss, Thomas A., and Jarat Chopra, *United Nations Peacekeeping* (New York, 1992).
Urquhart, Brian, *Hammarskjöld* (New York, 1973).

United States

Alexander, Charles C., *Holding the Line: The Eisenhower Era: 1952–1961* (Bloomington, IN, 1975).
Alteras, Isaac, *Eisenhower and Israel: U.S.-Israeli Relations, 1953–1960* (Gainesville, FL, 1993).
Ambrose, Stephen E., *Ike's Spies: Eisenhower and the Espionage Establishment* (New York, 1981).
———, *Eisenhower: The President*, ii (New York, 1984).
———, *Eisenhower: Soldier and President* (New York, 1990).
"America's Search for a Policy," *Foreign Report* 582 (31 July 1958).
Ashton, Nigel John, *Eisenhower, Macmillan, and the Problem of Nasser: Anglo-American Relations and Arab Nationalism, 1955–1959* (London, 1996).
Axelgard, Frederick W., "U.S. Support for the British Position in Pre-Revolutionary Iraq," in Robert A. Fernea and William Roger Louis, eds., *The Iraqi Revolution of 1958: The Old Social Classes Revisited* (London, 1991), 72–94.
Badeau, John S., *The American Approach to the Arab World* (New York, 1968).
Baldridge, Edward F., "Lebanon and Quemoy—The Navy's Role," *U.S. Naval Institute Proceedings* 87 (February 1961), 94–100.
Baldwin, Hanson W., "Strategy of the Middle East," *Foreign Affairs* 35 (July 1957), 655–665.
Barnet, Richard J., *Intervention and Revolution: The United States in the Third World* (New York, 1968).
———, "What Eisenhower and Dulles Saw in Nasser," *American-Arab Affairs* 17 (Summer 1986), 44–54.
———, *Cold Warriors: Eisenhower's Generation and American Foreign Policy* (New York, 1988).
———, *The Spectre of Neutralism: The United States and the Emergence of the Third World, 1947–1960* (New York, 1990).
———, *Into the Labyrinth: The United States and the Middle East, 1945–1993* (New York, 1994).
Bernkovitz, Morton, P. G. Bock, and Vincent J. Fuccillo, *The Politics of American Foreign Policy: The Social Context of Decisions* (Englewood Cliffs, NJ, 1977).
Biello, Daniele, "Gli Stati tra bipolarismo e polarizzazione. La diplomazia americana nel Medio Oriente e la Dottrina Eisenhower" [The United States Between Bipolarism and Polarization. American Diplomacy in the Middle East and the Eisenhower Doctrine] in Antonio Donno, ed., *Ombre di guerra fredda. Gli State Uniti nel Medio Oriente durante gli anni di Eisenhower, 1953–1961* [Cold War Shadows: The United States in the Middle East During the Eisenhower Years, 1953–1961] (Naples, 1998), 625–650.

Blechman, Barry M., and Stephen S. Kaplan, *Force Without War: U.S. Armed Forces as a Political Instrument* (Washington, DC, 1978).

———, "U.S. Military Forces as a Political Instrument Since World War II," *Political Science Quarterly* 94 (1979), 193–210.

Brands Jr., Henry. W., "Decisions on American Armed Intervention: Lebanon, Dominican Republic, Grenada," *Political Science Quarterly* 102 (1987–1988), 607–624.

Brendon, Piers, *Ike: His Life and Times* (New York, 1986).

Bryson, Thomas A., *American Diplomatic Relations with the Middle East, 1784–1975: A Survey* (Metuchen, NJ, 1977).

———, *Tars, Turks, and Tankers: The Role of the United States Navy in the Middle East, 1800–1979* (Metuchen, NJ, 1980).

Cable, James, *Gunboat Diplomacy, 1919–1991: Political Applications of Limited Naval Force* (New York, 1994).

Campbell, John C., *Defense of the Middle East: Problems of American Policy* (New York, 1960).

Cook, Blanche Wiesen, *The Declassified Eisenhower: A Divided Legacy of Peace and Political Warfare* (Garden City, NY, 1984).

Dietl, Gulshan, *The Dulles Era: America Enters West Asia* (New Delhi, 1986).

Divine, Robert A., *Eisenhower and the Cold War* (New York, 1981).

Drummond, Roscoe, and Gaston Coblentz, *Duel at the Brink: John Foster Dulles' Command of American Power* (Garden City, NY, 1960).

Dulles, Eleanor Lansing, *John Foster Dulles: The Last Year* (New York, 1963).

———, *American Foreign Policy in the Making* (New York, 1968).

Ewald Jr., William Bragg, *Eisenhower the President: Crucial Days, 1951–1960* (Englewood Cliffs, NJ, 1981).

Genco, Stephen J., "The Eisenhower Doctrine: Deterrence in the Middle East, 1957–1958," in Alexander George and R. Smoke, eds., *Deterrence in American Foreign Policy* (New York, 1974), 309–362.

Gurtov, Melvin, *The United States Against the Third World* (New York, 1974).

Halpern, Manfred, "The Morality and Politics of Intervention," in James Rosenau, ed., *International Aspects of Civil Strife* (Princeton, NJ, 1964).

Hart, Parker T., "Tensions and U.S. Policy in the Near and Middle East," Address before the Foreign Policy Association of Pittsburgh, 1 May 1959, *Department of State Bulletin* 40 (18 May 1959), 715–720.

Hoopes, Townsend, *The Devil and John Foster Dulles* (Boston, 1973).

Isenberg, Michael T., *Shield of the Republic: The United States Navy in an Era of Cold War and Violent Peace, 1946–1962* (New York, 1993).

Lenczowski, George, *American Presidents and the Middle East* (Durham, NC, 1990).

Lesch, David W., ed., *The Middle East and the United States: A Historical and Political Reassessment,* 2nd. ed. (Boulder, CO, 1999).

Little, Douglas, "Cold War and Covert Action: The United States and Syria, 1945–1958," *Middle East Journal* 44 (Winter 1990), 51–75.

———, "The Making of a Special Relationship: The United States and Israel, 1957–1968," *International Journal of Middle East Studies* 25 (November 1993), 563–585.

———, “Gideon’s Band,” *Diplomatic History* 18 (Fall 1994), 513–540.
———, “A Puppet in Search of a Puppeteer: The United States, King Hussein, and Jordan, 1953–1970,” *International History Review* 17 (August 1995), 512–544.
———, “His Finest Hour? Eisenhower, Lebanon, and the 1958 Middle East Crisis,” *Diplomatic History* 20 (Winter 1996), 27–54.
Lyon, Peter, *Eisenhower: Portrait of a Hero* (Boston, 1974).
Melanson, Richard A., and David Mayers, *Reevaluating Eisenhower: American Foreign Policy in the 1950s* (Chicago, 1987).
Mufti, Malik, “The United States and Nasserist Pan-Arabism,” in David W. Lesch, ed., *The Middle East and the United States: A Historical and Political Reassessment* (Boulder, CO, 1996), 167–186.
Nolte, Richard H., and William R. Polk, “Toward a Policy for the Middle East,” *Foreign Affairs* 36 (July 1958), 643–658.
Palmer, Michael A., *Guardians of the Gulf: A History of America’s Expanding Role in the Persian Gulf, 1833–1992* (New York, 1992).
Parker, Richard B., “The United States and King Hussein,” in David W. Lesch, ed., *The Middle East and the United States: A Historical and Political Reassessment*, 2nd. ed. (Boulder, CO, 1999).
Parmet, Herbert S., *Eisenhower and the American Crusades* (New York, 1972).
Polk, William R., “A Decade of Discovery: America in the Middle East, 1947–1958,” in Albert Hourani, ed., *St. Antony’s Papers, No. 11* (Middle Eastern Affairs, No. 2) (London, 1961), 49–80.
Quandt, William B., “United States Policy in the Middle East: Constraints and Choices,” in Paul Y. Hammond and Sidney S. Alexander, eds., *Political Dynamics in the Middle East* (New York, 1972), 489–551.
Quigley, John, *The Ruses for War: American Interventionism Since World War Two* (Buffalo, 1992).
Rosenau, James N., ed., *The Domestic Sources of Foreign Policy* (New York, 1967).
Schulzinger, Robert, “The Impact of Suez on United States Middle East Policy, 1957–1958,” in Selwyn Ilan Troen and Moshe Shemesh, eds., *The Suez-Sinai Crisis, 1956* (New York, 1990), 251–265.
Spiegel, Steven L., *The Other Arab-Israeli Crisis: Making America’s Middle East Policy from Truman to Reagan* (Chicago, 1985).
Tillema, Herbert K., *Appeal to Force: American Military Intervention in the Era of Containment* (New York, 1973).

Dissertations and Theses

Alin, Erika, “The 1958 United States Intervention in Lebanon,” D. Phil. thesis (American, 1980).
Abu-Diab, Fawzi, “Lebanon and the United States, 1945–1958,” D. Phil. thesis (Pennsylvania, 1965).

Abu el-Haj, Samira Ali, "Class Conflict and Political Revolution in Iraq: The Socioeconomic Origins of the 1958 Revolution," D. Phil. thesis (University of California, Los Angeles, 1987).

Al-Aiban, Mohammed Bandar, "United States Policy in the Middle East and Its Intervention in Lebanon, 1955–1958," D. Phil. thesis (Johns Hopkins, 1996).

Attie, Caroline C., "Lebanon in the 1950's: President Chamoun and Western Policy in Lebanon, 1955–1958," D. Phil. thesis (Texas, 1996).

Beal, Richard Smith, "Systems Analysis of International Crises: Event Analysis of Nine Pre-Crisis Threat Situations, 1948–1962," D. Phil. thesis (Southern California, 1977).

Bernstein, Paul Michael, "Values and Perceptions: Two Case Studies in American Foreign Policy," D. Phil. thesis (Pennsylvania, 1969).

Browne, Bernard G., "The Foreign Policy of the Democratic Party during the Eisenhower Administration," D. Phil. thesis (Notre Dame, 1968).

Ellis, Kail Claude, "United States Policy Toward Lebanon in the Lebanese Civil Wars of 1958 and 1975–1976: A Comparative Analysis," D.Phil. thesis (Catholic, 1979).

Korbani, Agnes G., "Presidential Working System: Style, Cognition, and Foreign Policy: A Comparative Study of U.S. Decisions to Intervene Militarily in Lebanon in 1958 and 1982," D. Phil. thesis (Northwestern, 1989).

Lambrakis, George B., "Perception and Misperception in Policymaking: The U.S. Relationship with Modern Lebanon, 1943–1976," D. Phil. thesis (George Washington, 1989).

Lipe, Rosanne Catherine, "Jordan's Foreign Relations, 1953–1978," D. Phil. thesis (North Carolina, 1980).

McGinnis, Harrill Coleman, "The Presidency and Crisis Decisions: The Application of an Analytical Scheme," D. Phil. thesis (Virginia, 1971).

Mustafa, Munawar Hassan Sabri, "The United States and Lebanon Before and During the Lebanese Crises of 1958," D. Phil. thesis (Duke, 1978).

O'Bannon, George W., "The Lebanon Crisis of 1958: A Case Study of United States Foreign Policy in the Middle East," M.A. thesis (Stanford, 1965).

Rifai, Abdul Halim, "The Eisenhower Administration and Defense of the Arab Middle East," M.A. thesis (American, 1966).

Wolf, John Berchmans, "An Interpretation of the Eisenhower Doctrine: Lebanon, 1958," D.Phil. thesis (American, 1958).

Yaqub, Salim Clyde, "Containing Arab Nationalism: The United States, the Arab Middle East, and the Eisenhower Doctrine, 1956–1959," D.Phil. thesis (Yale, 1999).

Index

ABOUT THE CENTER

The Center is the living memorial of the United States of America to the nation's twenty-eighth president, Woodrow Wilson. Congress established the Woodrow Wilson Center in 1968 as an international institute for advanced study, "symbolizing and strengthening the fruitful relationship between the world of learning and the world of public affairs." The Center opened in 1970 under its own board of trustees.

In all its activities the Woodrow Wilson Center is a nonprofit, nonpartisan organization, supported financially by annual appropriations from the Congress, and by the contributions of foundations, corporations, and individuals. Conclusions or opinions expressed in Center publications and programs are those of the authors and speakers and do not necessarily reflect the views of the Center staff, fellows, trustees, advisory groups, or any individuals or organizations that provide financial support to the Center.